THE BARBARIZATION OF WARFARE

'All things vanish. For each a time is due.
All things remain. I go. Now it's left to you.'

(*Journal of an Unseen April*, Odysseus Elytis)

In memory of my father, Andreas

GEORGE KASSIMERIS

editor

The Barbarization
of Warfare

NEW YORK UNIVERSITY PRESS

Washington Square, New York

First published in the U.S.A. in 2006 by
NEW YORK UNIVERSITY PRESS
Washington Square, New York, 10003
www.nyupress.org

Library of Congress Cataloging-in-Publication Data
The barbarization of warfare / George Kassimeris, editor.
    p. cm.
  Includes bibliographical references and index.
  ISBN-13: 978-0-8147-4796-4 (cloth : alk. paper)
  ISBN-10: 0-8147-4796-5 (cloth : alk. paper)
  ISBN-13: 978-0-8147-4797-1 (pbk. : alk. paper)
  ISBN-10: 0-8147-4797-3 (pbk. : alk. paper)
1. War--Moral and ethical aspects. 2. Atrocities. I. Kassimeris, George.
  U22.B36 2006
  355'.02--dc22   2006012756

Manufactured in India

ACKNOWLEDGEMENTS

In one of the greatest (counterfactual, I hasten to add) collection of essays *If It Had Happened Otherwise* published back in 1931, the editor J.C. Squire wrote, 'There is nothing more tedious than the preface that panegyrises the work introduced. Every right-minded reader is indignant with attempts to dragoon him.' I could not agree more.

The editor, however, should still exercise fully his/her right to a list of acknowledgements and I would like to take this opportunity to thank especially Joanna Bourke and Richard Overy who enthusiastically supported this project from the outset. I am also grateful to the British Academy for its generous assistance in funding it.

Carol Millwood, my best friend, mentor, editor and most forthright critic, read and mercilessly scrutinised the entire manuscript as she always does. I would also like to thank Jean Gilkison and Kristine von Oehsen for reading and commenting on sections of the book. Jean and Kristine took time out of their busy schedules to read parts of the manuscript and correct a host of errors at extremely short notice.

I cannot praise too highly my London and New York publishers, C. Hurst & Co. and New York University Press respectively. Michael Dwyer in London and Eric Zinner in New York have been outstanding once again. My sincere thanks are also due to Maria Petalidou, production manager supremo at C. Hurst & Co. — working with her has been a pleasure and an inspiration.

My deepest thanks, however, go to Kuzi Kassimeris-Salinas, love of my life. Without her support and confidence in me over the years, I would have never reached a point where such a project would have been contemplated, much less attempted.

Wolverhampton, April 2006   G. K.

CONTENTS

vii

THE CONTRIBUTORS

DAVID ANDERSON is Director of the African Studies Centre at the University of Oxford, and a Fellow of St Cross College. The paper in this collection was written while he was Stewart Visiting Professor in the Humanities at Princeton University. In 2005 he published *Histories of the Hanged: Britain's Dirty War in Kenya and the End of Empire* (2005). He has recently completed two further projects, one on Africa's drugs trades, and the other on criminality and violence in colonial eastern Africa. He is now working on a study of the Cold War in Africa.

JOANNA BOURKE is Professor of History at Birkbeck College, University of London. She has published seven books on Irish history, gender, 'the body', and modern warfare and the emotions. Her books have been translated into Chinese, Italian, Portuguese, Spanish, Catalan and Turkish. *An Intimate History of Killing: Face-to-Face Killing in the Twentieth Century Warfare* (London, 1999) won the Fraenkel Prize in Contemporary History for 1998 and the Wolfson History Prize for 2000. Her latest book *Fear: a Cultural History* was published in 2005 by Virago Press. She is currently writing a history of rapists in the nineteenth and twentieth centuries.

ANTHONY DWORKIN is executive director of the Crimes of War Project. He is a contributing editor of *Prospect* and has also written for the *Times Literary Supplement*, the *New Statesman*, the *Guardian*, the *Boston Globe* and other publications. He is co-editor of the forthcoming book *Crimes of War: what the Public Should Know* (2nd edn).

NIALL FERGUSON is the Laurence A. Tisch Professor of History at Harvard University. He is also a Senior Research Fellow of Jesus College, Oxford University, and a Senior Fellow of the Hoover Institution, Stanford. His books include *Paper and Iron: Hamburg Business and German Politics in the Era of Inflation 1897-1927* (1995), *The World's Banker: the History of the House of Rothschild* (2 vols., 1998), *The Pity of War: Explaining World War One* (1999), *The Cash Nexus: Money and Power in the Modern World, 1700-2000* (2001), *Empire: the Rise and Demise of the British World Order and the Lessons for Global Power* (2003), *Colossus: the Price of American Empire* (2004) and *The War of the World: History's Age of Hatred* (2006). He also edited *Virtual History: Alternatives and Counterfactuals* (1999). He is currently writing a biography of the banker Siegmund Warburg.

MARY R. HABECK joined the faculty of the Paul H. Nitze School of Advanced International Studies (SAIS) at Johns Hopkins University in the summer of 2005 after eleven years as a professor at Yale University. Dr Habeck teaches strategic thought and military history at SAIS, and is also consulting with the government on various aspects of the war on terror. She is the author most recently of *Knowing the Enemy: Jihadist Ideology and the War on Terror* (2006) and *Storm of Steel: the Development of Armor Doctrine in Germany and the Soviet Union, 1919-1939* (2003). She is the co-editor with Ronald Radosh of *Spain Betrayed: the Soviet Union in the Spanish Civil War* (2001) and *The Great War and the Twentieth Century* (1999) with Jay Winter and Geoffrey Parker.

RICHARD OVERY is now Professor of History at the University of Exeter after teaching at King's College for 25 years. He has written extensively on the Third Reich, the Stalin era in the Soviet Union and the Second World War. He is the author of 17 books, among which are *The Air War 1939-1945* (1980), *Goering: the 'Iron Man'* (1984), *War and Economy in the Third Reich* (1994), *Why the Allies Won* (1995), *Russia's War* (1998), *Interrogations: the Nazi Elite in Allied Hands* (2001) and *Dictators: Hitler's Germany and Stalin's Russia* (2004). He was made a Fellow of the British Academy in 2000, and was winner of the Samuel Eliot Morison Prize for military history in 2001. He is currently preparing a book titled *The Morbid Age: Cultures of Death and Dying in the Age of the World Wars*.

PAUL ROGERS is Professor of Peace Studies at Bradford University where he teaches courses on international security, arms control and political violence. His most recent books are *A War on Terror: Afghanistan and After* (Pluto Press, 2004) and *Iraq and the War on Terror* (2005). His next book will be *A War Too Far*. He is international security consultant for the Oxford Research Group, writes a weekly assessment of international security trends for the web journal *Open Democracy* (www.opendemocracy.com) and was Chair of the British International Studies Association, 2002-4.

DAVID SIMPSON is Distinguished Professor of English and G.B. Needham Fellow at the University of California-Davis. His latest books are *Situatedness: or, Why We Keep Saying Where We're Coming From* (2002) and *9/11: the Culture of Commemoration* (2006).

HEW STRACHAN is Chichele Professor of the History of War at the University of Oxford, Fellow of All Souls College, and Director of the Leverhulme Programme on the Changing Character of War. His books include *European Armies and the Conduct of War* (1983), *Wellington's Legacy: the Reform of the British Army 1830-54* (1984), *From Waterloo to Balaclava: Tactics, Technology and the British Army 1815-1854* (1985) (awarded the Templer Medal); *The Politics of the British Army* (1997) (awarded the Westminster Medal); the first volume of his three-volume *The First World War (To Arms)*, (2001); and (awarded two American military history prizes and nominated for the Glenfiddich Scottish book of the year) *The First World War: a New Illustrated History* (2003), published to accompany the 10-part Wark Clements television series for Channel 4. He is joint editor of the journal *War in History*, and was editor of the *Oxford Illustrated History of the First World War* (1998) and *The British Army, Manpower and Society into the 21st Century* (2000).

KATHLEEN TAYLOR studied philosophy and physiology at Oxford University before completing a research master's degree in psychology at Stirling University and a doctorate in computational neuroscience at Oxford. She did postdoctoral research in cognitive neuroscience and neuroimmunology and now works on the psychology and neuroscience of belief. Her first book, *Brainwashing: the Science of Thought Control* (2004), was short-listed for the MIND Book of the Year 2005 and runner-up in the *Times Higher Education Supplement* Young Academic Author award.

AMIR WEINER is an Associate Professor of History at Stanford University. He is the author of *Making Sense of War: the Second World War and the Fate of the Bolshevik Revolution* (2001) and *Landscaping the Human Garden: Twentieth-Century Population Management in a Comparative Framework* (2003). His current project, *Wild West, Window to the West*, concerns Russia's western frontier, from 1939 to the present.

JAY WINTER, Charles J. Stille Professor of History, joined the Yale faculty in 2001. From 1979 to 2001 he was Reader in Modern History and Fellow of Pembroke College, Cambridge. He is an historian of the First World War, and the author of *Sites of Memory, Sites of Mourning: the Great War in European Cultural History* (1995), editor of a collection of essays published by Cambridge University Press entitled *America and the Armenian Genocide*. In 2005 Cambridge published his work *The Great War in History: Debates and Controversies, 1914 to the Present*, written with the French scholar Antoine Prost. Next year Yale University Press will publish two of his books: *Remembering the Great War* and *Utopian Visions in the 20th Century*. In 1997 he received an Emmy award as co-producer of 'The Great War and the shaping of the twentieth century', an eight-hour series broadcast on PBS and the BBC, and shown subsequently in 28 countries.

MARILYN B. YOUNG is a Professor of History at New York University teaching courses on American foreign policy in the 20th century. Her published works include *Rhetoric of Empire: US China Policy 1895-1901* (1968); *Transforming Russia and China: Revolutionary Struggle in the 20th Century* (1982) (with William Rosenberg); *The Vietnam Wars, 1945-1990* (1991); and many co-authored anthologies and collections on gender and sexuality in China; feminist transitions to socialism; two documentary collections on the Vietnam War; one collection on current research on Vietnam and (with Lloyd Gardner) *The New American Empire*. A forthcoming anthology by the same authors will focus on comparisons between the current war in Iraq and past American wars.

THE BARBARISATION OF WARFARE

A USER'S MANUAL

George Kassimeris

Like all monuments to pain and cruelty, Potocari, on the north side of Srebrenica, where the photo on the cover of this book was taken, has an aura of dignity combined with its desolation. In the long, flat expanse of a former cornfield, with green hills rising on either side, lie a small flower-bed, a simple open pavilion topped by a tiny Islamic crescent, and a plain stone slab inscribed with a Muslim invocation: 'May revenge be turned into justice, may mothers' tears be turned into prayers that there should be no more Srebrenicas.' Then there are the graves. The green gravestones, about 1,438 of them so far, with space for many more as bodies are exhumed and identified, stretch almost as far as the eye can see and serve as a reminder of the capacity of men to inflict misery on each other.

Srebrenica is one of the worst and most shameful episodes of barbarism in post-war Europe. In mid-1992 this hitherto tranquil area of the Balkans grabbed the world's attention, when Serb forces swept across east Bosnia, unleashing a hurricane of violence that lasted six days and led to the murder of up to 8,000 Muslim men and boys, some in conditions of extreme horror. On one occasion, cited by the International Criminal Tribunal judge Fouad Riad, an elderly man was skewered to a tree by a knife and forced, before being shot at point blank-range, to eat the innards of his grandson. 'Truly scenes from hell, written on the darkest pages of human history,' said the judge.[1]

Yet what happened in Srebrenica also took place, sometimes on a huge scale, during the Second World War and later in Kenya, Algeria, Vietnam, Cambodia, Rwanda, Sierra Leone, East Timor, Kosovo and Chechnya, bearing witness to humanity's capacity to descend to acts of unspeakable barbarity if circumstances permit. What drives people to mistreat, humiliate and torment each other? What drives people into hatred, genocide, war, inhumanity and evil? What drove Japanese soldiers in 1937 in Nanking[2] to disembowel Chinese women, slice off their breasts and nail them alive to walls after raping them? What drove Hutus in 1994 in Rwanda[3] to kill young Tutsi children in front of their own parents, by cutting off one arm, then the other and then gashing the neck with a machete to bleed them slowly to death? What drove neighbours in the mid-1990s in former Yugoslavia, who had for years lived in relative harmony, to turn around and commit the vilest atrocities against each other? What drove young American soldiers to abuse, torture and sexually humiliate their defenceless detainees in Baghdad's Abu Ghraib prison?

The idea for this book came from an article Richard Overy wrote for the comment and analysis pages of *The Guardian* newspaper in May 2004 on the abuse of the Iraqi prisoners at Abu Ghraib. Entitled 'Like the Wehrmacht, we've descended into barbarity', the piece argued that the sadistic mistreatment of prisoners in Iraq was not an aberration. Although it horrified world opinion, such mistreatment had been the standard behaviour of soldiers for a long time and could easily be transferred to numerous other contexts. 'Barbarisation of warfare' was the phrase originally used in Omer Bartov's classic study to describe the murderous behaviour of German forces on the Eastern Front between 1941 and 1945, although it might easily have been used the other way around had the focus instead been on the mass rape, destruction and looting meted out by the Red Army first on the countries seen as having collaborated with Hitler's Reich and then on Germany itself in the closing months of the Second World War.[4] The battles of Stalingrad and Berlin, landmark military events of that conflict, revealed, apart from the vanity and horrifying callousness of political and military leaders, the terrible ferocity of modern warfare and the brutalisation of the individual under conditions of incessant killing and devastation.[5]

It is important, however, to recognise that excessive violence and barbarity are not phenomena exclusive to a 'world war' type of military conflict. Five years before Stalingrad, the Japanese, in the name of their Great East Asia Co-Prosperity sphere, were inflicting enormous, ingenious and unprovoked cruelties upon Chinese civilians and soldiers. And five years after Berlin, British battalions in Kenya were slicing off ears and flogging insurgents to death or setting them alight after pouring paraffin over them. Some British sub-units even kept scoreboards recording kills of 'terrorists', whose hands were often chopped off to make fingerprinting easier.[6] Those arrested 'terrorists' (i.e. any guerrillas/insurgents resisting British colonial rule) who did not make it on to the scoreboard were sent in their thousands to 1950s versions of Abu Ghraib, detention camps where they experienced forced labour, systematic brutality, humiliation and torture.

From Sparta to Darfur

Is it possible to talk about warfare and avoid at the same time talking about human viciousness and barbarity? Warfare and barbarity have been inseparable from each other throughout history, which we should have learned long ago. From Sparta in the 5th century BC to Darfur in the 21th century AD the use of indiscriminate terror, ethnic cleansing, genocide, and rape as familiar and effective tools of war-making has continued uninterrupted.

Consider, for example, this description of violence in a civil war:

When they had the prisoners in their hands [they] shut them up in a large building, and afterwards took them out in batches of twenty at a time and made them pass between two lines of [soldiers] drawn up to form a lane along which the prisoners went bound together, and were beaten and stabbed by those between whom they passed when anyone saw a personal enemy among them... [Later the captors] got up on to the top of the building, demolished the roof, and hurled down tiles...at the people below, who protected themselves as well as they could, though in fact most of them began to take their own lives... with cords taken from some beds that happened to be there, or with strips made out of their clothing...When it was day [the captors] piled up the bodies on to wagons and took them outside the city.[7]

This is not an extract from Primo Levi's Auschwitz memoirs, or a report of a *New York Times* correspondent in Kosovo, but Thucydides in his description of the civil war on the Greek island of Corcyra in 427 BC.

One cannot contemplate the cruel aspects of warfare for long without reflecting upon the impact and influence of war in the shaping of human instinct, character and institutions. In spite of the evidence about the horror of combat, and the catastrophe of defeat, people have always thought they had good reasons for going to war; to acquire new territory and resources, defeat their enemies or secure the release of captive or enslaved people.[8] Warfare, it has often been argued, fosters and provides an arena for the greatest human virtues: physical and moral courage, solidarity and comradeship, self-sacrifice, fraternity, loyalty, and patriotism.[9] No matter how many times the nature of the argument about the use and value of warfare has changed within the decades since 1945, the fact remains that war fascinates men more than it repels them. Its enduring attraction, writes *New York Times* veteran foreign correspondent Chris Hedges, in his powerful chronicle of modern war, is that it gives people's lives meaning.

Even with its destruction and carnage it can give us what we long for in life. It can give us purpose, meaning, a reason for living. Only when we are in the midst of conflict does the shallowness and vapidness [sic] of much of our lives become apparent... War makes the world understandable, a black and white tableau of them and us.[10]

People, as the Vietnam war veteran William Broyles Jr so eloquently put it, 'love war in strange and troubling ways.'[11] In Broyles's view, it is men in particular who love war because they love games; 'war is a brutal, deadly game, but [still] a game, the best there is'. But beyond that, he continues, 'it is an escape from the duties of everyday life, from the bonds of the family, community and work.'[12]

'Three thousand years have not changed the human condition' observes the classicist Bernard Knox; 'we are still lovers of the will to violence' but we are also its victims. There have always been warriors who, in Homer's words, 'call up the wild joy of war',[13] but what about the physical cruelty, the human degradation, the death and destruction that come with it? The twentieth century will certainly go down in history as one of the most violent, fanatical and brutal, which does not ensure the twenty-first-century will fare better, given that we have learned to tolerate the intolerable. 'Total war and cold war,' writes Eric Hobsbawm, 'have brainwashed us into accepting barbarity; even worse they have made barbarity seem unimportant.'[14]

Of course, one might argue that the twentieth century is a poor guide to the twenty-first, but any discussion of the new century should start with the previous one. The latter may not have ended well but as Jonathan Glover writes in his *Humanity: a Moral History of the Twentieth Century*, at the start there was optimism that 'the spread of a humane and scientific outlook would lead to the fading away, not only of war, but also of other forms of cruelty and barbarism'.[15] However, the twentieth century turned out to be the century of Hitler, Stalin, Pol Pot, Mohammed Aidid, Foday Sankoh and Slobodan Milošević who destroyed not only millions of lives but also the vision which came with the Enlightenment. In a powerful passage of his book *The Warrior's Honor* Michael Ignatieff explains why 'the idea of human universality', thanks to the twentieth century's large-scale cruelty and killing, now rests 'less on hope than on fear, less on optimism about the human capacity for good than on dread of human capacity for evil, less on a vision of a man as maker of his history than of man [as] the wolf towards his kind.'[16]

This brings us to the crux of the matter: can warfare be anything other than barbaric? Much historical evidence shows that there is little in recent history to prove that it can. The kind of dark barbarity that defined much of the world before the creation of the nation-state has largely character-ised the world that came after. The remarkable thing, however, is that it was only towards the end of the twentieth century that people in the West began to understand what Sri Lankans, Haitians, Liberians, Chechens, Somalis, Cambodians, Angolans, Sudanese and many others have long known all too well: that warfare prosecuted according to recognised laws of war has been the exception, not the rule.

For centuries we have debated the morality of going to war and the way in which it is fought, but international conventions are not sufficient in themselves to make soldiers adhere to the rules.[17] It is unnecessary to discuss how the International Committee of the Red Cross was formed in Geneva back in 1863 to see why the ideal of civilised warfare as a central element of European culture as propagated by Jean-Henri Dunant was doomed from the start. As the British military historian John Keegan puts it, 'there is no substitute for honour as a medium of enforcing decency on the battlefield, never has been and never will be. There are no judges, more to the point, no policemen at the place where death is done in combat.'[18] In other words, it is entirely up to the soldier himself to distinguish or not between combatants and noncombatants, legitimate and illegitimate targets and civilised and barbarous treatment of prisoners and of the wounded.

It was one of Dunant's successors, Cornelio Sommaruga, who in the early 1990s began talking openly about a new type of warfare where there was no respect for either the laws of war or the sign of the Red Cross, no clear lines of command, and in which civilians rather than enemy soldiers were the primary targets. In this new kind of warfare everyone and everything — from babies to crops and from livestock to houses and old people had become fair game.[19]

Whereas only one in ten of all casualties in the First World War was a civilian, this proportion has risen to nine out of ten today. Even more disquieting is the fact that a large number of them are children. However, what is less well-known is that a growing number of those responsible for the killings are children themselves. As P.W. Singer points out in *Children at War*, child soldiers, some no older than six, are to be found in three-quarters of the fifty or so conflicts currently being fought around the world.[20] In Sierra Leone's Revolutionary United Front (RUF), 80 per cent of the fighters were aged between seven and fourteen.[21] In Liberia 20,000 children are reported to have been involved in the country's protracted civil wars. Recruited from orphanages, refugee camps, city slums or from among those made destitute by AIDS, famine and war, children are easy to brainwash, quick to train, and readily drugged, terrorised and conditioned into committing reckless atrocities.[22]

What can be done once the point has been reached when child soldiers carrying Kalashnikovs larger than themselves commit vicious attacks? The answer would be that a great deal might be done if only we were able to explain both the complexity and psychology of such brutality. Yet explaining evil has turned out to be as difficult as preventing it.

Why We Need Monsters

On 17 December 1996 six Red Cross personnel were asleep in their beds in an ICRC hospital at Novye Atagi near Grozny in Chechnya. The hospital provided medical care for all factions in the conflict and was thus officially accepted by both Russian and Chechen authorities. The hospital compound was guarded by unarmed Chechen staff. At around 4 a.m., an unknown number of armed and masked men scaled the wall of the compound. They knocked one guard unconscious, pumped several shots into the hospital computers, and then made their way to the dormitory where the Red Cross staff were sleeping. The six Red Cross personnel — from Canada, Norway, New Zealand, the Netherlands and Spain — were shot dead at point-blank range. A male delegate who rose to meet his attacker took a bullet in the shoulder and escaped execution by feigning death. The members of the paramilitary squad took flight when one of the Chechen guards — who, against ICRC orders, was armed — fired a warning shot in the air. The incident represented the worst massacre of Red Cross personnel in history. As the coffins bearing the bodies of the six staffers were brought back to the organisation's headquarters in Geneva and placed in the room where a Christmas party was to have been held, staff, delegates and the press gathered to listen to a distressed Cornelio Sommaruga. He had received a message from a field delegate and he wanted to read it out:

All our endeavour is based on the belief that, even in the middle of the worst depravities of war, man retains a fundamental minimum of humanity. Events like this can make it very difficult to maintain this belief. But without it we would have to admit that nothing distinguishes man from beast, and that we will not admit.[23]

These are brave words, but history has taught us and continues to teach us that war survives all forms of outrage, that atrocities such as the one in Chechnya described above continue to occur and that it is idle to imagine a world where people are not hounded from their homes, starved to death or massacred. Then are we all human, or are some of us less human than others in times of war?

A few years ago the prominent Croatian writer now living in exile in Sweden, Slavenka Drakulić gave a reading in Berlin from her novel about mass rapes of Muslim women in Bosnia, *As If I Am Not There*. As is customary at such events, the reading was followed by a discussion with the audience when a young man stood up and asked Drakulić if she would consider writing a book from the viewpoint of a perpetrator. It is worth quoting Drakulić's answer in full, as she recollects the incident in her book about war criminals, *They Would Never Hurt a Fly*:

No, I will not! I answered almost too eagerly, as if doing so would be a crime. True, my books about the war were written from the perspectives of victims only. The horror of the war could truly be described only from their position, I thought. The world already knew enough about the perpetrators… If one attempts to write from the point of view of the perpetrators, to try to understand such people, how close does it come to justifying their acts? Can we actually understand war criminals? More important why should we even try? These were the questions that went through my mind as I thought about how ominous it was that this subject should be brought up in Germany of all places. I did not realise at the time that, in response to a young German reader's inquiry, I had reacted in a typically self-defensive way. Exactly in the same way as when, two years later, other people would react when I told them that I was writing about perpetrators, i.e. war criminals. Why are you interested in them? They are monsters, they'd say.[24]

Drakulić goes on to argue that although it is easy to understand such reactions, since war criminals have committed indescribable acts and nobody wants to be connected with them in any way, we still paradoxically need monsters— simply because not wanting to know takes us away from the essential question of how such unspeakable crimes were ever possible. If we believe that the perpetrators are monsters, writes Drakulić, it is

because we want to create as great a distance as possible between us and them, to exclude them from humanity altogether. We even go so far as to say that their crimes were 'inhuman', as if evil (as well as good) were not part of human nature. At the bottom of such reasoning there is a syllogism: ordinary people could not do what these monsters did. We are ordinary people, therefore we cannot commit such crimes. But once you get closer to the real people who committed those crimes, you see that the syllogism doesn't really work.[25]

Attempts to consider the humanity of perpetrators or the complicity of non-perpetrators can provoke outrage and accusations of 'excusing the inexcusable' or 'forgiving' or 'blaming the victim' but they are essential. It is not only the victims of war and atrocity whose permanently transformed worlds one has to enter if one wishes to understand the anarchy, cruelty and confusion of modern wars; it is also the world of perpetrators like Milošević, Karadžić and Mladić. Drakulić spent months continuously sitting in a Hague courtroom observing war criminals.

You sit in a courtroom watching a defendant day after day and at first you wonder, as Primo Levi did, 'If this is a man'. No, this is not a man, it is all too easy to answer, but as the days pass you find the criminals become increasingly human. You watch their faces, ugly or pleasant, the way they yawn, take notes, scratch their heads or clean their nails, and you have to ask yourself: what if this *is* a man? The more you know them, the more you wonder how they could have committed such crimes... And the more you realize that war criminals might be ordinary people, the more afraid you become. This is because the consequences are more serious than if they were monsters. If ordinary people committed war crimes, it means that any of us could commit them. Now you understand why it is so easy and comfortable to accept that war criminals are monsters.[26]

Drakulić's guide in her study is not Hannah Arendt, whose notion of the 'banality of evil' has been turned into something of a cliché, but Chistopher R. Browning, whose pioneering study *Ordinary Men* demonstrated the readiness with which good neighbours could become brutally efficient killers of each other.[27] Browning reconstructs from the records of a West German court of inquiry the activities of the 500 'ordinary men' of the Reserve Police Battalion 101 who, within a period of seventeen months from July 1942 to November 1943, shot and killed 38,000 Jews and crowded another 45,000 into freight cars to be transported to the extermination camps. These were not the Eichmann type of bureaucratic killers, issuing orders from behind their desks far from the killing fields, nor, with few exceptions, were they fanatical Hitlerites. They were working men in their thirties and forties, many of them police officers in civilian life, sent to Poland to do a job whose details were not disclosed in advance. When they were eventually told that their task was to murder Jews, nearly the entire battalion proceeded methodically and without apparent feeling. They killed their victims one by one, usually with a bullet to the base of the neck, including old men, women and children. To save time infants were not taken to the killing fields but murdered where they were found. When members of the battalion were interviewed by a German court in the 1960s nearly all of them claimed to have been 'horrified and disgusted' at first by what they were doing, yet nearly all overcame their repugnance and joined the killing, even though their commanding officer offered to exempt without penalty those who chose not to participate. A handful accepted his offer but soon rejoined their comrades. The rest pitched in at once. Some murdered eagerly. A few found the work sexually exciting. Some even made jokes about it. For most the assignment quickly became uneventful. The men of Reserve 101 might have been painting a house or moving furniture around for all the emotion they displayed.[28]

If nothing else, Browning's book discredits the notion that how human beings choose to explain and justify war does not necessarily account for why they wage it. And while Browning does not go so far as to suggest that people need little encouragement to engage in mutual slaughter or repression, Drakulić does. She even goes a step further by arguing that once you look at the type of people and the nature of the violence perpetrated and notice that so much of it has occurred in people's homes, in schools, in the familiar environment of everyday life, it no longer seems mindless, a throw-back to premordialism. The 'ordinary' killers of Reserve Battalion 101 had the same motives Drakulić's 'ordinary Balkan monsters': group conformity, peer pressure, racism, societal norms and a sense of superiority. The implication of all this is that normal-acting individuals (who have spent most of their lives as civilians in peacetime) are innately violent, needing only the opportunity of war to revert to primordial savagery. Drakulić asks, can ordinary men behave like this? 'Your neighbours, perhaps? Your relatives? No it cannot be. They look so normal'. Hence it is a lot easier to accept that war criminals are monsters than to agree with the view that 'evil arises out of ordinary thinking and is committed by ordinary people, [it] is the norm, not the exception'.[29]

The books by Drakulić and Browning together with others such as Michael Jackson's *In Sierra Leone*, Philip Gourevitch's *We Wish to Inform you that Tomorrow We will be Killed with our Families*, and Janine di Giovanni's *Madness Visible* on Sarajevo's 1,300-day siege, seek explanations for the phenomena of murder and violence. But ultimately they are books about the state of fear, they all seem to suggest, that war exposes the capacity for evil that lurks not far below the surface in each of us. We are all culpable. But are we all culpable because we are all afraid? Irrespective of how greatly the nature of warfare has shifted over the years, fear of being attacked as well as fear of the power of the Other remains a prime cause for conflict. One does not have to read Thucydides or Thomas Hobbes to know that when two groups are a potential threat to each other, the resulting fear gives each a reason for striking first. Each can see that the other has this reason, and the circle of fear is thus reinforced.[30]

Michael Jackson's *In Sierra Leone*, about the brutality of the country's ten-year civil war, helps one to understand those men and women who took to violence. In particular, he shows in convincing detail that atrocities were in fact the perpetrators' way of dealing with their own fear. Unless, writes Jackson, one has been caught up in

a war and experienced the terror that comes of knowing that thousands of heavily armed individuals are bent on one's annihilation, it is hard to realise that most violence is not primarily motivated by evil, greed, lust, ideology, or aggression. Strange as it may seem, most violence is defensive. It is motivated by the fear that if one does not kill one will be killed. Either by the enemy or by one's superiors. Against this constant anxiety, and the acute sense of fear and vulnerability that accompanies it, one conjures an illusion of power — torching buildings, shooting unarmed civilians, firing rocket grenades, smoking cannabis, shouting orders, chanting slogans, seeing oneself as Rambo, taunting, torturing, abusing the individuals one has taken captive. But all this display of might… simply reveals the depth of one's impotence and fear.

Writing on the tenth anniversary of the publication of his First World War novel, *Birdsong*, Sebastian Faulks remarks that at the early stages of writing, when trying from his readings about the war to understand why things turned out as catastrophically as they did, it became progressively more difficult for him to grasp the extent of how far one can go. The question 'what are the limits of humanity?' emerged naturally as Faulks kept reading about the millions of men who climbed over the sandbagged parapets of the trenches under which they lived to advance into the machine-gun fire which they knew would kill them. At no point, writes Faulks intrigued and repelled at the same time,

during the needless extermination of 10 million men did one of them say: enough, we cannot go on and still call ourselves human. In fact, the French army mutinied in 1917, but although the problem was widespread, it amounted to no more than a refusal to attack; some German machine gunners on July 1, 1916, did desist, appalled by what they did. But the big thematic question remained, and the answer seemed to be that there were no limits to which men could not be driven.[31]

Faulks deduces from this that it is not enough simply to assert that all war cheapens human life or to point out that war isolates combatants from the truth of their own actions. What needs to be understood more clearly — so that lessons can be learned — is that in battle 'one defence is to distance the people on the other side. The person you maim or kill is not seen as someone as frightened as you, whose mother and father want him to come back from the war.'[32] This view of human relations is born out of the fact that psychological distancing and dehumanisation of the enemy are quickly accomplished once the killing has started. [33] In the My Lai massacre Private Varnado Simpson killed about twenty-five people: 'Men, women. From shooting them, to cutting their throats, scalping them, to ... cutting off their hands and cutting out their tongue. I did it.' When asked how he could bring himself to perpetrate such atrocities, Simpson said:

I just went. After I killed the child, my mind just went. And once you start, it's very easy to keep on. Once you start. The hardest — the part that's hard is to kill, but once you kill, that becomes easier, to kill the next person and the next one. Because I had no feelings or no emotions or no nothing. No direction. I just killed. It can happen to anyone. [34]

Distancing between perpetrator and victim is one of the keys to such behaviour. Speaking of his first murder of a Tutsi, a young Hutu by the name of Pio says:

I had killed chickens but never an animal of the stoutness of a man like a goat, or a cow. The first person, I finished him off in a rush not thinking anything of it, even though he was a neighbour, quite close on my hill. In truth it came to me only afterward: I had taken the life of a neighbour. I mean, at the fatal instant I did not see in him what he had been before; I struck someone who was no longer either close or strange to me, who wasn't exactly ordinary any more... like the people you meet every day. His features were indeed similar to those of the person I knew, but nothing firmly reminded me that I had lived beside him for a long time... He was the first victim I killed; my vision and my thinking had grown clouded. [35]

If one wants to get closer to the truth of what happened and why, it is as important to listen to the victimisers as to the victims; to try to see things from the former viewpoint. In their award-winning documentary film *Massacre* Lokman Slim, a Lebanese writer and publisher, and his German wife Monika Borgmann, a journalist, tried to get inside the minds of six militiamen of Maronite Christian faith who described in detail their participation in the infamous killing spree at Sabra and Chatila Palestinian refugee camps in September 1982, one of the most brutal moments of Lebanon's 1975-90 civil war. [36] The Palestinian refugee camps were attacked at the height of that war on 16 September 1982, by gunmen from Christian militias who were occupying Beirut at the time, and allies of the Israeli army. For the next forty-eight hours they tore through the camps in an indiscriminate wave of killing. At least 2,000 people died, among them women and children.

In the film it is the precision of the men's accounts and their astonishingly limited emotional reaction to describing the brutal acts they committed that have the greater capacity to shock. Our initial orders, says one of them, were 'young and old, babies in arms, show no mercy. That became our slogan.' 'That was a good war, that was,' says another, before adding: 'After a while, killing gets to be like playing a game of marbles.' When the men are given photographs of the carnage taken by the first journalists on the scene, the camera studies their body language. The photographs would horrify any normal individuals but they fail to cause any distress to the men. The full realisation of how deeply these men dissociated themselves from the reality of their crimes comes when one of the six turns over one picture after another of these dead bodies and then stops at one of two dead horses. After a pause he says: 'Why kill the horses?'

Slim and Borgman have produced a film that is ultimately deeply depressing, but that is not their fault. As long as there is war and human conflict, there will always be people willing to commit atrocities in exchange for a little power and privilege. The twentieth century witnessed barbarity on a large scale that made victims of us all. However, this does not mean that there are no choices in warfare. People have a choice even when they have opted to march into battle. In the same way there are just wars and unjust wars, forms of killing that are necessary and forms that are not, there are human and inhuman soldiers. Saying this is not an attempt to establish a hierarchy of suffering, or to diminish the death and destruction of others, but the premeditated killing of non-combatants whether in Kosovo, Vietnam or Chechnya is different from acts committed in the heat of battle. Russian soldiers in Chechnya, for example, do have a choice when dropping a cartridge into the pocket of a man they are searching, then finding it, declaring him a terrorist and killing him on the spot.[37] And the same is true of American soldiers in Iraq who violate established military rules to subject prisoners to torture, abuse and sexual humiliation.

Democracy and Torture

Nobody has yet come up with a coherent plan for understanding and dealing with the murky depths of the human psyche. And this is not cynicism — just a sober understanding of how things are. There are torturers and potential torturers everywhere, even in the most civilised societies. The propensity for cruelty is in all of us, and it rises to the surface in many when they are given complete authority over other human beings. Add the unique environment of war, in which culture, religion, race, ethnicity and ideology often separate guards from prisoners and abuse becomes the norm instead of the exception.[38]

Excesses and errors in foreign wars are commonplace; invading and occupying armies have always behaved badly. The Germans under the Nazis during the Second World War, the Russians and the Japanese in the course of that war, the Belgians in the Congo, the British in Kenya, the French in Algeria, and the Dutch during the colonial wars committed atrocities and practised torture and sexual humiliation on natives who resisted but who above all were held in contempt. But most did it before the age of the digital pocket camera, and the possibility of images like the naked Iraqi prisoner cowering in front of barking dogs in Abu Ghraib, have forced us to come face to face with warfare's undiminished brutality and indiscriminate excess.

The late Susan Sontag, in an essay a few months after the Abu Ghraib scandal broke, expressed the notion that 'the photos are us'.

You ask yourself how someone can grin at the sufferings and humiliation of another human being — drag a naked Iraqi man along the floor with a leash? Set guard dogs at the genitals and legs of cowering, naked prisoners? Rape and sodomise prisoners? Beat prisoners to death? — and feel naïve in asking these questions, since the answer is, self-evidently: people do these things to other people. Not just in Nazi concentration camps (and in Abu Ghraib when it was run by Saddam Hussein). Americans, too, do them when they have permission. When they are told or made feel that those over whom they have absolute power deserve to be mistreated, humiliated and tormented. They do them when they are led to believe that the people they are torturing belong to an inferior, despicable race or religion.[39]

The real meaning of the pictures, insisted Sontag, is not that these acts were performed but that their perpetrators had no sense that there was anything wrong in what the pictures show. They were meant to be circulated for amusement. The problem, of course, runs deeper than the truth that some people take pleasure in the pain of others. The fact that the pictures were taken at all, and most of all the cheerful faces of the soldiers, suggest an atmosphere in which these soldiers had no reason to fear being punished for their behaviour.[40] The smiles of the tormentors confirm that as well as having lost whatever sense they had, these soldiers felt licensed to abuse.[41]

The female soldier in the case did not think there was anything wrong with holding a prisoner on a leash, because her superiors had sanctioned it. Her character becomes irrelevant as soon as we realise that what made her deeds possible was a very particular political culture created in Washington, DC, in which almost anything was permitted provided it was deemed to serve the 'war on terror', as waged by the United States.[42] This is where the abuse at Abu Ghraib has its origins. 'If White House and Pentagon lawyers seek ways to circumvent the Geneva conventions,' wrote Ian Buruma in the *Financial Times Magazine*, 'if torture is deemed permissible if the [US] president says so, if that same president divides the world into good guys and evil guys, and if it is unclear in Iraq who the enemies are, then it becomes hard to blame [the torturers] ...for playing pornographic games with real victims. The problem is not cultural, or personal but political...' [43]

There was 'a before 9/11 and an after 9/11' as Coffer Black, one-time director of the CIA's counterterrorist unit, put it in testimony to Congress in early 2002. Soon after the 9/11 attacks, Americans 'took the gloves off' and began torturing prisoners, and they have never really stopped. These words must by now be accepted as proven; not merely as an accusation. The problem stems in part from a moral equivalence that emerged after the events of 9/11 when America found itself under attack by a brutal, amorphous enemy, which would go to extraordinary lengths and use whatever means it could to destroy the West. President George W. Bush repeatedly declared that his country was 'in a different kind of war' and had an obligation to defend itself. Yet however 'different' that war was going to be, universal (and American) values required that civilised standards be maintained. A country as powerful as the United States has many choices, even when struck by a blow as heavy as that of 9/11. Ignoring international law and the norms of civilised behaviour as the US administration chose to do after 9/11 was always going to be self-defeating.[44] In its casual disregard for international public opinion and cavalier approach to human rights, the United States has not only damaged the nation's moral standing but, more crucially, undermined the very values

that the 'war against terror' was supposed to encourage.[45] Francis Fukuyama may have exaggerated in the past with his 'end of history' assertions
but he hardly did when he wrote of the 'seismic shift in the way much of
the world [now] perceives the US, [and] whose image is no longer the
Statue of Liberty but the hooded prisoner at Abu Ghraib'.[46]

Nothing destroyed the moral case for the US war in Vietnam quite
so effectively as the complicity of American forces in torture. Of the
many lessons of that conflict, which optimists hoped the United States
had learnt, this was surely one of the most important. Why the US army
in Iraq chose to ignore these lessons from Vietnam remains incomprehensible.[47] Years from now, the mistreatment of Afghan war detainees in
Afghanistan, Guantanamo Bay and Abu Ghraib is likely to rank with the
internment of Japanese civilians in the Second World War as a blot on the
good reputation of the United States.[48] Modern wars have come to be
defined by photographs, and the Abu Ghraib images are a public rebuttal
of Western claims that a criminal and depraved regime would be replaced
by an enlightened democratic government in which human rights would
be respected.[49]

The purpose of this introduction is certainly not to provide an analysis
of whether or not the occupation of Iraq turned out — in the words of
the liberal American magazine *The Nation* — 'to be a morally corrosive
imperial adventure.'[50] However, it needs to be said that the sight of Americans torturing Iraqis where Saddam Hussein tortured them destroyed
the credibility of the assumption that American and British troops would
help build a new democracy in a Middle East where human rights and the
rule of law would be respected.[51]

Now that we know all about the hidden prisons, the torture chambers
and the beatings, is there a moral difference between Saddam Hussein's
behaviour and that of American and British troops? As the months of the
Iraq war have turned into years, Iraqis, to use the bitter words of the Iraqi
cleric Sheik Mohammed Bashir, have discovered that

freedom in this land is not ours. It is the freedom of the occupying soldiers in doing what they like…abusing women, children, men, and the old men and women
who they arrested randomly and without any guilt. No one can ask them what
they are doing, because they are protected by their freedom…No one can punish
them, whether in our country or their country. They expressed the freedom of
rape, the freedom of nudity and the freedom of humiliation.[52]

When morality vanishes from the battlefield, a war can never be won. It does not matter much whether you choose to call this kind of treatment abuse or by some other euphemism; the point remains that torture, like any other atrocity, lives on in the mind of the tortured. And as any prisoner at Abu Ghraib or Guantanamo will tell you, every time a person is reduced to a howling beast by deliberately inflicted pain, our civilisation crumbles a little more, until in the end there will only be barbarism.[53]

At the start of the twenty-first century we should not be debating the use of torture. Questions such as whether torture works and whether the Geneva Conventions still hold should not be central moral issues of our age. No argument is more clichéd than that which asks why we should adhere to the Geneva Conventions when our terrorist enemies do not. Torture — no matter how 'light' and whatever the provocation— cannot be justified on any grounds.[54] For it is a sign of desperation, an admission that your side has no other resources left. Significantly, torture does not actually work; prisoners treated like those in Abu Ghraib will confess to anything. Torture is unjustified because it is wrong to inflict pain on defenceless captives, because it breaks the international conventions and because the costs outweigh the benefits of any intelligence it may elicit. Torture is a weapon of punishment and a terrorist method; not a path to democracy or freedom.[55]

And if the above arguments are not enough, there is an even stronger one for drawing a firm line against any use and any form of torture. It poisons and brutalises the society that allows it to happen. The days of France's bloody colonial war in Algeria may be long past, but its reverberations in French society continue. Alistair Horne wrote in his *A Savage War for Peace* that the use of torture in Algeria became for France a growing cancer, leaving behind a poison which would linger in the French body politic long after the war had ended.[56] Roughly a million and a half Frenchmen, including the future President of the Republic Jacques Chirac, fought in Algeria, and about a quarter of them are believed by the French health authorities to suffer from psychological traumas. The French military, unsurprisingly, still refuses to accept that the widespread use of torture was anything other than a necessary means of fighting a just war, but if it inspires widespread condemnation in France today, as it failed to do during the Algerian war, it is mainly because it can no longer be defended as an unfortunate necessity. Numerous recent studies on the

Algerian war show that French violence in Algeria was designed to terrify, subdue and exhibit power rather than to extract information.[57]

Ultimately the images of Abu Ghraib are a cause of shame for all of us because they show that barbaric behaviour needs little encouragement to flourish. These snapshots tell us what we need to know about who we are and the tissue-thin veneer of our civilisation. They also tell us that despite the profound socio-cultural changes that have taken place in Western society since 1914, barbarity, atrocity and terror continue to loom large. We have two kinds of motives for looking into history. There is curiosity about the past, what happened, who did what, and why; and there is the aim of understanding the present and how to place and interpret our own times, experiences and hopes for the future. And although no one could seriously claim that the history of twentieth-century warfare has been neglected by academics, only a small number of writers have tried to deal directly with barbarity in warfare, examining the rationale, motives, ideology and moral resources of people in wartime.

The principal aim of the chapters in this collection is to understand how and why this degradation of military ethics happens, and to attempt to offer explanations for its recurrence. In the bleak environment of the twenty-first century, when violence and torture are becoming addictive media spectacles, it is more necessary than ever to deepen our knowledge and understanding of the brutality displayed by human beings in times of war.

BARBARISATION vs CIVILISATION IN TIME OF WAR

Joanna Bourke

In the triptych of totalitarianism, total war, and terror, we might be persuaded to repeat Primo Levi's melancholic statement of 1946 that 'Today,
at this very moment as I sit at a table, I myself am not convinced that these
things really happened.'[1] The two world wars had reduced humanity to
rubble; the Holocaust had stripped even that rubble of meaning. It was
followed by the threat of nuclear annihilation. Humanity had fashioned
a world of suffering capable of dwarfing anything that went before. The
Enlightenment hopes of Voltaire and Diderot, the high-minded slogans of
Liberty, Equality, Fraternity, didn't simply peter out, but were purposefully crushed in the bestial milieu of the twentieth century.

Steeped (as we are today) in notions of trauma and seduced by apocalyptic fantasies, it is easy to forget that anxieties about humanity's slide
into barbarisation predate the horrors of last century. A dark vision even
shadowed the more typically optimistic rhetoric of the nineteenth century.
In 1869, for instance, an author simply known as 'A Truthseeker' penned
a pamphlet published in Dublin and entitled *Thoughts on Barbarism and
Civilisation*. In this pamphlet, he claimed that humanity was 'stand[ing] on
the shore, aghast at the stupendous and tumultuous breakers which thunder towards us'. Barbarism and civilisation had become indistinguishable,
he bemoaned. 'The dress of the people may differ',

but the souls are the same. Is the tomahawk a more dreadful weapon than the
bayonet? Is the war-cry of the Indian more horrible than the clamour of fifes and
drums in the battle-field? Is the attire of a New Zealander more grotesque than
the trappings of a Highland regiment? ...We are told that the difference between
their nature and our own is enormous. I cannot perceive it. Savages are cruel:

19

they kill women and children! Yes, they do, and so do we when it suits us. When a few years ago, New Zealand was ceded to the English, the [Maori] population numbered 200,000; now it is sunk to 20,000. Everywhere is room being made for the 'pale faces'. *Savages* cruel, indeed![2]

It was a heartfelt lament, a call for a renewed commitment to courtesy and respect towards strangers. We are right to be sceptical about his belief in the redeeming power of the blood of Christ in forging a less barbarous world, but his fears that cruelty and torture could once again become endemic in 'civilised' Europe were sound. Today's Tomahawk missiles are computer-guided, and they carry 1,000-pound warheads or 166 'soda-can-size bomblets'.[3] They are more terrible than bayonets. Unarmed women and children have become the target of choice; politicians and generals are keen to keep their expensive workforce — iron-garbed servicemen and servicewomen — from harm's way. It has become impossible to understand modern culture without directing ones' gaze into the abyss of the barbarian. Mass murder, torture, and gratuitous violence are no grotesque accidents. Barbarism is a cultural phenomenon.

The Threshold of the Human

No one is arguing that barbaric actions were absent in earlier times. During the Thirty Years' War, one-third of the German-speaking population of Europe died; anti-Semitism was there for all to see in Luther's *On the Jews and their Lies* of 1543; and Francisco de Goya's 'The 3ʳᵈ of May 1808 in Madrid' (1814) captured the carnage of that war. And we must not forget the actions of the original (and much maligned) Barbarians.

In the past century, however, the threshold of the human plummeted. It is possible to speak not of a *return* to barbarism, but a staggering inventiveness in novel forms of cruelty. The Holocaust is the pre-eminent instance of the wanton slaughter of non-combatants. Approximately six million Jews were killed, including around two million children. Other ethnic, social, religious, political, and sexual minorities were also singled out for elimination. These acts were calculated. Millions were implicated. The ideological and material infrastructures employed still numb the mind. The slaughter fused old and new; it included face-to-face killing with primitive instruments; it also included the new industrial murder of millions of people in gas chambers. Evil was not banal — quite the contrary; it infused every subtle nuance of the society from which it was born.

Even if we exclude the Holocaust, modern warfare is inseparable from barbarism. The war entered, uninvited, into people's homes and took up residence. The decisive conflict was the Second World War. While only five per cent of deaths in the 1914-18 war were civilian deaths, sixty-six per cent of deaths in the 1939-45 war were of civilians. Many more civilians than military personnel were killed in Belgium, China, France, Greece, Hungary, the Netherlands, Norway, Poland, the Soviet Union, and Yugoslavia. Furthermore, by whatever definition we use, large proportions of these victims were indisputably innocent. For example, of the six million Poles (Jews and non-Jews) who were killed by the Germans, one-third were children.

Today, ninety per cent of victims of war are civilians. Creating weapons of war that specifically target civilians has become a specialist endeavour. To take one example: in the 1960s and 1970s, aeroplanes of the United States scattered anti-personnel mines over Vietnam, Laos, and Cambodia. These missions became so routine that pilots had a word for these 'bomblets'; they were 'garbage', randomly chucked out of planes. Once 'seeded', these mines were forever primed to kill. Their location was unknown, meaning that even decades after the war ended, no-one was clear about where they were. By the mid-1990s, it was estimated that 110 million anti-personnel mines were scattered over 70 countries. The main victims — up to 75 per cent of victims in Somalia, for instance — were children, attracted by the shape or colour of these 'playthings'.[4] According to the Human Rights Watch, anti-personnel mines kill or maim 26,000 civilians every year.[5]

Technologies and Languages of Slaughter

Technologies of modernity facilitated these processes of brutality. Aerial bombardment not only increased the distance between combatant and victim, and thus depersonalised killing, it also provided a substitute language, a numbing glossalalia of techno-speak. As one earnest observer noted in 1945, after watching conscripts in action:

Keen discussions may develop spontaneously concerning the rival merits of particular weapons, and frequently these discussions become so involved with physics and ballistics that the participants neglect to realise that the weapon is used to facilitate death. A discussion on the most efficient ways of killing the enemy is not pleasant; however, a technological debate on the range and characteristics of a certain caliber rifle can be challenging and impersonal.[6]

Actions are separated from consequences; killing disconnected from the hypnotic cadence of iron mechanisms. As one bomb technician admitted: 'I don't *feel* like a war criminal. What I was doing is just like screwing fuses into sockets.'[7] The language of equipment and procedures stilled any intrusion of morbid thoughts.

High-tech warfare encouraged indiscriminate terrorising, especially from great heights. In aerial combat, this potential was recognised from the start. In 1924, James W. Garner, writing in the *American Journal of International Law*, warned:

The problem... is not the prohibition of aerial warfare, but its regulation in such a manner as to spare, so far as is practicable, unoffending non-combatants, private property and public institutions from indiscriminate destruction, and to insure that the wars of the future will not degenerate into struggles of reciprocal reprisals and barbarism, in which no distinction will be made between combatants and non-combatants or between public property and private property.[8]

Within a few years, such sentiments would be regarded as rather quaint or, in the patois of pragmatism, simply naive. As AAF (American Air Force) Commander General Ira C. Eaker replied when asked about his attitude to bombing German civilians during the Second World War:

I never felt there was any moral sentiment among leaders of the AAF.... A military man has to be trained and inured to do the job... The business of sentiment never enters into it at all.[9]

Yet, as Eaker was well aware, one-quarter of American bombs were dropped on residential or commercial sectors of German cities. According to the United States Strategic Bombing Survey, this was 'almost twice the weigh of bombs launched against all manufacturing targets together'.[10] Most of the victims were women. As Hans Rumpf shows, for every 100 male casualties there were 181 female casualties in Darmstadt, 160 in Hamburg, 136 in Kassel, and 122 in Nuremberg. Around one-fifth of those killed were children under the age of sixteen years and another one-fifth were over the age of sixty.[11]

At high altitudes, attacks upon unarmed civilians were rendered straightforward. Indeed, there was a strong correlation between altitude and guilt, with B-52 pilots and crews bombing at high altitudes being less liable to experience remorse than men on fighter-bomber missions who, in turn, were less guilt-ridden than men flying helicopter gunships where the victims were clearly visible.[12] In the words of John Glenn Gray, writing after the Second World War, from a distance pilots and artillery men could kill 'untold numbers of terrified noncombatants' without regret.[13] Anonymity in the slaughtering process even enabled the navigator of the *Enola Gay* which dropped the atomic bomb on Hiroshima to deny any adverse emotional reactions; he claimed to have 'come off the mission, had a bite and a few beers, and hit the sack, and had not lost a night's sleep over the bomb in 40 years'.[14]

If mechanical slaughter, technological numbing, and processes of distancing were all there was to it, barbarisation would be a mean thing. Unfortunately, the sense of moral confusion is palpable even in the accounts of servicemen and women engaged in intimate forms of killing. The hypnotic power of the peer-group is mentioned by nearly all. Take Jimmy Robertson. He was nineteen years old when he ended up in Vietnam and, one day, his superior officers decided to raze a village, killing men, women, and children. A year or so later, he painfully recalled the shock of participating in mass murder, the nightmare of his sudden surge of empathy, and his uncontrollable, numbed obedience to the norms of the group. In halting tones, he described his reactions:

Like, you know, as far as myself, you know, I happened to look into somebody's eyes, a woman's eyes, and she — I don't know, I looked, I mean, just before we started firing, I mean. You know, I didn't want to. I wanted to turn around and walk away. It was something telling me not to do it. Something told me not to, you know, just turn around and not be part of it, but when everybody else started firing, I started firing.... We were told that if we said anything, we'd be severely punished.[15]

Jimmy Robertson did end up feeling that what he had done (and, indeed, what he had not done — at the very least, turn his weapon towards non-human targets and, at the very most, protest and report the incident) was wrong. Not so with men like Lieutenant William Calley. He never felt remorseful for slaughtering hundreds of old men, women, and children on 16 March 1968 in My Lai: after all, 'what the hell *else* is war than killing people?' he queried. When he was first accused of mass murder, he was incredulous:

I couldn't understand it. I kept thinking, though. I thought, *Could it be I did some-thing wrong?* I knew that war's wrong. Killing's wrong: I realized that. I had gone to a war, though. I had killed, but I knew *So did a million others.* I sat there, and I couldn't find the key. I pictured the people of Mylai [sic]: the bodies, and they didn't bother me. I had found, I had closed with, I had destroyed the VC: the mis-sion that day. I thought, *It couldn't be wrong or I'd have remorse about it.*[16]

As I argue in *An Intimate History of Killing*, Calley was not alone in his delusions. War does not occur in a vacuum. It was not only those 'in the thick of things' that revelled in barbarism; civilians far from the killing fields were more liable to be either apathetic or enthusiastic than condemnatory about the actions of their loved ones. Within three days of William Calley's conviction for the murder of 22 Vietnamese civilians at My Lai, 200,000 copies of Nashville singer Tony Nelson's 'The Battle Hymn of Lieutenant Calley' had been sold.[17] Today, in the context of Iraq, we are hearing some unpleasant music — from country to rap — blaring out a belligerent message. In the time of the Vietnam War, the lyrics went:

> *My name is William Calley, I'm a*
> *soldier of this land,*
> *I've vowed to do my duty and to*
> *gain the upper hand,*
> *But they've made me out a villain,*
> *they have stamped me with a brand*
> *As we go marching on.*

Nixon received more than 100,000 telegrams and letters within twenty-four hours of Calley being arrested. Ninety-nine per cent deplored the arrest.[18] A Gallup poll showed that 79 per cent of Americans disapproved of Calley being court-martialled and half believed that the 'incident' for which Calley was tried was common in Vietnam.[19] When Calley was eventually released by presidential order, members of the House of Rep-resentatives stood and applauded. One book on Calley was entitled *The Making of a Hero.*[20]

This attitude was not simply an American one. America's Australian allies in Vietnam had a similar view. In a survey conducted by Leon Mann in Sydney in March and April 1971, 59 per cent of respondents thought that the perpetrators at My Lai should be left alone. Nearly one-third of respondents admitted that they would shoot civilians if ordered to do so. Because of the sampling technique used, Mann believed that the conclusions underestimated the proportion of people who agreed with the defence of 'obeying orders'. In attempting to uncover what type of person was most liable to accept atrocious behaviour, Mann found that it was not simply restricted to individuals of low socioeconomic status and educational level (who might, he assumed, be reluctant to assign responsibility to individuals since in their own lives they perceived themselves to be 'pawns, not independent agents'). Rather, he concluded, 'no single group was entirely free from the obedience response'.[21]

Most people accepted as legitimate the view that soldiers could massacre entire villages if ordered to do so by a legitimate authority. Thus, in another famous American study conducted during the Vietnam War, two researchers put forward a hypothetical situation where soldiers were asked to shoot all the inhabitants of a village, including old men, women, and children. Sixty-seven per cent of the respondents said that *most* people would follow orders and shoot. When they were asked 'What would *you* do in this situation?', slightly more than half said that they would shoot and only one-third said that they would refuse to shoot. The researchers were particularly struck by this latter response, observing:

Since it was a hypothetical question, it would have been easy enough for respondents to give themselves the benefit of the doubt and to say that they would refuse to shoot. But the important point... is that for many people it is not at all clear that this is the socially desirable response.

In other words, a majority of respondents felt that the desirable response was to follow orders. These respondents were 'not necessarily admitting to moral weakness; for many of them, in fact, this response represent[ed] what they would view as their moral obligation'. There was, these researchers concluded, a 'readiness for violence' in the American population.[22] These findings were consistent with experiments being carried out by researchers examining aggression more generally – the most well-known being the studies of Stanley Milgram, which were able to show how easy it was to persuade people to cause severe pain in others, particularly if ordered to do so by a figure of authority (such as a Yale-based social scientist).[23] Acting in barbaric ways makes sense to a large proportion of people, and not just in military contexts.

Nuclear Terror

However, the invention of a 'modern barbarism' reached new heights with the proliferation of nuclear weapons. Nuclear terror signalled a new, and most frightening, shift in the ways of waging war. On 6 August 1945, a 3,600 kg atomic bomb, nicknamed 'Little Boy', was dropped on Hiroshima. When it ignited, the temperature of the fireball (which was 100 meters in diameter) was 1,800 degrees centigrade at the outer edge and 300,000 degrees at the centre. The bomb killed approximately 140,000 people immediately. Three days later, a plutonium-type bomb was dropped on Nagasaki, killing around 24,000 people. These bland statistics don't include those who died days, months, or years later — nor do they include the 'pica babies' (pica is the Japanese word for 'flash') who were subsequently born with abnormalities because of radiation exposure in the womb.

This was barbarism at its worse: maiming and killing even the yet-to-be-born. As Tokyo radio insisted: 'Such bestial tactics reveal how thin is the veneer of civilisation the enemy has boasted of'. Some Americans agreed. General Dwight D. Eisenhower wondered if it had really been necessary to 'hit them with that awful thing'. Even the New York *Herald Tribune* found 'no satisfaction in the thought that an American aircrew had produced what must without doubt be the greatest simultaneous slaughter in the whole history of mankind', drawing a parallel between the Bomb and the 'mass butcheries of the Nazis or of the ancients'.[24]

With the start of the Cold War, these barbarous inventions only proliferated. In November 1952, the first hydrogen bomb was tested. While the bombs dropped on Hiroshima and Nagasaki were equivalent to 15,000 tons of TNT, the hydrogen bomb was equivalent to 25 million tons of TNT, and rising to 56 million tons in some tests.[25] What better way to signify the bond between modernity and barbarism than the pact between science and instruments of apocalyptic destruction? The philosopher Michel Foucault expressed the issue succinctly when he argued that 'what might be called a society's "threshold of modernity" has been reached when the life of the species is wagered on its own political strategies'. He continued: 'For millennia, man remained what he was for Aristotle: a living animal with the additional capacity for a political existence.' In contrast, now 'modern man is an animal whose politics places his existence as a living being in question.'[26] Hannah Arendt was equally dismayed. In 'Europe and the Atom Bomb' (1954), she concluded:

With the appearance of atomic weapons, both the Hebrew-Christian limitation on violence and the ancient appeal to courage have for all practical purposes become meaningless, and, with them, the whole political and moral vocabulary in which we are accustomed to discuss these matters.... The moment a war can even conceivably threaten the continued existence of man on earth, the alternative between liberty and death has lost its old plausibility.[27]

In this new world, courage, honour, and hope had no place. It was blasphemous: humanity securing the powers previously the exclusive reserve of God. Indeed, humanity's powers were ultimately more conclusive than those of the deity, in being able to annihilate irredeemably and without the possibility of redemption.

The Barbarisation of Language

In the forging of this new world, it is wrong to dichotomise civilisation and barbarism, or order and chaos. Indeed, the talk of barbarisation returns us to the same stark oppositions that got us into trouble in the first place: good versus evil; God versus Satan; Us versus Them; Civilisation versus Barbarism. These were the rhetorical figures which justified holy wars, jihads, apocalypses. In the modern world, barbarism has become very orderly. Indeed, it is evident that the most modern and the most scientific language we possess has been harnessed to the task. Thus, we see the development of a new science called 'wound ballistics'. It started in the 1890s, received a boost during the First World War, and took on institutional significance during the 1939-45 conflict when, for instance, the Wound Ballistics Research Group at Princeton employed physics to the 'game' of wounding. To take one example: in physics, the kinetic energy (K.E.) of an object is proportional to its mass (M) multiplied by the square of its velocity (v):

$$K.E. = \frac{Mv^2}{2}$$

As a consequence, the renowned Solly Zuchermann informed interested parties in 1940, that 'diminution of mass, as in small splinters, is more than compensated, from the point of view of destructive power, by increase in velocity'. He explained that:

If the mass (or weight) of a missile in motion is doubled, its kinetic energy also doubles; but if the velocity is doubled, its kinetic energy, available for wound production, is quadrupled. If mass is halved and velocity doubled, the energy also doubles, according to the formula. Thus, a wounding missile can be made smaller and still be as effective — or more so — if its velocity is increased.

Of course, if the missile, instead of stopping inside the body (and thus transferring its kinetic energy to the tissues) passes straight through the body, then 'it will not have lost much kinetic energy' and thus will not be as damaging. So, another formula was needed to calculate maximum 'retardation' of a missile due to 'drag'. The researchers at Princeton concluded that 'retardation' was 'proportional to the square of the velocity of the sphere, a general law for liquids expressed as a retardation coefficient, α'. The formula:

$$\alpha = \varrho \; \frac{ACD}{2M}$$

where ϱ is the density of the target medium, A is the projected cross-sectional area of the sphere, CD is the 'coefficient of drag' for the target medium in question, and M is the mass of the sphere.[28] This was lethality encapsulated in agreeable formulas on the blackboard.

The laws of physics yielded to the court of the barbarians, in the name of efficiency in mass killing. The results of this research were ready just in time for the wars in Korea and Vietnam; they included the M26 grenade that could spray more than a thousand fragments at a velocity of over 4,000 feet a second, 'new and improved' landmines, 'Sadeye' (a cluster bomb dropped from the air), and napalm. As US president Lyndon B. Johnson mused, 'Losing the Great Society was a terrible thought, but not so terrible as the thought of being responsible for America's losing a war to the communists. Nothing could possibly be worse than that.'[29] Eric Prokosch — whose book *The Technology of Killing* (1995) offers readers a tidy perspective — put the issue clearly:

A weapons designer is not, first and foremost, a killer; he is a statistician, a metallurgist, an engineer. He is trained for his profession and he thinks in its terms. Enter the world of the munitions designer. It is filled with 'lethal area estimate' and 'kill probabilities', 'effective casualty radius', and 'expected damage to a circular target area'. There are 'sensitivity studies' and 'compatibility tests' — not a form of marriage counselling, but a procedure for making sure than a given bomb can be used with a given airplane.[30]

It is the language of civility employed in the art of killing. Violence is underpinned by the force of reason and contained within the placid lines of a formula. As a result (in the words of Max Horkheimer and Theodor Adorno in *Dialectic of Enlightenment*),

The self-destruction of the Enlightenment... ultimately degenerates into a swindle, and becomes the myth of the twentieth century; and its irrationality turns it into an instrument of rational administration by the wholly enlightened as they steer society towards barbarism.[31]

In the midst of this terror, the barbarian speaks with a specialised language — as the ancient Greeks would have it, a 'bar-bar' — to tell of the new horrors. It is not simply that barbarisation was facilitated by shifts in language; shifts in language constituted an integral part of the barbarisation process. In the face of mass killing, language itself came under threat and was perverted. Words, which used to connect people, broke down. As Jan Gross argues, totalitarianism was not about mass organisation but the *prevention* of all association.[32] Speech became ritualised and the distinction between what 'is' and what 'ought to be' fractured. Syntax, grammar, and figure of speech were all distorted. Thus, it was important to encourage the fiction that the people being killed were not 'really' human. During the genocide of the Armenians, the Turks had a word for the men, women, and children they slaughtered: 'dog-food'. Dr Mehmed Reşid, Governor of Diyarbekir in 1915, nicknamed the 'Executioner Governor' in honour of the numerous tortures and murders he oversaw, explained that,

[e]ven though I am a physician, I cannot ignore my nationhood. I came into this world a Turk.... Armenian traitors had found a niche for themselves in the bosom of the fatherland; they were dangerous microbes. Isn't it the duty of a doctor to destroy these microbes?[33]

For the Turks, the Armenians were 'suspect' and needed 'resettlement'. The 'deportation' of women, children and the elderly was necessary for 'the restoration of order in the war zone by military measures, rendered necessary by the connivance of the inhabitants with the enemy, treachery and armed support.'[34]

A similar barbarisation of language took place during the Second World War. The virulent racism of all the participating countries was crucial in explaining the viciousness of the war. For instance, Shirō Azuma was a Japanese soldier who participated in the murders and rapes in Nanking (China) in 1937. He recalled:

> While the women were fucked, they were considered human, but when we killed them, they were just pigs. We felt no shame about it. No guilt. If we had, we couldn't have done it. When we entered a village, the first thing we'd do was steal food, then we'd take the women and rape them, and finally we'd kill all the men, women, and children to make sure they couldn't slip away and tell the Chinese troops where we were. Otherwise, we wouldn't have been able to sleep at night.[35]

Of course, racist attitudes were not the preserve of the Axis forces during the Second World War. The most vicious and prevalent atrocities carried out by British and American troops occurred in those theatres where the enemy was considered to be racially very different (as in the war in the Pacific 1939-45 and in Vietnam). It was a racism which lay at the heart of the military establishment (for instance, during the Second World War, drill instructors told recruits: 'You're not going to Europe, you're going to the Pacific. Don't hesitate to fight the Japs dirty',[36] and, in the Vietnam context, Calley was originally charged with the premeditated murder of 'Oriental human beings' rather than 'human beings'). Undeniably, men who carried out atrocities had highly prejudicial views about their victims. After a horrific recital of rape and murder, Sergeant Scott Camil of 1st Marine Division explained that '[i]t wasn't like they were humans. We were conditioned to believe that this was for the good of the nation, the good of our country, and anything we did was okay. And when you shot someone you didn't think you were shooting at a human. They were a gook or a Commie and it was okay.'[37] When the Japanese or Vietnamese were classified as inhuman, they all became fair game. The racism which led to such massacres was also tinged with fear, as the historian John W. Dower has pointed out in his exhaustive survey of racial attitudes in the Pacific theatre of war; Japan was the first non-white country to industrialise and become an imperial power, it was the first to claim a place among the Great Powers (at the Paris Peace Conference), the first to beat a Western power at war (Russia in 1905), and the first to raise the idea of Asia for the Asians.[38] These people needed to be put in their place.

Similarly in the Rwandan genocide, Tutsis were described as 'cock-roaches', with the Hutus simply engaged in 'bush-clearing'. Hutus were ordered to 'remove tall weeds' (adults) as well as the 'shoots' (children). Under genocide, language becomes divorced from experience — it is simply ideology. Again, in the case of Rwanda, many Hutu perpetrators knew that their Tutsi neighbours were innocent of the charges — but still insisted in killing them. In the words of one 74-year-old perpetrator who admitted that he knew the stories on Radio RTLM were lies but still killed: 'I regret what I did.... I am ashamed, but what would you have done if you had been in my place? ... I defended the members of my tribe against the Tutsis.'[39] Killing was re-conceptualised as 'action', 'severe measures', 'reprisal action', 'rendering harmless', 'evacuating', or 'giving special treatment'. Connections between people suddenly dissolved. Military personnel as well as some historians have over-emphasised the importance of comradeship in enabling people to engage in mass killing. Rather, instead of comradeship, atrocity became possible when individual perpetrators found themselves disoriented and alienated from each other. This was one reason why Vietnam was so susceptible to atrocity — ties of comradeship broke down, combatants barely knew the men they were serving alongside and, if they did, tended to feel hatred towards them second only to their hatred of the Vietnamese.

It is perhaps too easy, though, to identify the barbarian as the stranger — the one outside of us — in this case, the 'us' who are academic re-searchers. If the barbarian distorts language and fails to connect parts with wholes, so too do many academics working on war. Many military historians protest their pacifistic (not pacifist, but a general dislike of war-mongering, which might have to be set aside in extreme circumstances — such as in the context of Hitler's machinations) credentials with one breath while flaming plumes of bellicosity with the other. Take the example of rape in wartime. Gavin Hart conducted a major research project entitled 'Sex Behavior in a War Environment', in which he examined 718 Australian men who had seen active service. At one stage in this paper, he blandly noted that over ten per cent of the men had 'suffered penile trauma' on one occasion during their military service and five per cent had done so more than once. The cause of penile trauma? According to Hart, it was due to the refusal of some women to consent to certain sexual acts. In his words:

Failure [of the women] to indulge in fellatio at this stage often proved traumatic. Not infrequently, refusal caused the angry prostitute to violently wrench the erect penis causing severe preputial tears. A further cause of penile trauma was the strong desire of many soldiers, coupled with the unacceptance [sic] of prostitutes, to experience intraoral ejaculation.... At the onset of orgasm the soldier firmly held the girl's head in close contact with his penis and, in retaliation, the girl forcefully bit the penis to affect release.

This discussion of forced sex is positioned as if it constituted a natural aspect of wartime sexuality. The 'unacceptance' of women to engage in particular acts was (according to Hart) in itself, unacceptable. Hart does mention sexual ethics:

History continually relates how ethical and moral codes change radically under conditions of war. These altered standards together with absence from homeland and family, and ethical codes they represent, are conditions which favor promiscuity.[40]

The forced sexual acts carried out by soldiers are placed in the context of 'promiscuity'. Ethics were firmly positioned with the context of 'homeland and family'.

Torture

There are numerous other ways, in more recent times, that academics have become part of the brutalised community. Torture — officially ended in France in the 1780s and Europe generally in the nineteenth century — has made a comeback as an instrument of state policy. The Spanish government tortured ETA suspects; in Northern Ireland, the British government tortured IRA suspects. And today, powerful academic figures are calling for its return. Alan Dershowitz, an eminent professor of law at Harvard University, defends the use of torture using the patois of human rights. In his words, 'we cannot reason with them [meaning individuals he designates terrorists, while giving no way to make this designation accurately]... but we can — if we work at it — outsmart them; set traps for them, cage them, or kill them.' Dershowitz is an experienced lawyer, and the full flavour of his argumentation needs to be quoted. He wrote:

Constitutional democracies are, of course, constrained in the choices they may lawfully make. The Fifth Amendment prohibits compelled self-incrimination, which means that statements elicited by means of torture may not be introduced into evidence against the defendant who has been tortured. But if a suspect is

given immunity and then tortured into providing information about a future terrorist act, his privilege against self-incrimination has not been violated.... Nor
has his right to be free from 'cruel and unusual punishment,' since that provision
of the Eighth Amendment has been interpreted to apply solely to punishment
after conviction.

And the reasoning goes on and on. He proposed allowing judges to issue 'torture warrants' licensing authorities to torture individuals (he
calls them 'cunning beasts of prey') suspected of concealing information
about terrorist acts. The needle under the fingernail would, of course,
be sterilised; the dental drill through an unanesthetised tooth merely an
imitation of art — *Marathon Man* in this instance.[41]

Dershowitz is unfortunately not alone. Many other academics have
made similar arguments. Leonard Wantchekon and Andrew Healy, both
of Yale University, in an article entitled 'The "Game" of Torture' and published in the respected *The Journal of Conflict Resolution* in 1999, sought to
remove 'emotions' from the discussion of torture: 'The appalling practice
of torture is contrary to the foundations of human dignity and naturally
clouds judgment with anger', they wrote, calling for 'objective reasoning'. They developed an equilibrium model based on three 'players' —
the state, the torturer, and the victim — each with their 'strategies and
payoffs'. They concluded that 'when all parties act rationally to maximise
their utilities, the state might be able to torture to gain useful information
that exceeds any incurred cost'. After a lengthy series of calculus, they
concluded that the only way to stop torture was to 'eventually achieve a
situation in which most victims act in a strong manner, thereby altering
the state's utility, so that torture no longer is a rational decision'. If 'victim resistance becomes the standard, then the state has no incentive to
torture'. These comfortably-off Yale academics recommended teaching
potential victims of torture how to 'be strong', including '(a) say nothing
or give very terse answers, (b) stay calm and never look intimidated or
surprised, and (c) never panic and never confess'. They do admit that
international and domestic pressure on the state might also help create a
'culture of strong victims', but at the same time they noted that the state
needs to 'screen' potential torturers so that they would get the very best
for the task at hand: 'Entrance examinations to the military and police, as
well as interviews and psychological evaluations, can help to target the
correct candidates [for the job of torturer],' they concluded.[42]

The fact of the matter is: people get accustomed to barbarian ways. Even Simone de Beauvoir — an ardent opponent of torture during the French-Algerian War — admitted:

In this sinister month of December 1961, like many of my fellow men, I suppose, I suffer from a kind of tetanus of the imagination.... One gets used to it. But in 1957, the burns in the face, on the sexual organs, the nails torn out, the impalements, the shrieks, the convulsions, outraged me.[43]

It was a sentiment echoed by Eric Hobsbawm in his article 'Barbarism: a User's Guide', published over ten years ago but even more relevant today:

We have got used to it [barbarism]. I don't mean we still can't be shocked by this or that example of it. On the contrary, being periodically shocked by something unusually awful is part of the experience. It helps to conceal how used we have become to the normality of what our — certainly my — parents would have considered life under inhuman conditions.[44]

The terrifying fact is that the brutalities of this century have not only taken place in the milieu of Enlightenment values but have actually co-opted its framework. The ideals of the French Revolution and the Enlightenment have been used to (at the very least) tolerate and (at the worst) justify barbaric acts. In the words of Omar Rivabella in *Requiem for a Woman's Soul*, they 'torture in the name of justice, in the name of law and order, in the name of the country, and some go so far as pretending they torture in the name of God.'[45] This was particularly the case in regards to colonial peoples. Talking about torture (and its legitimation by state and military, as well as by many intellectuals) during the French-Algerian War, Rita Maran correctly observed that France's need to propagate its doctrines of human rights went hand-in-hand with its 'ideology of the *mission civilisatrice*'. She believed that this represented a 'contradiction between theory and practice', but perhaps (as she admitted a few pages later) the two processes were linked in some way. Maran observed that:

The civilising mission was an ideology simultaneously drawn from and undercutting the doctrine of the 'rights of man'. Those operating in its aura ignored or were oblivious to its inherent contradiction that restricted who might qualify for full status as 'man'. The shared understanding was that France's presence in Algeria was philanthropic, bringing civilisation to Algerians through education, roads and bridges, hospitals, an array of modern technical achievements, and last but not least, through notions of rights. When this process was disrupted by the Algerian revolution, the government, acting through its military and civilian agents took the position that unusual means were justified to restore order. By this logic, torture, one of the unusual means, was justified.

Notions of France's 'civilising mission' became both a 'rationalisation (in advance of torture)' and 'a justification (after the torture)'.[46]

As many theorists have stated, it wasn't simply the fact that the humanistic tradition proved too frail when assailed by barbarism, but that that tradition itself was sown with seeds of authoritarianism and cruelty. From the very start, the post-Second World War settlement and trials exempted the Allies from responsibility for certain of their actions. At the trial of German war criminals at Nuremberg, Allied representatives were understandably careful in ensuring that aerial bombardment and unrestrained submarine warfare were not placed on the agenda, despite the fact that The Hague Conventions had clearly outlawed both of those indiscriminate ways of waging war. When Winston Churchill heard the news about the death sentences passed on the Nazi leaders at Nuremberg he was alleged to have turned to General Sir Hastings Ismay and commented: 'Nuremberg shows that its supremely important to win. You and I would be in a pretty pickle if we had not'.[47]

What is important to acknowledge about barbarism in the twentieth century is that it is not a return to what used to be called the Dark Ages. The finest creations of the century were employed to terrorise. In Argentinean torture-chambers, intricate antibiotics were used to keep 'patients' alive for more of the same. The massacres and rapes in the former Yugoslavia were not a return to 'tribal brutality'; they arose out of familiar trials associated with the rise of the modern state, were witnessed by international agencies, and broadcast on television screens world-wide. The first war in Iraq was a very 'civilised' one, with smart bombs and all the technological expertise in the Western world thrown at it; the only result was a news-blackout about the casualties. Of course, the allies had copious accounts of the destroyed civilian homes and dead civilians. In addition to satellite data and photographs from reconnaissance aircraft, they had pilot reports and photographs taken by gun cameras on bombers. When asked to release video footage of bombs missing their targets, US Defence Secretary Cheney simply replied that such film would have been 'pretty dull, boring stuff'.[48] This antiseptic imagery enabled people to view the war in terms

of amusement, an exhilarating mix of docudrama and Nintendo entertain-
ment systems.

Return to the Present

Since 9/11 we live in an environment where the senior White House
lawyer (and now Attorney General), Alberto Gonzales, could call the
Geneva Convention a quaint relic. 'In my judgement,' he informed the
President, 'this new paradigm renders obsolete Geneva's strict limitations on questioning of enemy prisoners.'[49] The US policy of lending
detainees to other countries' jailers and torturers, known as 'rendition',
has spread to Britain. We are already exporting our suspects to regimes
capable of getting the information from them: the notion that it is sufficient to get 'diplomatic assurances' from these regimes that they will not
torture the deportees is naive at best.[50] This is not savagery — defined by
R.G. Collingwood as simply 'not being civilised' — it is barbarism, or a
conscious hostility towards civilisation.[51]

Today, the crisis is coming to a head, with the most powerful as well as
the most violent nation in the world openly flouting the most basic prohibitions of the enlightenment. In 1999 Daniel Bell, a leading human rights
commentator, confidently proclaimed that a 'thin' universalism regarding
human rights had been accepted ('at least in theory') by all governments
in the contemporary world. These 'thin' human rights included, amongst
others, the right not to be tortured or subjected to prolonged arbitrary
detention. He continued:

These rights have become part of customary international law, and they are not
contested in the public rhetoric of the international arena. Of course, many gross
human rights violations occur 'off the record', and human rights groups such
as Amnesty International have the task of exposing the gap between public al-
legiance to rights and the sad reality of ongoing abuse.

But, he observed, this was 'largely practical work, however. Theoreticians can contribute with suggestions for expanding, and rendering more
meaningful, this empirical, de facto consensus on universal rights'.[52]
Sadly for this American commentator, it was not to be: within less than
two years, theoreticians were no longer engaged in expanding this 'de
facto consensus' on fundamental human rights, but actively involved in
dismantling it. Gross human rights violations were not occurring 'off

the record' but in the full and approving glare of the American public. America overlooks serious human rights abuses in the name of its 'security' and in the 'war on terror'. In Guantanamo Bay, and other detention centres in Iraq, Afghanistan, and the British-owned island of Diego Garcia in the Indian Ocean, hundreds of prisoners are held without due process and 'stress and duress' tactics (that is, torture) are employed. No longer does the threat to basic human rights come from rogue dictatorships, but from the heart of the democratic empire. 'Thin' universalism is not slim but skeletal.

We are right to be shocked by the recent barbarism. Barbarisation of war does not take place in a vacuum. It is not simply linked to war, but also to the decline of the Enlightenment project more generally. In the modern period, it has taken place within the context of the 'advance' in weaponry, the Cold War and the proliferation of nuclear weapons, decolonisation (Kenya, Algeria, and Vietnam, to name just three), and now the 'war on terror'. We live in a world where millions of parents fear for the children — for the legacy of savagery that has been 'set at their heels'. Reflecting on the Holocaust, George Steiner put it thus:

at moments, when I see my children in the room, or imagine that I hear them breathing in the still of the house, I grow afraid. Because I have put on their backs a burden of ancient loathing and set savagery at their heels. Because it may be that I will be able to do no more than the parents of the dead children to guard them.[53]

Similar words might be being said by parents today — in Angola, Rwanda, Iraq. Indeed, they might also be said by parents in the relatively safe countries of Britain and America where the scapegoating of Muslims and the illegal war in Iraq are fanning the flames of hostility and hatred.

The words 'civilisation and barbarism' were the great watchwords of the nineteenth century. In the modern world, we see that the binary distinction is false; the barbaric has taken up residence in the house of the civilised. Indeed, it never left it. In *Thoughts for the Times on War and Death*, Sigmund Freud pointed out that disillusionment with the barbaric behaviour of warring countries was unfounded: 'In reality', he observed, 'our fellow-citizens have not sunk so low as we feared, because they had never risen so high as we believed'. Today, we can echo these sentiments: we have not become as barbaric as we feared, because we were never as civilised as we pretended. There is no true barbarisation' — simply the engagement of weapons and ideologies that were already present in the so-called non-barbarian or 'civilised' state. It was a short step from theory to practice.

But it may be wrong to allow ourselves to become tangled in the web of apocalyptic gloom. It is important not to exaggerate this mood of cultural crisis. In the light of the Holocaust, the Second World War, and the Cold War, current dangers pale in significance. I started with 'A Truthseeker', writing in 1869, and shall finish with him too. He wrote:

We stand on the shore, aghast at the stupendous and tumultuous breakers which thunder towards us. Is the time ever to arrive when a might natural force, when a universal moral power, shall completely overthrow and succeed that haughty, hallow, and artificial influence, which alone depends upon the sword's keenness? Is, indeed, the sword destined to rust? Nay, more, is it, indeed, to be converted into a plough-share for the benefit of the human family?[54]

The sentiments expressed by 'A Truthseeker' — with his appeal to a 'natural' morality — have a decidedly nineteenth century tone and, as we have seen, one of the most popular contemporary forms of 'universal moral power' — that is, human rights — has been co-opted by the barbarians. However, as in the past, there are small steps away from the path that seems to be leading us into that abyss. Instead of projecting our fears onto mythical scapegoats, we can set about forging a more equitable society. As during the Cold War, when millions of individuals throughout the world responded with a resounding 'no' to the nuclear-proliferating tactics of their governments, individuals and groups today can make themselves be heard. Instead of believing propaganda-fuelled rhetoric, we can insist on slaying the spectre of fear by acting in positive ways to perceived danger. Authoritarian versus egalitarian responses to perceived threats represent contrasting meditations on what it means to be human. Our future depends on which of these meditations we adopt.

THE SECOND WORLD WAR

A BARBAROUS CONFLICT?

Richard Overy

At the onset of the Second World War the British social historian R.H.
Tawney made the following categorical assertion: 'Either war is a crusade, or it is a crime. There is no half-way house.'[1] This view reflected the
widespread assumption in Britain and the United States that they were
conducting a just war, destroying militarism and political oppression in
the name of democracy. The post-war Nuremberg Trial of German leaders, largely organised and defined by the United States prosecution team,
was predicated on the argument that all the wars fought by Hitler's Germany were in themselves criminal.[2] Yet there is no doubt that Hitler and a
great many other Germans saw the war against the Soviet Union as a just
war to liberate Europe from the general menace of Jewish-Bolshevism
and the Slavic mass. Just as surely did the Stalinist Soviet Union publicly
define the contest with Germany as a war of liberation for the working
masses of Europe against the threat of fascist imperialism and militarism.
The discourses used by all the major wartime combatants presented the
war as just and the enemy as representative of the forces of darkness. The
many aspects of the conflict that are commonly regarded as 'criminal' or
'barbarous' arose precisely because war was viewed as some form of crusade. In an age that defined war as 'total', the frontier between crusade
and crime became first blurred then entirely eroded. The same United
States that argued in the 1930s for disarmament, the renunciation of
war and the outlawing of bombing ended up half a decade later dropping
atomic bombs on Japan.

This apparent paradox can only be explained satisfactorily by looking at the expectations about the nature of future warfare that shaped the way the war was fought between 1939 and 1945 and by examining the different ways in which the conduct of war was validated by those who fought it. The terms used by all sides were absolute to a degree exceptional in modern warfare (though more commonly found in civil conflicts). The nature of total war derived not just from the large-scale exploitation of the economic, social and mental resources of the nation but from the popular belief that victory or defeat would also be total. The world-historical terms under which the war was fought — civilisation against barbarism, race against race, democracy versus totalitarianism — were articulated in order to make legitimate forms of warfare that the liberal nineteenth century had tried to eradicate. The death toll of the Second World War was largely civilian, not military; in the First World War the ratio had been the reverse.[3]

Defining Barbarisation

The role played by ideology in shaping the criminal conduct of warfare in the Second World War lay at the core of Omer Bartov's classic study of the war between Germany and the Soviet Union, first published in 1985. The book's sub-title 'German Troops and the Barbarisation of Warfare' defined the way in which the subsequent debate about the barbarous nature of the war has been conducted. [4] The focus of Bartov's research was the criminal behaviour of German forces in the war against the Soviet Union. He demonstrated that the established view that only the security forces in the east — the SS, the security police, the regular police force and local police militia — had been responsible for atrocities against Soviet soldiers and civilians was wrong. The German army was also responsible, directly or indirectly, for much of the excessive violence and routine atrocity committed in the east. The argument was strongly underpinned by the work of the German historians Christian Streit, whose study of the maltreatment of Soviet prisoners-of-war pre-dated Bartov by almost a decade, and Christian Gerlach, whose detailed reconstruction of the activities of German forces in Belorussia exposed the deliberate nature of the barbarism.[5] In 1996 a controversial exhibition on the 'Crimes of the Wehrmacht' began a four-year tour of 34 German cities, bringing home to the German public the reality that soldiers had committed atrocities alongside the murderous security forces, whose atrocious behaviour had long been established and, in some cases, punished.[6]

The main contours of Bartov's argument, elaborated in a second book on the German army, can be briefly sketched. German soldiers in the east were the product of a system with a high level of indoctrination, some deliberate, some casual, which created a common set of assumptions about the nature of the enemy and the importance of defending Germany's future by smashing the threat of Jewish-Bolshevik Russia. This predisposition was reinforced by the so-called 'criminal orders' that emanated from Hitler's supreme headquarters in the course of 1941 permitting ruthless action against any opponent, military or civilian, and exonerating German soldiers in advance for anything they did which might under normal circumstances have been regarded as a violation of the rules of warfare.[7] The result was a process of degeneration in the behaviour of German forces, implied by the term 'barbarisation' rather than the simple adjective 'barbarous', which by the middle years of the war in the east made atrocity routine. The harder the war became, the more barbarous its conduct; but the driving force behind the process was the ideological imperative built into the war from the outset. The 'war of annihilation', as Hitler called it, was regarded as a battle between two world views in which ruthless severity was justified by the nature of the conflict.

The idea of barbarisation as a consequence of processes unleashed by deliberate disregard for the rules normally covering the conduct of war raises a number of issues. It suggests that the German conduct of war in the Soviet Union degenerated from a set of norms which were generally acknowledged to regulate the behaviour of armed forces in modern combat. Such norms certainly existed, enshrined in the Hague Rules and the Geneva Convention. But in reality many forms of combat in the first part of the twentieth century had ignored them (particularly wars of imperial pacification), or were outside international agreement. The Russian civil war of 1918-20 and the Spanish civil war of 1936-39 were fought by armies but were conducted with exceptional levels of ferocity and complete disregard for any rules of combat. Civilians were victims in both civil wars in large numbers. The intermittent war between Japan and China from 1916 to the Second World War was never fought in accordance with international law, nor was the war between

Italy and Ethiopia. In both cases atrocity was routine. In the case of war between Germany and the Soviet Union, the German side knew well that the Soviet state had not ratified the Geneva Convention and could be treated outside the normative conduct of war. When the Soviet government tried in the first weeks of the conflict to reach agreement through the International Red Cross on mutual respect for prisoners' rights, the German government refused to comply.[8] In all these cases warfare could be defined as 'barbarous' since it was conducted without respect for civilian life, or protection for prisoners-of-war, or acknowledgement of any rules of engagement. The German war on the Soviet Union was fought in ways consistent with almost all these examples of armed combat since the First World War. The way the war was fought between Britain, France and Germany in 1939-1940, in general according to the conventional laws of war, was the exception, not the rule in the Second World War.

The barbarisation of warfare is an elastic concept in another sense. Different forms of 'barbarism', or degenerate military behaviour, have to be identified, each with its own historical imperatives and historical context. Some were the product of the confrontation between army and army and were in this sense a direct relaxation of the rules governing the behaviour of one set of soldiers towards another. The abuse or murder of prisoners, or the killing of surrendering soldiers, or their torture and mistreatment all occurred in the fighting on the eastern front. Some were the product of conflict between armed forces and irregulars (first the popular militias raised in Soviet cities, then the formal partisan units which proliferated behind the German lines), which resulted in routine atrocity against non-combatants accused of complicity with guerrilla terrorism. Some were the result of deliberate destruction of civilian life through the bombing and shelling of civilian urban areas; other deaths resulted from the forced movement of populations or the requisition of foodstuffs desperately needed by the local population; in some cases the army gave assistance to the security forces which were engaged in murdering Soviet Jews or rounding up forced labour. Each of these different confrontations had its own cause and its own context even if the direct consequence for the victims of murderous violence was in the end the same.

Problems also emerge from the focus on the German armed forces, many of whom neither engaged in murder nor approved it. Many atrocities in the east were perpetrated by local nationalist militia and security forces; some were carried out by the forces of Germany's allies on the eastern front, Hungary and Romania. Above all, atrocity was not confined only to the invading armies. Part of the explanation for the cycle of barbarous behaviour lies in the dialectic of violence that developed between the German and Soviet side. This was a process with its own dynamic. Soviet civilian resistance and partisan attacks were ruthlessly suppressed by the German army. In turn Soviet irregulars murdered German soldiers, committed acts of terrorism and exacted vengeance on Soviet collaborators. The Red Army fought at times with tactics that encouraged German atrocity; there were cases where German prisoners were murdered rather than incarcerated. The predisposition to regard the Soviet enemy as a dangerous threat to European civilisation was reinforced by the experiences of many German soldiers when they came face-to-face with Soviet society.[9]

The degeneration of military behaviour on the Eastern Front as the war went on and Germany and her allies found themselves fighting a war of pacification alongside the formal military campaigns is a process distinct from the effect of indoctrination, though related to it. This explains the permanent tension that exists in most accounts of 'barbarisation' in the German-Soviet war, between arguments that suggest the primary role of propaganda and ideology in creating a predisposition to perceive the enemy in profoundly negative terms and those arguments that suggest that the environment of combat (the effects of poor climate, the hostile topography, the long time-span of fighting, deteriorating supply conditions, and fear) explains the increasing recourse to acts of barbarism.[10] The environmental explanation does not exclude the possibility that indoctrination played some part in determining the choices made by soldiers in the field, but it suggests that barbarisation is a circumstantial response, not something in the essence of the conflict itself.

The most problematic aspect of the thesis that barbarisation was a consequence of the special terms in which the German-Soviet war was conducted lies in the evident reality that the forms of violence defined as 'barbarous' — excessive, gratuitous violence, largely directed at civilians — occurred in many other contexts during the Second World War. The long war between Japan and China was not fought with regard to the laws of war. Guerrilla resistance in Europe and Asia was penalised by the occupying power with exceptional savagery. The war in Italy following the Italian surrender to the Allies in September 1943 involved a partisan war against German forces and a civil war between fascist and anti-fascist Italians, each of which provoked another cycle of atrocity and revenge in a theatre where German forces had already displayed the same brutality they had shown in the Soviet Union.[11] The barbarisation of warfare as it has been defined for the Eastern front has a much wider application. It is important, therefore, to be clear about what the concept of 'barbarisation' means before exploring general historical explanations for why the conduct of the war degenerated from normative notions of military violence.

There are three separate contexts in which violence perpetrated by armed forces (as distinct from violence carried out by security and police forces) occurred on a large scale outside the conventional laws of war:

1. violence between armed forces outside agreed rules of conduct (murder, torture or mistreatment of prisoners-of-war, murder of unarmed or surrendering soldiers, murder of the wounded);

2. violence between armed forces and irregular forces organised as militia, partisan units or underground resistance movements (summary executions, indiscriminate victimisation, terror attacks, assassination, torture and murder of prisoners);

3. violence between armed forces and civilians who were non-combatants (hostage-taking, murder of bystander populations, forced labour, deportations, bombing and shelling of civilian areas).

Of these three categories the third was by far the most murderous during the Second World War. In the Soviet Union an estimated 16 million civilians died, some at the hand of their own regime, some from starvation, but a very large number from the results of military action. In the Sino-Japanese war the estimates of civilian deaths vary widely, but run well into the millions, possibly as many as 20 million. The bombing of cities in Europe and the Far East cost the lives of at least 1.4 million people (a high proportion of whom were women and children) and dispossessed millions more. By any standard the Second World War was a barbarous conflict, and it became so not just as a result of German behaviour but on account of more widespread acceptance that the thresholds of violence should be lowered in order to avoid defeat or ensure victory.

The Paradox of Modern War

Though there are factors specific to the German-Soviet war which explain the way it was fought, the barbarous nature of the Second World War as a whole compels the argument that general or common factors may have been responsible for the descent into forms of warfare not usually experienced during the war of 1914-1918. This first war was a manifestation of the terrible power of modern weaponry against human beings; those human beings were in the main uniformed men, who could legitimately be blown to pieces, bayoneted or machine-gunned without violating accepted rules of combat. At the end of the war, when the victorious powers discussed prosecution of the enemy for war crimes the list of the actions regarded in international law as criminal was based on existing agreements.[12] The actions proscribed in 1919 were almost all engaged in by one or more of the combatant powers during the war that broke out twenty years later.

This fact alone suggests that in the intervening years the sanctions against forms of warfare previously regarded as illegitimate were eroded or ignored. By 1939, even before the start of the war, the ground had been prepared for forms of warfare that either were not covered effectively by existing international law or were regarded as the product of a new kind of war for which the old rules were inadequate or inappropriate. This was one of the more important consequences of the widespread acceptance of the concept of total war, which emerged in response not only to the exceptional levels of popular mobilisation achieved by 1918 but also to the idea that total war, as a war of national survival, legitimised military attacks against non-combatant targets. This second principle of total war was manifested in the campaign of unrestricted submarine warfare and in the use of dirigibles and long-range bomber aircraft against urban targets. German military thinkers assumed that the Allied sea blockade was also an expression of a new-found willingness to subject the civil population indiscriminately to economic and moral pressure sufficient to weaken the enemy's resolve, though the Royal Navy regarded it as consistent with the conventions of maritime warfare.

The involvement of non-combatants as legitimate targets of attack stemmed from an organic conception of modern society in which the existing, and easily-defined, distinction between a soldier and a munitions

worker or farmhand was eliminated on the grounds that in a modern
society, fighting a war over a sustained period of time, the munitions
worker and the farmhand made an evident contribution to the fighting
power of the armed forces and should be regarded as legitimate objects
of military activity. The potential for an enemy population under occupation to sustain resistance was limited during the First World War, but the
evolving view that much of an enemy's civilian population also contributed to sustaining the war effort from the very nature of its activities, its
labour or its moral stance undermined further the convention that the
non-military sections of a nation's population should be immune from
attack or punishment (a principle already breached by British behaviour
during the Boer War). During the Second World War the widespread
resistance to enemy rule in occupied Europe and Asia reflected a remarkable shift in the popular view of warfare and in military practice towards
civilians, the roots of which lay in the erosion of a discrete military sphere
during the first war.

Warfare waged as total war had about it much more the character of
a civil war. The Russian Civil War and the Spanish Civil War can both be
seen as varieties of total war; the many civil conflicts between 1939 and
1945 were by-products of total war and were waged mainly by civilians-
as-soldiers, not by armies. The civilian population in areas not subject
to occupation were encouraged by the authorities to see themselves as
soldiers on the factory front, or soldiers of labour, conferring on them a
status that only exacerbated the prevailing sense that the 'enemy' was the
enemy whether he held a gun in his hand or not. This was a status that the
workforce had to accept regardless. In Italy the war production commis-
sariat considered workers in 1940 to be a kind of production army: 'The
worker attached to war industry must be considered to be like a soldier,
who, in the face of enemy fire, has the requirement and obligation to remain at his proper combat post.'[13] Allied airborne propaganda directed at
the same Italian workers two years later told them that they were targets
because they sustained the fighting power of an enemy state, and could
not therefore be considered non-combatants, but instead, as one leaflet
put it, 'will be attacked with every means at our disposal'. Civilians were,
willy-nilly, defined as part of the social war effort.[14]

Historians have traced this shift in warfare back to the French Revolution and the birth of the idea of the 'nation in arms'.[15] Yet the level

of mobilisation implied by the concept of mass civilian participation in defence of the nation was only made possible in the last part of the nineteenth century by the revolution in transport, increases in the level of state supervision and the emergence of a maturing industrial economy. Popular nationalism and mass political participation also shaped the view of a future war as a war of national survival, but the military establishments in Europe still broadly favoured army-to-army conflicts and exclusive military control of the war effort. The shift that occurred after 1914, when the armed forces of every combatant power became civilian society in uniform and civilian politicians and officials began to organise the process of national mobilisation, often in the face of strong military objection, shaped what came to be called total war. In this sense mass mobilisation came to be regarded as an expression of modernity, in which the modern organic community, organised around the principle of the modern nation-state, fought for its survival by every means that the modern age had made available. The idea that modern social and economic developments were capable of generating savage industrialised wars and profound hatreds challenged many popular pre-war assumptions about social progress, and encouraged the argument that the war was the product of the survival of a decaying 'old regime'. In reality, as the work of Zygmunt Bauman and Omer Bartov has demonstrated, the age of mass violence (war, civil war and genocide) was an expression of the development of modernity in the context of, among other things, mass nationalism, scientific progress and modern bureaucratic practice. [16]

Indeed, science as such contributed a good deal to the wider syndrome that made possible the idea and acceptance of total war as an unavoidable reality of the modern age. The Darwinian revolution in biology was applied almost immediately by analogy to the human condition. The vulgar reception of evolutionary theory had at its core the idea that all of life represented some form of struggle for existence or survival; for human societies struggle was expressed as warfare. This conclusion was never simply a harmless platitude; the assumption that human beings could not escape their nature engendered ideas about national competition and the pursuit of national efficiency in order to ensure that particular peoples should survive the struggle for existence, always one at the expense of others. [17] The exploitation of ideas about war as an expression of natural selection and the struggle for survival between different groups of humans, current before 1914 though not universally accepted, hardened into a conviction that this was indeed so as a result of the war that followed. The new generation of post-war radical nationalist politicians was strongly influenced by this conviction. Popular biology can be found mobilised in much of what Adolf Hitler said and wrote in the 1920s. 'All of nature,' Hitler announced to a party meeting in 1923, 'is a constant struggle between power and weakness, a constant triumph of the strong over the weak.'[18] Hitler's *Mein Kampf* is littered with references to biological politics; his so-called 'Second Book', dictated in 1928, is full of ideas about the naturalness and necessity of violence. In Italy, Benito Mussolini made the idea that 'all life is struggle' a central feature of Fascist thinking about the purifying effects of violence. [19] Even more sober soldiers and statesmen were also seduced by the idea. The German general Wilhelm Groener, who played a key part in organising the mobilisation of German labour and resources in the Great War, concluded in a lengthy memorandum on modern strategy written in 1926 that 'the future of the race' would be at stake in any other great power war. [20] Georg Thomas, the officer chosen by the Defence Ministry in the 1920s to study secretly the possibility of future industrial mobilisation, defined modern war as 'no longer a clash of armies, but a struggle for the existence of the peoples involved'. [21]

To the natural character of the struggle between peoples was added the idea, popularised by pioneers of modern psychoanalysis, that human beings, even beneath the veneer of modern civility, were driven by an impulse to aggression. The most important exponent of the idea that there existed a perpetual struggle within man between the instinct to preserve and the instinct to destroy was Sigmund Freud, whose influence on thinking about human development in the early part of the twentieth century was as profound as that of Darwin forty years before. Freud's developed ideas about the instinct to aggression in man coincided with the experience of the Great War which Freud reacted to with a growing pessimism. In his essay on 'Our Attitude towards Death', written in 1915, Freud developed the idea that men all retain a primeval instinct for violence: 'The very emphasis on the commandment *Thou shalt not kill* makes it certain,' he wrote, 'that we spring from an endless series of generations of murderers, who had the lust for killing in their blood, as, perhaps, we ourselves have today.' The war, he concluded, 'strips us of the later accretions of civilisation, and lays bare the primal man in each of us.' [22] From these observations he went on in the 1920s to articulate a theory of the instincts that opposed love and hate, the urge for life and the urge for destruction. In 1933 he entered a widely publicised exchange with Albert Einstein on the subject 'Why War?' in which he returned to the thesis of instinctual aggression: 'It is a general principle, then, that conflicts of interest between men are settled by the use of violence. This is true of the whole animal kingdom, from which men have no business to exclude themselves.' [23] The efforts of warmongers, Freud told Einstein, was greatly facilitated by the 'instinct for hatred and destruction' present in man. Aggression, he concluded, was not something to be confined to history. It had 'a good biological basis' and was 'scarcely avoidable'. [24]

Neither Darwin nor Freud intended his science to make wars legitimate. Freud deplored the violence, even if it seemed to him unavoidable. Nonetheless, the effect of sciences that argued the natural character of species competition and instinctual violence as breakthroughs in a modern, scientific perception of the world was to create an intellectual framework which many non-scientists could use to explain why that part of the globe which claimed to be the most progressive and civilised was at the same time capable of organised violence and destruction on a scale scarcely conceivable before 1914. The paradox of European historical improvement and the disaster of the Great War was neatly captured by the novelist H. G. Wells in 1921 in a gloomy assessment of where the modern age had arrived: 'The spectacular catastrophe of the Great War has revealed an accumulation of destructive forces in our outwardly prosperous society, of which few of us had dreamt; and it has also revealed a profound incapacity to deal with and restrain these forces.' [25] Wells argued that the central problem was the mobilisation of massive industrial and technical power which transcended what he called the 'normal aspect' of conflict and substituted 'a terror and a threat for the entire species'. [26]

This paradox of progress also owed a great deal to science, for even without the impact of modern ideas about nature and violence, there existed a growing technological imperative for military forces to appropriate the fruits of scientific and mechanical development to avoid the danger of being overtaken by states whose scientific resources were mobilised more effectively or unscrupulously for military purposes. The relationship between scientific advance and the willingness to mobilise

science for military purposes had an inexorable logic to it for states that
rationalised conflict in terms of the necessity for national survival and the
rational exploitation of national advantage. This has remained down to
the present day the central paradox of modernity: on the one hand an
apparent capacity to generate high levels of economic well-being and
social order, on the other an enlarged capacity to produce weapons of
ever greater destructive power when applied to the structure of modern societies. This imperative could not be reversed except through acts
of collective self-restraint or mutual deterrence; it acted powerfully
during the Great War, from the introduction of poison gas at the front-
line in 1915 to the Allied decision, had the war continued, to launch an
Independent Force of heavy bombers against German cities and civilian
workers in the spring of 1919. No major military power could afford not
to make use of the resources offered by modern research. The apothe-
osis of the paradox of progress and dislocation was the development of
nuclear weapons which, though capable of obliterating a large part of
the developed world, were sustained and refined by states that at the
same time experienced after 1950 an exceptional period of economic
and social progress. This schizophrenic reality was explored by Robert
Lifton and Eric Markusen in *The Genocidal Mentality*, published in 1990,
an analysis of Western nuclear strategy which tried to show how it was
possible in the modern age for overwhelming destructive power and
democratic progress to co-exist, but it was a paradox well understood
in the inter-war years when the major powers failed again and again to
reach agreement on restraining the development of weapons whose use
would vitiate the very same economic and scientific progress that made
the new weaponry possible.[27] 'It is common knowledge,' Einstein told
Freud in their exchange of letters in 1933, 'that, with the advance of
modern science, this issue [war] has come to mean a matter of life and
death for civilisation as we know it.'[28]

These separate scientific discourses not only appeared to explain the
perennial resort to violence in recognisably modern scientific terms,
but also to supply the means to ensure that those violent propensi-
ties would be capable of unleashing the ever-greater destructive power
made available by science. Total war as a concept reflected a profoundly
pessimistic attitude towards violence as irresistible, biologically determined and, potentially, limitless.

A Crisis of Civilisation?

This pessimism was also fuelled by an evident moral crisis provoked by the reality of the Great War and its revolutionary aftermath. The crisis had many different faces, since the conclusions drawn from the war by conservative Europeans, or devout Christians, or democratic socialists or communists were self-evidently distinct. The crisis had one central characteristic: a belief that the war had weakened Western civilisation and made possible its catastrophic destruction. 'The present system,' reflected Wells in 1921, in the book he titled *The Salvaging of Civilisation*, 'unless it can develop a better intelligence and a better heart, is manifestly destined to foster fresh wars and to continue wasting what is left of the substance of mankind, until absolute social disaster overtakes us all.'[29] The sense that civilisation was doomed without remedial action, though by no means a sentiment confined only to the years after the First World War, was embedded in much of the intellectual and literary discourse of the inter-war years. The anxiety is reflected in the numerous titles printed throughout the developed Western world following the classic statement of crisis by the German philosopher Oswald Spengler in his *Decline of the West*, published in two volumes in 1918 and 1920. [30] The British historian Arnold Toynbee, much influenced by Spengler in his own work on the pathology of civilisation, eventually came to the conclusion that War (deliberately capitalised) in the modern age faced mankind with the prospect for the first time not only of destroying a given civilisation, as it had often done in the past, but of 'bringing to an end the history of mankind on this planet'. [31] In November 1938 the Federation of Progressive Societies hosted a symposium in London under the portentous title 'How Can Civilisation be Saved?' and were treated to an account by the British psychoanalyst Ernest Jones of the feebleness of modern populations in coping with the liberating effects brought about by the age of the French Revolution and the current descent into the 'primitive region of the mind' by many Europeans yearning for authority and violently fearful about the future. [32]

The sense that history was at a critical turning point which might end altogether the path of European progress was fuelled by the reaction of the West to the Bolshevik revolution in 1917, which was made to represent not only the triumph of barbarism in Russia but a permanent

standing threat of internal decay and subversion by communist forces
within states weakened by war and systems morally compromised by
its violence. In August 1936, Adolf Hitler wrote a long memorandum at
his retreat in Berchtesgaden in which he reviewed the state of the world
and of Germany's place in it. He bemoaned the threat posed by the Soviet Union to the survival of Western civilisation if communism should
ever sweep across Europe: 'The scale of such a catastrophe cannot be
predicted. For above all the thickly populated areas of Western Europe
(including Germany) would well experience after a Bolshevik breakout
the cruellest catastrophe to overtake mankind since the fall of the states
of antiquity.' [33] The violent anxieties and resentments that characterised
much of German society in the 1920s and 1930s were bound up with
the fear that after 1918 the German people stood on the brink of an
historical precipice. [34] These anxieties fed into the conflict with the Soviet
Union which began in 1941 with the 'war of annihilation' preached by
Hitler as the remedy for the threat to 'civilisation'.

    The consequences of the widespread sense of post-war *fin-de-siècle*
were not predictable or universal, but they contributed to the idea that
the next war, if it came, would be about more fundamental issues than
the first. The absolute quality of the political and ideological conflicts of
the inter-war years derived from conviction that the threat posed was
also absolute and unyielding. This view of war as a Manichean struggle
about the future embraced not only the contest between Fascism and
Bolshevism, but was articulated in the West in response to the threat
posed by the dictatorships. In the preface to *No Compromise: the Conflict
Between Two Worlds*, published in London just after the outbreak of war
in 1939, the author, the American philosopher Melvin Rader, told his
British public that they faced the 'grimmest of truths: there are things
worth dying for'. If the 'will-to-destruction' triumphed, he continued,
'our resolution to defend civilisation must become more implacable'.
In a brief foreword to the book, the British socialist Harold Laski applauded Rader's own lack of compromise: 'It is either we or they.' [35]
The popular culture of a 'war to the finish' gave war an essential rather
than instrumental character; war was no longer a means of achieving
limited ends, but became an end in itself. The moral 'crisis of civilisation'
blunted views about the moral object of war and encouraged popular
resistance even after formal national defeat. In most of the states that

contemplated or engaged in war in the 1940s, the moral absolutes of survival or decay, triumph or disaster, transcended the obligation to wage that war according to established norms of conduct, if the nature of the peril were sufficient to justify their abrogation. At the height of the Blitz in December 1940, Winston Churchill asked the Chief of the Air Staff to prepare for him a detailed analysis of how much poison gas could be dropped on Germany's major cities and for how long. He received the reply that supplies were very limited, but that the effect of gas bombs could be greatly enhanced by mixing them with quantities of high explosives in the attacking aircraft. [36] No operations resulted from the exchange; what is historically significant is the willingness of British leaders to contemplate such operations at all.

The extent to which the ideological gulf between differing political constituencies could generate exceptional levels of brutality was made evident in the course of the Spanish Civil War where atrocities were committed not only between the two opposed sides, Republican and Nationalist, but between factions supposedly engaged on the same side. The nature of the conflict was used to legitimise atrocity, just as it was used to give moral imperative to the conduct of the war waged between 1939 and 1945. The overbearing sense of moral responsibility — defence of civilisation, defence of the democratic way of life, defence of the race and so on — appeared to give a powerful moral impulse to the conduct of the war and permitted states to abandon humanitarian considerations on grounds of historical necessity, operational expediency or urgent self-defence.

Bombing: a 'New Means of Waging War'

These many strands of discourse about modernity and crisis between the wars did not cause war or determine strategic choices directly, but they help to resolve the historical paradox in which states otherwise committed to salvaging civilisation nonetheless willingly engaged in barbarous forms of warfare. One such paradox, already noted, was the enthusiasm of Britain and the United States for independent or strategic bombing during the Second World War directed at major urban areas, even though both states had publicly advocated in the 1930s the necessity for self-restraint in the exercise of air power against civilian targets.

The roots of Anglo-American interest in bombing lie in the First World War when, in response to German bombing of London and other British cities, plans were developed for a systematic attack on Germany's western cities in order to reduce German fighting power and to demoralise the civilian population. The first strategic bombing campaign began half-heartedly in 1918 but was in the end pre-empted by the Armistice. In the early 1920s a theoretical framework was given to bombing strategy in the context of ideas about total war. The classic statement of the idea that the civilian heartlands could be attacked from the air in order to produce a swift end to the war through the collapse of popular war-willingness and the massive dislocation of the structures of modern urban society was made in 1923 by the Italian General Giulio Douhet, but similar ideas were widely current in military circles throughout the developed world.[37] Bomb attack was regarded as the principal manifestation of the new kind of war ushered in by the conflict of 1914-1918. The entire enemy society came to be regarded as a legitimate target and bombing as the means to bring about economic decline and moral debilitation to a degree necessary to bring about the collapse of the enemy war effort. In all the major states, except for the Soviet Union, this shift in the view of future war was reflected in the development of a popular and collective fear of the apocalyptic consequences of bomb attack.[38]

Independent bombing operations represented modernity in several ways. Not only did they involve the development of an expensive modern weapons system (which only the most developed states could afford) and offer an apparently more rational and efficient form of warfare than the stalemate of the trenches, but bombing was also seen as a form of warfare uniquely adapted to exploit the potential vulnerability of modern urban life and of city populations regarded as less rooted and more prone to panic than were traditional communities. 'Direct air attack,' wrote the British Chief of the Air Staff, Hugh Trenchard, in 1928, 'on the centres of production, transportation and communications must succeed in paralysing the life and effort of the community and therefore in winning the war.'[39] At the American Air Corps Tactical School during the 1930s American airmen developed the concept of the 'social body' rooted in the industrial and population centres of a potential enemy. In analysing the ability of a state to sustain war the social and economic system were placed above the military system in importance, which validated the idea that war was really to be waged against enemy societies, not against the armed forces. 'Civilisation has rendered the economic and social life of a nation increasingly vulnerable to attack,' ran one lecture given on a course in 1935. 'Sound strategy requires that the main blow be struck where the enemy is weakest.' [40] The urban crowd, ran a British report following air exercises in 1923, would be 'infinitely more susceptible to collapse' than the armed forces. [41] There is almost no evidence that the British or American air forces had serious qualms about the fate of those civilians subjected to bomb attack, since the object was always expressed in abstract terms — 'the social body', the 'vital centres'. Concern that bombing violated the laws of war led to a high-level inquiry in Britain in 1928, but the conclusion arrived at by the Imperial General Staff was that air attacks against cities and civilian morale should properly be regarded as 'legitimate objectives of air attack'. [42] In the notes for a lecture given to British air force officers in 1936, the author observed that since war was now waged on a national basis, 'No longer possible to draw a definite line between combatant and non-combatant'. [43]

Air warfare against urban civilian populations and the economic infrastructure was widely expected in the 1930s and extensive civil defence precautions were taken to ensure that the civilian population had at least rudimentary protection against air attack. Although none of the combatant powers in 1939 wanted to be accused of starting the civilian war, there was no reluctance to assume that at some point a bombing war would begin if the military situation required it. When the Italian Air Staff was asked by the Italian Air Ministry in April 1939 what kind of enemy attacks to expect if war came, the reply listed military targets, 'industrial and logistical centres', and then 'in a total war — all the centres of population, in an order of priority based on the number of inhabitants.'[44] In this sense, the barbarous conduct of war against civilian centres was both premeditated and anticipated, but not outlawed. No international provisions existed sufficient to make bombing a war crime during the Second World War, while a general consensus about the military necessity, even legitimacy, of attacking centres of production and the populations who worked in them helped to create a wider sense that the '*new means of waging war*' [italics in original], as one Air Corps lecture put it in 1936, was permitted by the nature of modern weaponry, modern systems of production and distribution, and the voluntary participation of enemy non-combatants.[45]

'It is clear,' wrote Air Marshal Arthur Harris, Commander-in-Chief of RAF Bomber Command, 'that any civilian who produces more than enough to maintain himself is making a positive contribution to the German war effort and is therefore a proper…object of attack.' [46]

The mindset that could accept the deliberate targeting of non-combatant populations and the destruction of the social fabric of enemy cities was shaped by the changed expectations about the nature of war and the necessity of waging it to the full by bringing national power to bear as efficiently as possible against the entire enemy nation. In Britain and the United States the nature of the potential enemy — Hitler's Germany — encouraged the idea that the democracies should have no hesitation in doing anything that avoided defeat and secured unconditional victory. 'Against naked force the only possible defence is naked force,' wrote President Roosevelt for the Young Democrats' Convention in 1938. 'The aggressor makes the rules for such a war; the defenders have no alternative but matching destruction with destruction, slaughter with greater slaughter.' [47] Against Germany, as Churchill famously observed to Lord Beaverbrook in July 1940, only 'an absolutely devastating, exterminating attack by very heavy bombers from this country upon the Nazi homeland' would, he thought, bring the collapse of Hitler's Germany. [48] Both Britain and the United States could, on humanitarian grounds, have refused to engage in mass bombing attacks. The choice of bombing as a strategy was taken in the full knowledge that the effects would damage the civilian population, not the armed forces of the enemy state, and that this was consistent with a modern conception of what was permissible or necessary in the conduct of modern war against an enemy deemed to be a ruthless threat to civilisation. The result, already noted, meant that two liberal democracies deliberately caused the death of approximately 800,000 civilians and the maiming, dislocation and traumatisation of millions more. The intellectual framework that justified these excesses had a strong ideological core and lived on after 1945 to legitimise the coming of the nuclear confrontation when the nature of the perceived threat was sufficiently apocalyptic to explain why, in 1947, the US Joint Chiefs of Staff asked the Atomic Energy Authority for a programme of bomb production capable, by 1953, of 'killing a nation'. [49]

The Limits of the Permissible

The example of strategic bombing makes it clear that the barbarity of the Second World War was not confined only to the conduct of German forces on the Eastern front, though the contexts in which it was expressed were very different, the operational means employed quite distinct, and the victims chosen according to very different criteria. What united the many strands of a war that resulted in such high levels of civilian casualty and physical destruction were assumptions drawn from the war of 1914-1918 about the nature of modern conflict in the context of the apparently dissolving certainties of the post-1919 world and the sharper ideological and social conflicts that resulted from this.[50] The limits of the permissible in war were reshaped to take account both of the nature of modern society and economy but also of the deep ideological and racial fissures that modern political conflict generated. These conflicts were articulated as part of a more general crisis of humanity, or civilisation. Alongside the optimistic expectations of a 'war to end all wars', there developed in the 1920s a strong sense that the existing order had been irreversibly crippled by the Great War, and that further wars even bloodier than the first were likely to result from the failures of the modern age that the war exposed. The sense that a purifying violence might rescue European humanity, regenerate its culture and heal the social body was not confined only to the radical nationalist dictatorships. Much more research needs to be done on how the morbid discourses of modernity and crisis were communicated, understood and instrumentalised in the interwar years, but it is evident that the barbarous character of the war that followed after 1939 was determined to no small extent by an exceptionally morbid world view drawn from the experience and consequences of the earlier war and the willingness to adapt that world view to the circumstances of the second.

TIME, SPACE AND BARBARISATION

THE GERMAN ARMY AND THE EASTERN
FRONT IN TWO WORLD WARS

Hew Strachan

On 25 January 1904, Halford Mackinder delivered a lecture at the Royal Geographical Society in London, which geographers in Britain regard as the founding moment of geopolitics. Mackinder, who had read natural sciences and history at Oxford before qualifying as a lawyer, was the pivotal figure in the establishment of modern geographical studies in British universities. A serial pluralist, he was never happy doing one job when he could be doing several. In 1904 he was Reader in Geography at Oxford University, a Student (i.e. Fellow) of Christ Church, and Director of the London School of Economics. He would later become a Member of Parliament, and he was the British High Commissioner in south Russia in 1919.[1]

His lecture, which was attended by Spenser Wilkinson, appointed Oxford's first Professor of Military History in 1909, and Leo Amery, the strongest advocate of Britain's war aims in the Middle East in 1917-18, was called 'the geographical pivot of history'. Mackinder sought 'a formula which shall express certain aspects ... of geographical causation in universal history. If we are fortunate, the formula should have a practical value as setting into perspective some of the competing forces in current international politics.'[2] For Mackinder Europe and Asia were not two continents but one. He called it Euro-asia. A continuous land mass of 21 million square miles, it embraced, he calculated, half the world's land surface if the deserts of Arabia and the Sahara were excluded. He defined

58

Euro-asia as the world's 'heartland' and Russia, placed at its centre, as the 'pivot state'. 'The most remarkable contrast in the political map of modern Europe,' he declared, 'is that presented by the vast area of Russia occupying half the continent and the group of smaller territories tenanted by the Western Powers.'[3]

Mackinder drew attention to the succession of invaders who had moved from east to west, the horse-mounted warriors of the steppes — Mongols, Tatars and Cossacks. He argued that thus far in the world's history Russia's latent potential had been restrained by the problems of communication: road building across such a vast area had been too challenging a task. Instead sea-power had provided the basis for global economic links. His own country, Britain, a land mass on the periphery of Euro-asia, had been its most conspicuous beneficiary. However, that, Mackinder reckoned, was an era which was now drawing to a close. Alfred Thayer Mahan's theory of maritime supremacy drew on evidence from the eighteenth and early nineteenth centuries; it would not prove applicable to the twentieth. 'Trans-continental railways are now transmuting the conditions of land-power, and nowhere can they have such effect as in the closed heart-land of Euro-Asia.'[4]

In 1904 Mackinder feared an alliance between Russia and Germany. Such a relationship would give the 'pivot state' of the Eurasian 'heartland' direct access to the oceans in the west. It would place the divide between east and west not on the Bug or the Vistula but on the Atlantic seaboard. Britain's maritime supremacy would be directly challenged by a state whose eastern extremities would also abut the Pacific. After the First World War, in 1919, when Mackinder wrote a text designed to influence the peacemakers at Versailles, *Democratic Ideals and Reality*, he was more explicit about geopolitical probabilities and their likely impact on immediate policy. 'Who rules East Europe commands the Heartland: who rules the Heartland commands the World Island: who rules the World Island commands the World.'[5] He feared that Russia, after the Bolshevik revolution of 1917, would be too weak to resist German penetration, and that Germany would therefore dominate eastern Europe and also — following his own logic — the world. For Mackinder, although he was British, the Eastern Front, the place where Germany and Russia clashed in the two world wars, was the front from which all other outcomes would flow.

Geopolitics is hardly fashionable, at least in European academic circles. The disciplines of geography and military history have directed their attentions in divergent directions, so much so that the latter neglects the former even in its more prosaic and conventional forms. Historians of war too often discuss their subject matter as though mountains, rivers and deserts are of little consequence: battlefield maps show troop dispositions in preference to contours. But military operations are conditioned by climate and terrain. Next to time, space — and the relationship between time and space — is the bread and butter of a general's life. In seeking the reasons for the 'barbarisation' of war in the twentieth century, historians are in danger of looking too far beyond the ends of their own noses. Ideological confrontation, racial hatred and economic mobilisation may be constituent elements of what became 'total war' in the years 1937-45, but for most soldiers these issues were subliminal and even secondary. Far more military attention was directed to the study of the map than to the reading of *Mein Kampf*.[6] 'What is possible [in war] will depend firstly on geography, secondly on transportation in its widest sense, and thirdly on administration,' Montgomery declared after the Second World War. 'But geography,' he went on, 'I think comes first.'[7]

As the First World War closed, Mackinder accused the democratic powers of the West, Britain and the United States, of being particularly neglectful of the implications of geography. Germany, he argued in *Democratic Ideals and Reality*, was not: 'We have had for a byword in these times the German war map. It may be questioned, however, whether most people in Britain and America have fully realised the part played by the map in German education in the past three generations. Maps are the essential apparatus of Kultur, and every educated German is a geographer in the sense that is true of very few Englishmen or Americans. He has been taught to see in maps not merely the conventional boundaries created by scraps of paper, but permanent physical opportunities — 'ways and means' in the literal sense of the words. His Realpolitik lives in his mind upon a mental map.'[8]

What Mackinder was doing with geography when he developed his ideas about geopolitics was using it as a basis for what in the 1920s British thinkers like J.F.C. Fuller and Basil Liddell Hart would call grand strategy, the incorporation of social, political, economic and military means in one all-encompassing approach to national policy. For Mackinder geography was the determinant of strategy and he believed that that conviction also shaped the outlook of Germany. However, he was not quite right, because *Realpolitik*, as Mackinder called German policy, could also expose problems and obstacles as well as 'ways and means'.

The German General Staff and the Russian Threat 1904-1914

Mackinder's sense of the opportunities and tensions in the relationship between Germany and Russia before 1914 was hardly new to the Germans in general or to the German general staff in particular. On the one hand, the possibility of cooperation itself flickered in 1904. In October Germany offered Russia a defensive alliance, and in July 1905 the Kaiser and the Tsar reached an agreement at Björkö. It was the Russians, not the Germans, who broke off these contacts. The belief that a Russo-German pact made sense continued to fuel the long-term designs of many Germans, including Erich von Falkenhayn, the chief of the general staff in 1914-16.[9] On the other hand, the awareness of latent conflict took a number of forms. Racially it was characterised by the clash between Teuton and Slav. Culturally — and consequently — Germany saw itself as the outer bastion defending European civilisation against Asiatic backwardness. The rapidity of Germany's modernisation in the decades after unification made it more aware both of progress as a force in its own right and of the contrast between itself and a neighbour who was medieval and even primitive. Politically, Germany in this context was not a monarchy dogged by arrested constitutional development, but the representative of political enlightenment. Possessing universal male suffrage and the largest socialist party in Europe, it was the very opposite of Russia, an autocracy and a police state, which sent its socialists to Siberia or into exile.

However, Germany could not afford to be self-confident in its superiority. Mackinder's views were widely shared: given its land mass, its natural resources and its population, Russia had the potential to dominate not only Germany but all Europe. Germans, like others, saw Russia as the coming power. Its gross domestic product before 1914 was greater than that of any other European state, including both Germany and Britain, and its annual growth rate between 1908 and 1913 ran at 3.25 per cent. Over the same period its output from its metal industries rose 88.9 per cent.[10] This was the key sector of the economy in terms of raw military power.

In 1914 the Russian army mustered 1.4 million men before mobilisation, as opposed to 800,000 men in the German army. Russia's so-called 'grand programme' of 1913 aimed to increase the army's annual recruit contingent from 455,000 to 585,000. By 1917 the Russian peacetime army would be three times the size of Germany's.[11]

To successive chiefs of the German general staff between 1871 and 1914, therefore, Mackinder's insight was hardly novel. Helmuth von Moltke the elder was convinced of Russia's potential as a result of his visit there in 1856. In 1871, even before the war with France was concluded, he turned his thoughts to Russia, identifying between it and his own country 'an unmistakable mutual aversion in faith and custom, a conflict in material interest'.[12] Alfred von Schlieffen told his sister in 1892 that Russia was 'our special enemy'.[13] Helmuth von Moltke the younger shaped his own attitude to preventive war around the growth of the Russian threat. Although it was Britain that prompted the Kaiser to convene the notorious 'war council' of 8 December 1912, it was Russia which caused Moltke the younger to declare at that meeting that the sooner the war came the better.[14]

It was not just the nature of the threat that made Germany's Eastern Front so central to German policy. It was also the nature of Germany's response. Both the elder and the younger Moltke reckoned that, if war came in Europe, it would be long, and that one reason for this was that it would be a war fought by coalitions. In 1866 and 1870 single campaigns had won wars in short order because they were fought by single powers. But in 1914 no power stood alone; each, if defeated, could be rescued by an ally. In Germany's case, that ally was Austria-Hungary.

This was the second geopolitical or grand strategic reason why the Eastern Front was so pivotal to Germany. The First World War began in the Balkans, and it was triggered by Austria-Hungary's need to reassert itself as a Balkan power. The state that could deter it from doing so was Russia, and it was to bolster Austria-Hungary's resolve against Russia that Germany issued the so-called 'blank cheque' at the beginning of July 1914. Germany entered the war as a consequence of its alliance obligations. Moreover, it was on the Eastern Front, not the Western, that the German-Austrian alliance was played out. Vienna had no interest in what happened in France and Belgium.

In the days of Moltke the elder, he and his Austrian counterpart as chief of the general staff, Friedrich von Beck-Rzikowsky, had reflected these geopolitical and grand strategic assumptions in an operational solution. The German army from the north and the Austro-Hungarian army from the south, the one moving from East Prussia and the other from Galicia, would aim to envelop a portion of the Russian army by converging east of Warsaw in what is today Poland.[15] But extraordinarily, in February 1913, with war being fought in the Balkans, Moltke the younger told his Austrian counterpart, Franz Conrad von Hötzendorf, that 'the centre of gravity of the whole European war, and consequently the fate of Austria, will be decided not on the Bug, but on the Seine.'[16] Thus by the eve of the First World War the operational solution was out of step with the geopolitical, grand strategic and alliance imperatives. It was so above all for geographical reasons — and herein is the relevance of Mackinder.

Moltke the elder had planned an offensive into Russian Poland, but Schlieffen progressively abandoned such thinking. He set little store by the Austro-Hungarian army and so let the two armies' joint planning fell into abeyance. He focused his attention on the northern sector of Germany's Eastern Front, on East Prussia rather than the middle Vistula. If the Germans advanced at all, their axis was more likely to be due east, rather than south-east. Instead of staying close to the Austro-German frontier, they would move away from it, lengthening their lines of communication as they did so. Russia's ability to trade space for time by withdrawing into Asia would increase the danger of over-extension. When the German advance passed beyond Warsaw and entered Russia proper, it would be shouldered north once more. The Pripet marshes divided the front at its centre, forcing any army deployed on a broad front in two divergent directions. The Pripet river, into which the marshes drained, flowed eastwards to the Dnieper. The latter was one of a series of rivers, running north-south, which seemed to form natural lines of defence. Schlieffen concluded in 1894: 'The expanse of the country, the great distances of Russia, cannot be defeated.'[17]

A British military commentator, Colonel A.C. Macdonnell, in *The Outlines of Military Geography*, published in 1911, itemised the waterways of the Niemen, the Augustow canal, the Vistula, the Wartha and the Prosna as natural defences in west Russia, and those of the Pruth, Dniester, Bug and Pripet in south-west Russia. He characterised Warsaw and Novo

Georgievsk as 'one huge entrenched camp'. Furthermore, he appreciated, as Schlieffen had done, that getting to Warsaw was only the beginning; from there to St Petersburg or Moscow was another 650 to 700 miles. 'This long distance over difficult and inhospitable regions,' Macdonnell warned, 'still presents as formidable an obstacle to the advance of the invader as it did in the time of Napoleon'.[18] However, Macdonnell then added a rider to his historical analogy: 'if we exclude the increase to railway communications'. Here was the rub. Mackinder had reckoned that railways were transforming the geopolitics of Euro-Asia.[19]

There is no reason to imagine that Schlieffen or the younger Moltke read Mackinder's 1904 lecture. It is more probable, even if by no means certain, that they were familiar with the work of Friedrich Ratzel, the founder of geopolitics in Germany. Mackinder was right: Germany took geography seriously. By 1914 the German general staff's land survey section had a complement of over 500 officers. The trigonometric, topographic and cartographic sections each contained ten sub-sections. It had seven map series in production.[20] Ratzel published the first edition of his great text, *Politische Geographie*, in 1897. He saw states as organically linked to the soil on which they found themselves, and argued that their cultural influence radiated out from their centres, compelling smaller neighbours to cluster under their suzerainty: 'Culture has always created more grounds and means for the fusion of a nation's members and so broadened the circle of those who are aware of their political connectedness.'[21] He traced this process of cultural development and expansion over two millennia, placing Rome at its beginning and Russia at its end. For him, as for Mackinder, Russia was a potential world power, which would in due course bring the land mass stretching from the Pacific to the Atlantic under its sway.[22]

Ratzel said nothing in his 1897 edition about war itself, but he remedied the omission in the second edition, published in 1903. However, this was not a polemical tract which concluded that Germany would have to fight Russia for possession of the 'heartland'. Geography was a constraint, not an opportunity. He warned against campaigns of over-extension, quoting as examples Napoleon's campaigns of 1807 in Poland and 1812 in Russia. 'The conditions of a normal campaign did not apply. Reconnaissance was almost impossible; orders which were sent did not arrive. The distances, the mud, the ice, the snow, the accidental played the key role. Force of circumstance began to dominate the fall of the dice, and to gain superiority over human genius.'[23] Ratzel disagreed with those who were inclined to say that railways had changed the balance between offence and defence (and Mackinder was one of them, albeit to show how the Russians, like the Mongols, might break through to the west). Ratzel believed that railways favoured the defence — allowing the power that had been attacked to concentrate to meet the threat and to deliver a counter-stroke. Events on both the Eastern and Western Fronts in 1914 would prove him right.[24]

Ratzel cited the Swiss military theorist, Antoine-Henri Jomini, to support his case. Jomini was the best-known Francophone interpreter of the Napoleonic wars, but by the beginning of the twentieth century most German soldiers were more likely to refer to the works of a Prussian, Carl von Clausewitz. Unlike Jomini, Clausewitz had actually served in Russia in 1812. In 1804 he had anticipated that Napoleon would be defeated if he invaded Russia, a prophecy which was fulfilled to an extent that surprised even Clausewitz. His separate historical study of the campaign found theoretical reflection in book 6 of *On War*, that which discussed the defensive war. In chapter 26, devoted to a national insurrection against an invading army, Clausewitz explored the relationship between time, space and the decisive battle. He believed that a popular uprising did 'not lend itself to major actions, closely compressed in time and space'. This was because 'its effect is like that of the process of evaporation: it depends on how much surface is exposed. The greater the surface and the area of contact between it and the enemy forces, the thinner the latter have to be spread, the greater the effect of a general uprising [the German word is *Volksbewaffnung*]'.[25] Clausewitz reckoned that Russia alone of the states of Europe was big enough for a national uprising unsupported by a regular army to have this effect on an invader. German military thought before 1914, while praising Clausewitz, paid little attention to book 6, beyond endeavouring to counter its contention that the defence was stronger than the offence; Ratzel's apparent ignorance of Clausewitz's thoughts on the subject was symptomatic, if instructive.

Ratzel confronted his military readers with a conundrum. Too large a theatre of operations, and the effort would disappear into thin air; too small, and the objective of the war would not be achieved. In his view the optimum was to seek a theatre of war that was restricted enough to enable a decision, but not so small that that decision was minor in its effects.[26] The German general staff therefore confronted a paradox — the threat lay to the east, but the operational possibilities were greater to the west. It took counsel of its geopolitical fears and the geographical possibilities. Its review of the terrain went no further across the frontier than Poland. The conclusions it drew were pragmatic. It planned a battle that was defensive in East Prussia, exploiting the shield of the Masurian lakes and using its own railway network not just for deployment but also for operations themselves. In August 1914 its thinking on the defensive counterstroke was duly carried into brilliant effect at Tannenberg. Here was the fruit of Schlieffen's legacy, of staff rides and map exercises.[27]

Transport, Supply and Terror

The general staff favoured the offensive in the west for very similar operational reasons — the geography meant its goals were closer and its highly developed railway network facilitated the movement of mass armies. Sigismund von Schlichting, a veteran of the campaigns of 1866 and 1870, and an interpreter of the legacy of the elder Moltke, observed in his *Taktische und strategische Grundsätze der Gegenwart* (1897-9): 'Civilians, who promote the means for peaceful exchange, at the same time open the gates to enemy invasion'.[28] His books laid down principles which made it clear that he, like Ratzel, never countenanced the possibility of Germany invading Russia. His general rule was that the more a country was civilised and cultivated the more it favoured invasion. Its landscape, shaped by roads and railways, prompted movement, and its agriculture fed the army. He did not mention Russia by name, in itself perhaps an example of how inconceivable he considered a German attack on that country to be. But he was clear that operations in uncultivated land (he took Bulgaria as his example) would require totally different strategic measures and methods from those used by the German army hitherto, and stressed that large rivers would be the greatest obstacles to the armies of the future. It is worth adding in parenthesis that he thought that waging war in two different theatres of war would expose Germany's war leadership to contradictory strategic pressures.[29]

Geography was therefore the key determinant as to where the army would fight — because geography shaped operational possibilities regardless of political considerations or the wider strategic context. Schlichting's assumptions about the benefits of fighting in the more developed parts of Europe rested on the primacy of transport and supply. He was unusual: despite their importance, logistics were not a fashionable topic. In 1913 the German general staff's historical section published a tactical and strategic examination of army supply. It proceeded by way of case studies drawn from nineteenth century wars. One of these was Napoleon's 1812 invasion of Russia, which it declared had 'opened a new epoch in the development of army supply. It made crystal clear how the difficulties of provisioning had grown with the increase in army size, and how especially in under-developed lands special consideration ha to be given to logistics in the execution of operations, or else manpower would melt away like snow in the sun.'[30] The study concluded that Napoleon's supply system could not cope with the strains of invading Russia, which required a totally different approach to logistics. The only feasible solution to such challenges was the railway.

However, in 1913 the railway network of Eastern Europe and Russia was insufficient to sustain an invasion. Moreover, the German army still planned, despite the general staff study's observation about the growth in army size, to feed off the land. The text's relevant passage study revealed not only that the German army had failed to develop a new approach to supply but also how cavalier it was as to the possible consequences: 'One of the most important principles of military supply since the wars of the French Revolution has been that the first recourse is to exploit the resources of the land. That principle must hold as good for one's own territory or for that of an ally as for the enemy's, even if the forms of exploitation are different. What matters is to make the army mobile by starting off with smallest possible amount of baggage. Misplaced concerns about the local population must not be a constraint. They have often inflicted serious damage on one's own troops and then created the circumstances which have delivered the resources of the land to the enemy.'[31]

Herein is one further explanation for the atrocities visited on the civilian populations of Belgium and northern France in 1914.[32] For the German army struck west when the war came. It could not go east, not least because it planned to feed off the land. In this respect it obeyed the logic spelt out by Schlichting. But events proved Schlichting wrong and Ratzel right. In September 1914 railways, and indeed the level of industrialisation enjoyed by Western Europe in general, favoured the defensive at the Marne, and continued to do so during 'the race to the sea'.

Now time — alongside space, the other standard imperative in the formation of operational concepts — kicked in. Before the war successive chiefs of the German general staff had confronted a paradox. They knew that a major European war was likely to be long. This was not just a consequence of the alliance blocs. It was also the result of tactical developments: defensive firepower, delivered by breech-loading rifles, machine guns and quick-firing artillery, was likely to cause attacks to bog down. But once nations had gone to war their peoples would be unlikely to accept compromise. The incipient clash between Teuton and Slav, once evoked in German public consciousness, played on popular prejudices sufficiently deep for them not to be easily defused. The challenge that confronted Schlieffen and then the younger Moltke was that Germany could not live with the consequences of those insights. It was not economically strong enough to sustain a long war. In the first place it was outnumbered. The German army could not match the combined strengths of France and Russia. Britain's entry into the war did not make this equation much worse, at least not immediately, but it had massive economic consequences. London became the Entente's arsenal and financier, and its strategy in 1914, using sea-power to impose a blockade, underlined its readiness to engage in a long war. Germany therefore needed a quick operational success so that what happened on the battlefield could overturn the bigger and longer-term inevitability of defeat. In other words, Germany had to fight a short war because it could not — it seemed — sustain a long one.[33] In Belgium and northern France its armies pillaged to feed themselves, but they also used terror to speed their advance. In 1870, the campaign in France had achieved rapid success on the battlefield at Sedan but the war had been prolonged into 1871 by the *francs tireurs*. In 1914, the Germans tried to combine both phases in one, acting pre-emptively against civilians as they advanced and using the argument of military necessity to justify the ethical consequences.

The Eastern Front in the First World War

In the event, however, the outcome of the fighting on the Western Front in 1914 reversed Germany's original conundrum. Before the war, geo-politics and alliance considerations pointed Germany to the east, but op-erational considerations took it west. By November 1914 grand strategy (if we can use a phrase that the Germans not only never used but also did not comprehend) pointed Germany to the west, because Britain had become the mainstay of the enemy coalition and therefore had become the logical focus of their main effort. But the operational possibilities seemed greater in the east.

In the winter of 1914-15 this imbalance manifested itself in a bitter feud between Falkenhayn at supreme headquarters, OHL, and Paul von Hindenburg and Erich Ludendorff on the Eastern Front, at what became OberOst. Falkenhayn saw Britain as the enemy's centre of gravity and therefore the proper goal for German strategy, but he could not marshal the operational means to fulfil the strategic ends. Germany lacked a navy big enough to take on the British Grand Fleet, and it lacked the military punch to finish off France, Britain's principal ally on land. Hindenburg and Ludendorff extrapolated from the defensive victory at Tannenberg to argue along Schlieffenesque lines. Envelopment battles were achievable in the east because the force to space ratio was more favourable, and therefore strategy should be bent to the operational possibilities.

Broadly speaking, that was what Germany did in 1915. It adopted the defensive in the west in November 1914, digging deep trenches, so that it could create a *masse de manoeuvre* for use in the east. It overran Poland in the summer of 1915, and it precipitated Russia into the 'great retreat'. On 25 June 1915, Hans Delbrück wrote in the *Preussische Jahrbücher*: 'A short while ago we stood in front of Przemsyl, but now Lemberg is in our grasp. It is a campaign for which there is scarcely a parallel in the history of the world. The triumphs of Alexander the Great dissipated themselves over colossal spaces and were executed with such demands on his resources that they exhausted them. The fighting which was done as a result of these victories could not be more different; the enemy's strength was completely shattered and scattered through decisive battle.'[34] On 27 August 1915 his comparison was not with Alexander but with Napoleon. He recognised that the Russians could trade space for time as in 1812.

But, he went on, 'Today all is totally different. The land itself yields more, because it is more densely populated and better cultivated than in 1812. A scorched earth policy is easier to order than to execute, as Poland has already shown; there is always plenty left behind.'[35]

These were the greatest German and Austro-Hungarian victories of the war — in terms of armies broken, cities captured and ground conquered. But the operational possibilities still did not march in step with strategic goals. Many of the reasons for this were geographical. The German army was designed to fight close to its frontiers. It was now engaged on something which exceeded its geographical range — in terms of transport and supply, in terms of operations, and in terms of grand strategy.

Logistically, Delbrück was wrong. Hindenburg and Ludendorff's plans for massive envelopments in the east exceeded the reach of the German army's transport systems. Falkenhayn modified their scale, but Polish *panje* wagons were no substitute for railways. The Russians' scorched earth policy proved more effective than Delbrück anticipated. The armies of the Central Powers plunged forward across a land stripped bare.

Operationally, Hindenburg and Ludendorff failed to recognise that envelopment was not the panacea that Schlieffen and his followers maintained it was. Envelopment battles made sense where there were fixed points that were also reasonably proximate — frontal positions where the enemy could be pinned, frontiers against which he could be driven. But on the Eastern Front space for manoeuvre allowed space for the Russians to retreat. The geography enabled envelopment on paper but invalidated it in practice. In October 1915, Falkenhayn wrote to Hindenburg, 'One cannot hope to achieve a massive and decisive envelopment of a numerically superior enemy, who refuses to stand, despite the loss of land and people, and has the whole of Russia and good communications behind him.'[36] Russia's geography undermined Germany's operational competence in 1915.

Strategically, the war which Germany now waged required it to develop a new conception that went beyond operational possibilities, that recognised its political, economic and social aspects, and that united these into what later observers would call grand strategy. Germany in 1914-18 lacked the institutional structure to develop such a broad approach to strategy. The powers to do so were vested in the Kaiser, who was not equal to the challenge, and OHL was at bottom no more than an operational headquarters. This lack of an institutional and conceptual base for the development of grand strategy was far more significant on the Eastern Front than it was on the Western for two reasons. The first was the size of the theatre of war. Issues of supply and manpower were intimately connected with the war's political and economic direction. Significantly Ludendorff was one of the first to canvass the independence of Poland. His reasons were military; he wanted it to raise men. But it soon became clear that the independence he had in mind was notional, albeit again for narrowly military reasons. He wanted Poland to form a protective buffer for Germany in the east. However, the real charge behind the Polish question was not military, but political. A commitment to Poland's independence would undermine efforts to seek a separate peace with Russia, and the establishment of any form of German suzerainty would prejudice relations with Germany's ally, Austria-Hungary. Vienna wanted Poland, or a large chunk of it, to be subordinated to the Dual Monarchy.

Such considerations brought into relief the second consideration. The war on the Eastern Front was a coalition campaign in a way that was not true of any other major front for the Central Powers. Germany ran the Western Front, Austria-Hungary the Italian, Bulgaria the Macedonian, and the Ottoman Empire the Caucasian and Arabian. But all four powers had stakes in the war against Russia. OHL proved itself totally unable to work out command structures appropriate to the conduct of coalition warfare. The Austro-Hungarians felt that they had been let down from the very start of the war, because the Germans had not honoured the plan to envelop Warsaw. Their anger was deepened by the humiliation of 1914-15: that winter, as the Russians stood poised to break into Hungary, they were rescued by the Germans. OHL did nothing to poor oil on these wounds. Falkenhayn subordinated Austrian troops to German command. The victories of 1915 were the work of two Germans, August von Mackensen and his chief of staff, Hans von Seeckt, not of Austro-Hungarian commanders. For a whole month at the end of that year, Falkenhayn and Conrad did not speak to each other, and instead set about developing their own plans for 1916. In Falkenhayn's case that meant attacking the French at Verdun, in Conrad's attacking the Italians in the Trentino. Both neglected their common front in Russia.

The logical outcome should have been defeat and collapse for the Central Powers. That of course was what happened in the war as whole. But the Central Powers did defeat Russia in 1917 and were able to impose a 'German victory' at Brest Litovsk in 1918. Crucially, however, they achieved it in spite of military victories, not because of them. Russia collapsed from within. Here was a frightful portent. Brest Litovsk pointed the way to two conclusions.

First, it suggested that what mattered in war were not operational ideas, let alone grand strategy, but just plain fighting. Tactical capabilities themselves became a device for shaping strategic outcomes. In 1914-15 Ludendorff had argued in terms of great envelopment battles. In 1917-18, when planning the offensive in the west, Ludendorff memorably said: 'I object to the word 'operation'. We will punch a hole into their line. For the rest, we shall see. We also did it this way in Russia!'[37]

Secondly, the treaty of Brest Litovsk seemed to demonstrate that when victory came it would be because the enemy nation would implode, as Russia had done in 1917. Germany's own defeat seemed to confirm the argument. In the west the allies achieved a series of tactical successes in the so-called 'hundred days' of late 1918, but not a victory that could be explained in operational terms. There was no envelopment or even much of a breakthrough. Instead the German defeat was attributed to revolution, hunger and governmental instability. When Ludendorff came to reflect on it in 1935 in *Der totale Krieg*, he stressed that the bases for victory in war were national mobilisation, totalitarian government, and the subordination of the nation's resources to the waging of war: strategy as defined by Clausewitz — the use of the battle for the purposes of the war — fell into a black hole.

German Geopolitics Between the Wars

In the interwar period German war planning was preoccupied with the defence of its now reduced frontiers. In relation to the Eastern Front this meant little change from its pre-1914 assumptions: the issues were the constraints and opportunities of Poland, not penetration into Russia proper. Again the sorts of offensive options reviewed even in the 1930s concerned Germany's immediate neighbours and therefore lay within the bounds of a tactical-operational approach to the conduct of war, rather than the setting of grander objectives. Moreover, time was as important as space. The message of 1914-18 was that a war fought over several fronts was much more difficult to conclude and therefore became protracted. The use of greater violence in war, not as an end in itself but as a means to an end, could even be morally defensible. If it made the war short then the case for breaching non-combatant immunity through bombing, for example, was justified not just by military necessity but also by the fact that in overall terms lives would be saved. In Britain, Liddell Hart, whose desire to limit war was unimpeachable, developed exactly these sorts of arguments in *Paris, or the Future of War*, published in 1924.

The campaigns fought by the German army between 1939 and 1941 delivered quick victories with low casualties. Crucially, moreover, they achieved strategic outcomes through tactical-operational success. How great a victory Hitler hoped to achieve when he invaded France in May 1940, and how quickly he would do it, are still contentious questions. Indeed the uncertainty is itself indicative. Hitler's own instructions for this campaign — as for that in Poland — said that the aim was the destruction of the enemy army; there was no reference as to what the political or geographical goals might be. The plans focused on achieving a breakthrough in the Ardennes and getting across the Meuse. What would happen then would depend on how the situation developed on the ground. The link between the initial breakthrough and the ultimate defeat of France was not clear. As in 1914, however, the range set for penetration lay within the logistic grasp of the German army. It was able to get to just short of Dunkirk and then had to halt to regroup. Having expected a long war, the German army was astonished to find it had triumphed in a short one.[38]

No serious thinking had gone into the invasion of the Soviet Union in the interwar period — any more than into that of Russia before 1914. In 1941 Mackinder (now an old man) was proven right. His prediction of 1919 — that Germany and Russia would clash for control of the 'heartland' — came to pass. But for the subsequent twenty years German geopoliticians resisted this apparent inevitability. Fully aware of the geographical constraints on waging war in the east, they answered Mackinder's heartland problem by proposing cooperation, not confrontation, with Russia. Karl Haushofer, himself a professional soldier who had served with the Bavarian army in the First World War, not least on the Eastern Front, was Mackinder's greatest admirer and the most obvious exponent of geopolitics in interwar Germany. He presented a copy of Ratzel's *Politische Geographie* to Hitler when he was in prison in 1924.

For Haushofer, military geography, the conditions imposed by terrain on the operations of armies, proved a powerful constraint on geopolitics. He was opposed to the annexation ideas of the Pan-German League, and hoped instead that a robust frontier could be created which allowed Germans to be on German territory. He welcomed the Russian Revolution as a blow to capitalism, and therefore a greater danger to Britain than to Germany. Russo-German antagonism could only play into Britain's hands. Established as not only professor of geography in Munich but also president of the party-approved association of German academics, he applauded the Russo-German pact of 1939. In a memorandum of 1940, 'Der Kontinentalblock', he declared that the most important task of 'our time' was the creation of a Eurasian block: his aim was not to follow Mackinder but to prove him wrong. The Axis needed to complete its work by co-operating with the Soviet Union not by fighting it. He was appalled by the campaign in Poland, especially by its consequences for military thought if generals concluded from the speed of the war that military operations could surmount geopolitical realities: 'It would be a mistake to believe that changes in the world political order in areas like India and in the Orient, as well as in places nearer to hand, could be played out with the same lightning speed as the geopolitically defensive [wehrgeopolitisch] campaign in Poland in the autumn of 1939.'[39]

Haushofer developed a new branch of geopolitics, which he called 'Wehrgeographie', by which he meant the use of resources for the purposes of national defence. Its major exponent in the 1930s was a Bavarian general and First World War veteran, Oskar Ritter von Niedermayer, who in 1915 had led an expedition across Persia to Afghanistan in a bid to rouse India to revolt against the British.[40] In his own writings on 'Wehrgeographie', Niedermayer likened it to the British idea of grand strategy, but also said that all issues of war and policy should take account of the needs of space and time, in other words of operational considerations. Between 1924 and 1931 Niedermayer was the Reichswehr ministry's representative in Moscow. The covert rearmament of Weimar Germany was heavily dependent on the training and development opportunities which the Russians provided in exchange for German technological and industrial expertise. Like Haushofer, Niedermayer did not see a hard line against communism within Germany as incompatible with close military cooperation with the USSR. Another of Niedermayer's circle, Hans von

Seeckt, the head of the Truppenamt and therefore the *de facto* chief of the general staff, adopted a similar stance, determined that Russia should be Germany's ally, not its enemy. Seeckt rejected notions of class or racial conflict, seeing Germany's position in geopolitical terms, and identifying Britain as its principal enemy. In April 1933, Niedermayer wrote 'Wehrgeographische Betrachtungen über die Sowjet-Union', an article published in the *Zeitschrift für Geopolitik*. His opening line declared that 'the whole space of which the Soviet Union is the master is established for defence' — '*auf Abwehr, auf Verteidigung*', as he put it, so covering both parrying an invasion and countering it. He stressed the value to the defence of being on interior lines, and he reiterated all the familiar points about the weather, the distances, and the advantages vouchsafed the defence by the river lines and the Pripet marshes. The article concluded on a directly political level, endorsing Seeckt's call for amicable relations between German and Russia, and seeing the two states as potential allies not only in Germany's domestic recovery but also in the struggle to overthrow the Versailles treaty.[41]

Three pressures worked against these arguments. The first, itself geopolitical in nature, was the legacy of the allied blockade of the Central Powers in the First World War. As the conviction grew, not only in Britain but also in Germany itself, that sea-power had been decisive in winning the war, and that starvation had precipitated Germany into revolution, so one possible conclusion to be derived from the imperatives of 'Wehrgeographie' was that Germany should expand to the east. Barred by the British and the sea from establishing economic security to the west, Germany had to find the resources it needed for self-sufficiency from Poland and Russia. The summons for cooperation with the Soviet Union was the pacific side of this coin, the demand for its invasion the bellicose.

Hitler's rise to power and the call for 'Lebensraum' made expansion, not alliance, the long-term geopolitical solution. The second pressure was therefore that of political ideology. Seeckt opposed the Nazis' ambitions to push eastwards, but Niedermayer was more equivocal. He needed a job, and in 1933 he was given responsibility for developing academic studies at the interface between the Wehrmacht and the universities. Dependent on the Nazis, he distanced himself from Haushofer, who became an increasingly marginal figure. Haushofer was put under house arrest in 1941 and interned at Dachau in 1944. As a result geopolitics too changed direction — the last of the three pressures. Niedermayer was now persuaded that geography was not as determining a factor as Haushofer had believed. The challenge to political and military leaders was to work with geography but, Niedermayer argued, the greatest commanders could, by understanding its constraints, overcome them. He cited in his support Alexander the Great and even, more oddly, Napoleon. In an argument reminiscent of Mackinder's about the impact of railways, he contended that new technologies — in Niedermayer's case airpower — could change the relationship between time, space and geography. In an article of 1940 on 'Wehrgeographie am Beispiel Sowjetrusslands', Niedermayer reflected the influence exercised on his thinking by his reading of Clausewitz, pointing out that it was the state which underpinned the concepts of 'Wehrgeographie', and that politics not geography shaped war. Whereas before he had argued that Stalin was confronted by too many domestic problems to be able to wage war, now he stressed that the Soviet Union wanted world revolution. Niedermayer's article produced a thorough review of the USSR's war-making capacity and paradoxically stressed that geography was still its best defence.[42]

So Niedermayer's principal point was not a denial of geography's role in war but an argument that military capability could overcome it. In 1934, Alfred Franke re-examined the 1812 campaign in an article for the *Zeitschrift für Geopolitik*. He argued that Napoleon had made sufficient allowance for the problems of geography and supply. His failure in Russia had been the result not of geopolitical imperatives but of military factors, as he had been unable to inflict an overwhelming defeat on the enemy in the early stages of the invasion. The Russians retreated not because they were using geography to trade space for time but because they were militarily inferior to the French. Not until September 1812 did Kutuzov realise the value of space to Russia. Time and space had, therefore, been given their chance as a result of decisions reached for other reasons. Franke then went on to use the Central Powers' conquests on the Eastern Front in 1915 to emphasise that an army could have too much space for manoeuvre — that, paradoxically, space could undermine manoeuvre rather than enable it. Russia provided plenty of space within which armies could manoeuvre, but that space itself made manoeuvres useless. The German and Austrian victories in Poland in 1915 had weakened Russia but had not destroyed it: that had been accomplished by internal collapse. For

Franke, unlike Niedermayer, nothing had changed: German operational competence in the First World War, like France's in the Napoleonic Wars, had been forfeit to Russia's principal ally, its space.[43]

Franke's analysis of the 1812 campaign differed little from Clausewitz's, to whose book, *On War*, he referred. After 1918 *On War* was revisited: admonitions to take the text as a whole, and not to cherry-pick quotations in self-serving fashion, were taken seriously by those like Haushofer and Niedermayer who were trying to put German conceptions of strategy on a broader footing than those rooted only in operations and even tactics. More attention was paid both to book 6, with its precepts on the inherent strength of the defensive, and to book 7, with its argument that the diminishing power of the attack leads to 'the culminating point of victory'.[44] In 1937 Friedrich von Cochenhausen, a retired general and president of the Deutschen Gesellschaft für Wehrpolitik und Wehrwissenschaften, prepared an abridged edition of *On War*. Although prefaced with a quotation in praise of Clausewitz from Hitler himself, its message on war with Russia was pessimistic. Despite cuts elsewhere, Cochenhausen left intact chapter 26, book 6, with its reflections on time, space and the national defence of Russia. In his introduction, he quoted from Clausewitz's history of the 1812 campaign: 'The land of Russia is not a land which can be formally conquered or can be occupied, at least not with the resources available to contemporary European states'. And he went on specifically to reject the notion that things had changed since Napoleon's day. 'We have proof for this argument in the world war. The offensive which we launched with insufficient manpower against Russia in the summer of 1915 got stuck half way. That situation lasted almost two and half years, until the inner collapse of the army forced our enemy to the peace table.'[45]

For analysts of the 1812 and even the 1915 campaign, Russia's economic backwardness had been one of the obstacles to its invasion. However, for Russians themselves it was a source of vulnerability. Stalin's five-year plans were testimony to his own attention to 'Wehrgeographie'. The forced pace of industrialisation enhanced Russia's defensive capabilities, and not just in terms of military equipment. Haushofer saw urbanisation as one of the biggest challenges confronted by 'Wehrgeographie': 'Every street a trench, every house a fortress'.[46] The fight for Warsaw in 1939 had appalled him: the civilian population confronted disease as its infrastructure was destroyed, the attacker confronted a natural defensive zone. Presciently he pointed to the rapid urbanisation of the Soviet Union. When Schlichting had anticipated that economic progress could aid the invader, he was referring in part to agriculture and the feeding of troops. Cities were adding to Russia's defensive strengths, not subtracting from them. The 1933 edition of *Truppenführung*, when discussing defensive obstacles, was less concerned about rivers than the pre-1914 writers had been, but was very well aware of how 'combat in built-up areas wears forces down very quickly, often without having a decisive effect on the action'. It suggested that the main force should aim to bypass cities, but acknowledged that the 'wider and deeper' and 'the longer the time the enemy has to fortify it', the more a built-up area would have to be attacked frontally.[47]

Operation Barbarossa

When it was told to get on with planning the invasion of the Soviet Union by Hitler in the summer of 1940, the solutions produced by the army's general staff, OKH, followed the implications of Niedermayer's post-1933 views — that military competence could overcome geographical constraints. This was not simply the consequence of subordinating professional standards to ideological imperatives or to the Nazi dictatorship. There was abundant evidence in 1940 to support the contention that the Red Army was peculiarly vulnerable and inefficient. The purges had cut a swathe thought its officer corps, particularly in the senior ranks, and the results had been evident in the Finnish war. Those German generals who saw the Soviet forces at first hand when the two sides had met in the carve-up of Poland in 1939 confirmed such judgements. Therefore OKH tackled the proposed invasion of the Soviet Union as an operational task. Having been amazed by the rapidity and scale of its own success in France, the German army fell into the trap of believing in its own legend and so institutionalised it as 'Blitzkrieg'. Its solutions, as in the campaigns which had worked in 1939-41, were tactical-operational. The generals' thinking had advanced little since Ludendorff.

Walther von Brauchitsch, the commander-in-chief of the army, told Hitler on 21 July 1940 that the campaign would require one hundred divisions, as the Soviet Union had only 50 to 75 good divisions, and that it would be over within a month. His optimism rested on four general but pervasive assumptions. First, the war with Russia would be short — no more than ten weeks. Second, the aim would be to create pockets close to the frontier, and so to envelop the Russian forces and destroy them. Third, the main thrust would be delivered to the north of the line of the Pripet marshes, which divided the front into two sectors, and the marshes would guard the German right flank as the attack swung north. Fourth, the campaign would end on a line running north-south through Smolensk. In other words the shape and size of the theatre of war were limited by the forces available for the task, and by what was to hand for their transport and supply, rather than by political objectives. Franz Halder, the chief of the army's general staff, reckoned that the objectives were limited — the occupation of the Baltic states, Belarus and part of the Ukraine: Russia, like France, would become a second rate power. Hitler did not disabuse him. Halder's diary entry of 28 January 1941, reporting on a planning conference for Operation Barbarossa, begins, 'Purpose is not clear', and goes on: 'At conference proceed from: Operational mission. Space – no pause; that alone guarantees victory. Continuous movement is a supply issue. Everyone must help with resolution. Distances!'[48]

Time and space were therefore the crucial considerations for Halder. He did not seek to clarify the 'purpose'. Alfred Jodl of the armed forces staff, OKW, recalled in May 1945, 'We did ...not conduct the attack against Russia because we wanted space, but because the advance against the Russians developed further day by day, and finally led to ultimate demands.'[49] In a memorandum of 5 August 1940, Erich Marcks, the officer entrusted with the initial planning, claimed that the Russians could not avoid a decision as they had in 1812 by withdrawing into the interior, since 'a modern army of 100 divisions cannot sacrifice the sources of its strength.' In an accurate reflection of the Red Army's initial deployments in 1941, Marcks stated that 'it is a given that the Russian army is positioned for a defensive battle to protect Great Russia and eastern Ukraine.' But as the paper progressed Marcks modified these assertions. He warned that 'a decision against the Russian army cannot be achieved in a single blow.' His proposed target was not Smolensk, but Moscow, with the north-south line running from the northern Dvina, through the central Volga, to the lower Don. Marcks reckoned that the maximum logistic reach of the army was 400 kilometres, provided a fresh supply base was created

200 kilometres from the German border. However, the northernmost tip of this advance suggested an extension to Archangel, where the Dvina drains into the White Sea, over 1,000 kilometres from East Prussia as the crow flies. Even Moscow was more than 400 kilometres distant, but it was Marcks's calculation that 'its capture would destroy Russia's cohesion'. Marcks thought the fall of Moscow would be sufficient to persuade the Russians to agree terms, and that could be achieved within nine to seventeen weeks. Marcks did not of course suggest what those terms might be, nor elaborate on how they might be simultaneously acceptable to Hitler and to Stalin. But he did conclude with a warning dire enough for anybody who paused to consider the point. 'If the Soviet government does not collapse or does not make peace, it will be necessary to go on to the Urals. Although Russia, after the defeat of its armed forces and the loss of its most valuable European lands, will not be capable of continued active operations, it can still carry on holding out, supported by its Asian territories, for an incalculable period of time.'[50]

The implications of his warning — that the campaign could expand in terms of time and space — were not followed through. Halder demanded the freedom to plan at the operational level. Hitler, in allowing him to do so, never forced OKH to align its concepts and their military limitations with his own grandiose objectives. Military geography and Nazi geopolitics remained at odds. Even Niedermayer was dismayed, describing an invasion of the Soviet Union in a memorandum of 30 November 1940 as 'insane'. He, rightly, no longer saw air power as the panacea to overcome the limitations of the army's reach. In 1942 he would be restored to general's uniform as the commander of an infantry division in the Caucasus, but when in the same year he came to publish his thoughts on 'Wehrgeographie' in book form, he wrote as an academic: 'The geographer has the right to warn when an overestimation of the power of human ambition leads to an underestimation of the physical and spatial realities, and to a neglect of the relationships between space, time and human strength.'[51] On 2 February 1941, Fedor von Bock, designated as commander of Army Group Centre, remarked to Hitler that a military victory over the Red Army was possible, but he did not see how the Russians could be made to come to terms. The army was condemned to penetrate further and further into the Soviet Union, as it tried to convert battlefield success into a political outcome. Gerd von Rundstedt, the commander of Army

Group South, ruefully remarked on bidding farewell on 4 May 1941 to Wilhelm Ritter von Leeb, the commander of Army Group North , 'See you again in Siberia'.[52]

Siberia lay far beyond the German army's logistical reach. The supply plan, based on a short war and reckoning on a pause for recovery after an advance of 300 to 400 kilometres, assumed that 'the army would essentially live off the land and provide itself with everything that could be manufactured within the country or was to be found there.'[53] Russia and its peoples would be ransacked. This was the point where ideology came in — after the planning outline was already clear. Requisitioning was designed to aid tempo, but if practised on this scale it could provoke resistance. The population might fight back, and thus slow the German advance. The consequent loss of tempo could enable the Russians to avoid defeat close to the frontier, and allow them to retreat into the interior; thus the war would become extended in time and in space. Partisans threatened the Germans with protracted war, as they knew from 1870-71, and as they knew from 1914 brutality could nip such resistance in the bud. Therefore terror would be part of the package designed to get quick victory. In early 1941 army officers began to move from seeing the invasion of the Soviet Union purely in operational terms, as a re-run of the fall of France, and instead clothed it as a struggle waged by National Socialism against Bolshevism. The use of the term 'partisan' covered over this elision of military necessity, with its focus on time, space and their impact on operations, and the issues of ideology and race. The quartermaster general on the Eastern Front, Eduard Wagner, had only nine security divisions for the Wehrmacht's rear areas. He therefore needed both the SS and the police to make up his manpower deficit. Wagner's instructions in February 1941 for the administration of the war zone made the consequences clear: 'On the principle that preservation of the army's mobility was the supreme law of warfare, security and ruthless utilization of the country were to have precedence initially over an orderly administration in the interest of the Soviet population.'[54]

Hitler's own way out of the dilemma was one which temperamentally the army could embrace: Russia would collapse from within. Here were the lessons from 1917-18. Tactical success would be enough to shake the structure internally. In 1914, the German army had used terror as a means to aid it in its achievement of operational success, not as a substitute for it. In 1941 it still pursued operational successes, but such triumphs could no longer be ends in themselves, because it knew that they could not themselves produce final victory. 'The stab in the back legend' is central to understanding many of the assumptions which underpinned the conduct of the Second World War, on both sides. But in adapting its lessons to the Eastern Front in the Second World War, the German army neglected one other element in its defeat of Russia in 1917-18. Its policy on the Eastern Front after the February revolution of 1917 had been one of fraternisation, not coercion. Moreover, Germany itself had supported the Bolsheviks. On 17 March 1941, Halder wrote in his diary, 'In Great Russia force must be used in its most brutal form. The ideological ties holding together the Russian people are not yet strong enough, and the nation would break up once the functionaries are eliminated.'[55] The tensions between geopolitics and geography were to be resolved not by operational excellence but by brutality and terror.

THE MODERN AND THE PRIMITIVE

BARBARITY AND WARFARE ON THE EASTERN FRONT

Mary R. Habeck

The Second World War was supposed to be the very model of modern conflict. The countries of Europe spent twenty years after the end of the First World War acquiring the latest military hardware and developing the most up-to-date strategies and tactics based on a fundamental reconsideration of warfare. The result, each was certain, would be a quick, clean war of technology — a showcase of modernity in action. To all outward appearances, the war started that way. The armed forces of Germany that marched off to Poland in September 1939 learned from their defeat in the Great War and rethought tactics and technology in a fundamental way. The Wehrmacht would fight a lightning war, carried through with such speed and surprise that there would be no chance for the enemy to even react. To make certain that the military would have the tanks, aeroplanes and heavy weaponry that twentieth-century warfare demanded, the Weimar and Nazi governments spent millions of marks, circumvented the Versailles Treaty, and risked war with France and Britain. Throughout September the two decades of effort seemed to pay off, as the army showed itself an exemplar of modern efficiency, precision and effectiveness, rolling across the Polish military as if it did not exist and then turning to dispatch the French and British armies with similar ease the following year.

Yet it was precisely the German army, which imagined that it set the standard for modernity, that degenerated earliest and furthest from the modern ideals of warfare. Beginning with the invasion of Poland and reaching its height on the Eastern Front against the Soviet Union, the Wehrmacht was involved in deliberate massacres of civilians, the mistreatment and executions of millions of prisoners of war, the plundering of everything from individual homes to entire economies, the intentional devastation of cities small and large, and the enslavement of millions of Soviet and Polish citizens. The Nazi government systematically and purposely undermined the rule of law — including the developing field of international law — while demanding that the military carry through draconian punitive measures that had not been seen in Europe since the Peace of 1648. Meanwhile, both the way that the Wehrmacht fought the war and the conditions of the battlefield 'demodernised' combat on the Eastern Front, creating an army that, by the end of the war, was little more than a horde of starved, unwashed and walking men.

What is striking about the degeneration of the German army is that every part of the behaviour of the German military on the Eastern Front can be found in earlier stages of warfare in Europe. Limitations on what is justified and permitted during war, such as the legal protection of civilians and their property, are a modern development; combat from antiquity through the Thirty Years War had seen precisely the same sort of large-scale plundering, massacres and enslavement that characterised the conflict on the Eastern Front. I would argue, in fact, that what happened to the war on the Eastern Front was not so much a degeneration of warfare as it was a regression of warfare, a deliberate turning away from the advances that began to transform conflict after 1648 and a return to a more ancient and barbaric vision of war. The Nazi regime planned and ordered this regression of warfare, and the Wehrmacht assented, using modern techniques and technologies to commit the most primitive of crimes. The demodernisation of the army may have been unintentional, but, as Stephen Fritz and Omer Bartov have suggested, the regression of the Wehrmacht was the result of deliberate policy.[1]

Setting the Conditions for the Regression of War

The first step backward was the very basis for the wars against both Poland and the Soviet Union. Unlike the limited wars of the past two centuries, which had been fought for modern ideals like '*raison d'Etat*', 'balance of power', or 'national integration', these would be total wars over the most primitive of issues: life or death.[2] Only one nation would survive the conflict; the other would necessarily be completely destroyed. Even more importantly, only one nation deserved to survive the war. The concept of the common humanity of all men, derived from Christian ideals and the Enlightenment, and gradually widened throughout the nineteenth and early twentieth centuries to include the entire human race, was rejected by the Nazis in favour of a two-tier ordering: true humans, who deserved certain rights and privileges, and the sub-humans, who deserved none.[3] The identification of the enemy with the 'Asiatic hordes' that had menaced Europe hundreds of years before or with the Jewish threat as in the Middle Ages, also located this war as an ancient struggle and not the modern conflict that it might have seemed.

The dehumanisation of the enemy, and the definition of the war as a fight for existence, allowed all the other steps for the regression of warfare to take place. The next stage was to undermine the generally accepted laws of war, an absolutely vital precondition for the planned degeneration of warfare. Since the eighteenth century, European nations had developed international customary laws governing acceptable behaviour during war, and especially the treatment of non-combatants and prisoners of war. These customary laws had no legally binding basis — no signed agreements — nor were they enforced by any recognised international body, but most nations of Europe acknowledged their validity and attempted to live up to their standards, at least when fighting each other in continental Europe. Exceptions to the laws were recognised by other nations as barbarous behaviour and condemned as such.[4] The informal nature of these agreements began to change in the mid-nineteenth century and two international conferences finally codified the customary rules in the Hague Rules of Land Warfare in 1907 and its complement, the Geneva Convention in 1929.[5] Hitler and the Nazi regime realised that these agreements would prevent them from carrying out the war of annihilation that they wanted on the Eastern Front.[6] They argued that the specific characteristics of the enemy meant that the laws of war had to be set aside and that there had to be a return to as Major General Eugen Müller, an influential staff officer, put it 'an earlier form of warfare.'[7] As Müller saw it, the present rules of warfare were only established after World War I and in a war in which 'one of the two enemies must die', there could be no mercy for the other. But what was this 'earlier form of warfare'? Admiral Wilhelm Canaris, the head of military intelligence, noted in a memorandum on the legality of the new regulations that this was not just a rejection of the Hague and Geneva Conventions, but rather a dismissal of the entire corpus of customary laws that had defined European behaviour in war for the past two hundred years.[8] By an 'earlier form of warfare' Müller must have meant a return to the way that wars were fought before 1648, and perhaps even earlier than that.

The special instructions on the limitations of military jurisdiction distributed before the invasion of the Soviet Union (Operation Barbarossa) gave commanders the legal justification to allow the men under their command to ignore the Hague and Geneva Rules as well as all previous customary law.[9] The 13 May 1941 'Barbarossa Jurisdiction Order' argued that military jurisdiction was primarily designed to maintain discipline — rather than to protect the lives of innocent civilians. As long as discipline was preserved, it was legally permissible to prosecute the ruthless war required by the special nature of the battlefield and 'the peculiar qualities of the enemy' or, as another version of the order put it, the 'specific quality of the Eastern enemy' and his 'Jewish-Bolshevik ideology'.[10] Efficiency and effectiveness were, in other words, more important than questions of right and wrong, as Hitler himself argued before the beginning of the war with Poland.[11] This decree and similar orders from the same time made three other important inroads into the accepted laws of war. First, they made it impossible for the army to bring civilians who committed or *were suspected of committing* offences against German soldiers before any courts or even to hold them for later trial. Judgement was to be made on the spot by the commanding officer with the only alternatives death or freedom. The orders also ruled out the prosecution of any Wehrmacht personnel who committed crimes against enemy civilians unless the 'maintenance of discipline or security of the troops calls for such a measure.'[12] Finally, the rules of evidence were done away with since, as Müller said, 'In cases of doubt of guilt, suspicion will often have to suffice. Clear evidence often cannot be established.'[13]

Developing the Regression of War

Undermining the rule of law was but the first step. As the war on the Eastern Front developed, a series of orders imposed by the Nazi regime and the Wehrmacht built on this foundation and encouraged barbarism from German soldiers. Deliberate policy deprived prisoners of war of the protections that had developed during the past two hundred years, allowed or even ordered German soldiers to shoot civilians out of hand, mandated the confiscation of property, and enslaved men, women and children. The new orders on POWs were especially deadly, because they implied that captured Soviets did not have a normative right to life. As in wars of the distant past, men were shot while surrendering, beaten after capture, and starved to death in captivity. Just before the war in the East began, the army issued regulations to ensure Soviet captives were treated as harshly as possible. German soldiers were reminded that Bolshevism was the deadly enemy of Nazi Germany and that they should expect insidious behavior, especially from the prisoners of 'Asiatic origin'. The call for a 'complete eradication of all active and passive resistance' meant that any hint of disobedience led to the death of the offending prisoner. The regulations also prescribed that POWs could be required to work without pay for their enemy, another clear violation of the Geneva Conventions, but reminiscent of the enslavement of captives once common to warfare, a point to which we will presently return.[14] When it became apparent that the war in the Soviet Union would not end as quickly as the Wehrmacht had expected, Reinhard Heydrich, Heinrich Himmler's chief lieutenant in the SS, issued directives in September to deal with the millions of Soviet soldiers taken prisoner during the summer campaign. The directives began with the principle that all Soviet soldiers were illegitimate combatants. They were, in fact, criminals, who had lost 'all claims to treatment as an honourable soldier and according to the Geneva Convention.' Their guards were to use bayonets, rifle butts and firearms to ruthlessly stamp out any resistance and it was expressly forbidden to fire warning shots at escaping prisoners of war. Instead, the directives ordered them to be shot out of hand, in direct contravention of the army's own regulations. The basic principle, the directives stressed, was that it was perfectly legal to use weapons against unarmed Soviet prisoners.[15] The results of these (and other orders) were stark: of approximately 5.7 million Soviet soldiers who surrendered during the war in the East, 3.3 million died.[16]

The 'Commissar Order', which prescribed the immediate separation of political commissars from other prisoners and their summary execution, took the barbarisation of warfare further. The genesis of the com-

missar execution order is telling and shows that, even while his orders
were pushing his military into the past, Hitler wanted the war to make
the Soviet Union itself more primitive as well. On 17 March 1941,
Hitler summoned the high command to a conference in which he stated
that the intelligentsia created by Stalin had to be exterminated.[17] Two
weeks later, he clarified what he meant by 'intelligentsia': the Bolshevik
commissars and other members of the new Communist intellectual
class. Halder wrote in his diary that Hitler wanted the creation of several new states from the old Soviet Union, but states without 'an intellectual class of their own. Formation of a new intellectual class must
be prevented. A primitive Socialist intelligentsia is all that is needed.'[18]
A later draft order prepared from Hitler's directives gave completely
different justifications for the Commissar Order. Now the charge was
that commissars had to die because they rejected any 'European culture, civilisation, constitution and order'.[19] The final order offered a
third set of reasons for the summary executions. First, that the enemy
would not follow any of the principles of humanity or international law
himself; second, that 'in this fight it is wrong to treat such elements
with clemency and consideration in accordance with international law';
and finally, that the political commissars were 'the originators of the
Asiatic barbaric methods of fighting'.[20] The expected barbarism of the
enemy justified taking pre-emptive barbaric action against him. It is
worth noting that the order followed the new guidelines on evidence
as well, stressing that 'when deliberating the question of 'guilty or not
guilty,' the personal impression received of the commissar's outlook
and attitude should be considered of greater importance than the facts
of the case for which there may not be proof.'[21]

General Erich Hoepner, the commander of Panzer Group 4, placed
the orders for the ruthless extermination of the commissars within
the larger context of the war. He reminded his commanding officers
that the war against the Soviet Union was 'a fundamental part of the
German people's fight for existence. It is the old battle of the German against the Slavs, the defence of European civilisation against the
Muscovite-Asiatic flood, the resistance against Jewish-Bolshevism.'
Therefore, there could be no mercy for the commissars, those 'bearers'
of the Bolshevik system.[22]

Regression of War and the Jews

The labelling of the enemy as 'Jewish-Bolshevism' was significant since the Nazis argued that Bolsheviks and Jews were the same people.[23] The assent of the Wehrmacht high command to this identification allowed the army's active participation in the Holocaust and the deliberate murder of unarmed civilians. Before this order was issued the German army was involved in rounding up and killing Jews, but they had insisted that the SS and SD carry out the majority of the actual massacres.[24] Not that their hands were entirely clean even then. In his diary Lt. Col. Helmuth Groscurth, a staff officer in the 295th Infantry Division, recorded that Heydrich berated the army for not killing enough people in Poland, specifically noting Jews as well as the Polish nobility and priests as targets for execution by the army, not the SS.[25] The complete identification of Bolshevism with the Jews, however, allowed Hitler to fold the war against the commissars and the Soviet system into the larger attempt to wipe out the Jews. The 'special instructions' for troop conduct in Barbarossa called for the extermination of Bolshevik agitators, guerrillas and the Jews.[26] Another order issued in July 1941 specifically demanded the execution of 'Jewish functionaries'.[27] The army's participation in rounding up Jews for death camps, in individual killings, and in the destruction of entire communities increased dramatically.[28] The Wehrmacht now acknowledged that the Jews, as a whole, were enemy combatants who could be killed out of hand and for whose slaughter no soldier would ever be held accountable.

The Wehrmacht also justified killing unarmed Jewish men, women and children by arguing that all Jews were partisans. The war against these guerrillas consumed a great deal of the army's energy, and caused frustration and anger among the ordinary soldiers as they struggled to secure their rear and protect lines of communication. However, the decision to use the most primitive of measures against them was decided not in the heat of battle and after the death of comrades, but methodically and in cold blood before the war in the Soviet Union began. In taking action against the guerrillas the Wehrmacht did have some support from the existing laws of war. The Hague Rules for instance recognised only soldiers in uniform as combatants deserving legal protection. The army's response to the partisans, however, went far beyond the bounds of international norms and, as with so much else, led them to commit atrocities that had not been seen since the Thirty Years War. Significantly, the reprisals carried out against the partisans, the Jews and anyone suspected of helping them fit into the overall war of annihilation waged by the Nazis. Martin Bormann, who had just been made head of the Nazi Party Chancellery, welcomed the Soviet declaration of a partisan war since it gave Germany the opportunity 'to eradicate all those who oppose us'.[29] In pursuit of this policy, the Wehrmacht would regress to flogging civilians, burning entire villages, shooting all males over 15 years of age, exemplary hangings, and other barbaric acts to terrorise the conquered peoples into submission.

The deliberate nature of these actions is obvious from the forethought that went into the rules allowing them. The Nazis expected the Soviets to fight a guerrilla campaign, and included regulations on how to deal with irregular fighters in the original orders on jurisdiction and troop behaviour in the invasion zone. These explicitly stated that partisans were to be 'ruthlessly liquidated by the troops, either in combat or in flight.' Anyone suspected of partisan activity could be brought before an officer who could shoot the prisoner on the spot, while higher-ranking officers were authorised to carry out collective punishments against villages involved in partisan attacks 'if circumstances do not permit a speedy determination of individual perpetrators.'[30] The army high command version of this order included a slight modification that allowed the troops to treat as guerrillas any of the indigenous inhabitants who even *intended* to participate in hostilities.[31] It must again be stressed that the changes in legal jurisdiction made it impossible to prosecute any German soldier who accidentally or purposely killed innocent civilians while involved in the war against the partisans.

As the invasion progressed and the partisan war actually began, Wilhelm Keitel — the Chief of the Supreme Command of the Armed Forces (OKW) — issued another order for dealing with irregular fighters that would further push the conflict in the East into barbarism. Keitel stated that all attacks by the guerrillas were to be blamed on communists (i.e. Jews), whatever their source, and since he believed that a man's life was worth nothing in that part of the world, then 'it should be considered appropriate to put to death 50-100 communists to atone for one German soldier's life.' The killings were to take place in the manner most likely to terrorise the population into submission.[32] Another decree in

December 1941, issued by Hitler himself, urged the army to include
women and children in any reprisals, 'without reservations'. After all, as
he reminded the Wehrmacht, this war was a matter of life or death and
had nothing to do with 'soldierly chivalry or with the agreements in the
Geneva Convention.'[33]

The implicit accusation that the Jews were responsible for the partisan war was soon made explicit. The Jews as a whole would be identified
with the partisans and the summary execution of all Jews regardless of
age or gender became part of the Wehrmacht's war on the guerrillas.[34]
The official signal for this shift came in the 'Reichenau Order' of 10 October 1941. Here Walter von Reichenau, the commander-in-chief of the
army, reminded his officers that the 'fundamental goal of the campaign
against the Jewish-Bolshevik system is the smashing of its instruments of
power and the eradication of Asiatic influence in the sphere of European
civilisation.'[35] The ordinary German soldier was more than a warrior, he
was also

the bearer of a ruthless national ideology and the avenger of all the bestialities
which have been inflicted on the German and racially related nations.

This is the reason why the soldier must have full understanding of the necessity
of a severe but just retribution upon the Jewish subhuman elements. Its second
purpose is to nip in the bud revolts in the rear of the armed forces, which, as
experience shows, are always fomented by Jews.

Reichenau then proceeded to issue new orders to combat this fresh
danger. The occupied population, which was already on starvation rations, could no longer be fed from army kitchens. Houses that caught fire
during the war were not to be saved because 'the disappearance of the
symbols of the former Bolshevik regime...is part of the framework of
the war of annihilation.' Finally, he prescribed the collective execution of
male populations, as necessary to fulfil the army's historic mission of free-
ing the German people once and for all from the 'Asiatic-Jewish danger.'
The army understood exactly what was expected of it from this order.
In a situation report dated nine days later, a commander in Byelorussia
wrote, 'The Jews, as the spiritual leader and bearer of Bolshevism and
the communist idea, are our deadly enemy. They are to be annihilated.
Always and everywhere, when reports about sabotage, incitement of
the population, resistance, and so on compelled us to action, Jews were
confirmed as the initiators and people behind them, and in most of the

cases, as the culprits themselves.'[36] With the issuing of these orders the Holocaust and the other atrocities committed by the Wehrmacht became inextricably linked.

Despite their expressed conviction that what they were doing was right and necessary, both the Wehrmacht and the Nazi regime knew that their new regulations did not fit into modern ideals of warfare. This is obvious from three features of these and similar 'criminal orders' issued by the Wehrmacht. They were given extremely limited distribution, so that only the highest-ranking commanders were privy to any written evidence. There was also a specific requirement that lower-ranking commanders were to be informed about the orders orally, and not permitted to see or read the written orders. Finally, there was an added stipulation that the executions be carried out away from the troops, so that their modern moral sensibilities would not be outraged by the atrocities.

Booty, Slavery and Sieges

Additional sets of guidelines, issued in May and June just before the invasion, gave the Wehrmacht the right to engage in the oldest of military practices; pillaging by the ordinary troops and plundering on a massive scale by the army itself. The guidelines had in fact two separate but related purposes — to allow the German troops invading the Soviet Union to live off the land and to ruthlessly exploit the mineral and industrial resources of the newly occupied territories for the greater good of the German economy and the resupply of the Wehrmacht. By ordering German soldiers to feed themselves as best they could from the territory they moved through, the Nazi regime killed two birds with one stone. On the one hand, it kept the logistical strain on the Wehrmacht to a minimum and preserved the food supply of the German homeland. On the other hand, it deprived Soviet citizens of their necessary provisions and made certain that they would either move out of the war zone (i.e. resettle themselves) or starve to death, both of which the Nazi government wanted to encourage. The decision to exploit the raw materials and industrial capacity of the Soviet Union was no less important and amounted to nothing less than looting on an unprecedented scale. Specific industries necessary for the war effort were targeted for preservation and exploitation, while precious commodities such as fuel, foodstuffs, animal feed and even articles of clothing — all described as 'military booty' by the German army itself — were to be gathered and immediately shipped back to the homeland.[37] In effect, the decision to plunder the economy of the Soviet Union forced the Soviets to pay for their own conquest.

The Soviet Union could provide another commodity that the Nazi regime intended to exploit: manpower. Even before the demands of the war in the East created shortages in the German labour pool, the Nazi government had decided to 'recruit' Polish and Soviet citizens to work in specific industries. By the end of the war 2.8 million workers would leave their homes and travel to Germany to work for their enemy under wretched conditions.[38] While at first the recruitment of workers was voluntary and they were promised good pay for their work in Germany, the exigencies of the war would soon turn recruitment into conscription. During late 1942, just as the demands for labour in the homeland increased, the Wehrmacht experienced increasing difficulties in finding volunteers for work both in the occupied territories and in Germany. The army's solution was to begin forced conscription of labourers, many of whom had to be dragged away and guarded closely to keep them from fleeing.[39] By 1943 the army was drafting entire 'year classes' of young adults,[40] compelling them to work 12-hour days,[41] using them to build fortifications for the Wehrmacht's defences, and shooting all those Soviet citizens who attempted to evade their captors.[42] If the decision to use forced labour began as an answer to the demands of modern industry, by 1943 it had turned into the enslavement that had so often been the lot of conquered peoples of the past.

The treatment of cities under siege, an ancient part of warfare that European customary law and The Hague Rules had fundamentally altered, returned to its older form under the Nazis. In early July 1941, as the progress of the invasion seemed certain to lead to the collapse of Stalin's regime, Hitler told his commanders that he intended to level Moscow and Leningrad and make them uninhabitable. *Moscow et Leningrad delendae sunt.* Ironically enough, Hitler specifically ordered the use of the most modern of weapons — the air force — to carry out the rasing.[43] As the siege around Leningrad tightened throughout the summer and autumn, the Wehrmacht set about planning the destruction not just of the physical buildings of Leningrad, but of its entire male population. In a memorandum on the issue, the Wehrmacht argued that they should declare the

entire city a military target, seal the area so that no one could leave, and
then use artillery and aircraft to destroy the city. Afterwards the women
and children who survived would be allowed to leave, but the rest of the
inhabitants would be shut into the city without food for the winter. Those
few who made it through to the spring would be led away into captivity
and then the army would level the rest of the city with explosives.[44] An
order from the head of the XXVII Army Corps just one month later emphasised to the soldiers taking part in the siege that they should not share
their food with the Soviets and that 'every civilian, even woman or child,
trying to cross our encirclement around Leningrad, is to be fired on. The
less mouths to feed at Leningrad, the longer will be its resistance there,
and each refugee is inclined toward espionage and the partisans; all these
things cost the lives of German soldiers.'[45]

The Regression of War in Action

The collective result of the 'criminal orders' was to give the Wehrmacht
the license to conduct a war the likes of which Europe had not seen in
three hundred years. Officers and soldiers who fought on the Eastern
Front recognised that the war in the East was far different from that in
the West and that they were involved in a more primitive and barbarous
undertaking.[46] In some cases, it was the economic development of the
land in which they fought or the supposed character of the enemy they
faced that made the Germans feel as if they had stepped back in time.
They wrote in diaries and letters about the backward economy of the
Soviet Union,[47] that the Russians seemed trapped in the Middle Ages,[48]
and that the land was in a time warp 'of centuries.'[49] One officer entered
a village where the inhabitants were unaware that the Tsar was dead, and
had missed entirely the Russian Revolution, Stalin and the start of the
Second World War.[50] Another soldier saw the collision of past and present
as he watched the Wehrmacht's supply train of trucks and armour drive
past fields with donkeys and camels at work and later saw a camel caravan
used to carry fuel to the front.[51]

But it was the character of the conflict and the nature of enemy they
fought which convinced others in the Wehrmacht that this war was
something from the past that would require barbarous methods to win.
Soldiers agreed with Hitler that this was a struggle for the very existence

of the German people, a war over life or death with all the cruelty and violence that this implied.[52] 'It's either us or the Jews,' one soldier wrote, understanding with others in the Wehrmacht that the fight they were in was a war between two absolutely opposed ideologies and not between two countries.[53] Foreign volunteers were likely to see it as a crusade by all of Europe against communism, another definition of the war that looked to the past to understand the current conflict.[54] The comparison with the Thirty Years War occurred to two high-ranking officers, both of whom were well aware that the orders issued by the Nazi state contravened the established rules of law from the previous two centuries.[55] As for the enemy himself, soldiers and officers thought of the Russians and Jews as 'animals',[56] Asiatic hordes,[57] and beasts created by the Jewish-Bolshevik system that had to perish.[58] Dehumanising the enemy allowed German soldiers and officers to agree with the Nazis' new vision of warfare and to fight without granting the Soviets any mercy or quarter.[59]

By the time the order to execute commissars was issued, the army had few qualms about implementing it. One officer, who did protest that this was murder, stopped objecting once he heard that the orders came from Hitler himself.[60] In general, however, officers and soldiers seem to have been well-prepared ideologically for the task in front of them. They agreed that the execution of the commissars was necessary because the Soviets made it that way, and because only thus could they liberate both ethnic minorities and the Russians themselves from this 'cruel government'.[61] The emphasis on informing the soldiers orally about the order and on making certain that the commissars were killed away from the troops shows that uneasiness remained during the early days of the campaign.[62] As the conflict progressed, however, shooting commissars became part of the ordinary duties of the war.

The order to kill Jews as well as commissars was seen as a natural extension of the war on communism. As one soldier would write home, 'the great task that lies before us in the battle against Bolshevism is the destruction of eternal Jewry.'[63] Individual officers and soldiers did understand that this was wrong and raised objections, but the most serious complaints seem to have occurred only when small children were massacred in front of the troops.[64] In a particularly telling incident, troops refused to allow the execution of ninety Jewish children at Belaya Tserkov, but had apparently not protested when the children's mothers and fathers were killed. Overall, the army had few problems with their new duties, however distasteful they might be. The comparison by one soldier of killing Jews to exterminating pests or destroying dangerous animals could have come directly from any Nazi propaganda of the time.[65] The discovery of mass executions carried out by the communists as they retreated from their part of occupied Poland only convinced the troops of the barbarity of their enemy and the need to be equally barbarous in return. [66] As the war dragged on, the troops became more convinced that the Jews were responsible for the conflict and that they had to be wiped out entirely.[67] A sergeant was not alone when he wrote at the end of 1942 that annihilation was all that was left for the Jews.[68]

Regression and the Partisan War

The partisan war, as Bormann had foreseen, would become intertwined with the larger war of annihilation. It did not start that way. At least some Ukrainians welcomed German soldiers and saw them as liberators from Stalin's regime. The Soviet declaration of a guerrilla war against the invaders was, however, taken up enthusiastically by the population, showing that there was far more discontent with the way that the Wehrmacht conducted its conquest and occupation than with Stalinism. This is almost certainly, as historian Hannes Heer has argued, because of the seemingly random way in which — right from the beginning — the army carried out reprisals and executions against the guilty and innocent alike.[69] By September 1941 the German army was deeply involved in 'pacification' operations throughout the occupied zone, although the modern term is misleading. The Wehrmacht predicated the conduct of their new war on the Nazi directives, which assumed that the behaviour of the German army would be anything but modern. When the guerrillas attacked German troops and installations or whenever civilians provided aid to the Red Army, the response was swift and brutal and became more so over time. As spelled out in the regulations, even suspicion was enough to put Soviet citizens to death.[70] In September, when camp fires and signal flares were lit to guide Red Army attacks on German forces in Dnepropetrovsk, the commander in charge ordered the taking of hostages and their execution if aid was given again.[71] Just two months later, the guidelines for reprisals had become much more brutal. The deaths of a few German and

Romanian soldiers in partisan attacks led to the rounding up of hostages, with ten shot for each occupation soldier killed by the partisans and one killed for each wounding. The bodies were also left hanging three days to terrorise the rest of the populace into cooperation.[72] This was actually mild compared to the actions taken in Kiev and Kharkov. In the former the Wehrmacht shot 300 hostages for acts of sabotage while fifty were executed in Kharkov with the threat of another 200 to be killed for each additional act of terrorism.[73] A few weeks later, the Wehrmacht shot 400 residents of Kiev for an attack on an intelligence installation.[74] The worst reprisals were probably in Zhitomir, where ten inhabitants were killed for shooting *at* a German, while the actual wounding or killing a member of the Wehrmacht led to the rounding up and killing of one hundred Soviet citizens — men and women.[75] The same brutality informed counterinsurgency measures in the countryside. By the autumn of 1941 the German army was answering attacks from villages with tactics straight from their new (primitive) regulations: burning down entire villages and shooting their inhabitants.[76] By the time the commander of the 4th Panzer Army ordered all males over fifteen from the town of Bratskaya Zemlya shot for the participation of some in fighting against the Wehrmacht, it was not an exceptional atrocity, but a normal part of the wholesale regression of the war on the Eastern Front.[77]

Ordinary soldiers who witnessed or participated in the reprisals at times regretted the need to be cruel, but generally found ways to excuse their actions and to blame the victims for the barbarity of the war.[78] After a detailed description of his unit's destruction of a Ukrainian village and the shooting of most of its inhabitants, Peter Neumann told himself that they might be ruthless, 'but the partisans also wage an inhuman war and show no mercy. Perhaps we cannot blame them for wishing to defend their own land; but all the same, it's clearly our duty to destroy them.'[79] In answer to a question about the partisans, a soldier wrote his friend that it was wrong to treat these 'swine' humanely — they had to be shot immediately.[80] Officers and soldiers accused the Jews in particular of fighting against them, and justified the mass murder of entire Jewish communities as necessary to ensure peace.[81] In any case, whenever the army needed hostages or decided on reprisals, it was often the Jews that they chose to massacre first.[82] Over time, as with the shooting of commissars, the brutal struggle against the guerrillas — including torture, the killing of innocent civilians, and leaving the dead bodies of partisans hanging for days — became part of the normal business of this abnormal war.[83]

The Wehrmacht learned to treat Soviets who surrendered in battle with similar barbarity. A soldier, new to the front, was shocked at the use of whips on Soviet POWs and actually protested at the murder of one prisoner. His complaint was not even understood by the veteran who had done the shooting. 'This is no kindergarten,' the shooter told the newcomer. 'You'll soon get that baby talk knocked out of you.'[84] Not many months later the newcomer — now a veteran himself — beat a Soviet prisoner senseless and told a friend that they should all be wiped out.[85] Peter Neumann went through the same transformation, at first stunned at the shooting of Soviet soldiers who attempted to surrender, but later a willing participant in battles in which, as in past centuries, no quarter was given.[86] German officers and soldiers often blamed the brutal behaviour of the Soviets for their decision to kill enemy soldiers attempting to surrender, but there were many times when the officers simply allowed bloodlust to take its course.[87] Indeed, behind the apparently uncontrollable violence was the new legal reality that no German soldier would be brought to account for any atrocities committed against the enemy. This not only excused past actions, but also encouraged future butchery. Added to the belief that the enemy was not quite human,[88] the new regulations allowed Soviet prisoners to be purposefully starved to death,[89] shot for refusing to obey orders from a German soldier,[90] or even killed in revenge for a perfectly legitimate attack by their former units.[91]

Laying Waste the Land

Meanwhile, the 'criminal orders' forced soldiers at the front to live off the land, seize any excess foodstuffs for the home country, and thus starve the indigenous peoples. Even before the invasion of the Soviet Union, the Nazi government began experimenting with the mass starvation of people in Poland. By May 1941 the food rations for Poles were 100 grams of meat per week and 75 grams of bread a day. Polish Jews were only allotted 75 grams of bread a day and no meat at all.[92] Once the campaign against the Soviet Union began, German troops were forced to forage for themselves, seizing everything from vegetables and fruit to milk, eggs, chickens, cows and pigs to feed themselves. Anything edible that crossed their path was fair game and, although they sometimes took every bit of food in the village for themselves, the German soldiers never paid for what they stole, nor did they pay for their billeting in the villages they passed through.[93] By 1942, Ukrainian and Russian peasants were starting to feel the effects of the deliberate plundering of the countryside.[94] Many of the elderly people, women, and children — generally the only remaining inhabitants of the land through which the army moved — became dependent on the field kitchens for their daily food, which explains why Reichenau's order forbidding this sort of aid was so devastating for Soviet citizens.[95] Meanwhile Soviet cities under German occupation were placed on iron rations that made even the Polish situation look bright.[96] Once the advance into the Soviet Union bogged down, the army itself began to experience difficulties finding enough to eat. The high command tried to stop the 'wild' requisitioning of food — not out of concern for the native population but because there was no longer enough being sent back for Germany and for the rest of the Wehrmacht.[97] Only with the return of spring and summer did the soldiers eat well, by once again taking away all that the Soviets had to feed themselves.[98]

As they crossed the vast Ukrainian and Russian plains, German soldiers also 'requisitioned' other items from the native population — clothing, weapons and horse-drawn carts.[99] But this small-scale looting paled in comparison to the massive plundering that the Wehrmacht and other agencies, at the behest of the Nazi government, carried out in the occupied territories. One participant in the war on the Eastern Front was almost certainly right when he commented that 'any significant looting by German armed forces, of which I am aware, was usually officially sanctioned and carried out on specific instructions from a higher authority.'[100] The large-scale seizure of goods brought back desperately needed raw materials that the German government used both to maintain its own economy and to prosecute the war against the Soviet Union.[101] Some smaller-scale plundering took place in conjunction with 'pacification' operations against suspected partisans and the villages that supported them. The detailed lists of cattle, pigs, sheep and horses taken during these actions read like the booty from a Viking expedition.[102] Just as with the plundering of the Jews in the Holocaust, when money was involved, each denomination from the various countries had to be carefully itemised and any gold or silver jewellry listed separately.[103]

One of the most astonishing inventories lists the cattle, pigs, sheep, and 'workers' seized during an operation: men, women, and children who were to be sent into slavery.[104] At last the German army had reached its nadir: a return not just to the days before the Peace of Westphalia, but a regression to the Middle Ages and before — to the classical age, when defeat in war meant the enslavement of the conquered.[105] Over the next four years the Wehrmacht would round up and send back to the homeland millions of Poles, Russians, Ukrainians and Byelorussians to work in the factories, fields and homes of their conquerors.[106] The barbarisation of the German army — from the most modern of armies to one that purposely engaged in mass murder, pillaged and plundered, gave no quarter to cities under siege and surrendering enemies, and now led away captive its conquered foe — was complete.

SOMETHING TO DIE FOR, A LOT TO KILL FOR

THE SOVIET SYSTEM AND THE BARBARISATION
OF WARFARE, 1939-45

Amir Weiner

Zinaida Pytkina was not by nature a bloodthirsty woman. Forced into the ranks of SMERSH (acronym for 'Death to Spies'), the young communist was actually frightened that she had done something wrong since 'they look[ed] for offenders, and I thought in the beginning that maybe I have broken the law, too.' She soon became an offender, but not against Soviet law, rather against international law, by actively taking part in 'washing prisoners until they sang' (a euphemism for torture and beatings), often concluding with their execution. Told by her commanding officer to 'sort out' a young German major whose interrogation had been completed, Pytkina ordered the German to kneel beside a pit outside the interrogation building, drew her pistol ('my hand didn't tremble'), pointed it at his neck and pulled the trigger. Recalling her emotions, Pytkina pointedly said, 'It was a joy for me. The Germans didn't ask us to spare them and I was angry...I was also pleased. I fulfilled my task. And I went back into the office and had a drink.'[1]

Meanwhile, nineteen-year-old Mitia Khludov proudly wrote to a family friend from his deathbed:

My battery has done wonders in knocking the hell out of the Fritzes. Also, for our engagement, I have been recommended for the Patriotic War Order, and better still, I have been accepted to the party. Yes, I know, my father and my mother were *burzhuis*, but what the hell! I am a Russian, one hundred percent Russian, and I am proud of it, and our people have made this victory possible after all the

101

terror and humiliation of 1941; I am ready to give my life for my country and for
Stalin; I am proud to be in the party, to be one of Stalin's victorious soldiers.[2]

And on 9 February 1942, Viacheslav Balakin, an 18-year-old partisan operating north of the Smolensk-Viazma railway entered in his diary:

Monday. Dreamed of Ira G. Woke up in a good mood. Drove with Siomik to
Nekasterek to fetch bread —without success. We shot a traitor. Morale 'gut.'
In the evening I went to do the same to his wife. We are sorry that she leaves
three children behind. But war is war!!! Toward traitors any humane consideration is misplaced.[3]

What accounted for these three youngsters' unquestioning willingness
to kill and die in the crucible of war? What were they fighting for? Why
did they kill so easily and eagerly? What compelled them to sacrifice their
own lives without hesitation? On its face, the answer to all these questions does not appear overly complex, and is one to which most students
of the wartime Soviet Union adhere by and large. The Germans did not
leave much of an alternative, having launched a war of extermination
against the Jewish-Bolshevik menace and its subhuman Slavic population.
The Soviets had no choice but to fight to the bitter end. Faced with mass
murder of civilian population and millions of prisoners of war, every
imaginable daily abuse, a conscious strategy of intentional starvation of
entire cities, and the literal obliteration of thousands of small towns and
villages across the countryside, the Soviets reacted in kind. The regime
mobilised the population around its fighting men and women for the defence of the Russian Motherland. Themes of age-old Russian nationalism
and Orthodoxy supplanted the failed rallying cry of revolutionary ideology. Needless to say, there is some truth to this thesis.

However, this conventional wisdom practically leaves out the contribution of the Soviet system to the brutalisation of its fighting men and
women before and during the war. When circumstances and opportunism
are overwhelmingly weighted, the omnipotent and omnipresent system
that for better or worse shaped the lives of its members is rendered im-
potent and its distinct features vanish, blurred by ahistorical universality.
Indeed, a fuller and more satisfying answer to the question *what they were
fighting for?* should begin with an inquiry into the worldview, values, and
preconceived biases the Soviets acquired within the system that brought
them up and now demanded their ultimate sacrifice. This essay seeks to
elucidate the Soviet system's input to the brutalisation of warfare during

the Second World War, arguing that such brutality was both conditioned by and integral to the Soviet ethos.

If the study of the horrifying wartime losses and destruction inflicted by the Germans helps to explain the harsh retaliation by the Soviets, then the weaving of the war into the evolving revolutionary narrative clarifies the distinct choice of methods. For the Soviets, the war was not merely an unpleasant accident, nor was it a traditional clash of two major powers. It was the realisation of an historical nightmare, one that Soviet power expected from the moment of its inception. Throughout the 1930s, Soviet citizens were constantly warned against the evils of German fascism and its implications for the USSR. The dominant theme of the Terror in 1937-38 was the excision of fascist agents from the Soviet body politic.[4] If the alleged crimes of the sinners in the late 1930s were presumed to anticipate the forthcoming catastrophe of capitalist encirclement, then the alleged crimes in the 1940s were seen as the full-blown actualisation of the worst fears of the preceding decade. The war and its accompanying horrors, concluded Stalin, were the inevitable outcome of historical forces, 'not a casual occurrence or the result of errors of particular statesmen, though mistakes were made.'[5] Soviet military planners envisioned a short war that would be carried swiftly into the enemy's territory, rather than the actual desperate, prolonged fighting within the gates of Moscow, Leningrad and Stalingrad. But the unexpected efficiency of the Nazi war machine did not alter the essential understanding of the German threat or the role of the war in the overall Soviet enterprise. The war was anticipated, fought, and reflected upon as the Armageddon of the Bolshevik Revolution.

The Face of Things to Come

The imprint of the Soviet domestic order on the conduct of the fighting troops could already be seen during the annexations of eastern Poland, the Baltic states, Bessarabia and northern Bukovina, and the botched Winter War with Finland in 1939-40. Militarily, these operations were rather insignificant. Politically and socially, however, they precipitated the brutalisation of the troops' conduct on several levels.

The events of 1939-40 launched a prolonged process in which ordinary citizens were personally exposed to a growing and tangible tension between official claims and the actual turn of events and social-political realities. For the first time since the brief and unsuccessful Polish campaign in 1920, Soviet troops stepped out of their borders. The ensuing territorial expansion might have softened the shock had it been a smooth operation. But it was not, and the sluggish campaigns revealed a certain fragility. [6] Two decades of intense propaganda regarding the superiority of the Soviet system over the decaying outside world proved too successful for its own good when challenged directly by actual experience. The results varied. The annexation of the Western Ukrainian and Belorussian provinces seemed to win broad support. Coupled with a low number of fatalities — 1,475 in all — the consolidation of these peoples and lands was in line with Soviet nationality policy from the early 1930s. Yet, although the Red Army was marching into some of the backwater areas of Europe, even these pauperised regions posed a problem for its servicemen. Prepared to encounter a backward country, populated by oppressed class brothers, soldiers were puzzled and humiliated. 'We have been in towns and villages, but I have seen no class brothers of mine,' observed one chauffeur. 'To me they all look like kulaks and bourgeois. A peasant has three or four horses, five or six cows; there is a bicycle in front of every house. Workers wear suits, hats — the same as a big Soviet director. There is something here that I don't understand!' [7] By all accounts, including those of the Red Army, the chauffeur and his comrades soon overcame their puzzlement and joined the looting orgy (and, to a lesser degree, rape) of those who 'looked and dressed like kulaks and bourgeois'. In an ironic twist that most Poles did not necessarily appreciate, the Soviet system reincarnated itself in the fictitious world it created.

There was another catch. The annexation struck a chord even with those who would later turn against the regime, but for the wrong reasons. 'We were not bloodthirsty,' recalled Pavel Negretov, 'but when western Ukraine and the Baltic Republics were annexed, we were glad about the successes of our policy. I remember that at that time one of my schoolmates said: 'well, now the NKVD will clean things up there.' And none of us said anything against him.' [8] It would be left to hundreds of thousands of Soviet soldiers and partisans to live with the consequences of the NKVD's 'cleaning things up' in these territories, which climaxed with the mass murder of political prisoners on the eve of the Soviet retreat in the summer of 1941. By the time the Germans arrived, the good will that locals exhibited toward Soviet power in the autumn of 1939 had long been exhausted. Instead of a single anti-German front, the Soviet treatment of the annexed territories guaranteed several additional foes: powerful nationalist-separatist guerrilla movements supported by thoroughly embittered populations.

Moreover, the successful Polish and Mongolian campaigns in 1939 created an illusion that future wars would be similar. The alarmed voices of Konstantin Simonov and Aleksei Surkov who witnessed the hardships and brutalities first-hand and cautioned against the 'common superficial notions of the romantic [essence] of war' barely registered with decision-makers and servicemen.[9] The Polish campaign in particular whetted the appetite for more. Officials and rank-and-file soldiers agreed that the 'liberating mission' of the Red Army should now be directed toward the oppressed peoples of the Baltic states, Bessarabia, and Finland.[10] The Winter War came as a cold shower. With about a quarter of a million dead and wounded servicemen in the course of barely three-and-a-half months of fighting, scepticism ignited over the justification and mission of the war and the actual state of the army spread among the rank and file. Red Army agitators were confronted by servicemen inquiring about the difference between Soviet policy in Finland and Japanese policies in China, just as diarists expressed confusion and misgivings about the entire enterprise. The exposure to the better technology of the poor Finnish army and to the higher living standards in Finland and the Baltics caused sceptical soldiers to express doubts regarding the officially proclaimed desires of local Baltic populations to join the Soviet family. It also spelled devastation for these societies. Soldiers' strong sense of humiliation at the sight of the much higher living standards of the easily vanquished opponents was detrimental for locals subjected to looting, rape, and killings. It was then and there that the popular image of the Red Army as marching eastward with trainloads of looted property and of the Soviet soldier wearing several wristwatches stolen from civilians was recast.[11] The sad state of affairs was only exacerbated by the comparison with the Wehrmacht. The Red Army's own admission of the shabby appearance and performance of its troops corresponded with locals' low impressions.[12] Once again, it was left to the victorious troops to endure the condescension of the occupied population. The outcome was not difficult to imagine.

Yet all of this would soon be dwarfed by the rapid and total collapse of the Red Army in the face of the German invasion. Once again Soviet propaganda proved too effective for its own good. Self-styled true believers like Lev Kopelev admitted to being delighted with the news of the war. 'This is the holy war. Now the German proletariat will support us, and Hitler will be overthrown immediately.' Other Soviet soldiers were shocked that German soldiers captured during the early days of the war did not respond to the food and smoke they offered them in joining the 'Red Front', but rather offered insolent looks and belched 'Heil Hitler!' in their faces.[13] The perceived Nazi arrogance fueled hatred and vengeful pride. During the first days of the invasion, young enthusiasts on their way to the front bragged that 'Hitler became full of himself, rejoicing with the success in the war with the little powers. But the USSR is neither Belgium nor Greece. We'll crush the fascist hounds even faster than we crushed the White Finns.' A year later and despite the catastrophic defeats they were identically echoed by other angry and humiliated servicemen who assured their relatives that 'this is not the marches [the enemy] led into Belgium, Denmark, and France. Here, in this gullied, pitted steppe, death, and only death, awaits him at every step.'[14]

Enthusiastic youngsters were also the ones most devastated at the sight of German soldiers roaming in the streets of their hometown. One woman recorded her shock shortly after she saw the first German soldier in her Ukrainian town in August of that year. 'I was choked and tears rolled from my eyes. A short, strongly built German approached me. 'Crying? Cry for the Russian soldier. The German soldier is better than the Russian soldier.' But it was not for the Russian soldier that she was crying. Rather it was the overwhelming sense of humiliation in the face of completely unexpected defeat. 'The belief in the invincibility of the Soviet Union collapsed, the gilded facade fell away, the falsity showed its real face. What was the point in fortifying the defence for such a long period and all the talk about the invincibility [of the Soviet Union], when everything collapsed in one month?'[15]

Such a realisation was a tremendous blow to a system built on total commitment and belief. It would require a decisive victory to stop, or at least delay, the corrosive effect. In the meantime, the bitter humiliation of colossal defeats and exposure to the full wrath of racial policies under occupation, in captivity, and on the battlefield led to an immediate about-face change in views and practices. Or rather, it led to a return to the pre-Soviet-Nazi-Pact notions of the enemy and ways to cope with him. The shock over the pact with Nazi Germany was genuine enough for a populace whose vilification of this arch-enemy for over a decade left deep imprints. 'Why do our newspapers not scold Goebbels nowadays? Did he become a Bolshevik?' exemplified comments officials encountered from baffled citizens in 1940.[16] In more than one way, the German attack and conduct forced the Soviet machine and its fighting cogs back into their normal habitat.

Integral Brutality Unleashed

Why did Soviet soldiers keep fighting literally to the death in conditions to which so many other societies throughout wartime Europe had succumbed? What was it that astounded the equally zealous Nazi invaders? Following two and a half decades of socialism in power, these questions should have been easily answered. But neither the war nor the regime's use of a variety of mobilising battle cries provided easy answers. The making of the Soviet fighting men and women reveals two sources that complemented each other. The Soviet system functioned at its utmost efficiency under conditions of total war. It was, after all, a world based on constant and ruthless mobilisation campaigns and relentless demonisation of any group the regime marked as hostile to its cause. The result was a profound institutional, cultural and socio-political brutalisation of society well before it entered the war, and even more so once it found itself in the throes of a life-or-death struggle. However brutal the operations of the Soviet regime were, they were credited — if not universally endorsed — as means to instil order and a sense of direction where chaos ruled. Simply put, the relentless and harsh experiences of collectivisation, famine, and terror produced a tough people who could and did endure difficulties that had defeated others. Their commanders were of the same mould, largely of peasant and worker origin, who had climbed the military ladder without forgetting where they had come from.

In this light, the draconian orders Nos. 270 (August 1941) and 227 (July 1942) that classified falling into captivity and unauthorised retreat as acts of treason were not aberrations for Soviet people, but rather an integral part of their world. Hence, even the criminalisation of captivity

regardless of circumstances seemed to have been internalised by combatants. After watching a group of Soviet POWs who survived German
captivity in liberated Kharkiv in February 1943, and whom he described
as 'weird ghostlike figures in terrible rags... with breath [that] smelled of
death,' an incensed British correspondent called the attention of a Soviet
soldier. 'Don't you get het [sic] up about them. For all we know, they may
have been left here by the Germans as spies or diversionists,' came the
answer. [17] These orders were not taken simply at face value, but more in
the spirit they inculcated in the face of total collapse during a low point
of the campaign. The execution of at least 158,000 Red Army servicemen, including 13,500 soldiers during the battle of Stalingrad alone —
compared to a total of 15-20,000 such executions in the German army
throughout the entire war — at the time of severe manpower shortages,
was not only an *ad hoc* enforcement of military discipline. It was also part
of an ethos tracing back to the Civil War that assigned primacy to the
purity of the ranks over other dire needs regardless of circumstances. [18]
Similarly, the iron discipline adopted by the Red Army following the
Finnish fiasco, including public flogging of straying soldiers, reinforced a
violent atmosphere that was instantly applied by the troops to the civilian
population it conquered. [19]

At the same time, one cannot underestimate the weight of the traditional Russian and Soviet way of war that underscored the primacy of
the collective over the individual, and was partially responsible for the
acceptance of colossal sacrifice for the larger cause and community. Even
as the top command gained fame for its skilled strategic operations, the
age-old habit of wearing out Russia's enemy by sacrificing its own enormous human fodder remained intact. The resulting catastrophic losses in
human lives went hand-in-hand with the rigidity of the troops' attitude
and conduct. Equally important was a sense of deeply rooted traditions
of fatalism and resilience that had only recently helped so many to endure the horrors of civil war, collectivisation, famine and terror. Just as
the latter planted deep resentment, so did they help in withstanding an
onslaught that did not distinguish between town and village, but rather
treated all as Slavic *Untermenschen*. Born into the Soviet system or passing
through its formative experiences, the frontline generation was mostly a
Soviet product. [20] The writer Viacheslav Kondrat'ev and poet Iurii Belash
were probably right recalling that soldiers in the trenches did not debate

the tenets of Marxism-Leninism; they were not consumed by unqualified admiration for the *Vozhd'*, but rather by patriotic love for the Mother-land.[21] Still, what patriotism and what fatherland did they have in mind? By their own admission they had known no other alternative system at the time. As one of them put it years later: 'We knew our motherland, we knew Stalin, we knew where we were going.'[22]

This worldview and system followed servicemen to the fronts and into the trenches, as Gabriel Temkin pointedly noted. Less than two months into the war, with the Germans inflicting one defeat after another on the collapsing Red Army, Temkin, who had escaped earlier from Ger-man-occupied Poland, was separated from his unit along with all Soviet ethnic Germans who had already been engaged in battles against the Ger-man invaders, and sent to a labour battalion in the rear. The unit was soon captured by the Germans. While in captivity, Temkin, a Jew, was confronted by the legacy of Soviet ethnic relations and their functions under new circumstances. Some prisoners helped the Germans to sniff out Jews, stripping them of their boots before they were led to execu-tion. But none other than a rabid Ukrainian anti-Semite saved Temkin. 'Did you really think, you motherfucker, that I would be after you for a loaf of bread,' the Ukrainian reproached Temkin, forging friendship in the least expected place and circumstance. A certain universal sense of dignity overpowered entrenched animosities. Temkin later escaped and rejoined the Red Army forces. But not immediately. Like all other POWs, this young Jewish man had to go through an NKVD verification camp to make sure he was not a German agent or infected by his German captors. As always, cleansing the ranks was paramount to even the direst needs of manpower. Having survived the verification, which he contends was genuinely concerned with collaborators (had there been a certain quota, his Polish background would have done him in), he was allowed to rejoin the army. His squad was sent directly to the front, and they still had no rifles as they were crossing the Donets River. 'Don't worry, you'll find them there' [i.e., left by fallen soldiers] the commissar promised them, which is exactly what happened. His real war had started, recalls Temkin, with undisguised pride. [23]

Moreover, this was a system that was now offering a second chance to millions of inmates, and a clean slate to everyone and itself. For many convicts — nearly 1.1 million people — fierce fighting on the battlefield was motivated by the prospects of political and legal rehabilitation.[24] The redemption of past sins through wartime exploits, particularly the stain of wrong social origin, was ordained by the regime itself. During the war, the trickle of rehabilitated common (and, to a smaller degree, political) criminals in the Gulag camps turned into a tidal wave of several hundred thousand 'former people' who won rehabilitation for themselves and their families. Many of them were driven equally by patriotism and guilt over sitting in prison while their country was at war, as many of them related at the time.[25] Some 440,000 of them ended up in penal battalions, the units with the highest rate of combat fatalities. '[I knew] that in the penal battalion my old sins could only be pardoned through my blood,' recalled Vladimir Kantovskii, one of the released inmates. 'And in spite of everything, some opportunities were opening for me. There was a small chance of survival — even if 10 people survived out of 250 it meant that you had a chance.'[26] Indeed, he was one of the few who won release from the battalion after having severely wounded, only to be sent back to complete his sentence in the Gulag.

However, many more former inmates who survived won their freedom and even more. Their service won them internal passports, which elevated them at once on par with the urban population and above the rest of the peasantry, which was still deprived of this document and consequently of the right of free movement. For others, it was nothing less than the beginning of a political career. Dmitrii Triastov, a self-described former recidivist, knew the penal system rather well. By early 1943, however, Triastov had already become a company commander in the Red Army. Writing to his former wardens on 11 April 1943, Triastov implored the Chekists to read his letter to other prisoners as a living example of the possibility to rebuild their lives through service at the front. 'Here, each of them can vindicate himself, be a good commander, and also receive high decoration, as I had,' wrote Triastov.

For my good exploits in the fight against fascism I was awarded not only with the Red Star medal, but I was also admitted to the ranks of the Communist Party. I don't have on me anymore this past, filthy stain of my [criminal] record. It was dropped. Therefore, a bright path for a happy life is open for me.[27]

The reinstatement into the party ranks of scores of front-line veterans who had committed various offenses, ranging from conducting religious rites to embezzlement, that otherwise would have led to expulsion accentuated this change.[28] By all accounts, these people had a lot to kill for, and equally, a lot to die for. And they did.

In the same vein, the Soviet wartime system had also provided millions of peasants in uniform with an unprecedented incentive for fighting as hard as they could against the foreign invader. For the first time in two decades of humiliation as second-class citizens, peasant servicemen were endorsed as the core of a new rural constituency. Having assumed power positions in the villages, often with the active popular support of fellow peasants, this group displayed a remarkable sense of entitlement based on their service to the motherland and at the expense of those who had not shared their wartime ordeal. Families of Red Army servicemen were a key group in this development. Concern for dear ones (many had several relatives in service), discrimination at the hands of the Germans and collaborators (most important, at the hands of 'former people' who returned from exile and assumed positions of power, especially in the villages) forged a cohesion that developed into loyalty to Soviet power. Finding shelter in Cossack and Ukrainian villages, between his escape from a German prison camp and his reunion with Red Army forces, Gabriel Temkin observed that for locals the Red Army was the army of their husbands, fathers and sons. 'More than once,' recalled Temkin in reference to the numerous occasions when he was saved from inquisitive local policemen or the Germans, 'I saw a mother looking at me tenderly, as [she held] back tears or shed them profusely she would whisper: 'Perhaps your mother is now taking care of my boy'.'[29] As we shall see in the discussion of the partisan warfare in the countryside, compassion for one's own went hand-in-hand with violence against all others.

Not necessarily communists, they became the face and body of Soviet power in the wartime and postwar countryside. The travails of the Soviet peasantry were far from over and it would continue to be a second class long after the war. Nonetheless, the war ushered in a new village, dominated by vast networks of Red Army veterans and their families. For them, the war erased past humiliation and heralded a new beginning, this time as legitimate members of the Soviet family and not simply as the symbol of obstacles and backwardness.

Early on, the Soviet wartime hate campaign did away with all restraints. But there was nothing novel to the demonisation and de-humanisation of the enemy, both pillars of Soviet political culture from its very birth. This time, however, the enemy lived up to and exceeded Soviet official allegations. The destruction was tangible and visible, personal and national, and unlike the prewar purge campaigns, the enemy was not the often improbable relative, friend, next-door neighbour, or hitherto admired hero. Popular wartime correspondents constantly reminded the soldiers of the German devastation not only of the country as a whole, but even more so of their most intimate environment, such as Vasilii Grossman's immortal executed schoolteacher. In the immensely popular poem 'Kill Him!' Konstantin Simonov exhorted soldiers to 'Kill a German every time you see one!' and Il'ia Ehrenburg scolded the servicemen that a day passing without killing a German is a wasted day: 'If you have killed one German, kill another. Nothing gives us so much joy as German corpses.' And as the Red Army was closing on Germany, so did the vehemence and vengeance grow. 'Germany is a witch [and] the Germans have no souls,' exclaimed Ehrenburg and reminded the Soviet troops that they were not marching alone on Berlin, but accompanied by 'all the corpses of the innocents, all the cabbages of Maidanek, all the trees of Vitebsk on which the Germans hanged so many unhappy peoples, and the boots and shoes and the babies' slippers of those murdered and gassed in Maidanek,' namely, 'the dead [who were] knocking on the Joachimsthaler strasse... and all other cursed streets of that city.' The final call for revenge was quite expected: 'We shall put up gallows in Berlin... We shall forget nothing... A German is a German everywhere... Germany, you can now whirl round in circles, and burn, and howl in your deathly agony; the hour of revenge has struck!'[30]

From the Kremlin, Stalin insisted that the Red Army was devoid of racial hatred. Despite the foreign press jabbering that the Red Army exterminated German soldiers just as Germans out of hatred of everything German, Stalin protested, '[It] annihilates them, not because of their German origin, but because they want to enslave our motherland.'[31] On the ground, however, it was Ehrenburg who set the tone, and much in line with Stalin's earlier statement on 6 November 1941 that 'if the Germans want to have a war of extermination, they will get it.' And they did.

The Germans' fanatical fighting and fear of captivity in the hands of the Soviets (in itself a product of the successful Nazi indoctrination on the Jewish-Bolshevik Asiatic menace) played their part in minimising the number of German POWs — far less than a million by 1944. An absolute majority of the approximately two-thirds who survived Soviet captivity were taken prisoners *after* the end of hostilities. But when the war was still raging in 1943 the mortality rate of German POWs in Soviet hands reached a peak of over 50 per cent. Moreover, German soldiers were fully aware of the fate expecting them in Soviet hands.[32] Soviet policies and warfare were not anchored in genocidal ideology and institutions, nor did they carry out such practices. But they did bring to the front an already brutalised and hardened constituency that could and did go head to head with the Nazis.

In a statement on 23 February 1942, Stalin denied rumours that the Red Army was not taking German prisoners. Moreover, he issued a specific order that called on the troops to spare the lives of surrendering Germans. But in a conversation with fellow Communists, he also took care to let his true sentiments be known. When Milovan Djilas mentioned that Yugoslav partisans did not take German prisoners 'because they killed all our prisoners', Stalin responded with this anecdote:

One of our men was leading a large group of German prisoners and on the way killed all but one. They asked him, when he arrived at his destination: 'And where are all the others?' 'I was just carrying out the orders of the commander in chief,' he said, 'to kill every one to the last man — and here is the last man.'[33]

In a system where 'working toward the *Vozhd*'' echoed its Nazi counterpart of 'working toward the *Führer*', namely constant effort by subordinates to interpret and implement the leader's will and the ensuing radicalisation of measures, such a comment in the presence of top lieutenants amounted to a green light. On the ground, there were millions of soldiers willing to execute any German they laid their hands on. David Dragunskii, two-time Hero of the Soviet Union, had no qualms about relating his exploits in public. 'All of us hate the Germans!' exclaimed Dragunskii in a speech before the Jewish Anti-Fascist Committee in the summer of 1945.

But I hate them doubly. For one, because I am a Soviet man; for another, because I am a Jew! ... I yearned to get to Germany. I got to Germany... The Germans knew that my brigade was headed by a Jew. They posted notices that they would flay me alive...That very night [in Berlin] we caught five hundred SS troops whose commander had posted that notice. We made shashlik and beef stroganoff of them all. We caught the colonel of the SS swine. He complained that someone had taken his watch. 'Take care of his complaint,' I commanded one of my men. The colonel is not around anymore.[34]

Notably, most of Dragunskii's soldiers were not Jews nor did they need any ulterior motives to 'make shashlik and beef stroganoff' of the Germans they had captured.

Until very recently, the tale of the Red Army soldiers' systematic rape of millions of German women (if eight-year-old girls qualify, too) had been a taboo in Russia. At the time, however, mass rapes were rather a public horror show. 'Women, mothers and daughters, lie right and left along the highway, and a cackling armada of men with pants pulled down in front of each of them,' recalled Leonid Rabichev. 'Pulling aside bleeding and unconscious [women], shooting children rushing to help. Cackles, growls, laughter, cries, and moans. And their commanders, Majors and Colonels stand on the highway, some chuckle, some conduct — no, more likely regulate the traffic so that all of their soldiers, with no exception, would take part. No, this was not circling the wagon [but] a hellish terrible group sex.... The Colonel who was just conducting the movement, cannot hold himself and joins the line, and the Major fires at the witnesses, hysterical children and old people.'[35] The rate of two million illegal abortions a year performed in Germany between 1945 and 1948 points not only to the unprecedented and horrifying magnitude, but equally defies mono-causal explanation. Several aspects, however, are most relevant for the present discussion. For one, the winds blowing from the Kremlin were certainly tolerant. There was no concerted, systematic effort to curtail these phenomena for the sake of maintaining operational discipline. At times, rape and looting were punished by officers on-site, but it was only two years after the end of hostilities that Soviet troops in Germany were confined to their garrisons and separated from the civilian population.[36] Here, too, the pattern of 'working toward the *Vozhd*' was on display. When Milovan Djilas complained to Stalin about the Red Army soldiers raping in Croatia, Romanian, and Hungary, the latter dismissed it as boys having fun after going through hell. And this was only on the way to Germany. In this light, it came as no surprise to hear a Soviet Marshal articulating an almost identical reasoning in response to inquiry by a Western correspondent. 'Of course,' responded the officer, 'a lot of nasty things happened.'

But what do you expect? You know what the Germans did to their Russian war prisoners, how they devastated our country, how they murdered and raped and looted? Have you seen Maidanek or Auschwitz? Every one of our soldiers lost dozens of his comrades. Every one of them had some personal scores to settle with the Germans, and in the first flush of victory our fellows no doubt derived a certain satisfaction from making it hot for those *Herrenvolk* women. However, that stage is over. We have now pretty well clamped down on that sort of thing — not that most German women are vestal virgins. Our main worry is the awful spread of the clap among our troops.[37]

In a macabre way, some Soviet officers viewed the rapes as 'justice from below', compensating the deprived rank-and-file with what their superiors enjoyed all throughout the war. After explaining to a British correspondent that German women practically understood that 'it was now the Russians' turn', a Soviet major reasoned that 'for nearly four years, the Red Army had been sex-starved. It was all right for the officers, especially the staff officers, so many of whom had a 'field-wife' handy — a secretary, or typist, or a nurse, or a canteen waitress — but the ordinary Vanka had very few opportunities in that line.' And since raping Russian women and even Polish women was not a real option, continued the officer, things erupted in Germany. Hence, Vanka could finally compensate himself for the privileges he was denied by his own military system.

Humiliation at the sight of prosperity and perceived arrogance of the enemy, even when vanquished and ruined, added fuel to the anger over the loss of relatives, friends and comrades. Crossing into Romania — a country not necessarily known for its wealth even before the wartime destruction — and Hungary, Soviet soldiers were stunned by the relative prosperity they encountered, just like they were in 1939-40 in eastern Poland and the Baltic states. Similar scenes of mass looting repeated themselves, only this time without any inhibitions. The regime's reaction was telling. Indeed, the Soviet authorities were alarmed, but not by the pervasive looting. Rather, they worried that the exposure to the higher standard of living would 'dazzle [soldiers'] eyes' and trigger negative reflections on the Soviet system.[38] So, as long as they remembered their cultural superiority, the soldiers had a free hand to loot, rape and maim.

Further to the west, Soviet servicemen were even more shocked and angered at how well the Germans were dressed, the quality of their housing, tidiness, running water and indoor toilets. Rage over the gap between the Soviet and the German condition was translated to an orgy of destruction. 'They lived well, the parasites,' uttered a 19-year-old soldier who made the way from Stalingrad to Berlin. 'Great big farms in East

Prussia, and pretty posh houses in the towns that hadn't been burned out or bombed to hell. And look at these dachas here! Why did these people who were living so well have to invade us?'[39]

Such reasoning was probably unfamiliar to those who endured the Nazi occupation and had never seen the outside world. They had, however, plenty of other reasons to act with equal ruthlessness.

Integral Brutality Unchecked

The tale of Soviet men and women living under and fighting German occupation is largely one of exposure and involvement in an unprecedented brutalisation of public life. Enactment of genocide, intentionally induced famines, and deportation to forced labour took on new qualitative and quantitative levels for a population already seasoned by the relentless violence of the Soviet state. Side by side with the overwhelming German brutality and the outcome of the total collapse of state authority, Soviet partisans had to confront daily the consequences of Soviet policies, such as lingering bitterness over recent mass deportations, expropriation of property, false elections, and destruction of civil society by way of systematic denunciations. Even for the local men and women who joined the Soviet partisan movement, home was an alien, foreign country, at least until the tide of war changed in mid-1943. Soviet partisans, especially those operating on the recently annexed territories, where the bulk of the partisan activity took place, had to cope constantly with multiple fronts: Germans, local nationalist guerrillas, and the local population. There, brutalisation was both instant and enduring, personal and institutional.

A Soviet partisan leader and a career NKVDist was blunt when he summarised the hostile environment that surrounded him in his own native region in Ukraine until the autumn of 1943. The population could be divided into two categories. The first consisted of anti-Soviet elements already dissatisfied with Soviet power who, with the arrival of the Germans, entered the service of the fascists as spies, servants, and so on. The second category included those who did not understand the essence of fascism and, in their pursuit of private property and land, sided with the Germans, immediately reporting to German authorities the arrival of partisans in one town or another. The reaction to this situation was uncompromising. 'If we heard that someone complained about Soviet power or the partisans and the Red Army, we found him and punished him.... The population of the surrounding villages and districts was 90 percent pro-Soviet since we shot all the hostile elements,' wryly noted the commissar of the same brigade.[40]

Indifference to the suffering of the civilian population under occupation was justified on ideological grounds and as a part of the Bolshevik ethos. A *Pravda* editorial on 30 July 1942 reminded readers that during the civil war, Lenin used to say: 'He who does not help the Red Army wholeheartedly and does not observe its order and iron discipline is a traitor.' And so the lives of civilians forced to work under the Germans were expendable. Grigorii Linkov, a party official parachuted into western Belorussia to revive partisan activity there, and one reputed for his basic decency, did not hesitate to provoke the Germans' wrath on the local population:

I understood, of course, that the Hitlerites might send a punitive expedition to the village, accuse its citizens of contacts with the partisans, and cruelly avenge themselves on the peaceful population. But I also understood that the population that was driven to repair the enemy's roads, whether voluntarily or involuntarily, delayed the hour of victory for a while. But who can determine what a minute of military activity costs?[41]

As early as December 1941, the Wehrmacht Commander-in-Chief in Ukraine observed that 'Death by strangulation inspires fear more particularly.'[42] His Soviet counterparts opted for identical logic and measures. Public hanging of captured anti-Soviet guerrillas became a didactic spectacle. Quite likely the ritual of hanging was intended to add an element of humiliation and terror, since the Soviet Criminal Code spoke only of shooting as the exceptional measure of punishment for extremely serious crimes. Already in July 1943, eight Soviet citizens convicted of collaboration were hanged in the city square of Krasnodar in front of thirty thousand people, and newsreels of the trial and the hanging were shown in local cinemas. The ever-brutish Nikita Khrushchev, in charge of the Ukrainian partisan movement and eradication of anti-partisan forces, aspired for a landscape filled with gallows. Literally. '[In order] to terrorise the bandits,' Khrushchev wrote to Stalin, 'we should not shoot [them], but hang them. The courts-martial must be conducted openly, with the local population in attendance.'[43]

By the time he made the proposal, public hanging of suspected collaborators had already become commonplace. Soviet partisan units turned
the public execution into a pillar of their military-political activity. In one
village alone, the Lenin Mounted Brigade executed 56 prisoners from a
Cossack regiment, shot and hanged another 84 alleged collaborators and
'counterrevolutionary elements' in the course of a raid into an occupied
territory, and overall executed some 825 village elders, policemen, and
other traitors in less than two years of activity.[44]

Taking prisoners was a temporary act on the way to execution. 'We
did not take prisoners as a rule,' calmly noted a commissar of a partisan
detachment. 'If we did take prisoners, we shot them after a preliminary
interrogation.'[45] Killing and mutilating captured enemy combatants,
especially of suspected collaborators, was the rule, and often was carried out with obvious satisfaction. Leo Heiman, a sixteen-year-old Polish
Jew, had his first encounter with Soviet partisans near Brest Litovsk, all
former Red Army servicemen, when they looted the house where he
and other refugees were staying and assaulted the women, 'by mistake,
as they apologised later when they learned that we were Jews.' When the
middle-class lad from Warsaw joined the partisan ranks shortly thereafter,
he immediately embarked on a similar pattern of rape, mutilation, and
looting. Interestingly, his first commander who schooled him in partisan
life was a former Gulag prisoner who instituted a Gulag-like code in the
detachment. As his batman, Heiman was responsible for a steady supply
of minors and alcohol. Captured informants were subjected to a grisly
death as happened to two policemen from Slonim. 'First of all, Pete the
Lawyer and Vasy the Gipsy broke their arms and legs,' Heiman related in
matter-of-fact tone.

They fainted and we poured cold water over them until they came to. The operation was repeated and I had to run to the kitchen for more cold water. Since
all the men, except those on lookout duty, wanted to take part in the fun, the
room became rather crowded. After the volunteers [the policemen] came to [and
admitted their service in the Gestapo] they begged to be shot. As they lay on the
floor, we all kicked them in the ribs until they spat blood and fainted once again.
We revived them for the third time, before finally kicking them to death.

However, the same applied to all Soviet partisans in the area, including
the most disciplined ones. German prisoners and local collaborators and
informers, women included, were literally skinned, burnt with hot iron

rods, often beheaded, their eyes gauged, or simply drowned in outhouses to the amusement of the participants and observers. [46] At this point, the common rule was no rules at all.

Collective punishment became the order of the day from entire na-tionalities down to the village level. 'We won't be respected if we don't take harsh measures. We must arrest even the most unimportant ones. Some must be tried, others simply hanged, the rest deported. For one of ours, we will take a hundred of them... [You] haven't used enough violence! When you seize a village where they killed two women, you must destroy the entire village,' Nikita Khrushchev exhorted the chiefs of political and punitive organs under his command in November 1944. [47]

There was little need to drive this point home, since it had already been the norm. A Ukrainian nationalist guerrilla who admitted that his own side was 'quite cruel.... We didn't take any prisoners of war and they didn't take any prisoners either, so we killed each other. That was natural,' was nevertheless shocked by the brutality of the Soviet partisans. 'The Germans just killed us,' recalled Oleksii Bris. 'But with the Red partisans the bestialities were different. Some of them were cutting the ears off our members. In rare cases they have this Asian way of torturing people — cutting your ear and tongue off. I don't know if they did this to people who were still alive, but these events happened quite often. It's sadism that exists in every system. The Germans just hanged people, but I never saw tortured bodies.'[48]

He must have kept his eyes closed. One may grant Bris the benefit of doubt when claiming he had never witnessed or participated in mutila-tion of prisoners, but his comrades did, as in the case of fifteen Jewish girls captured by a Ukrainian unit operating in western Belorussia. They were raped, tied to each other with barbed wire and burned alive.[49] Mass murder was already taking place in the very midst of the local population, at times with its active participation. The slaughter of Jews certainly hor-rified most, if only because of the fear of who would be next. For others, mass executions became a macabre spectacle, and a significant number actively participated. The level of collaboration with the German occupa-tion authorities was more widespread than recognised hitherto. By 1943, some 300,000 people served in the local police (*Schutzmannschaft*) in Ukraine and Belorussia. Most were not volunteers or active participants in the extermination, and more often than not were motivated by greed and power rather than commitment to the Nazis. But their sheer numbers and willingness to carry out such activities created an environment in which the most astounding atrocities were routinised and normalised. The local police, never in short supply, were indispensable for the 'Final Solution.' This was especially true during the 'second wave' of killings in 1942 when the Germans opted for total extermination of the Jews and the liquidation of Soviet POWs and other non-Jewish groups. The pool of killers who often switched their allegiances to the dominant power in the territories was vast indeed, including the Soviet partisans who opened their ranks to able-bodied Jews, but also executed them on the smallest excuse and used their family camps as bait for ambushing the Germans and the local police.[50]

Indeed, the pursuit of ethnic cleansing and mass extermination was not limited to movements in power. Each ethnic group and its political-military representatives sought the physical removal of other ethnicities. The Ukrainian nationalist movement, the largest anti-Soviet guerrilla organisation, had never concealed that its goal of unifying all Ukrainian lands went hand-in-hand with the cleansing these lands of all foreign elements, i.e., non-ethnic Ukrainians. Armed with the cohesive ideology of integral nationalism (often referred to favourably by its ideologues as 'zoological nationalism') and mottos such as, 'The road to Golgotha can be magnificent, if you know where you are heading and to what end,' the movement sought the extermination of Russians, Poles, and Jews wherever and whenever it could.[51] Alas, it was not alone. In a rare memoir of a perpetrator portraying his involvement in atrocities, not in a report to superiors or under interrogation by captors, Waldemar Lotnik reflects on the Polish-Ukrainian massacres in 1943-44 along the Buh River on the eve of the Soviets' return. Along with his comrades in the Polish Peasants' Battalion, 18-year-old Lotnik literally obliterated Ukrainian villages, murdering most people in sight, indiscriminately raping women, mutilating corpses, and burning villages to the ground. The Ukrainian nationalist forces which for a while manned the local police units under German auspices were doing just the same, sinking these provinces into a bloodbath that stood out even by the standards of that era. Killing was personal, with neighbours who had lived together for decades, if not centuries, turning against one other with ferocity that in rare moments of reflection astounded even themselves.[52]

For sure, the craze for blood built upon existing animosities. But why did they burst out at this time and with such intensity? From the First World War on, these territories had been subjected to relentless social engineering drives by every movement that operated there, either in power or in opposition. The Polish government's policies from the mid-1930s on assumed an increasingly racial character regarding the Jews, and regarded the Ukrainian population collectively. The nationalist movement of the latter was practically similar in ideology and action. The arrival of the Soviets brought mass deportations of socio-ethnic 'hostile elements,' and was soon followed by the Nazis. By that time the population was functioning within a warlike, aggressive ethos, in which familiar rivals turned into abstract, undifferentiated enemies, previously untouchable women and children became legitimate prey, and compromise was passed over for a violent 'zero-sum game'. Coupled with a sense of urgency in the face of an uncertain future, the actual power vacuum in large parts of these regions, and the illusion that statehood was an actual possibility, provided a fertile environment for the worst atrocities. Lotnik makes clear that by the time the Ukrainian-Polish slaughter started, he (like the rest of the population) was well aware of the fate of the Jews whose murders took place 'in our midst'. Still, nothing but amazement at the passivity of the victims is recorded. When he set out on his bloody path, not only were there practically no Jews in what had been a densely populated territory, but there were also few regrets. He might have added that four years earlier, straggling Polish army units that escaped the German onslaught attacked Jewish and Ukrainian settlements suspected of harbouring 'communist sympathies' — a thinly veiled code for ethnic animosity. Invading from the East, the Soviets only inflamed these animosities by releasing Ukrainian and Belorussian POWs, but not Poles.[53] Although Lotnik is incapable of drawing the link between German treatment of the Jews and the Ukrainian-Polish mutual atrocities, the logic and methods of all three were indistinguishable. Ironically, if not surprisingly, Zygmunt Bauman's 'gardening state' flourished in the stateless territories that conditioned and endured the worst bloodletting of the war.

War and State Terror

The course of warfare and the fate of Soviet state terror were closely intertwined. What were the features of this pillar of the Soviet system following the encounter with its totalitarian other? The ordination of the war as the revolutionary Armageddon spelled a drastic shift in the purge paradigm from cleansing certain areas to cleansing entire groups of people. The prewar partiality and focus on specific border regions were replaced by the targeting of each and every member of a stigmatised group regardless of the geographical location or service it rendered to the Soviet state. Excision was intended to be total, irreversible, and pursued relentlessly. The resettlement of all ethnic Germans at the beginning of the war — despite an earlier official recognition of their heroic contribution to the war effort — underlined that exigency was not the driving motive in Soviet cleansing operations, especially not in the midst of the cataclysmic war. With its very existence hanging by a thread and the Red Army being routed by invaders, the regime opted for the largest cleansing operation since collectivisation, removing hundreds of thousands of capable young men from the Red Army ranks. At the same time, the phenomenon of targeting elusive enemies from within — a peculiar innovation of purification campaigns that followed the 'Great Transformation' in the early 1930s — remained intact. Entire nationalities were deported on charges of harbouring hostile attitudes toward Soviet power. The number of deported nationalities, 'kulaks' in the newly annexed territories, repatriated Soviet prisoners of war and forced labourers who had been in Germany, and Axis POWs — all political categories by definition — surpassed the total of those deported throughout the preceding two decades, collectivisation and Terror included. Correspondingly, the Gulag population reached its climax in the early 1950s, with over 2.5 million inmates in the camps and colonies alone, approximately a half million more than at the height of the Great Terror, including the prison population. Not least, about a quarter of the deportees died during the first three years of incarceration.[54]

NKVD officers who participated in the deportations professed uncompromising commitment to the enterprise based on their professional and ideological convictions. Lieutenant Nikonor Perevalov who took part in the deportation of the Kalmyks in December 1943 felt pity for the miserable people he brutalised. Still, stated Perevalov, 'If we had been ordered to shoot them down, we would have shot them down. I would have fulfilled this order...this is the requirement of the oath that we all swear and this is the rule... we were told why the Kalmyks had to be evicted — because they had shown such a negative side of their character during the German occupation. I saw them as someone on the enemy's side, not just because I was a Communist but from a personal point of view as well.'[55] In this light, the NKVD's burning alive of several hundred Chechens, deported for their alleged collaboration with the Germans, in the snowbound village of Khaibakh may not have been the operational rule, but to Soviet contemporaries was not incomprehensible either.[56] In the same vein, many of his generational cohort viewed wartime collaborators as the realisation of the party's constant warning against elusive enemies in their midst. Expressing her disgust with those who eagerly awaited the Germans' arrival at her hometown in Nikopol, a Young Pioneer who dreamed of killing the kulaks who killed Pavlik Morozov (the model Soviet child informant), but who was also confused by her friends being targeted as 'enemies of the people', entered in her diary: 'Yes, there are many enemies. The party is right when it says every third person is a traitor or informer and we have to watch out. I see for myself now.'[57] Both could have added that at this point their worldview had already been shaped not only by professional loyalties and the information provided by their superiors, but even more so by the avalanche of demonising literature and propaganda that called attention to the internal weeds — both individuals and entire nationalities — who did not rise to the occasion or, even worse, betrayed the Soviet cause. Mass-circulation popular short stories conveyed the message of revenge against these weeds who could redeem themselves only through sacrificial death. Wanda Wasilewska's *Raduga*, Losev's *Konets Andreiia Chubarova*, Leonid Leonov's *Nashestvie*, and Aleksei Tolstoy's *Strannaia istoriia* all preached uncompromising official, communal, and individual intolerance toward women fraternising with Germans or Soviet soldiers falling into German captivity. Regardless of the circumstances, such people had no place in Soviet society. At least not alive.

In Possession of Some Infallible Truth

Asked to explain why she felt such a sense of joy and fulfilment after killing the German officer in cold blood, Zinaida Pytkina, who opened our discussion, replied:

I am sorry for my people. When we were retreating we lost so many 17-, 18-year-olds. Do I have to be sorry for the German after that? This was my mood... As a member of the Communist party, I saw in front of me a man who could have killed my relatives... I would have cut off his head if I had been asked to. One person less, I thought. I understand the interest in how a woman can kill a man. I wouldn't do it now. I would do it only if there was a war and I saw again what I had seen during the war... Should I have kissed him for that? ... I even used to ask to be sent on reconnaissance missions to capture a prisoner, but it was not allowed. Women were not sent on such missions — but I wanted to go. I wanted to crawl to the enemy's side and capture a prisoner, perhaps kill him.[58]

The urge to avenge the humiliation of 1941 and the ensuing occupation; anger at the exposure to the higher living standard of a despised enemy; the stunned realisation that the enemy was even worse than ever portrayed; excitement at sheer action and killing and genderless desire to go to further extremes; official and self-ordained feelings that the war offered a clean slate after an oblique past; and not least, a sense of mission and double-duty as members of a unique polity and its extraordinary political and punitive organs whose violence and harshness they internalised long before the war. Zynaida Pytkina, Mitia Khludov, Viacheslav Balakin and millions of their compatriots had it all.

Wars, especially of the magnitude and endurance of the Second World War, are not merely events that happen to people, just as their conduct is not the outcome of an ideological genetic code. Rather, they are processes affected by the participants, who bring along certain worldviews through which they measure circumstances and react in certain ways. As they often did, Vasilii Grossman and Milovan Djilas the great wartime writer-philosopher and the partisan-philosopher turned dissident, respectively, offered the most astute and complementary summations of the driving force behind the carnage: 'The extreme violence of totalitarian systems proved able to paralyse the human spirit throughout whole continents,' argued Grossman, ever sensitive to the overwhelming power of the interwar, pan-European ethos.[59] Always attentive to the unique role of ideology, Djilas opined:

No matter what your ideology may be, once you believe that you are in the possession of some infallible truth, you become a combatant in a religious war. There is nothing to prevent you from robbing, burning, and slaughtering in the name of your truth, for you are doing it with a perfectly clear conscience — indeed the truth in your possession makes it your duty to pursue it with an iron logic and unwavering will… ideology demands the liquidation of your enemies, real or imagined.[60]

The violence unleashed during the war involved practically all sides, albeit in varying degrees, forms and levels of endurance. But the common features that accompanied it — whether the undifferentiated approach to the enemy, the application of abstract identities to the 'other', or the resulting pursuit of total annihilation of both soldiers and civilians — require students of the wartime Soviet Union to examine the ethos that made this development possible, as well as those ideological contours that established unique modes of action. The final word belongs to Vladimir N. Shubkin, a veteran-turned-sociologist:

[I]t was the pre-war country that entered the war. Everything in that country was taken by the people to the front: the capacity for self-sacrifice; the suspicion of others; cruelty, and spiritual weakness; baseness, and naive romanticism; officially demonstrated devotion to the leader, and deeply concealed doubts; the thick-headed rigidity of bureaucrats and people playing safe, and a lively hope that something would turn up; the heavy burden of indignity, and the feeling that the war was just. Nothing was left behind, nothing was forgotten. And both soldiers and Marshals had to cope with all this.[61]

It was a system that overwhelmed and politicised every sphere of public and private life and valued and institutionalised violence. It could and did offer its citizens something to die for, and a lot to kill for.

PRISONER TAKING AND PRISONER KILLING

THE DYNAMICS OF DEFEAT, SURRENDER AND
BARBARITY IN THE AGE OF TOTAL WAR

Niall Ferguson

'*Pochemu?* Why did you continue to fight?' This was the question one Red Army officer asked of a German commander after accepting his surrender in May 1945.[1] This essay seeks to answer that question by sketching a hypothesis about the dynamics of military defeat, and in particular the phenomenon of surrender. It seeks to explain why it proved so difficult to end the Second World War, even after the overwhelming economic advantage of the Allied powers had turned the strategic tide decisively against the Axis. In particular, it offers a suggestion as to why both Germany and Japan continued to fight so tenaciously — and so lethally — long after any realistic chance of victory had disappeared.

A significant part of the explanation, it is argued, lies in the extremely violent battlefield culture that developed in two key theatres of the war, which deterred soldiers from surrendering, even when they found themselves in hopeless situations. This culture had its origins on the Western Front during the First World War.[2] But in the Second World War it became official policy on both sides, not only on the Eastern Front but in the Pacific theatre as well. Only when the Allied authorities adopted techniques of psychological warfare designed to encourage rather than discourage surrender did German and Japanese resistance end.

I

In common with most combatants in the world wars, my vantage point is that of a fundamentally unheroic individual with minimal military train-

126

ing. Millions of such men all over the world found themselves trying to kill one another between 1914 and 1918 and again between 1939 and 1945. And although the development of artillery in the First World War and aerial bombardment in the Second meant that the majority of military casualties were not victims of 'face to face' combat, nevertheless infantry engagements, supplemented by tanks and mobile artillery, continued to be of decisive significance.[3]

For men who fought in the great battles of the mid-twentieth century, there was a finite number of alternatives — at most five, a number which grew smaller as the moment of engagement drew closer:

    a) To stay in one's place, obey orders, fight and risk death;

    b) To attempt to flee, that is to desert;

    c) To refuse, along with one's comrades if one could persuade them, to obey orders to engage the enemy, that is to mutiny;

    d) To mutilate oneself in the hope of passing off a self-inflicted wound as an authentic 'Blighty' and getting sent back to a dressing station; or

    e) To give oneself up to the enemy, that is to surrender.

Of these, perhaps the most important is option e) — surrender. This is for a simple reason: when it happens on a sufficiently large scale, surrender is what ends wars.

It was a common misconception of the age of total war that victory went to the side that killed the most of the enemy in battle. As Elias Canetti put it: 'Each side wants to constitute the larger crowd of living fighters and it wants the opposing side to constitute the largest heap of the dead.'[4] But if killing the enemy had been the key to victory, the Central Powers would have won the First World War and the Axis Powers the Second (table 1, next page).

Clausewitz, however, knew that the 'net body count' was not the key, as he made clear in the fourth book of *On War*:

> Now [it] is known by experience that the losses in physical forces in the course of a battle seldom present a great difference between victor and vanquished respectively, often none at all, sometimes even one bearing an inverse relation to the result, and that the most decisive losses on the side of the vanquished commence only with the retreat.[5]

It is in the retreat, Clausewitz pointed out, that soldiers 'lose their way and fall defenceless into the enemy's hands, and thus the victory mostly

Table 1 : The 'Net Body Count' in Two World Wars (millions)

	First World War	Second World War
Allied Military Deaths	5.4	11.3
Central Powers / Axis Military Deaths	4.0	4.6
Difference: The 'Net Body Count'	1.4	6.7
As a Percentage	35	145

Sources: Author's own calculations based on the figures in Jay M. Winter, *The Great War and the British People* (London, 1985), p. 75; Richard Overy (ed.), *The Times Atlas of the Twentieth Century* (London, 1996), pp. 102-5; Mark Harrison, 'The Economics of World War II: An Overview', in idem (ed.), *The Economics of World War II: Six Great Powers in International Comparison* (Cambridge, 1998), pp. 3f., 7f.; *idem*, 'The Soviet Union: the Defeated Victor', in idem (ed.), *The Economics of World War II: Six Great Powers in International Comparison* (Cambridge, 1998), pp.268-301, p. 291; Richard Overy, *Russia's War* (London, 1997), pp. xvi, 287; John Erickson, 'Red Army Battlefield Performance, 1941-45: The System and the Soldier', in Paul Addison (ed.), *Time to Kill: the Soldier's Experience of War in the West 1939-1945* (London, 1997), pp. 235ff.; Rüdiger Overmans, 'German Historiography, the War Losses and the Prisoners of War', in G. Bischof and S. Ambrose (eds), *Eisenhower and the German POWs: Facts against Falsehood* (London: Baton Rouge, 1992), p. 141; John Ellis, *The World War II Databook: the Essential Facts and Figures for all the Combatants* (London, 1995), pp. 253-6.

Note: It should be emphasised that the figures for the Second World War are especially problematic, not least because of the large numbers of quasi-military formations (e.g. Soviet 'partisans', German *Volkssturm*). As in all wars, a proportion of deaths was due not to enemy action but to disease, accidents and other factors unrelated to enemy action. However, the proportion was smaller than in previous wars because of improved medical provision.

gains bodily substance after it is already decided'. This was a paradox he attempted to resolve with his famous emphasis on morale:

The loss in physical force is not the only one, which the two sides suffer in the course of the combat; the moral forces also are shaken, broken, and go to ruin. It is not only the loss in men, horses and guns, but in order, courage, confidence, cohesion and plan, which come into consideration when it is a question of whether the fight can still be continued or not. It is principally the moral forces which decide here, and in all cases in which the conqueror has lost as heavily as the conquered, it is these alone. ... In the combat the loss of moral force is the chief cause of the decision.[6]

And hence it follows that:

The losses in a battle consist more in killed and wounded; those after the battle, more in artillery taken and prisoners. The first the conqueror shares with the conquered, more or less, but the second not; and for that reason they usually only take place on one side of the conflict, at least they are considerably in excess on one side.

[Captured] artillery and prisoners are therefore at all times regarded as the true trophies of victory, as well as its measure, because through these things its extent is declared beyond a doubt. Even the degree of moral superiority may be better judged of by them than by any other relation, especially if the number of killed and wounded is compared therewith ...

If prisoners and captured guns are those things by which the victory principally gains substance, its true crystallisations, then the plan of the battle should have those things especially in view; the destruction of the enemy by death and wounds appears here merely as the means to an end.[7]

A logical inference from this was that enemy troops should be encouraged to surrender – or, at least, not discouraged from doing so.

There were, in any case, humanitarian arguments for not killing those enemies who laid down their arms. The merciful treatment of prisoners of war was widely recognised as a hallmark of civilised nations in the eighteenth and nineteenth centuries. It was one of Napoleon's maxims that 'Prisoners of war do not belong to the power for which they have fought; they all are under the safeguard of honour and generosity of the nation that has disarmed them.'[8] European colonisers protested — perhaps rather too much — whenever they encountered customs of prisoner-killing among indigenous peoples, whether native Americans or Afghan tribesmen. Before the First World War, prisoner killing was explicitly proscribed by two Regulations of the Hague Convention. Regulation 23(c) stated that it was forbidden to kill or wound a prisoner who had surrendered by laying down his arms. Regulation 23(d) prohibited the order to that no quarter be given.[9]

Yet the laws of war can seem very remote to men in battle; there is no right of appeal after a foe decides to ignore Regulation 23(c). The decision to surrender — to become a prisoner — therefore involves weighing up not the terms of the Hague Convention but:

a) the likelihood of one's being killed if one continues fighting;

b) the likelihood of one's being killed by one's own side if one attempts to surrender;

c) the likelihood of one's being killed by the enemy if one attempts to surrender and

d) the differential between the recent quality of life as a fighting soldier as compared with the anticipated quality of life as a prisoner, including, of course, the possibility that one might be sooner or later be killed.

On the other side, there are the countervailing influences of e) discipline and f) aversion to dishonour, the importance of which, relative to naked self-preservation, varies according to the quality of a soldier's training and the culture of the army he fights in.

The factors that keep men fighting have been neatly summarised by W.L. Hauser as submission, fear, loyalty and pride.[10] Of these, loyalty to the 'primary group' — the small unit to which a soldier belongs — is sometimes said to be the most important: men often fight on in desperate situations in order not to let their 'pals' down, so the argument runs.[11] Wesbrook, on the other hand, has argued that military disintegration may have more to do with a failure of loyalty to the bigger entities of regiment, nation, leadership or cause. Men will only fight on if they feel a 'legitimate demand' is being made on them to risk their lives.[12] On reflection, these are neither mutually exclusive nor wholly sufficient explanations of military resilience. The bonds of the primary group may be an important determinant of morale, but by themselves they cannot explain large-scale military outcomes. Comradeship within small groups tends to be found in most armies. On the other hand, armies that lack such small-scale solidarity can still continue to fight. When casualties are exceptionally high — as on the Eastern Front after 1941 — primary group identities are hard to sustain. Yet in that case men on both sides kept fighting. This may partly have been because they felt the causes they were fighting for were legitimate. But it will be argued here that there were also negative reasons for keeping fighting which have nothing to do with either primary group loyalty or the legitimacy of political demands. The dynamics of defeat can be understood equally well in terms of primary groups and legitimate demands; for most surrenders are part of a collective action by a unit or a whole army, rather than individual actions. It is clearly safer to surrender as a group than to surrender as an individual, and the primary group sometimes was the unit that agreed to enter captivity together. In the same way, surrender can be a reflection of good discipline if a large group of men is ordered to lay down its arms by its own commanding officer and does so in good order.

To illuminate the predicament of the potential *captor*, it is helpful to imagine a schematised game: instead of the prisoner's dilemma, the captor's dilemma. The captor's dilemma is simple — accept the enemy's surrender or kill him. The captor has been fighting an opponent who has been trying to kill him, when suddenly the opponent makes as if to surrender. If he is sincere, then the rational thing to do is to accept his surrender and send him back through the lines towards a prisoner of war camp. There are four arguments for doing so, namely the prisoner's value as:

a) a source of intelligence

b) a source of labour

c) a hostage, and

d) an example to his comrades, if by treating him well you can induce them either to imitate him by giving themselves up too or to reciprocate by acting mercifully if the tables are subsequently turned.[13]

It should be noted, however that most if not all of these benefits flow to the captor's army as a whole and may not be discernible to the individual captor.

What are the arguments — on the other side of the captor's dilemma — against taking prisoners? Here the immediate interests of the individual captor come to the fore. One possibility, as we have seen, is that the supposed surrenderer may be bluffing. Accepting surrender is therefore itself risky. It may also be quite difficult to transport a prisoner back to the lines — in the First World War the British army specified a ratio of between one and two escorts to every ten prisoners[14] — and anyone given this job has to be subtracted from the attacker's force (which may of course have some appeal for the individual captor). The problem is increased if the man surrendering is wounded and incapable of walking unassisted. The simple solution is obviously to shoot the prisoner and forget about him; had he kept fighting that would have been his fate anyway, and while he was fighting he probably inflicted casualties on the attacker.

This then is the captor's dilemma: to accept a surrenderer, with all the personal risks entailed; or to shoot the surrenderer, with the likelihood that resistance may be stiffened, increasing the risks to one's own side as a whole.

It is important to distinguish here between killing that happened in the heat of battle and more cold-blooded killing — or, indeed, fatal neglect — away from the battlefield. In his *Middle Parts of Fortune*, a thinly fictionalised memoir of the Battles of the Somme and Ancre, Frederic Manning vividly captures the experience of killing surrendering men when the 'blood is up'. Almost deranged by his young friend Martlow's death, the hero Bourne runs amok in the German lines:

Three men ran towards them, holding their hands up and screaming; and he lifted his rifle to his shoulder and fired; and the ache in him became a consuming hate that filled him with exultant cruelty, and he fired again, and again ... And Bourne struggled forward again, panting, and muttering in a suffocated voice.

'Kill the buggers! Kill the bloody fucking swine! Kill them!'[15]

Such things happen in most wars. As George S. Patton succinctly put it: 'Troops heated with battle are not safe custodians.'[16] Winston Churchill implied as much when he sardonically defined a prisoner of war as 'a man who tries to kill you and fails, and then asks you not to kill him'.[17] It is hardly surprising that during or immediately after intense fighting such requests often go unheeded. Nevertheless, there has been considerable variation between different armies, as well as within armies, in the readiness of troops to kill surrendering men or newly-taken prisoners, as well as in the readiness of commanders to condone such behaviour. There has also been a great deal of difference in the way prisoners have been treated by those in charge of POW transports and camps. Decisions to surrender were clearly influenced by expectations of treatment in enemy hands at every stage of the process of capture and internment. To understand why some armies surrendered before others therefore requires knowledge of how those expectations were formed.

II

For those who had not read or who had forgotten their Clausewitz, the First World War provided a colossal reminder that it was capturing, not killing the enemy that was decisive. Despite the huge death toll inflicted on the Allies by the Germans and their allies, outright victory failed to materialise: demography meant that there were more or less enough new French and British conscripts each year to plug the gaps created by attrition. However, it did prove possible, first on the Eastern Front and then on the Western, to get the enemy to *surrender* in such large numbers that his ability to fight was fatally weakened. Thus the large-scale surrenders (and desertions) on the Eastern Front in 1917 were the key to Russia's military defeat. Overall, more than half of all Russian casualties took the form of men who were taken prisoner — nearly 16 per cent of all Russian troops mobilised. Austria and Italy also lost a large proportion of men in this way: respectively a third and quarter of all casualties. One in four Austrians mobilised ended up a prisoner (see table 2). The large-scale surrender of Italian troops at Caporetto came close to putting Italy out of the war.[18]

Table 2: Prisoners of War, 1914–1918

Country of origin of POWs	Minima (POWs Nov. 1918)	Maxima c.	Prisoners as a proportion of total casualties	Total mobilised	Prisoners as a proportion of total mobilised
France	446,300	500,000	11.6	8,340,000	5.4
Belgium	10,203	30,000	11.0	365,000	2.8
Italy	530,000	600,000	25.8	5,615,000	9.4
Portugal	12,318	12,318	37.2	100,000	12.3
Britain	170,389	170,389	6.7	6,147,000	2.8
British Empire	21,263	21,263	3.3	198,000	10.7
Romania	80,000	80,000	17.8	1,000,000	8.0
Serbia	70,423	150,000	14.6	750,000	9.4
Greece	1,000	1,000	2.1	353,000	0.3
Russia	2,500,000	3,500,000	51.8	15,798,000	15.8
USA	4,480	4,480	1.4	4,273,000	0.1
Total Allies	*3,846,376*	*5,069,450*	*28.0*	*45,001,000*	*8.5*
Bulgaria	10,623	10,623	4.2	400,000	2.7
Germany	617,922	1,200,000	9.0	13,200,000	4.7
Austria-Hungary	2,200,000	2,200,000	31.8	9,000,000	24.4
Turkey	250,000	250,000	17.2	2,998,000	8.3
Total Central Powers	*3,078,545*	*3,660,623*	*19.9*	*25,598,000*	*12.0*
Total	6,924,921	8,730,073	24.2	70,599,000	9.8

Sources: War Office, *Statistics of the Military Effort of the British Empire during the Great War, 1914–20* (London, 1922), pp. 237, 352–7; John Terraine, *The Smoke and the Fire* (London, 1980), p. 44; Winter, *Great War*, p. 75.
Note: Percentages calculated using minima. Greek prisoners figure includes missing and so probably overstates the number of prisoners. Romanian figures are very approximate.

By comparison, surrender rates for the British, French and German armies were low. Around 5 per cent of all Germans and French mobilised ended up as prisoners, and less than 3 per cent of Britons. The low point of British fortunes in the war — from around November 1917 to May 1918 — saw large increases in the numbers of Britons in captivity: in March 1918 alone, around 100,000 British prisoners were taken, more than in all the previous years of fighting combined.[19] In August 1918, however, it was German soldiers who began to give themselves up in large numbers. Between 30 July 1918 and 21 October, the total number of Germans in British hands rose by a factor of nearly four. This was the real sign that the war was ending.

Contemporaries clearly understood the benefits of taking prisoners alive. A substantial proportion of the British film *The Battle of the Somme* consists of footage of captured Germans. Official photographers were encouraged to snap 'wounded and nerve-shattered German prisoners' being given drink and cigarettes.[20] Sergeant York's capture of 132 Germans was one of the highlights of American war propaganda in 1918.[21] Nevertheless, men on both sides on the Western Front were deterred from surrendering by the growth of a culture of 'take no prisoners'.[22]

Despite its illegality, the practice of prisoner killing appears to have evolved more or less spontaneously among front-line troops. In part, it was the product of what would now be called a cycle of violence. Prisoners might be killed by men eager to avenge slain comrades. In his diary for 16 June 1915, A. Ashurt Moris recorded his own experience of killing a surrendering man:

At this point, I saw a Hun, fairly young, running down the trench, hands in air, looking terrified, yelling for mercy. I promptly shot him. It was a heavenly sight to see him fall forward. A Lincoln officer was furious with me, but the scores we owe wash out anything else.[23]

Private Frank Richards of the Royal Welch Fusiliers recalled seeing another man in his regiment walk off down the Menin Road with six prisoners only to return some minutes later having 'done the trick' with 'two bombs'. Richards attributed his action to the fact that 'the loss of his pal had upset him very much'.[24] Alternatively, prisoners might be killed as revenge for earlier atrocities committed by the other side. There were numerous stories of fake surrenders, in which gullible soldiers were gunned down after responding to a disingenuous white flag or cry of 'Kamerad'.

The vengeful mentality was certainly encouraged by war propaganda, which made much of the civilian victims of (for example) submarine warfare. In May 1915 the *avant-garde* sculptor Henri Gaudier-Brzeska wrote from the Western Front to Ezra Pound, describing a recent skirmish with the Germans: 'We also had a handful of prisoners – 10 –and as we had just learnt the loss of the "Lusitania" they were executed with the [rifle] butts after a 10 minutes dissertation [*sic*] among the N.C.[O.] and the men.'[25]

This kind of thing also seems to have been encouraged by some commissioned officers, who believed the 'take no prisoners' order enhanced the aggression and therefore fighting capability of their men. A brigadier was heard by a soldier in the Suffolks to say on the eve of the battle of the Somme: 'You may take prisoners, but I don't want to see them.' Another soldier, in the 17th Highland Light Infantry, recalled the order 'that no quarter was to be shown to the enemy and no prisoners taken'.[26] Private Arthur Hubbard of the London Scottish also received strict orders not to take prisoners, 'no matter if wounded'. His 'first job', he recalled, 'was when I had finished cutting some of the wire away, to empty my magazine on 3 Germans that came out of their deep dugouts, bleeding badly, and put them out of their misery, they cried for mercy, but I had my orders, they had no feelings whatever for us poor chaps.'[27] In his notes 'from recent fighting' by II Corps, dated 17 August 1916, General Sir Claud Jacob urged that no prisoners should be taken as they hindered mopping up.[28] Colonel Frank Maxwell, VC, ordered his men (the 18th Division battalion of the 12th Middlesex) not to take any prisoners in their attack on Thiepval on 26 September 1916, on the ground that 'all Germans should be exterminated'.[29]

An argument often used was that prisoners would be a burden on those who took them prisoner. Private Frank Bass of the 1st Battalion Cambridgeshire Regiment was told by an instructor at Étaples: 'Remember, boys ... every prisoner means a day's rations gone.'[30] Others offered arguments with almost genocidal overtones. In June 1916 a 'Major Campbell' was quoted as follows in the Young Citizen Volunteers' magazine, *The Incinerator*:

If a fat, juicy Hun cries 'Mercy' and speaks of his wife and nine children, give him the point — two inches is enough — and finish him. He is the kind of man to have another nine 'Hate' children if you let him off. So run no risks.[31]

Such incidents occurred in other theatres of war. At Gallipoli in May 1915 Captain Guy Warneford Nightingale of the Royal Munster Fusiliers and his men 'took 300 prisoners and could have taken 3,000 but we preferred shooting them'.[32] Sometimes this 'preference', as we shall see, was simply to avoid the inconvenience of escorting prisoners back to captivity. John Eugene Crombie of the Gordon Highlanders was ordered in April 1917 to bayonet surrendering Germans in a captured trench because it was 'expedient from a military point of view'.[33] That this kind of thing happened during the First World War was acknowledged by senior British officers. As Brigadier General F.P. Crozier observed: 'The British soldier is a kindly fellow and it is safe to say, despite the dope [propaganda], seldom oversteps the mark of propriety in France, *save occasionally to kill prisoners he cannot be bothered to escort back to his lines.*'[34]

Exactly how often such prisoner killings occurred is impossible to establish. Clearly, only a minority of men who surrendered were killed this way. Equally clearly, not all of those who received (or indeed issued) such orders approved of them or felt able to carry them out.[35] But the numbers involved mattered less than the perception that surrender was risky. Men magnified these episodes: they passed into trench mythology. The German trench newspaper *Kriegsflugblätter* devoted its front page on 29 January 1915 to a cartoon depicting just such an incident. 'G'meinhuber Michel' advances on a Tommy ('Hurra! – Wart', Bazi, di Kriag i!'); the Tommy puts his hands up (Hat eahm scho …'); the Tommy then shoots at the advancing Michel (Bluatsakra!!! Teifi! Teifi!'); Michel then gets the Tommy by the throat ('Freindl! Jetzt gehst Maschkera'); he proceeds to beat him to a pulp with his rifle butt ('Doass muass a englisches Boeffsteck wer'n'); and is duly rewarded with the Iron Cross.[36] The more such stories were repeated, the more reluctant men were to surrender. John Keegan is therefore surely wrong to dismiss prisoner-killing incidents as 'absolutely meaningless … in "win/lose terms"',[37] for *future* decisions about surrender plainly were affected by the belief that the other side were taking no prisoners.

Why did German soldiers, who had hitherto been so reluctant to give themselves up, suddenly begin to surrender in their tens of thousands in August 1918? The obvious interpretation — following Clausewitz — is that there was a collapse of morale. This was primarily due to the realisation among both officers and men that the war could not be won.

Ludendorff's spring offensives had worked tactically but failed strategically, and in the process had cost the Germans dear, whereas the Allied offensive of 7–8 August outside Amiens was, as Ludendorff had to admit, 'the greatest defeat the German Army has suffered since the beginning of the war'. Unrestricted submarine warfare had failed to bring Britain to her knees; occupation of Russian territory after Brest-Litovsk was wasting scarce manpower; Germany's allies were beginning to crumble; the Americans were massing in France, inexperienced but well-fed and numerous; perhaps most importantly, the British Expeditionary Force had finally learned to combine infantry, artillery, armour and air operations. Simply in terms of numbers of tanks and trucks, the Germans were by now at a hopeless disadvantage in the war of movement they themselves had initiated in the spring.[38] Victory was out of the question, and it was the rapid spread of this view through the German ranks that turned non-victory into defeat, rather than the 'draw' Ludendorff appears to have had in mind. In this light, the mass surrenders described above were only part of a general crisis of morale which also manifested itself, as Deist has convincingly argued, in unprecedented levels of sickness, indiscipline, shirking and desertion.[39]

III

The numbers of men who ended up being taken prisoner in the Second World War were huge — much larger than in the First. Altogether between 1914 and 1918, as we have seen, somewhere between 6.9 and 8.7 million men were held as prisoners of war — around a tenth of the total number of men mobilised, and rather fewer than the 9 or 10 million who were killed or died as a result of the war. In the Second World War around 96 million people served in the armed forces of all the belligerent states, of whom approximately 35 million — more than a third — spent at least some time in enemy hands.[40] In the case of the German army, virtually every soldier still on active service at the end of the war spent at least some time as some kind of camp inmate or other. However, as we shall, the overwhelming majority did not become prisoners until *after* the war was over — after the surrender had been signed and they had been ordered to lay down their arms. Indeed, up until that point the impressive point about the German army was the extreme reluctance of both officers and men to surrender.

In the first phase of the war, the most spectacular prisoner haul was in France. Here, even more than in 1918, the importance of morale in determining defeat was apparent. On paper, the Wehrmacht did not enjoy a decisive superiority over the French army; indeed, in many respects it was the defending force that enjoyed the advantage. Though inferior in the air, the French had twice the number of wheeled vehicles and 4,638 tanks to the Germans' 4,060. Moreover, French tanks had thicker armour and bigger guns.[41] Yet the weakness of French morale was obvious even during the 'Phoney War',[42] and when the German offensive was launched, many units put up only token resistance. On 15 May Rommel's men were able to take 450 prisoners in the course of two small skirmishes; later they captured 10,000 in the space of two days. Rommel himself was struck by the readiness of the French officers to give themselves up, and by their insouciant 'requests, including, among other things, permission to keep their batmen and to have their kit picked up from Philippeville, where it had been left'.[43] Another German officer saw 'several hundred French officers who had marched 35 kilometres without any guard from a prisoner of war dispatch point to a prisoner of war transit station ... with apparently none having made their escape.'[44] Karl von Stackelberg was baffled: '20,000 men ... were heading backwards as prisoners. ... It was inexplicable ... How was it possible, these French soldiers with their officers, so completely downcast, so completely demoralised, would allow themselves to go more or less voluntarily into imprisonment?'[45] British soldiers captured in 1940 could not help noticing that 'the French had been prepared for capture and so were laden down with kit, while we were all practically empty-handed.'[46]

In all around 1.8 million French troops were taken prisoner in 1940, of whom nearly a million were kept in Germany as forced labourers until 1945.[47] It is true that perhaps as many as half of those who surrendered did so in the period between 17 June, when Pétain announced that he was seeking an armistice, and the implementation of the armistice eight days later.[48] But it is still remarkable that more than a third of the French army had already been taken prisoner before 17 June. It is indicative of the poor state of French morale that colonial troops from French Africa felt that they had fought with more determination than their supposed masters; their units certainly took heavier casualties.[49]

What lay behind the French collapse? In part, as Marc Bloch argued shortly after the débâcle, it was abysmal leadership; [50] perhaps, as Ernest May has recently contended, the Germans were simply lucky in their decision to switch the direction of their main attack from Belgium to the Ardennes.[51] But at root this was a collapse of morale. In the words of one German officer: 'French spirit and morale had been ... broken ... before the battle even began. It was not so much the lack of machinery ... that had defeated the French, but that they did not know what they were fighting for. ... The Nazi revolution had already won the Battle of France before our first armoured divisions went to work.'[52] To use Wesbrook's term, there was a failure of legitimate demand on the French side: the cause of defending the Republic did not seem worth dying for. A related factor was that the French had learned defeatism from the Pyrrhic victory of 1918. This was the mood that had been foreshadowed in Louis-Ferdinand Céline's *Voyage au bout de la nuit*, with its ghastly evocation of the slaughter of the Great War's opening phase. The same mood inspired the Nobel laureate Roger Martin du Gard's letter to a friend in September 1936: 'Anything rather than war! Anything ... even Fascism in Spain ... Even Fascism in France: Nothing, no trial, no servitude can be compared to war: Anything, Hitler rather than war!'[53] Yet it is inconceivable that the French would have surrendered in such large numbers and in such an orderly fashion if they had not expected to be treated comparatively well by the Germans. The assumption clearly was that, with the war seemingly over, they would swiftly be returned to their native land.

On an even larger scale were the Soviet surrenders that followed the launch of Operation Barbarossa against the ill-prepared Red Army in June 1941. In a series of encircling manoeuvres, the Germans captured hundreds of thousands of Soviet troops who appeared to the invaders to be not only ill-equipped but demoralised. By 9 July the German forces west of Minsk had already captured 287,704 prisoners.[54] It was a similar story at Bialystok and Smolensk. By the autumn, the more than three million had been marched off into captivity. There were many reasons for the Soviet collapse, not least Stalin's pig-headed refusal to heed intelligence about the impending German invasion, which compounded the damage he had already done by purging the Red Army's officer corps.[55] Ill-prepared, ill-trained, ill-equipped and above all ill-led, hundreds of thousands of Russian soldiers found themselves outmanoeuvred and encircled. There was certainly little incentive to break out of the German 'cauldrons': the NKVD units sent by Stalin to punish shirkers and sabo-teurs were the devil the soldiers knew, while the German forces were initially seen by some naive souls (in the Ukraine especially) as liberators. In other words, Soviet prisoners in 1941, like the French in 1940, 'came quietly' partly because they did not expect to be killed by the Germans, merely incarcerated for the duration of a war which, to judge by its open-ing phase, seemed unlikely to last long. At this stage in the war, being Hitler's prisoner seemed to many Soviet conscripts preferable to being Stalin's cannon fodder.

No collapse of this magnitude disgraced the armies of Britain and the United States during the war: less than 3 per cent of British forces and less than 1 per cent of Americans ended up as prisoners, despite the fact that they were fighting on foreign soil rather than defending the *patrie*.[56] Unlike their French counterparts, British, Dominion and American sol-diers tended to surrender not because of a loss of confidence in the wider aims of the war, but because officers sought to avoid futile sacrifice of life when a position became indefensible. The typical capture narrative in Anglophone war memoirs has the enemy completely surrounding a unit and the officer ordering his men to lay down their arms rather than die 'pointlessly'.[57] This was what happened, for example, when nearly two thousand Canadians were captured at Dieppe.[58] It was the same story when the American forces surrendered in the face of overwhelming odds at Guam.[59] Characteristic was the view of the American Marine Chester Biggs, captured by the Japanese in 1941: 'It is all right to die for a cause if the cause is a good one, but to die just for the sake of saying "We fought to the last man and didn't surrender" is not a very good cause.'[60] By contrast, surrenders by individuals or small groups were frequently unpremedi-tated: the classic experience was of getting lost and inadvertently stum-bling into an enemy position, a situation in which the captors were more surprised than bloodthirsty.[61] Men who simply 'cracked' after too long in the field were more likely to flee than to surrender (hence the fact that such men usually ended up being court-martialled for desertion).[62]

Yet despite the consolation that 'discretion is the better part of val-our',[63] British, Dominion and American servicemen taken prisoner were often taken aback by their own feelings of guilt after having been captured, which was not something they had been prepared for.[64] In the words of the American POW Andrew Carson:

We had been trained to act instinctively, immediately to commands like 'Attention', 'At ease', 'About face', 'Man your battle stations' and 'Fire when ready', but the word 'Surrender' was foreign. It had not been programmed into our minds and therefore brought no response.

He and his comrades could only weep, swear and try to convince themselves that 'we had done our very best'.[65] Not all British soldiers went into the 'bag' passively, however — even when ordered to destroy their arms by their own commanders. 'Not fucking likely, you yellow bastard!' was the furious reaction of one member of the 51ˢᵗ (Highland) Division when ordered to surrender by an officer of the Kensington Regiment in June 1940.[66] This attitude found its echo among some Australian and New Zealand troops in similar situations. Rather than surrender on Crete, Donald Watt's unit of Australians opted to split up and try to escape; when cornered, his friend Frank was ready to try 'punching his way out, as though in some sort of Western movie'.[67] But these were the exceptions.

What of German surrenders? Beginning with the surrender of Paulus's 6ᵗʰ Army at Stalingrad on 30 January 1943, the war ended with a succession of large-scale surrenders: the collapse of Central Army Group in July 1944, when twenty-five divisions gave themselves up; the surrender of more than eighteen divisions at Jassy in August 1944.[68] On closer inspection, however, there were important differences between the endings of the two world wars. It is, unfortunately, far from easy to make a precise comparison between the events of 1918 and 1945 as the available statistics were computed on different time-scales. But this much can safely be said. The vast majority of German prisoners were captured only *after* the official surrender signed by General Jodl at 2.41 a.m. on 8 May 1945. According to Zabecki, for example, the Western Allies had captured just 630,000 Germans prior to the capitulation.[69] The Maschke commission put the total number of Germans held prisoner in the first quarter of 1945 at more than 2 million, roughly shared between the Eastern and Western theatres of the European war.[70] Overmans estimates that the number of POWs at the time of the German capitulation 'cannot have exceeded 3 million, of whom some 2 million would have been in the East'.[71] In other words, at least 8 million of the final total of 11 million German captives laid down their arms after the official surrender. Not untypical was the Kurland Army, which resisted to the bitter end despite having been surrounded by the Red Army as early as January 1945. Moreover, an incalculable but large proportion of the 3 million pre-capitulation prisoners clearly gave themselves up in the very last weeks of the war. By contrast, the biggest prisoner hauls of the First World War came (according to the British statistics) in the period 24 September – 21 October 1918, i.e. before the armistice was signed on 11 November. Although we should not exaggerate the completeness of the collapse in 1918 — there is indeed some evidence that German resistance was stiffening as the fighting neared the German border — it nevertheless seems fair to say that German forces were slower to surrender in the Second World War.

Germany's allies responded to military adversity in diametrically opposite ways. Italian soldiers, as is notorious, surrendered quite readily. By contrast, the Japanese resisted even more tenaciously than the Germans. In the Pacific War, the Western armies' ratio of captured to dead was around 4:1. The Japanese ratio was 1:40.[72] Only 1,700 Japanese prisoners were taken in Burma, compared with 150,000 who were killed; of the prisoners, only 400 were physically fit and in the first week of captivity all of them tried to commit suicide.[73] It was only when they were on the verge of starvation in the closing months of the war that large numbers of Japanese troops began to give themselves up.[74] And even as late as July 1945 17,000 Japanese lost their lives in a futile attempt to break out of Sittang.[75] Unlike other nationalities, the Japanese tended to be captured singly and only when incapacitated.[76] One Japanese soldier refused to lay down his arms until 1974.[77] The question is therefore straightforward: how can we explain the relative tenacity of the German and Japanese armies in the Second World War? Why did they keep fighting after any rational hope of victory had evaporated?

IV

One possible explanation might be sought in the realm of military discipline. Armies during and after the First World War had sought to deter men from surrendering or running away by increasing the perceived likelihood that they would be killed by their own side if they attempted to do so. During the First World War, British military justice was a good deal harsher in this regard than German. In the British army, 266 soldiers were executed for desertion, 18 for cowardice, 7 for quitting their posts and

2 for casting away their arms: 293 in all. By contrast, only 18 Germans were executed for comparable offences, despite the fact that the German army was twice as large.[78] Only on 23 June 1918 did Ludendorff issue the desperate order: 'Every man going to the enemy will be punished with death on return to Germany.'[79]

In Britain the death penalty for desertion was abolished in 1930;[80] and although British war leaders — notably Churchill and Montgomery — were fond of phrases like 'never surrender', it was never restored.[81] The Americans too were lenient: only one GI was executed for desertion during the entire Second World War.[82] But in Germany and Russia the penalties for desertion were significantly stiffened before and during the Second World War. It was Trotsky who pioneered the draconian rule that if Red Army soldiers advanced they might be shot, but if they fled, they would definitely be shot.[83] Under Stalin, the principle was extended to include the commanding officers or families of deserters.[84] Those Soviet prisoners of the Germans lucky enough to survive the war found themselves imprisoned once again under equally harsh conditions for 'Betrayal of the Motherland'.[85] The Wehrmacht executed between 15,000 and 20,000 of its own men, mainly in the later stages of the war for the so-called political crimes of desertion or *Wehrkraftzersetzung*; and effectively sentenced many thousands more to death by assigning them to 'punishment battalions', the standard sentence for soldiers who lost their weapons.[86] Such draconian discipline became increasingly important on the Eastern Front when very high casualty rates (up to 300 per cent of the original strength of some divisions) prevented the formation of primary group loyalties and desertion rates began to rise.[87] Phrases like 'most severe punishment' and 'ruthless use of all means' became routine euphemisms for summary executions. By the end of the war, German *Landsers* faced what might be called Trotsky's choice: 'Death by a bullet from the enemy or by the "thugs" of the SS.'[88]

Did the threat of the death penalty or some other sanction deter men from deserting or surrendering? There is some evidence that it did: as one German deserter who made it to the Russian lines explained in October 1942, the reason more of his comrades did not surrender was fear 'that if they deserted their families would be punished, that if they were seen trying to cross over they would be shot, and that if they were caught they would be executed'.[89] Another German deserter who gave himself up to the Americans in France later explained how he had weighed up his conflicting fears — of his own side's military discipline as against the enemy's superior firepower:

I remember very well the say that it was all made clear to me, the impossibility of Germany prevailing. It was July 26, 1944. There had been an air raid by 1,500 American 'Flying Fortresses' and I didn't see one Luftwaffe plane in the sky to challenge them. Of course, superior forces don't always win, but when the superiority is as enormous as that, there's nothing you can do. Close by us was the SS Tank Division Das Reich and contingents from the Hitler Youth. They were totally smashed up from the air. They didn't even have the chance to show how brave they were. When that sort of thing happens, you know it must be the end … it was hopeless, we couldn't possibly have won the war. Of course, you didn't dare say so to anyone, you didn't know if they would tell your superior officers, and then they'll have you for betraying your country by talking about defeat. It was possible that you would end up hanged.

Yet there is reason to doubt that the deterrent effect of the death penalty alone kept the majority of Germans fighting to the bitter end. Ahrenfeldt's figures reveal that the desertion rate for the British army was no higher during the Second World War than during the First: indeed the average was slightly lower in the Second World War (7 per thousand compared with 10 per thousand).[90] The calculus of desertion is clearly rather different from the calculus of surrender; still, the British evidence is suggestive.

Another possibility is that men refused to surrender not out of fear of punishment but out of fear of dishonour. As is well known, the Japanese military sought to stigmatise rather than prohibit surrender.[91] Although there was no formal prohibition of capture in either the Army's or the Navy's pre-war criminal codes and disciplinary regulations, by 1940 surrender had become taboo.[92] 'Never live to experience shame as a prisoner' was the stark message of the 1941 Field Service Code, and the Japanese army simply refused to acknowledge the existence of Japanese prisoners of war.[93] Many Japanese servicemen certainly seem to have absorbed this message. Even at the end of the war, there was extreme reluctance to make use of 'Surrender Passes' bearing the word 'surrender' in either Japanese (*kosan, kofuku*) or English: 'I Cease Resistance' was the preferred euphemism.[94] Some Japanese soldiers refused to lay down their arms until the Imperial Headquarters issued an order on 15 August 1945 that 'servicemen who come under the control of the enemy forces ... will not be regarded as POWs'.[95]

There was something of this aversion to surrender in Nazi Germany too. In *Mein Kampf*, Hitler had bitterly recalled the trauma of 1918, when 'political discussions' among new conscripts — 'the poison of the hinterland' — had undermined the morale of the army.[96] Twenty years later, when Goebbels concluded a speech at the Sportpalast with the words 'a November 1918 will never be repeated', Hitler 'looked up to him, a wild, eager expression in his eyes ... leaped to his feet and with a fanatical fire in his eyes ... brought his right hand, after a great sweep, pounding down on the table and yelled ... "Ja"'.[97] 'As long as I am alive,' he told General Franz Halder in August 1939, 'there will be no talk of capitulation.'[98] It was a refrain repeated until the suicidal end. His last official proclamation of 24 February 1945 envisaged a protracted war of resistance on German soil, which implied the complete destruction of the country and something close to collective suicide.[99]

Again, there is evidence that such ideas were internalised by serving soldiers. When the American psychologist Saul Padover interrogated Lieutenant Rudolf Kohlhoff after his capture in December 1944, he elicited a revealing response to his question about the possibility of a German defeat:

But I tell you Germany is not going to be defeated. I don't know how long it will take to achieve victory, but it will be achieved. I am convinced of it, or I would not have fought. I have never entertained thoughts of losing. I could not tell you how victory will come but it will. Our generals must have good reason to fight on. They believe in the *Endsieg*. Otherwise they would not sacrifice German blood. ... the Wehrmacht will never give up. It did not give up in the last war either. Only the civilians gave up and betrayed the army. I tell you, the Americans will never reach the Rhine. We will fight to the end. We will fight for every city, town and village. If necessary we will see the whole Reich destroyed and the population killed. As a gunner, I know that it is not a pleasant feeling to have to destroy German homes and kill German civilians, but for the defence of the German Fatherland I consider it necessary.[100]

Another prisoner, a young parachutist, told the same interrogator that he was 'deeply humiliated for having permitted himself to be captured' and felt he 'should have died "on the field of honour".'[101]

Such attitudes were obviously more prevalent among those troops who had been most thoroughly indoctrinated by the regime. As Ameri-

can troops neared Marienbad in the Sudetenland in April 1945, Günter Koschorrek — a disillusioned veteran of the Eastern Front — had
no doubt that 'in this endgame, some brain-damaged troop leaders ...
[would] follow Hitler's orders to the letter and fight to the last round of
ammunition'.[102] Yet even self-consciously unpolitical professionals were
influenced by Hitler's orders to fight to the death. When Martin Pöppel, an experienced paratrooper officer, found his unit surrounded by
the Gordon Highlanders in Rees in April 1945, he and his men found the
decision to surrender far from easy:

I discussed the situation with the last Unteroffizier. The Führer order was very
much in my mind: 'If a superior officer no longer appears in a position to lead,
he is to hand over command to the nearest rank below.' Personally, I was ready to
surrender – me, who had been a paratrooper from the very first day of the war.
Yet although the struggle was completely hopeless, men came to me in tears. 'As
paratroopers, how will we be able to look our wives in the face, if we surrender
voluntarily.' A phenomenon, incredible. ... Then, after long silence, they said
that if the 'Old Man' [Pöppel was 24] ... thought we should surrender, then they
would follow me.[103]

One American corporal noted that 'the Krauts always shot up all their
ammo and then surrendered' — unlike (by implication) American soldiers, who would surrender when in a hopeless situation. It was exceedingly hazardous to try to parley with Germans who still had bullets left to
fire, even if they were surrounded.[104]

   In the final analysis, however, it was not only the fear of disciplinary
action or of dishonour that deterred German and Japanese soldiers from
surrendering. More important for most soldiers was the perception that
prisoners would be killed by the enemy anyway, and so one might as well
fight on.

V

Though tolerated by a few senior officers, as we have seen, the 'take no
prisoners' culture of the Western Front was never legitimised by any government during the First World War. Even during the Russian Civil War,
the Bolsheviks — draconian in their treatment of their own deserters
— drew the line at sanctioning prisoner killing. Trotsky explicitly forbade
it in an order of 1919.[105]

   It was Nazi Germany which first adopted an official policy of prisoner-killing. The decision systematically to shoot Red Army prisoners

— foreshadowed by the brutal way the war in Poland had been fought
— was taken on the eve of Operation Barbarossa and subsequently
elaborated on during the campaign. The 'Guidelines for the Conduct of
Troops in Russia' issued on 19 May 1941 called for 'ruthless and vigorous measures against the Bolshevik inciters, guerrillas, saboteurs [and]
Jews'.[106] The 'Commissar Order' of 6 June 1941 required any captured
political commissars to be shot out of hand. The justification for this
was that 'hate-inspired, cruel, and inhumane treatment of prisoners can
be expected on the part of *all grades of political commissars. ...* To act
in accordance with international rules of war is wrong and endangers
both our own security and the rapid pacification of conquered territory ... Political commissars have initiated barbaric, Asiatic methods
of warfare. Consequently they will be dealt with *immediately* and with
maximum severity. As a matter of principle, they will be shot at once
...'[107] The Wehrmacht High Command reiterated this by decreeing that
the army was to 'get rid of all those elements among the prisoners of
war considered Bolshevik driving forces'; this meant handing them
over to the SS *Einsatzgruppen* for execution.[108] 'Politically intolerable
and suspicious elements, commissars and agitators' were to be treated
in the same way, according to an order issued by the Army Quartermaster General Wagner.[109] In September 1941 the High Command issued a further order that Soviet troops who had been overrun but then
reorganised themselves should be regarded as 'partisans' and hence shot
on the spot.[110] Such orders were passed on by front-line commanders in
less euphemistic terms. Troops were 'totally to eliminate any active or
passive resistance' among prisoners by making '*immediate* use of weapons'.[111] The commander of the 12th Infantry Division told subordinate
officers: 'Prisoners behind the front-line ... Shoot as a general principle! Every soldier shoots any Russian found behind the front-line who
has not been taken prisoner in battle.'[112] In the confusion that reigned
after the huge German advances into Soviet territory, this could be interpreted as a licence to kill. According to Omer Bartov, the Germans
may have summarily executed as many as 600,000 Soviet prisoners;
by the end of the first winter of the campaign some two million were
dead.[113]

As we have seen, German soldiers themselves were subject to draconian discipline; in return, however, they were licensed to treat the sup-

posedly 'subhuman' enemy without pity. The recollections of one *Landser*,
Guy Sajer, give a flavour of the attitudes that quickly took hold:

Sometimes one or two prisoners might emerge from their hideout with their
hands in the air, and each time the same tragedy repeated itself. Kraus killed
four of them on the lieutenant's orders; the Sudeten two; Group 17, nine.
Young Lindberg, who had been in a state of panic ever since the beginning of
the offensive, and who had been either weeping in terror or laughing in hope,
took Kraus's machine gun and shoved two Bolsheviks into a shell hole. The two
wretched victims ... kept imploring his mercy ... But Lindberg, in a paroxysm
of uncontrollable rage, kept firing until they were quiet. ...

We were mad with harassment and exhaustion. ... We were forbidden to take
prisoners. ... We knew that the Russians didn't take any ... [that] it was either
them or us, which is why my friend Hals and I threw grenades ... at some Russians who were trying to wave a white flag.

[Later] ... we began to grasp what had happened. ... We suddenly felt gripped
by something horrible, which made our skins crawl. ... For me, these memories
produced a loss of physical sensation, almost as if my personality had split ...
because I knew that such things don't happen to young men who have led normal
lives. ...

We really were shits to kill those Popovs ... [Hals said.]

He was clearly desperately troubled by the same things that troubled me. ...
'[That's] how it is, and all there is,' I answered. ... Something hideous had entered our spirits, to remain and haunt us forever.[114]

Quite apart from its illegality, some Germans saw the folly of prisoner-killing, and not just because of the value of prisoners as intelligence
sources.[115] Wolfgang Horn, who admitted to shooting 'cowardly' Russians
himself if they were too slow to raise their hands, nevertheless deplored
the decision of the lieutenant commanding his unit to shoot prisoners.
It was not only 'unchivalrous' but also 'stupid' because 'Russians hid-
ing in the forest might have seen the prisoners being shot and so they
might fight better the next time'.[116] Alfred Rosenberg, Minister for the
Occupied Eastern Territories, saw as 'an obvious consequence of [the]
politically and militarily unwise treatment [of prisoners] ... not only the
weakening of the will to desert but a truly deadly fear of falling into German captivity.'[117] The 18th Panzer Division came to the same conclusion:
'Red Army soldiers ... are more afraid of falling prisoner than of the
possibility of dying on the battlefield.'[118] So did the commander of the
Grossdeutschland Division, who appealed to his men to 'understand that

the ultimate result of the maltreatment or shooting of POWs after they had given themselves up in battle would be ... a stiffening of the enemy's resistance, because every Red Army soldier fears German captivity.'[119] Such views went largely unheeded by soldiers on the ground, however; and orders against 'senseless shootings' of POWs by commanders like General Lemelsen were simply ignored.[120] Nor did the suspension of the Commissar Order have much impact. Indeed, the practice of prisoner killing became routine: 'We take some prisoners, we shoot them, all in a day's work.'[121]

This kind of experience explains why some Germans found the prospect of surrender once their own position had become patently hopeless so unpalatable: fear of retaliation. Even while they were advancing, the Germans were plagued by fear 'of falling into the hands of the Russians, no doubt thirsty for revenge'.[122] When things started to go wrong, therefore, many Germans were willing to fight to the death rather than surrender. By no means exceptional was the intransigent officer who declared after the capitulation at Stalingrad: 'There'll be no surrender! The war goes on!' and then shot a Russian officer.[123] In July 1944, the lieutenant in charge of Eduard Stelbe's unit shot himself rather than fall into the hands of the Red Army.[124] Eight months later, Edmund Bonhoff's commanding officer — who for months had exhorted his men to 'stick it out' until the French and British belatedly joined the German war against the Soviets — simply 'ran away, just leaving us there [in Courland]'.[125] Gottlob Bidermann's description of the 132nd Infantry Division's surrender to the Russians provides further evidence of the extreme reluctance of some frontline officers to obey direct orders to capitulate, even as late as 8 May 1945. One officer shot himself through the head; another ran back screaming 'No surrender! I refuse to surrender!' to the next German line, where he tried to force the commander of a self-propelled gun to engage the enemy. He had to be knocked out by a rifle butt. 'Why did you continue to fight? Hitler is long dead,' asked the Red Army colonel who accepted Bidermann's surrender. His answer was: 'Because we are soldiers.'[126] But this was not a sufficient explanation. A part of the reason was that, having committed war crimes themselves, Wehrmacht troops expected no quarter from the Red Army if they surrendered. 'If we should lose tomorrow,' wrote Guy Sajer, 'those of us still alive ... will be judged without mercy ... accused of an infinity of murder ...

spared nothing.'[127] This dread of defeat was, of course, compounded by the involvement of the Wehrmacht in massacres of civilians, particularly Jews. One soldier who witnessed the slaughter of thousands of Jews at Paneriai in Lithuania could say only: 'May God grant us victory because if they get their revenge, we're in for a hard time.'[128]

In many cases retribution was indeed swift. German prisoners were routinely shot after interrogation if not before, a practice explicitly justified as retaliation for German treatment of Soviet prisoners. Zinaida Pytkina, a SMERSH interrogator, recalled how she executed a German officer with a shot in the back of the neck:

It was joy for me. The Germans didn't ask us to spare them and I was angry. . . . When we were retreating we lost so many 17-, 18-year olds. Do I have to be sorry for the German after that? This was my mood . . . As a member of the Communist Party, I saw in front of me a man who could have killed my relatives. . . . I would have cut off his head if I had been asked to. One person less, I thought. Ask him how many people he killed – he did not think about this?[129]

In turn, German troops on the other side were 'told that the Russians have been killing all prisoners'.[130] Ruthenians drafted into the Wehrmacht would have deserted in larger numbers had they not 'believe[d] the officers' stories that the Russians will torture and shoot them'.[131] Eduard Stelbe was genuinely surprised when the first words of the Russian officer to whom he surrendered were simply: 'Does anyone have a cigarette.' When some female soldiers pointed their pistols at him and his comrades as they trudged to captivity, he fully expected them to fire; in fact the pistols had been emptied. It was just, he recalled, 'a little show of sadism'.[132]

It was not only on the Eastern Front that such a cycle of violence manifested itself. In the Pacific theatre too, the ill treatment and murder of prisoners were commonplace. It is clear from many accounts that American and Australian forces often shot Japanese surrenderers during the Pacific War.[133] It happened at Guadalcanal, especially after twenty Marines fell victim to a fake Japanese surrender that turned out to be an ambush.[134] The Marines' battle cry on Tarawa was 'Kill the Jap bastards! Take no prisoners!'[135] In his diary of his experiences in New Guinea in 1944, the celebrated aviator Charles Lindbergh noted:

It was freely admitted that some of our soldiers tortured Japanese prisoners and were as cruel and barbaric at times as the Japs themselves. Our men think nothing of shooting a Japanese prisoner or soldier attempting to surrender. They treat the Japs with less respect than they would give to an animal, and these acts are condoned by almost everyone.

This behaviour was not merely sanctioned but actively encouraged by Allied officers in the Pacific theatre. An infantry colonel told Lindbergh proudly: 'Our boys just don't take prisoners.'[136] The testimony of Sergeant Henry Ewen confirms that Australian troops killed prisoners at Bougainville 'in cold blood'.[137] When Indian soldiers serving with the British in Burma killed a group of wounded Japanese prisoners, George MacDonald Fraser, then serving in the 14th Army, turned a blind eye.[138]

As in the First World War, the practice of killing prisoners was sometimes justified as retaliatory. At Okinawa in May 1945, the orderly of a popular company commander who had died of his wounds 'snatched up a submachine gun and unforgivably massacred a line of unarmed Japanese soldiers who had just surrendered'.[139] However, there is evidence that 'taking no prisoners' simply became standard practice. In the course of the battle for the island, 75,000 Japanese soldiers were killed; less than a tenth of that figure ended up as prisoners.[140] 'The [American] rule of thumb,' an American POW told his Japanese captors, 'was "if it moves, shoot it".'[141] Another GI maxim was 'Kill or be killed.' The war correspondent Edgar L. Jones later recalled: 'We shot prisoners in cold blood, wiped out hospitals, strafed lifeboats … finished off the enemy wounded.'[142] War psychologists regarded the killing of prisoners as so commonplace that they devised formulae for assuaging soldiers' subsequent feelings of guilt.[143] Roughly two-fifths of American army chaplains surveyed after the war said that they had regarded orders to kill prisoners as legitimate.[144] This kind of thing went on despite the obvious deterrent effect on other Japanese soldiers who might be contemplating surrender.[145] Indeed, it is far from easy to distinguish the self-induced aversion to surrender discussed above from the rational fear that the Americans would kill any prisoners. In June 1945 the US Office of War Information reported that 84 per cent of interrogated Japanese prisoners had expected to be killed by their captors.[146] This fear was clearly far from unwarranted. Two years before a secret intelligence reported that only the promise of ice cream and three days' leave would suffice to induce American troops not to kill surrendering Japanese.[147]

To the historian who has specialised in German history, this is one of the most troubling aspects of the Second World War: the fact that Allied troops often regarded the Japanese in the same way that Germans regarded Russians — as *Untermenschen*. The Australian General Blamey, for example, told his troops that their foes were 'a cross between the human being and the ape', 'vermin', 'something primitive' that had to be 'exterminated' to preserve 'civilisation'.[148] On 22 May 1944 *Life* magazine published a picture of a winsome blonde gazing at a human skull. A *memento mori* perhaps, in the tradition of the Metaphysical poets? On the contrary:

When he said goodby [sic] two years ago to Natalie Nickerson, 20, a war worker of Phoenix, Ariz., a big, handsome Navy lieutenant promised her a Jap. Last week Natalie received a human skull, autographed by her lieutenant and 13 friends, and inscribed: 'This is a good Jap – a dead one picked up on the New Guinea beach.' Natalie, surprised at the gift, named it Tojo.[149]

Boil[ing] the flesh off enemy skulls to make table ornaments for sweethearts' was a not uncommon practice.[150]

VI

Thus, when American met German in the battlefields of Western Europe after the invasion of Italy, both sides had experience of lawless racial war, even if the scale of the German experience was vastly greater. Not surprisingly, prisoner killing was carried over into the new European theatres. Perhaps the most notorious example was the murder of 77 American prisoners at Malmédy by the SS Battle Group Peiper on 17 December 1944.[151] That taught Allied troops to fear Waffen SS units more than regular Wehrmacht units.[152] Yet such atrocities were committed by both sides. On 14 July 1943, for example, troops of the American 45th Infantry Division killed seventy Italian and German POWs at Biscari in Sicily.[153] Sergeant William C. Bradley recalled how one of his comrades killed a group of German prisoners captured in France.[154] On 7 June 1944 an American officer at a SHAEF press conference declared that US airborne forces did not take prisoners but 'kill them as they hold up their hands coming out. They are apt in going along a road with prisoners and seeing one of their own men killed, to turn around and shoot a prisoner to make up for it. They are tough people.'[155] Stephen Ambrose's history of E Company, 506th Regiment, 101st Airborne Division, suggests this was not wholly without foundation.[156] As one Foreign Office official noted:

'American troops are not showing any great disposition to take prisoners unless the enemy come over in batches of twenty or more. When smaller groups than this appear with their hands up, the American soldiers ... are apt to interpret this as a menacing gesture ... and to take liquidating action accordingly. ... there is quite a proportion of 'tough guys', who have experienced the normal peace-time life of Chicago, and other great American cities, and who are applying the lessons they learned there.'[157]

As in the Pacific theatre, American troops often rationalised their conduct as retaliation. The tenacity of German troops — their reluctance to surrender, and their ability to inflict casualties until their supplies of ammunition were exhausted — was intensely frustrating to Americans, certain of victory, who saw their resistance as futile. However, prisoner killing continued to be overtly encouraged by some American officers. Patton's address to the 45th Infantry Division before the invasion of Sicily could not have been more explicit:

When we land against the enemy ... we will show him no mercy. ... If you company officers in leading your men against the enemy find him shooting at you and, when you get within two hundred yards of him, and he wishes to surrender, oh no! That bastard will die! You must kill him. Stick him between the third and fourth ribs. You will tell your men that. They must have the killer instinct. Tell them to stick it in. He can do no good then. Stick them in the liver.[158]

Major-General Raymond Hufft ordered his troops to 'take no prisoners' when he led them across the Rhine.[159] And, as in the Pacific, American troops were encouraged to regard their foes as sub-human. One American interrogator described an eighteen-year-old parachutist captured after the Ardennes offensive as a 'fanatical Hitler youth', a 'totally dehumanised Nazi' and a 'carefully formed killing machine':

I wondered why the M[ilitary] P[olice] had not fulfilled his wish [to die in battle], particularly after he had killed one of their comrades. They had merely knocked him out cold. Hard-eyed and rigid of face, he was arrogant with an inner, unbending arrogance. He aroused in me an urge which I hope never to experience again, an urge to kill. I could have killed him in cold blood, without any doubt or second thought, as I would a cockroach. It was a terrible feeling to have, because it was without passion. I could not think of him as a human being.[160]

German soldiers also came to fear falling into the hands of Australians ('because of the way the Aussies treated their prisoners'), New Zealanders ('We were told they would cut the throat of every POW') and French North African troops, whose 'reputation for fairness was bad'.[161]

Such behaviour might have been expected to encourage retaliation. When Corporal Donovan C. Evers found himself trapped by a German tank in a basement near Hamburg in March 1945, he

started up the steps to surrender. I had a lot of thoughts walking up those steps about all the atrocities that we had committed on the German soldiers. We didn't know what to expect from the Germans. When I walked out the door of the house with my hands up, a young German soldier about sixteen years old stuck an automatic pistol in my stomach and said, 'For you the war is over.' I thought that was it, that he was going to shoot me.[162]

Yet the scale of prisoner killing — the extent to which soldiers fought to the death — was far less in Western Europe than in Eastern Europe. Throughout the war, the Germans tended to treat their Anglophone foes relatively well when they surrendered; certainly far better than their Soviet counterparts. One New Zealander taken prisoner in Italy was plied with schnapps, pork and potatoes by his Anglophile captor.[163] John Verney, captured in Sardinia by the Italians after a successful commando mission, feared that he would be shot if handed over to an incandescent German officer; but his anxiety was probably overdone.[164] Massacres of POWs were the exception, not the rule in the West. Likewise, only a minority of American soldiers regarded prisoner-killing as legitimate. In March 1945 Major John Cochran very nearly killed a sixteen-year old German boy — a Hitler Youth officer candidate — who had surrendered only after killing one of his men:

I was very emotional over the loss of a good soldier and I grabbed the kid and took off my cartridge belt. I asked him if there were any more like him in the town. He gave me a stare and said, 'I'd rather die than tell you anything.' I told him to pray, because he was going to die. I hit him across the face with my thick, heavy belt. I was about to strike him again, when I was grabbed behind by Chaplain Kerns. He said, 'Don't!' Then he took the crying child away. The chaplain had intervened not only to save a life but to prevent me from committing a murder. Had it not been for the chaplain, I would have.[165]

This was the kind of restraint absent on the Eastern Front, where Christianity was overridden by what Michael Burleigh has called the totalitarian 'religions' of National Socialism and Stalinism.[166]

VII

The crucial determinant of an army's willingness to fight on or surrender was, as we have seen, soldiers' expectations of how they would be treated

if they did lay down their arms. In the case of prisoner-killing in the heat
of battle, information about enemy conduct in this regard was relatively
easy to obtain: eye-witness accounts of prisoner-killings tended to circu-
late rapidly and widely among frontline troops, often becoming exaggerated in the telling. By contrast, news of the way prisoners were treated
away from the battlefield was slower to spread, depending as it did on
testimony from escaped POWs or the letters from POWs to their families relayed by the International Committee of the Red Cross. It should
be borne in mind that both of the latter channels were effectively closed
between Germany and the Soviet Union. It was exceedingly difficult for
POWs to escape from camps on either side because of the geographical
distances between enemy camps and safe territory, the harsh discipline
of camps and the refusal of the Germans to acknowledge Stalin's belated
signing of the Geneva Conventions.

The notorious Japanese maltreatment of prisoners during the Second
World War (which stood in marked contrast to their conduct towards
captured Russians in 1904–5) was partly a consequence of the stigmatisa-
tion of surrender *per se* mentioned above. Because the Japanese despised
capture for themselves, they despised those who surrendered to them
in equal measure.[167] Physical abuse of prisoners — including slaps in the
face and beatings — was a daily occurrence in some camps.[168] Executions
without due process were frequent. Official policy encouraged such brutality by applying the Geneva Convention only '*mutatis mutandis*', which
the Japanese chose to translate as 'with any necessary amendments'. In
practice, POWs were used as slave labour.[169] And because the Japanese
regarded prisoners as having been spared and expected submission in
return, they treated them with extreme harshness. Some prisoners set to
work on notorious railways like the Burma–Thailand line were made to
wear armbands bearing the inscription: 'One who has been captured in
battle and is to be beheaded or castrated at the will of the Emperor.'[170] Attempting to escape — which the Western powers regarded as a prisoner's
duty — was treated by the Japanese as a capital office, though the majority of Allied prisoners who died were in fact victims of malnutrition and
disease exacerbated by physical overwork.[171] In addition, as a wartime
British report noted with good reason, there was 'an official policy of
humiliating white prisoners of war in order to diminish their prestige in
native eyes'.[172] (That said, the Japanese used even more extreme violence

towards the indigenous populations of the territory they occupied, undermining their specious claims to be the liberators of Asia.[173])

There is no question that British, Australian and American attitudes towards the Japanese hardened as reports filtered out about the way the Japanese were treating POWs. Even the relatively rare occasions when the Germans shot British POWs — notably the fifty men who had attempted to escape from Stalag Luft III in March 1944 — caused the mood of British servicemen to harden in advance of D-Day. In the same way, Russian wives wrote to their husbands at Stalingrad: 'Don't let them capture you, because prison camp is worse than death.'[174] If prison camps were merely death camps then there was every reason to fight to the death, and little reason to show mercy to German prisoners. The Germans too soon formed a clear enough idea of what their fate would be if they survived surrender and became prisoners of war: Siberia became the shorthand for incarceration in conditions of barely imaginable harshness. Günter Koschorrek knew full well that the Soviets did not 'treat their prisoners in accordance with the terms of the Geneva convention … We have fought against the Soviets — we can imagine what awaits us in Siberia'.[175]

VIII

Precisely for this reason, the key to ending the war lay in psychological warfare: in persuading German and Japanese soldiers that, contrary to their own expectation, it was safe to surrender. Accordingly, the many leaflets fired by Allied artillery onto German positions — as well as radio broadcasts and loudspeaker addresses — emphasised not only the hopelessness of Germany's military position but also, crucially, the lack of risk involved in surrendering.[176] Key themes of 'Sykewar' were the good treatment of POWs — in particular, the fact that German POWs were given the same rations as American GIs, including cigarettes — and Allied observance of the Geneva Convention.[177] Typical was the leaflet which read simply:

EINE MINUTE, die Dir das Leben retten kann
ZWEI WORTE, die 850,000 Leben retteten
DREI ARTEN, nach Hause zu kommen
SECHS ARTEN, das Leben zu verlieren.[178]

The 'two words which had saved 850,000 lives' were of course 'I surrender' — or rather 'Ei Ssörrender', spelt out phonetically.

Though it is not easy to assess its effectiveness — POW questionnaires revealed persistent trust in Hitler and belief in the possibility of victory until as late as January 1945 — W. H. Hale was probably close to the mark when he concluded that 'Sykewar ... implanted in many enemy minds facts and arguments that speeded individual disaffection or surrender.'[179] According to Janowitz and Shils, once primary group solidarity began to break down in the Wehrmacht in the last months of the war, Allied propaganda began to be effective; indeed, it cannot be ruled out that the line of causation went the other way.[180] Perhaps the best evidence of the effectiveness of such psychological warfare was the evident preference of German troops to surrender to American units. 'God preserve us!' one German soldier wrote in his diary on 29 April 1944. 'If we have to go to prison, then let's hope it's with the Americans.'[181] That was a widespread sentiment. Until the third quarter of 1944, more than half of all German prisoners were held in the East. But thereafter, the share captured by the Americans rose rapidly. It is clear that many German units sought to surrender to the Americans in preference to other Allied forces, and particularly the Red Army. With the benefit of hindsight, they would have done better to look for British captors, since the British treated German prisoners better than the Americans and were also less willing to hand them over to the Soviets.[182] But successful psychological warfare led the Germans to expect the kindest treatment from US forces.

Similar efforts were made to encourage Japanese soldiers to surrender. 'Surrender passes' and translations of the Geneva Convention were dropped on Japanese positions, and concerted efforts were made to stamp out the practice of taking no prisoners. On 14 May 1944 General Macarthur sent a telegram to the commander of the Alamo Force demanding an 'investigation ... of numerous reports reaching this headquarters that Japanese carrying surrender passes and attempting to surrender in Hollandia area have been killed by our troops.'[183] The Psychological Warfare Branch representative at Tenth Corps, Captain William R. Beard, complained that his efforts were being negated 'by the frontline troops shooting [Japanese] when they made an attempt to surrender'.[184] But gradually the message got through, especially to more experienced troops. 'Don't shoot the bastard!' shouted one veteran when a Japanese emerged from a foxhole waving a surrender leaflet.[185] By the time the Americans took Luzon in the Philippines, '70 per cent of all prisoners surrendering made use of surrender passes or followed exactly the instructions contained in them'.

IX

The importance of encouraging the other side to surrender was a lesson not everyone learned from the First World War. On the contrary, a number of the combatant countries in the Second World War elected to elevate the practice of killing and mistreating prisoners to the status of official policy. The effect was to create 'cycles of violence', particularly in the East European and Pacific theatres of war, which tended to prolong hostilities. Of course, there were many reasons why the death toll of the Second World War was so much higher than that of the First, not the least of which was simply the superior destructive power of weaponry. But another important reason was that, particularly on the Eastern Front but also in the Pacific theatre, men on both sides of the conflict were reluctant to surrender. No doubt their reluctance had something to do with stern military discipline and codes of martial honour. But quite apart from these, there was the very good reason that prisoners were routinely killed or subsequently treated so badly that their chances of survival could be as bad as 1 in 2.

Only quite late in the war was it remembered — and only on the Allied side — that prisoner-killing was in fact counterproductive; and that the best way of bringing the war to a swift end was to make surrender seem a more attractive option for enemy soldiers than fighting on. It was a lesson of the First World War that Adolf Hitler was not alone in failing to learn. It is a lesson that bears repeating.

SURROGATES OF THE STATE

COLLABORATION AND ATROCITY IN KENYA'S MAU MAU WAR

David Anderson

Kenya's Mau Mau rebellion was by far the most violent, and the most savagely fought of Britain's many wars of decolonisation after 1945.[1] From its beginning in October 1952, with the declaration of a State of Emergency, through to its conclusion in January 1960, official estimates reckon that British security forces killed over 11,500 rebels in combat, and hanged another 1,090 after prosecution on charges relating to the rebellion. At the peak of the conflict, in 1955, not less than 78,000 Africans were held in British prisons and detention camps, the vast majority being incarcerated only on suspicion of support for the rebels and without charges having been brought against them. However, these official figures tell only part of the story. Unofficial estimates, based upon the traces to be found in the archives, inflate the number of rebel deaths in combat to some 20,000, and careful scrutiny of the prison records reveals that there may have been a further 25,000 African detainees.[2] The war's impact should also be measured in relation to the size of the community most directly affected in its prosecution — the one million Kikuyu-speakers inhabiting the fertile, hilly districts of the Central Province and Mount Kenya. At least one in ten of the entire Kikuyu population, and as many as one in four adult males, were killed or imprisoned as a consequence of this war. It was Kikuyu who raised this rebellion, and despite efforts to broaden it to incorporate other African communities they never succeed in bringing about the nationalist insurrection that some had hoped to provoke. The British counter-insurgency was therefore not a war waged against the

159

African community writ large, but a war focused almost exclusively upon one ethnic group, the Kikuyu.

The British public of the 1950s caught only glimpses of this war in newspaper reports and cinema newsreels.[3] Mau Mau was portrayed not as the product of frustrated, legitimate nationalist aspiration against colonial oppression, but as an atavistic, barbaric, anti-European and anti-Christian sect, which used anarchic terror and intimidation to halt the modernisation of Kenyan society. The brutality of Mau Mau attacks was presented as evidence of these assumptions.[4] To the British mind, Mau Mau's violence seemed especially frightening. At a time when the technologies of war had rendered killing a more mechanical act, the machetes, swords and axes that were the principal weapons in Kenya marked this conflict as one of shockingly intimate violence, while the hunt for and chasing of a victim gave the individual acts of killing a macabre, adrenalin-fuelled fury. Face-to-face killing completely dominated this war.[5]

The British press, in particular, concentrated upon Mau Mau attacks on Europeans, reporting the hacking and mutilations of the bodies of apparently defenceless civilian victims. Because of the pervasiveness of this image, Mau Mau continues to be remembered — quite wrongly — as a war against white settlers. The threat to Kenya's white settlers was always present, but in fact only 32 European civilians were murdered by the rebels — a figure dwarfed by the 2,800 civilian Africans, the vast majority being Kikuyu, officially recorded as having been killed or wounded for their *opposition* to the rebellion.[6] These African civilians who took a stand against the rebels were not accidental casualties of the fighting; rather, their prominence in the conflict was the product of a deliberate British strategy to create a civilian militia of African surrogates who would defeat the rebellion for them. This essay considers the consequences of that surrogacy strategy.

Surrogacy allowed the British to fight crucial parts of the war by proxy, permitting their Kikuyu allies to behave in ways that would not be allowed to conventional British forces. This was a war without rules that enveloped the entire Kikuyu civilian population. In its most common manifestations, surrogacy led to the terrorisation of local communities, to the torture of suspects, and to criminal extortion and physical menacing of the general public. British administrators, military commanders, and police officers repeatedly denied responsibility for the actions of their

African surrogates, claiming not to have sanctioned such behaviour. In a pattern familiar to other struggles that have descended into a form of civil war of this kind, the denial was often cloaked in expressions of regret that African forces should seek to settle their differences by such means, tinged with discreet recognition that the intensity of their feelings was understandable in the context of the war. This amounted to a variant on the common apologists' notion that 'war is hell, so bad things happen'.[7] But the policy of surrogacy was itself the primary cause of those 'bad things'. To put it bluntly, the British administration chose to fight Mau Mau's terror with state counter-terror. In its most extreme manifestations, the surrogacy strategy led to massacres as severe as any witnessed in modern warfare since the end of the Second World War. The massacres offer the most spectacular evidence of state complicity, though the daily ordinariness of the surrogacy strategy, in its control of the local economy and especially through denial of food to the rebels, more profoundly reveals the character of the coercive police state that oppressed the Kikuyu rural districts of Kenya over the course of the war. We will explore these consequences of surrogacy through two specific cases: one a gruesome massacre, the other an example of the systemic torture and extortion of civilians. But first we need to consider the formation and remit of the surrogates themselves — the Kikuyu Home Guard.

The Kikuyu Home Guard

A complex set of affiliations determined the architecture of this conflict. The core support for the Mau Mau movement was to be found among Kikuyu who had been evicted from European-owned farmland, among those excluded from property-owning by changes to land tenure in the rural districts of Central Kenya, and among the growing band of urban poor gathered in the slums of the eastern portion of Nairobi. This was an anti-colonialism driven by grievance, but the movement failed to achieve a nationalist momentum. Instead, Mau Mau remained bound to cultural, economic and political debates centred on the Kikuyu peoples. Mau Mau activists were mostly younger Kikuyu males, men in their late-teens and twenties dominating the movement. Other sectors of Kikuyu society, including senior elders who were secure property holders, had strong sympathies with the ideals of the movement, but the majority of Kikuyu objected to the coercive and violent methods adopted by Mau Mau to secure its support-base. A covert campaign of political oath-taking was used to obtain funds and to bond communities to the movement, and it was this that raised the first signs of opposition and anti-rebel sentiment in the Kikuyu countryside. Like many other peasant rebel movements, Mau Mau did not unite the rural communities, but divided them.

Once the Emergency was declared, from October 1952, British counter-insurgency endeavoured to exploit and cultivate this internal opposition. Kikuyu who stood against the rebels were lionised as 'Loyalists', in an echo of earlier imperial struggles in North America and Ireland where communities had been divided in rebellion.[8] To nurture Loyalist Kikuyu communities and guard them against Mau Mau attack, a militia was created and armed by the state.[9] Styled the Kikuyu Home Guard, this militia grew to a force of 25,600 by March 1954, more than matching the rebel armies that had taken to the forests and hills.[10] The Home Guards were not trained soldiers, but civilians whose participation in the state's militia was a matter of circumstance. The vast majority were reluctant recruits, men pressured to take sides when they would rather have been left alone. A substantial proportion of Home Guard recruits held rebel sympathies, and it was acknowledged that 50 per cent or more of them had taken Mau Mau oaths — whether willingly, or under duress. Kikuyu, in the words of Sorrenson, 'had to accept the facts of power'[11] and bow before coercion from either side. Infiltration and defection were therefore constant troubles for the British in this messy guerrilla war, but the essential strategy of pushing the Kikuyu militia into the forefront of the counter-insurgency campaign guided the state's strategy throughout the peak of the fighting, from January 1953 to March 1955. If this struggle came to have the appearance of a civil war, then it was because British strategy purposefully made it so.

This was to be seen in several respects. Home Guard units were compulsorily recruited in each of the Kikuyu-speaking districts, with chiefs and headmen who showed reluctance in creating such a force being summarily dismissed from service. Tactical decisions were taken on the positioning of Home Guard posts in areas where they were most likely to 'lure' the rebel forces into an attack — essentially using them as bait. This placed the Home Guard at the very heart of the fighting, yet left them highly vulnerable. Home Guards were especially important to the British in areas where the military and colonial police found it most difficult to operate — the villages and rural farms of the Kikuyu homelands, where passive support for the rebellion was at its strongest, and where reliable intelligence was most difficult to glean. These surrogates were therefore a very real danger to the rebel movement, and within the first six months of the war it was already clear that the bulk of the fighting would involve the Home Guard. As the threat of rebel attacks became more apparent, especially in the wake of the Lari massacre at the end of March 1953, more fortified posts were built — there would eventually be 550 — and the Home Guard were equipped with a larger number of weapons and given extended operational powers and greater freedom of action. Although each unit was ostensibly under the supervision of a junior European administrative officer, training was rudimentary and discipline poor. The general, day to day running of the force was left entirely in the hands of African chiefs and headmen. This would normally include the identification of suspects, detentions, interrogations, and even the prosecution of alleged offenders through courts presided over by the same chiefs who ran the Home Guard units. Lax state supervision characterised all of these aspects of Home Guard activity. Lastly, and most significantly, the force was never incorporated within the military command structure of the campaign, remaining as a civilian unit controlled through the political administration.[12] As we shall see, this allowed the state to use the Home Guard to prosecute war against the wider civilian population, punishing the rebels and their supposed supporters through extra-judicial harassment, theft of property, and food denial.[13]

Surrogacy and Atrocity — Mununga Ridge

Though it is not easy to precisely define what an atrocity is, the gratuitous slaughter of unarmed civilians is accepted as a war crime, regardless of contingent circumstances or the contemporary views of the combatants. There were several civilian massacres carried out by the security forces during the Mau Mau war, three infamous examples coming in the hours and days immediately following the Mau Mau attack upon Loyalists at Lari in March 1953. Retaliation and vengeance motivated these events, and although British army commanders and police officers were implicated in these and many other instances, it was most commonly the

Kikuyu Home Guard who did the killing. Civilian massacres such as those that took place after Lari, and the one at Mununga Ridge we will describe here, were not covert actions. The Kikuyu Home Guards involved in the attacks made little effort to cover their tracks, and although the British authorities played a role in suppressing information about these events, or spinning the reporting to make them appear as 'legitimate' military engagements, the events themselves were only very rarely shrouded in secrecy.[14] Indeed, the brazen and open character of such atrocities in Kenya strongly suggests that the perpetrators did not feel themselves to be in anyway accountable for their actions; Kikuyu surrogates took the war to the enemy in ways that conventional forces could not, and that was precisely what the British intended. The story of the massacre at Mununga Ridge illustrates this point very clearly.

Mununga Ridge lay close to the fringe of the Aberdares Forest, in Murang'a District. Villages and settlements here were important to the food supply of the Mau Mau rebels based in the nearby forests, and in the hottest period of the war, from March 1953 to March 1954, there were repeated actions fought in this location. Staunch loyalist resistance had been organised here under the local chief, Njiri Karanja. At his fortified Home Guard post, located nearby at Kinyona, the chief defiantly flew the Union Jack from a tall flagpole. The area was a stronghold of the African Inland Church, many of whose Christian members had rallied to reject the Mau Mau oath and spurn the rebel cause. But Njiri had a fierce reputation in dealing with the rebels and their supporters, of whom there were many in his location, especially on Mununga Ridge, one of the chief's most troublesome areas. Mau Mau found Njiri's Kinyona base so tough a nut to crack that they named it 'Berlin', and around 'Berlin' the war was fought with bitterness and determination on all sides.

Njiri Karanja was a principal target for the rebels, and so was constantly accompanied by a bodyguard of African soldiers. Mau Mau had successfully assassinated other chiefs and headmen, so Njiri and his family knew that their lives were in very real danger. As rebel activity in Murang'a intensified from April 1953, there was a spate of attacks on Home Guard posts, roadside ambushes of government staff, and a series of night-time raids on the homes of loyalists. One of the victims, at the end of June 1953, was Chief Njiri's eldest son, Thigiru, who worked as a headman under his father and was the leading organiser of the local Home Guard.

Thigiru was caught by a rebel band laying in wait for him on Mununga Ridge. There, in front of agricultural labourers whom Thigiru had gone to supervise, the headman was killed, and his body savagely mutilated.[15]

Chief Njiri's grief-ridden rage at the murder and mutilation of his son was the catalyst for the massacre that followed. Njiri's Home Guard units were deployed on Mununga Ridge that same morning. They rounded up 'known' rebel sympathisers for interrogation about Thigiru's death. Despite beatings and other intimidation, the population of Mununga Ridge were too afraid to speak. Such conspiracies of silence were a common feature of the Kenyan war, as was the assumption on the part of the Home Guard that some members of the local community must have been in league with the rebels. Frustrated by this passive resistance when they knew that many locals must have witnessed the killing, Njiri and his Home Guards returned to Mununga the next day, first set fire to the huts and grain stores along the ridge, and then seized the livestock. All through the morning, the smoke could be seen rising from the burning buildings. The killings also began that morning, and went on over the next two days. Some were shot with the rifles that had been issued to the Home Guard only in April, while other victims were hacked with pangas — heavy-bladed machetes favoured by Kikuyu for agricultural work. Those who could fled from the ridge to seek refuge with friends in neighbouring locations, or to take their chances in the forest. By the end of the second day, some 400 civilians had been slaughtered by Njiri's Home Guards.

How do we know of this atrocity? The official histories of the role of the Home Guard in the war have little to say about the incident, other than to record the killing of Thigiru,[16] and there are no detailed reports that have yet come to light in the archival record. Local memories of the event remain strong, however, and Caroline Elkins has recorded the testimony of survivors of the massacre.[17] These personal, eyewitness accounts are vivid and compelling on the brutality of what occurred, unequivocally placing the blame upon Chief Njiri Karanja: but we need to look to other, written accounts to understand the deeper history of this massacre. Two of these are of particular importance, both authored by Europeans who witnessed the aftermath of the massacre, the first being published only three years after the event, the second coming into print 50 years later.

Virginia Blakeslee was a missionary worker with the African Inland Mission, an American Christian organisation from which the members of the African Inland Church had split in Murang'a only a few years before the Mau Mau war began.[18] During the first year of the war, Blakeslee worked at a mission hospital a few miles to the east of Chief Njiri's fortified post at Kinyona. She knew Njiri well, in effect being under his protection, and in a chapter in her memoirs entitled 'Terror on the Ridges' her loathing of the Mau Mau rebels is apparent. The candour with which Blakeslee describes the massacre of Mununga Ridge in the chapter that follows is therefore all the more remarkable. 'Over on Mununga Ridge billows of smoke rolled heaven-ward early one morning', wrote Blakeslee:

Awestricken men came from Kinyona to the hospital, speaking in low tones and holding their hands over their mouths — a Kikuyu gesture expressing great consternation and deep emotion. "The head of Thigiru, Njiri's favourite son on whom he depended to execute his orders, has been brought to the chief's village," they said faintly. "Njiri is very angry. He sent all the Home Guards and the King's African Riflemen [his personal bodyguard] stationed at his village to Mununga to kill every man on the ridge. The men of Icamuguthi and Gathukiini, hundreds of them, are lying all about the villages and in the bushes dead. Their villages have been burned. Their cattle and sheep have been taken. Their gardens have been destroyed. The women and children have fled to the caves and thickets to hide. ... Njiri says all the people on Mununga ridge are Mau Mau and helped to kill his son."[19]

Blakeslee spoke with many survivors of the massacre, and hunted for some of her church members who had been among those affected by the violence. She reports that many of those who survived the massacre were subsequently rounded up and taken to a British detention camp.

Leonard Gill's memoir of his service with the Kenya Regiment gives us a second account of the Mununga Ridge atrocity. Gill's company was stationed in central Murang'a, where the massacre was reported to them two days after the event. On making his way to the area with other British officers, Gill describes the scene they encountered:

Before going to see Njiri, we drove across the Erati Valley and up onto the [Mununga] ridge. We had to drive around bodies left everywhere. Not only did we see human corpses, we saw dead donkeys, cows, goats, sheep, dogs and chickens. Nothing moved. The stench of death permeated everything.[20]

Gill also provides a full account of how the massacre occurred, explaining that when Njiri went up on to the ridge 'with a well armed patrol' after the killing of Thigiru, he discovered that 'outside every hut were sacks of food, with head-straps tied around them ready to be carried up to the forest for the terrorists', and that the tracks along the ridge toward the forest showed that they were in 'constant use by terrorists'. It was this evidence of the 'aiding and abetting the enemy' through provision of food that provoked Njiri into the premeditated and callous atrocity.[21] 'Over the next two days,' continued Gill,

Njiri took a large squad of armed Kikuyu Guard, first down the Erati [Mununga] Ridge and then down the river valley. Every living creature was shot and killed — about 225 men, women and children on the ridge and about 175 in the valley. This he did entirely on his own authority.[22]

Though nationalist views of the Mununga Ridge massacre, expressed in oral reminiscences, demonise Chief Njiri Karanja as 'a beast' and present the event purely as an act of state atrocity, it should be noted that the massacre in fact revolved around the control of food supplies to the rebel forces. A classic bone of contention in all such wars, the denial of food to the enemy was one of the principal purposes of the Home Guard, and it was also the issue that most commonly brought them into conflict with other Kikuyu civilians. Caught in the *Realpolitik* of this, Gill makes it clear that Njiri's loyalist son Thigiru had sought to 'face both ways' on Mununga Ridge, turning a blind eye to and perhaps even facilitating the supply of food to the rebels in the nearby forests.[23] Such arrangements were not uncommon, being the way by which local communities negotiated a truce between the warring factions. Tellingly, it was not the local Mau Mau commanders benefiting from this food supply that killed Thigiru, but another band of rebels led by General Kago. His rebel force, styled by some as *komerera* — or 'renegades' — raided and pillaged across Murang'a throughout the bloody summer of 1953, their activities cutting across the local ties between civilian communities and other forest gangs, and bringing the war into the very heart of the Kikuyu homesteads.[24] Thigiru was ultimately betrayed by his inability to negotiate this decentralised character of the rebel command, though his father, Chief Njiri, appears to have been unaware that his son was conspiring with the rebels over food supplies.

In these dilemmas we capture both the power of the surrogacy strategy to compel local communities to 'take sides', and its capacity for indiscriminate destruction. In such acts as the Mununga Ridge massacre, the state displayed its willingness, through its surrogates, to deploy terror and violence within a culture of impunity. Though British officials and army officers knew what Njiri had done on Mununga Ridge, no action was taken against him. In other aspects of the war against Mau Mau, this complicity would become institutionalised as part of the fabric of daily administration, as we shall now see in the case of Ruthagathi.

Surrogacy as Institutionalised State Terror — Ruthagathi

The British decision to create the Home Guard as surrogates created a security dilemma for all Kikuyu, by forcing everyone to choose a side.[25] The dilemma was driven by uncertainty and fear, not by hatred or prejudice toward a known enemy. Those joining the Home Guard were aware that to do so threatened the years of social capital they had built up in their communities. They made what choices they could, and then hoped to negotiate the outcome. However, the decision of the British to place the administration of the Kikuyu rural areas fully in the hands of the police and the Home Guard from the summer of 1953 — a move designed to relieve the army of the need to operate in such a difficult political and social environment — cleared the way for the emergence of a predatory, criminal economy run by and for the benefit of the state's Kikuyu allies. This initiated new ways of punishing those on the other side, and brought about other kinds of atrocity.[26]

In March 1954, Colonel Arthur Young arrived in Kenya to take up duty as Commissioner of Police. Previously Commissioner of the City of London Police, and with experience of the emergency in Malaya, Young was a highly respected and experienced officer and an outspoken advocate of consensual and community based policing. Intelligent and highly principled, he had clear views on the standards of professionalism required in a modern police force. And, as his Malayan experience showed, he did not believe that those standards should be any different in a colonial context than at home. By 1954 it was no secret that the Kenya police needed 'sorting out', and Arthur Young seemed eminently well suited to the task.[27]

But on reaching Kenya, Young was shocked to discover that the problems of indiscipline in the police force, the district administration, and the Home Guard had reached a level that was difficult to fathom. It was clear to him that discipline could only be restored if prosecutions were brought against the offenders. The difficulty lay in assembling the evidence. To do this, Young established a special internal investigations unit within the CID, to be headed by Donald MacPherson. To ease its workload, the unit focused on a single district, Nyeri, where there were known to be deeply rooted problems of indiscipline in the Home Guard. Within a few months, MacPherson had opened 16 prosecution cases files, all of them deemed 'serious' and each arising from incidents since April 1954.

Once it became apparent that MacPherson did indeed intend to prosecute the cases, the investigation unit met with concerted and well-organised obstruction. This came from all levels of the administration, up to and including the Central Province Commissioner, C.M. Johnson, and the Member for African Affairs, Windley. There is nothing to suggest that these senior officials denied that beatings, torture, and murders were carried out by the police and Home Guard in Nyeri, only that they thought such matters should not be brought before the courts. It was more important to protect the reputation of the security forces, and especially to nurture the fragile morale of the Kikuyu Home Guard, than to bring people to justice. This became a struggle over the methods to be employed in combating Mau Mau. Young wanted discipline and the rule of law; his opponents defended the use of 'counter-terror'.[28]

The first of MacPherson's cases to come before the court concerned the goings-on at the Ruthagathi Home Guard post. This post, in Chief Joshua's part of Nyeri District, was under the command of Muriu Wamai, a renowned local loyalist of formidable repute.[29] Wamai had joined the Home Guard at its initiation, in January 1953, and was promoted to the position of headman one year later. Six months into his command, on the evening of 18 July 1954, a series of shots rang out close to Ruthagathi. When two European officers arrived to investigate, they found Wamai and his men waiting by the gate to the Ruthagathi post. Wamai described how they had detected a Mau Mau gang nearby, killing two of them in a fierce exchange of fire. The British officers were shown two bodies, lying nearby in the bush. Both were dead from gun shot wounds. The dead men were apparently unknown, and the deaths were simply recorded as two more Mau Mau kills.

Within a month of this event a number of documents had come into MacPherson's possession suggesting that this account of the events of 18

July could not be true. First, a series of unsigned letters were given to the CID, alleging that the dead men were not strangers at all, but well-known local farmers. Claims such as this were not unusual, although the administration characteristically dismissed them as rebel attempts to smear good Home Guard and police officers. But on this occasion the claims were soon supported by the sworn testimony of the headmaster at Ruthagathi, who explained that the deceased men had been arrested several days before their deaths. And the headmaster had good reason to know this was true, as he, too, had been subjected to 'screening' by Wamai at this time: he was beaten and tortured in the Ruthagathi Home Guard post, and the two deceased men were treated in the same fashion before being summarily shot. Next, a wife of one of the deceased men was found by MacPherson, and she also made a statement corroborating the allegations of unlawful detention, torture and murder at Ruthagathi.

The prosecution of Muriu Wamai, and five other Home Guards, for the murder of two Kikuyu farmers came before the court in late November 1954. Having been taken in by Wamai on suspicion of 'Mau Mau activities', the prosecution explained, the two deceased farmers, Marathe and Mathenge, were severely beaten and tortured at Ruthagathi. Evidence was produced showing that Ruthagathi was, in fact, a government interrogation centre, to which suspects were routinely brought for 'screening' from the surrounding countryside. Beatings and torture were allegedly part of the daily routine. Numerous local Kikuyu witnesses were produced, each having been victims of Muriu Wamai's 'reign of terror' at Ruthagathi. Suspects who confessed to Mau Mau crimes under torture in Ruthagathi would then be taken before the local African court, the prosecution explained, where Chief Joshua would hand down heavy fines. To ease this procedure, Wamai kept a log of the 'confessions' of his suspects, presenting this to the court as 'evidence'. The fines were enormous, and it was noted that wealthier Kikuyu were hauled before this court with greater regularity. This was little more than an elaborate extortion racket, and one that could not possibly have functioned without the knowledge of British officers.

The prosecution's evidence, all of it from African witnesses, appeared to provide a rare and disarmingly frank insight as to the 'methods' of the Home Guard, but it was fundamentally contested by a string of European witnesses who appeared for the defence. These included the District

Commissioner, Hughes, the officers attached to the Ruthagathi post, and several police officers. The evidence was utterly consistent from one witness to the next, in support of Wamai's original story and alleging that the evidence against him was nothing less than an elaborate rebel plot to frame a staunch loyalist.

It was the evidence of Wamai himself that finally turned the case, when, on his third day of questioning by the court, the headman broke down and made a dramatic confession. He admitted that the two deceased were local men who had been brought in for questioning, under suspicion of having taken an oath. Both refused to confess, despite interrogations and torture over three days. Wamai had then shot them both at close range and in cold blood. Further highly incriminatory revelations followed. Wamai now provided the court with a detailed account of what went on at Ruthagathi. It was a special interrogation centre. Prisoners were taken there to be beaten and tortured. Chief Joshua and all the British officers knew this — Wamai had merely done what he was told. Moreover, the screening of prisoners from the Ruthagathi location was a deliberate policy to wage 'economic war' against Mau Mau's passive wing in the area, slowly draining it of wealth and property.

There was worse to come. Wamai had frankly told Chief Joshua and the local district officer, Richmond, what had happened on 18 July. It was they who mounted the cover-up, making alterations to the Home Guard post record book and assisting in the concoction of sworn statements from the other five accused supporting the defence. Another district officer had lied to the court about the supposed battle. Wamai also now claimed to have made a confession of the murder to the Karatina police in August, when MacPherson's team had exhumed the bodies of the deceased men for examination. If this was indeed true, then two police officers had committed perjury, and a third had made a false statement to the court. An African chief, five other Home Guards, and five British officers were therefore among those complicit in the conspiracy to cover up the crimes at Ruthagathi.

Justice Cram accepted all this evidence as amounting to a substantive description of the conduct of affairs at the Ruthagathi Home Guard post. In a trenchantly worded judgment, he found the accused guilty of murder, pointed out that several British officers may have perjured themselves (and therefore should be subject to prosecution), described the Kikuyu Home Guards as the equivalent of 'Gestapo men' and their post as a 'Kenya Nordhausen, or Mauthausen', and ordered that the African courts in the district should be closed immediately, pending a full investigation into their operation.

Governor Baring was horrified by Justice Cram's outspoken criticisms and made every effort to have the judgement embargoed, but a copy soon found its way back to London, where it circulated under the heading 'Kenya's Belsen?' There were other consequences besides bad publicity. Everything about the Ruthagathi case had confirmed Arthur Young's belief that the Kikuyu countryside was run by a 'rule of fear', and that the highest officials in the land, including Baring himself, condoned this. After Ruthagathi, Young wanted further prosecutions but Baring insisted that MacPherson's investigations be halted. It was too much for Young; he tendered his resignation to Baring on 14 December. A few months later Young explained the reasons for his resignation to the Labour Party's Barbara Castle, and gave her assistance in trying to pursue other cases of gross abuse. But, in public, Young kept his silence, and therefore spared the British Secretary of State, Lennox-Boyd, from a worse scandal.[30]

A second consequence of the Ruthagathi case was the decision to issue a surrender offer linked to an amnesty. This would give the rebels amnesty from prosecution for all past crimes, including murders, and wipe the slate clean for the Home Guard by halting the other CID investigations.[31] Baring got approval for this from London early in January and made his public announcement of the amnesty at a gathering of Home Guard in Nyeri on 18 January.[32] The amnesty also provided the excuse to issue a pardon for the murderer, Muriu Wamai. The Ruthagathi case exposed the 'reign of terror' in Kikuyuland to public scrutiny, but in the end no one at all was to be punished for the crimes exposed in the court.

The extortion and torture at Ruthagathi were part of a wider pattern of Home Guard abuses that was a function of their surrogate role in the Kikuyu countryside. The Home Guard at Ruthagathi could have cleared all Mau Mau suspects out of the location very easily in a matter of a few weeks, but to try to do so would have invited greater conflict with the rebels, bringing the war very directly to Ruthagathi as it had come to Mununga Ridge. Rather than take this risk, they opted to exploit their advantage by selectively preying upon the civilian population, slowly squeezing the local wartime political economy for whatever they could gain. They did so with the compliance of the state, whose gaols and courts were used as the mechanisms of extraction, and whose European officers shielded the Kikuyu militiamen from scrutiny.

'We Didn't Do It, but they Deserved it Anyway'

Atrocity, brutality, excess and extortion by the Kikuyu Home Guard did not begin or end on Mununga Ridge or at Ruthagathi. There were other massacres and other interrogation centres where torture and beatings were the norm. It is clear from the surviving documents on the investigations inspired by Arthur Young that several senior administrative officers were well aware of the abuses and atrocities committed by the Home Guard, but that they considered these actions to be among the necessary costs of war. C.M. Johnston, the British Provincial Commissioner for Central Province, was among those officials. On at least one occasion Johnston deliberately sought to halt the investigation of Home Guard atrocities. It is also clear that Governor Baring was fully aware of the widespread character of misdemeanours such as those committed at Ruthagathi, and that he, too, argued against the prosecution of Home Guards on the grounds that this would 'lower morale'. In short, the prevailing view among the senior British administrators held that 'State terror' was needed to fight rebel terror.[33]

The Governor's amnesty of January 1955 nipped in the bud the prosecutions that Young had initiated, sparing the British government from further (and more significant) embarrassment in the courts. Britain has hidden its deeds under the cloak of this amnesty ever since. The amnesty itself amounted to a tacit admission of British culpability, but it did not stop the abuses. When the Labour Party MP Barbara Castle visited Kenya toward the end of 1955, she still found plenty of evidence of the 'rule of fear' in the rural areas and published articles in the British press claiming the Home Guard to be 'guilty of some of the worst atrocities'. She also poured scorn on the disingenuous claims of British officers supervising the Home Guard that they were not involved in brutalities and had no knowledge of them.[34] There were other highly credible witnesses too. David Martin, a young teacher at Alliance High School in Nairobi, witnessed the beating and torture of suspects by Home Guard 'while the D.O. [European District Officer] looked on and took no action.'[35] Martin's colleague Carey Francis, the headmaster at Alliance, put it even more bluntly in an article published in 1955: 'men boast openly of brutality', he wrote; 'Injustice persists because many in the [security] forces believe in injustice'.[36]

The official attitude of the British government in Kenya to reports of atrocity and abuse by the Home Guard is best captured in the notion that 'We didn't do it, but they deserved it anyway'. They did, indeed, 'believe in injustice'. Using the Home Guard as surrogates, British officials ignored gross atrocities such as at Mununga Ridge, and contracted out interrogation and torture to their allies at places such as Ruthagathi. These examples of war crimes were not the excesses of 'a few bad apples', as too many British officials liked to contend, but were the product of the system of coercive government imposed on the Kikuyu countryside by British policy under the Emergency. The surrogates of the colonial state, Muriu Wamai, Chief Njiri Karanja and their like, cannot escape responsibility for their actions at Mununga Ridge, Ruthagathi and elsewhere. But will the British government ever accept responsibility for the barbarity of its actions in Kenya?

THE AMERICAN EMPIRE AT WAR

Marilyn Young

War as you undoubtedly appreciate, presents civilisation with a great opportunity and a great challenge. It is in a time of war that great fortunes are often made. It is between wars that economic conditions tend to deteriorate. If mankind can just discover some means of increasing the duration of wars and decreasing the intervals between wars, we will have found a permanent solution to this most fundamental of human ills, the business cycle.

(Love Dad, Joseph Heller)

The phrase 'barbarisation of warfare' is likely to evoke two automatic responses from most people. First, that war is *always* barbarous and second, in only partial contradiction, that *of course* warfare has become more barbarous as the means to fight wars have become more lethal. While the first proposition, in my view, holds, I have come to wonder about the second. The number of Iraqi casualties, over the past three years, even at the maximal estimate, is lower than for a similar period of time in either the Korean or the Vietnam War. The same is true for US casualties. The benefits of high tech war have been achieved: war in which surgical air strikes are not an oxymoron but a description and bombs are anyway smarter than they used to be. If many non-combatants are nevertheless killed, it is because of faulty intelligence rather than the disproportionate use of force; not saturation bombing, then, but precise bombing of the wrong target.

These technological developments have not made warfare less barbarous, they have replaced one mode of barbarity with another. The war on terror the Bush administration announced on 12 September 2001 is by design a war of indefinite duration and therein lies its barbarity. In

175

the language of Joe Haldeman's science fiction novella, it is a 'forever war', since a war against a tactic must last as long as people in a world of asymmetric power use it.[1] Wars, as the US used to fight them, were intended to end in peace. That barbarity of warfare, however repugnant, was assumed to have an end point.

The end of the Cold War could be imagined. Indeed, many analysts believed it would end in some sort of convergence between the two systems. In the meantime, détente was a reasonable substitute for peace. From the middle of the last century almost to its end, Western Europe and Japan enjoyed a more or less comfortable period of US hegemony. In the rest of the world, anti-colonial and anti-imperialist movements challenged the US with a little help from friends in the Soviet Union and China. The US responded with a wide array of tactics, by preference covert, and using local armed forces (Guatemala, Iran, Indonesia, Laos, Cuba for example) but overt and direct when nothing else would do: Korea, Vietnam. With the exception of Cuba, covert means worked well enough — for the US, if not for the inhabitants of the countries to which they were applied. Direct military intervention proved to be less satisfactory: devastation of the country being saved from a fate worse than devastation, Communist domination, and large numbers of US casualties, public disaffection and a peace well short of victory (stalemate in Korea, defeat in Vietnam).

The lessons learned by post-Korean War administrations could be summarised in three words: keep China out. The lessons of Vietnam were equally direct and they were fully applied in the Bush family's first war against Iraq: choose a single, demonic enemy (Saddam Hussein, the new Hitler; not the shadowy Viet Cong nor, worse yet, the avuncular Ho Chi Minh); establish total control of the media as quickly as possible (untamed images alienate the average television viewer or newspaper reader); pre-empt atrocity stories (not My Lai but fictive Iraqi raids on maternity wards); move major military forces into place quickly (incremental escalations prolong the agony and multiply opportunities for dissent); announce simple, clear, achievable goals and then come on home (victory parades, yes; quagmires, no).

On the whole, things worked out well for President George H.W. Bush. In speeches serving both as prologue and epilogue to the war, he drew on Second World War Grand Alliance imagery: a clearly defined aggressor had been denied his ill-gotten gains; the US had brought the possibility of stability to the Middle East and could now see 'a new world coming into view. A world in which there is the very real prospect of a new world order.'[2] Yet despite the care taken not to revisit any part of the Vietnam War during Operation Desert Storm, that war continued to haunt the American public and its politicians. Returning veterans, despite the homecoming parades whose absence was said to have upset Vietnam veterans, wrote sour reflections on the war and many suffered ongoing physical disabilities they (and their doctors and lawyers) called 'Gulf War Syndrome', as if every American war created its own diseases.[3] Surprisingly, the Gulf War fared badly in films as well. Given the speed and decisive nature of the US victory over Saddam Hussein's forces, one might have expected films that glorified the immense power of US military forces. Instead, one film, *Courage Under Fire*, was an extended argument as to why America needed heroes and a more ambiguous statement that it had them. The only notable film to come out of the war, *Three Kings*, depicted the conflict as Vietnam on crack cocaine: a war of multiple betrayals and massacres; a war without honour or sense.

Although combat in Iraq lasted only a little over a month, Americans seemed no readier to send US troops abroad after it was over than they had been before.[4] Eric Dean, in a book which compared Vietnam to other American wars, insisted on the similarities between Vietnam and other, more acceptable American wars. It wasn't the singularity of the war, but rather that it was 'fought at a time and in a cultural context when a protracted war in which thousands of young Americans were being killed or coming home with serious physical or mental wounds became — and will remain — intolerable and absurd.' He viewed the prospect with ambivalence: 'It may be that in a society which is unwilling to accept pain, suffering, and death...that death in battle has simply become unspeakably obscene. Perhaps this is a good thing; perhaps it has created serious handicaps for American foreign policy.'[5] From the point of view of the state, the unwillingness of the populace to accept battlefield death was a sign of serious social disorder, first diagnosed as the 'Vietnam syndrome' by President Nixon.

A wide variety of American policymakers, both Republican and Democratic, became increasingly frustrated by the public aversion to war. The end of the Cold War made matters worse. The global danger of Communism, that had justified a half-century of defence budgets, academic agendas and foreign policy initiatives was suddenly gone. There was talk of a 'peace dividend', of the possible reduction in Pentagon budgets. That was one way of thinking about a unipolar world. Another, increasingly influential way sought to maintain global US military dominance.

The problem was that not all Americans shared this dream. President Ronald Reagan's Ambassador to the UN, Jeane Kirkpatrick, complained of America's 'whole world view and view of history which predisposes us to believe that peace is a norm and that war and violence are abnormal.' Kirkpatrick was not alone in her conviction that war was the necessary normal state of human affairs, though not everyone was as pessimistic about the American public. Michael Ledeen, for example, a senior fellow at the American Enterprise Institute, believed that 'all the great scholars who have studied the American character have come to the conclusion...that we love war. ... .What we hate is not casualties but losing.' Yet Ledeen too felt he had to remind his countrymen to face the fact that 'peace is *not* the normal condition of mankind and moments of peace are invariably the result of war. Since we want peace, we must win the war.' The world is an evil place, Ledeen warned, and because 'our enemies are inclined to do evil, we must win decisively and then impose virtue on their survivors so that they cannot inflict further evil upon us.' It is possible to lead by 'high moral example', but Ledeen did not recommend it. 'Fear is much more reliable and lasts longer. Once we show that we are capable of dealing out terrible punishment to our enemies, our power will be far greater.'[6]

In the last decade of the twentieth century, political commentators close to the Republican Party beat the drums of war steadily. America, the most powerful nation on earth, must demonstrate its willpower, its readiness to use force in pursuit of its interests, its capacity to project force anywhere in the world at a time of its own choosing. President Nixon had presciently named the problem decades earlier when the country erupted to protest against his invasion of Cambodia in 1970. The world had arrived at an 'age of anarchy', he warned, when even in the United States, there were 'mindless attacks on all the great institutions which have been created by free civilisations in the last 500 years.' If, at such a time, 'when the chips are down, the world's most powerful nation, the United States of America, acts like a pitiful, helpless giant, the forces of totalitarianism and anarchy will threaten free nations and free institutions throughout the world.' American power was not being tested, but rather 'its will and character. ... The question all Americans must ask and answer tonight is this: Does the richest and strongest nation in the history of the world have the character to meet a direct challenge by a group which rejects every effort to win a just peace, ignores our warning, tramples on solemn agreements, violates the neutrality of an unarmed people, and uses our prisoners as hostages? If we fail to meet this challenge, all other nations will be on notice that despite its overwhelming power the United States, when a real crisis comes, will be found wanting.'[7]

Americans remained divided as to whether the ensuing destruction of Cambodia was necessary but, in this and future conflicts, administrations anxious to be able to deploy US troops abroad would consistently pose the issue in Nixonian terms: the world's most powerful nation must *act* like the world's most powerful nation. Democratic administrations embraced American military force with a fervour equal to that of their Republican rivals. As Madeline Albright put it, in explaining Operation Desert Fox, the intense bombing of Iraq in December 1998, 'If we have to use force it is because we are America. We are the indispensable nation. We stand tall. We see farther into the future.' The press response to this and earlier Clinton bombing attacks against Iraq was positive: 'the president's limber trigger finger is making it hard for the yahoo right to keep portraying him...as President Sissy.'[8]

Prominent journalists joined the war party, chief among them the foreign policy analyst for the country's most important newspaper, the *New York Times*. In 1999, Thomas Friedman begged President Clinton to 'give war a chance' in Serbia: ... 'Let's at least have a real war... It should be lights out in Belgrade: every power grid, water pipe, bridge, road and war-related factory has to be targeted...the stakes have to be clear: Every week you [Serbs] ravage Kosovo is another decade we will set your country back by pulverizing you. You want 1950? We can do 1950. You want 1389? We can do 1389 too.... Give war a chance.' Two years later, Friedman raised the cry once more: 'A month into the war in Afghanistan, the hand-wringing has already begun over how long this might last. Let's all take a deep breath and repeat after me: Give war a chance. This is Afghanistan we're talking about. Check the map. It's far away.'[9] Four years later, when war had been given many chances in Iraq, Friedman still believed that the administration of George W. Bush 'were the right guys' to deal with terrorism. 'One thing I can assure you about these guys,' he told a TV reporter, 'is that they know how to pull the trigger.'[10]

The worriers continued to worry. Norman Podhoretz, editor-at-large for *Commentary* magazine and a prominent neoconservative, contemplated the coming of World War IV against international terrorism and wondered if the US could win it. 'I fully realize,' he wrote, 'that we are judged both by others and by ourselves, as lacking the stomach and the skills to play even so limited an imperial role as we did in occupying Germany and Japan after World War II.' He had himself occasionally doubted the country's capabilities in this regard. 'Yet,' he concluded hopefully, 'given the transfiguring impact of major wars on the victors no less than on the vanquished, who can tell what we may wind up doing and becoming as we fight our way through World War IV?' The prospect of what the US (or any other warring state) might become as it fought its way through the 21st century did not give Podhoretz pause. He was confident that everybody in the world would be better off and that victory in World War IV would mean, as President George W. Bush proclaimed, 'an age of liberty here and across the world.'[11]

Stephen Peter Rosen, director of the Olin Institute for Strategic Studies and a professor in the Government department at Harvard University, sought to explain why, in a new era of total American dominance, wars had to be constant: 'We are an informal empire, to be sure, but an empire nonetheless. If this is correct, our goal is not combating a rival, but maintaining our imperial position, and maintaining imperial order.' Imperial wars, Rosen observes, are different from conventional wars, which end with the troops coming home. 'Imperial wars end, but imperial garrisons must be left in place for decades to ensure order and stability.' Moreover, imperial strategy requires preventing the emergence 'of powerful, hostile challengers to the empire: by war if necessary, but by imperial assimilation if possible.'[12]

Rosen's understanding of the world was codified in the 2002 National Security Strategy which ordained that American forces would be such as to 'dissuade potential adversaries from pursuing a military build-up in hopes of surpassing, or equalling, the power of the United States.' The policy was not to be mistaken for unilateralism, however: 'The U.S. national security strategy will be based on a distinctly American internationalism that reflects the union of our values and our national interests.

The aim of this strategy is to help make the world not just safer but better.'[13] As Condoleezza Rice put this in a radio interview, no power will ever again be allowed 'to reach military parity with the United States in the way that the Soviet Union did.' Why? Because 'when that happens, there will not be a balance of power that favors freedom; there will be a balance of power that keeps part of the world in tyranny the way that the Soviet Union did.'[14]

To facilitate the wars necessary to maintain that balance, the US would have to achieve 'global force projection'. And to achieve that, a radical expansion of the already massive string of US bases would have to be secured. General Jay Garner, the first US administrator in Iraq, explained the model he had in mind as he thought through post-war planning: 'We used the Philippines. And the Philippines, for the lack of a better term, it was in essence a coaling station for the navy. And it allowed the US navy to maintain presence in the Pacific. They maintained great presence in the Pacific. I think....' Worried a bit by the association (it took almost 13 years to pacify the Philippines), Garner admitted it might be 'a bad analogy'. Nevertheless, he went on, 'I think we should look right now at Iraq as our coaling station in the Middle East, where we have some presence there and it gives a settling effect there, and it also gives us a strategic advantage there...'[15]

The mobilisation of support and resources to fight for coaling stations is as difficult today as it was at the end of the nineteenth century, when a major anti-imperialist movement protested at the annexation of the Philippines and the counter-insurgent war that followed. The Bush administration tactic has been the frequent invocation of the memory of 11 September 2001 and the ongoing danger of another terrorist attack on American soil. Hence the frequent announcement of states of high, colour-coded alerts, often timed to coincide with Bush administration political needs. At the same time, the broader public has not been required to make sacrifices. Secretary of Defence Donald Rumsfeld's vision of an imperial military force called for a lean, fast moving high-tech military that could drive quickly to military victory without straining the professional, volunteer military force. Such a force would impress all possible enemies, allies and also one's own population with its ability to reach into any corner of the world and pound it. When the Chief of Staff of the Army, General Erik K. Shinseki warned, before the invasion of Iraq, that the task would require hundreds of thousands of troops to secure the country, his testimony was dismissed as alarmist and he was forced to retire.[16]

Instead of the major land army the first Bush administration had employed, the second Bush administration relied on a concept, 'shock and awe,' developed by Harlan Ullman, a senior associate at a strategic policy think-tank. Ullman's plan, repeated throughout the 'countdown' to the war, looked forward to 'showering' Baghdad with more bombs in the first 48 or at most 72 hours of war than were used for the 39 days of Gulf War I so as to 'take the city down'. The idea of shock and awe is to gain 'rapid dominance,' Ullman wrote. 'This ability to impose massive shock and awe ... will so overload the perception, knowledge and understanding of [the] adversary that there will be no choice except to cease and desist or risk complete and total destruction.' [17]

Yet the sharp outlines of a victorious war story quickly blurred. Instead of the victorious, orderly march into the defeated capital past the cheering thousands: looting, arson, anarchy and peaceful demonstrators shot and killed. Instead of a ceremonial turning over of power to the new rulers, historically the moment that legitimised the new order, senior American officers sat alone on the plush sofas of an empty palace. A historian, Wolfgang Schivelbusch, observed that the 'absence of the vanquished from their place at the table of surrender resonated as a sinister silence, like a tragedy ending without a dying hero's last words.' The scene of the generals in the palace was a 'scene of ersatz surrender, for the simple reason that the defeated regime had vanished without a trace.'[18]

Meanwhile, demonstrating that he had, after all, learned something when he was in the National Guard and in apparent imitation of Tom Cruise in the movie *Top Gun,* George W. Bush, the straps of his flying costume pulled a bit tighter than is usual, co-piloted a Navy jet onto the deck of the aircraft carrier *Abraham Lincoln* which had had to put out to sea a bit in order to make the landing feasible. There were no Iraqis there, of course, only cheering American sailors and a largely admiring press corps. But if the surrender was ersatz, so was the victory speech, for openly to declare victory would require the release of Iraqi prisoners of war. Nor did the president announce the return of peace, as General Macarthur had on board the *Missouri* to mark the end of the Second World War in the Pacific. Instead, stirring a great stew of historical references,

Bush called upon the spirits of war presidents past (Roosevelt, Truman, Kennedy and Reagan), in the course of announcing that America's mission had been accomplished. What neither Bush nor the press had foreseen was the rapid development of armed resistance to US occupation, the slow pace of 'Iraqification', the need for far more US troops than are available, the ongoing failure to provide the most basic services to the Iraqi population and the growing impatience of the American public to be done with it.[19]

The genius of the American empire has been its ability to persuade ordinary Americans that it does not exist *and* that it exists solely for their protection; that America used force only in retaliation, never aggressively; that it was necessary to fight abroad so as not to have to fight at home, and finally, after the bloodletting of Vietnam had turned the public's stomach, that if the US had to fight, only its enemies would die. The guardian at the gate could be represented by Sgt Christopher Potts, of Tiverton, Rhode Island, who died last October. Writing to his wife about the trip from Kuwait into Iraq, Potts described the 'children of all ages from God knows where begging for food and water. The dust was blowing all over them, and some had torn outgrown clothes, and some were barefoot.' Potts said that after a few miles both he and his driver were weeping. 'I said to him, You know, this is why I'm here, so that my kids won't ever have to live like that. Then we just drove in silence for a while.' He died convinced that somehow, by killing people over there, he was protecting his family, over here. One marine who survived his tour in Iraq had a more acerbic sense of the value of his service. At a party in his honour at an expensive home in Malibu, California, one he himself was unlikely ever to own, he told the group toasting him as a hero: 'I'm not a hero. Guys like me are just a necessary part of things. To maintain this way of life in a fine community like this, you need psychos like us to go out and drop a bomb on somebody's house.'[20]

On the other hand, there was Corporal Daniel Planalp, whose sense of what was going on Iraq was quite different from that of both the Sgt. Potts and the cynical marine: 'This is Vietnam,' he told a reporter. 'I don't even know why we're over here fighting. We're fighting for survival. The Iraqis don't want us here. If they wanted us here, they'd help us.'[21] There are increasing signs that, like its predecessor, the enterprise is unravelling faster than Washington's masters of spin can control. The military is

having a harder and harder time meeting its recruitment quotas, despite
a steady lowering of standards, more aggressive recruiting tactics, large
cash bonuses and 'spending $200 million on upbeat television ads'. Low-
ering standards, one retired officer observed, in the language of our day,
'impacts on a moral issue. If young people aren't enlisting, that tells me
we are not doing the right thing over there (in Iraq). If our leaders can't
see that, the damage will go deeper than it did in Vietnam.' In an effort
to improve retention statistics, army recruits are no longer subject to
dismissal for drug or alcohol abuse, or even for lack of physical fitness.[22]

Meanwhile, the president's overall approval ratings fell from a high
of 80 per cent in September 2000 to 39 per cent exactly five years later,
while 65 per cent were convinced the country was on the 'wrong track'.[23]
In September 2005, over half of the population (62 per cent) disapproved
of Bush's handling of the war in Iraq; and percentages were similarly pessimistic for those who believed the war in Iraq had been worth fighting or
that it made the US safer, or that the war on terrorism was going well.[24] 'I
don't think it's going well,' a worker in Louisiana told a reporter, 'there's
too much killing.'[25] At the end of May 2005, Vice-President Dick Cheney
declared that the insurgency was in its 'last throes', but military officers
in Iraq, like Lt- Col. Frederick P. Wellman, agreed with the worker from
Louisiana: 'We can't kill them all. When I kill one I create three.'[26]

Forms of resistance made familiar during the Vietnam War reappeared:
extensive failure to report for military service; the appearance of an anti-
war veterans association (Iraqi Veterans against the War); the organisation
of Gold Star Families for Peace; a marked increase in both applications for
conscientious objector status and desertion rates. In Congress, a biparti-
san group, all of whom had voted for the resolution authorising the war,
introduced a resolution calling for an explicit plan for the withdrawal
of American troops.[27] It was voted down, but the effort to force the
withdrawal of troops continued in various forms — from putting the
issue on local ballots to the fierce demand by Cindy Sheehan, one of the
founding members of Gold Star Families for Peace, that the president
himself should account for the death of her son in Iraq.[28] Such opposition,
falling short of a principled anti-imperialism, could yield to the creation
of yet another narrative of lost American innocence, in which the US is
the victim, this time, of an ungrateful Iraqi people. As J.M. Coetzee has
written, empire has only one thought: 'how not to end, how not to die,

how to prolong its era.'[29] But it is worth thinking about Corporal Panalp, whose despair at finding himself in a war he cannot justify is reflected in Bush's radically declining support.

Not long ago, Niall Ferguson, Harvard historian, fellow contributor to this volume and admirer of empires past, scoffed that Americans did not really 'have what it takes to rule the world'. [30] Let us hope that he is right.

THE GLOBAL WAR ON TERROR AND ITS IMPACT ON THE CONDUCT OF WAR

Paul Rogers

In the aftermath of the attacks in New York and Washington on 11 September 2001, the United States embarked on a 'global war on terror', initially with the strong support of many other countries. In its first three years this war involved a sustained campaign against the al-Qaida network, the termination of the Taliban regime in Afghanistan and the subsequent termination of the Saddam Hussein regime in Iraq.

Close to five years after 9/11, and over three years after the initial military occupation of Iraq, there are few signs of an early end to this war. The al-Qaida network remains active, having been involved in a far larger number of paramilitary actions than in a similar period prior to 9/11, and its core elements are largely at liberty, aided by enduring support in parts of Afghanistan and Pakistan. Osama bin Laden himself remains at large and is able to deliver detailed statements on al-Qaida strategy and tactics. In Iraq, an anticipated early withdrawal of occupation forces has proved a chimera, and an insurgency is persisting that is tying down some 200,000 US troops in Iraq itself and neighbouring countries. The US defence budget is rising rapidly and is even beginning to approach the levels reached at the height of the Cold War.

There is little prospect of any early end to the American global war on terror, but nor is there any prospect of a change in US policy. George W. Bush was re-elected with a clear majority in November 2004, the Republican Party gained control of both Houses of Congress, and there was a strong feeling of vindication in Washington. Experienced independent analysts in the United States may be persistently critical of the effects of current policies, and there was a marked decrease in support for the administration during the middle months of 2005, but there is little or no sign that these developments will have much impact on the conduct of the war. Indeed, neoconservatives in the United States believe that the Republicans' electoral successes mean that the 'Project for a New American Century' is very much on course and that the first three years of President Bush's second term represent the clearest opportunity to further this great idea.

This is in marked contrast to opinions across much of Europe, where threats of possible military action against Iran and Syria are viewed with deep misgivings. There is even more concern in much of the majority world, with a rise in anti-Americanism that further fuels support for radical movements. The aim of this essay is to review the factors that lie behind current US policies in the war on terror, make an assessment of the results of the first four years of this war, suggest the likely impact of current US policies over the next three years, during the remainder of George W. Bush's second term, and then discuss whether the manner of the pursuit of the war on terror is likely to have a more general impact on the conduct of war in the coming years. In particular, there have been substantial changes in the manner in which the US war on terror has been conducted, such as to suggest that there is a 'barbarisation' effect that could have an enduring impact. This might not just be on the manner in which the United States conducts warfare but more generally on the conduct of war by Western states that might be engaged in the war on terror. This might encompass the pursuit of vigorous counter-guerrilla operations in urban areas, use of area impact munitions, long-term detention without trial, torture and pre-emption as more commonly used military tactics.

The US Political Context

Although neoconservatism has been a feature of US politics for several decades, it came to the fore in the late 1990s during Bill Clinton's second term. While it ranges across many areas of policy, it has developed a particular resonance in relation to US foreign and security policy, itself rooted in a belief in an historic role for the United States in the twenty-first century. Much of this was encapsulated in the Project for a New American Century, founded in 1997 and supported by Dick Cheney, Donald Rumsfeld and many others who were to become key people in the Bush administration after November 2000.[1]

At the root of the neoconservative outlook is the belief that there is only one viable economic system, a belief supported powerfully by the collapse of most centrally-planned economies after 1989. That system is the globalised free market developed along the lines of the domestic US economy. Moreover, the United States has a pivotal and historic mission to be a civilising force in world affairs, promoting free-market values to ensure a world economy and polity that is broadly in the US image.[2] This sense of mission came to the fore immediately prior to George W. Bush's election victory in 2000 and is deep-seated in significant parts of the US political and electoral system. Major elements of it have substantial religious overtones and these speak to some of the more evangelical elements of American Christianity, a religious orientation with well over 100 million adherents. To some extent, neoconservatism has elements of a faith-based system, so strong are the views of many of its adherents. In particular, it is not possible to accept that there is any legitimate alternative, and the war on terror is essentially being fought against forces that represent a fundamental threat to the vision of an American Century.

Prior to 9/11, the new vigour of US foreign and security policy was particularly evident in a belief that multilateral cooperation was only appropriate when it was directly in favour of American interests. Indeed, there were many examples where it was deemed highly inappropriate. Even in the closing years of the Clinton presidency, Congress made it unacceptable to attempt ratification of the Comprehensive Test Ban Treaty, there was antagonism in Republican circles to proposals for an International Criminal Court, and even efforts to ban anti-personnel land mines and control some forms of arms transfer were thought to be restrictive to the United States.

After George W. Bush came to power in 2001, the extent of opposition to multilateralism increased rapidly, including withdrawal from the Anti-Ballistic Missile Treaty and the Kyoto Protocol, opposition to the strengthening of the 1972 Biological and Toxin Weapons Convention and a refusal to participate in talks on limiting the weaponisation of space. Coupled with vigorous policies on trade issues, this amounted to a substantial change of attitude on the part of the Bush administration and represented a very different outlook for those who had anticipated a consensus administration, given the narrowness of its electoral victory in November 2000.

The approach was summarised succinctly by conservative American commentator Charles Krauthammer shortly before the 9/11 attacks:

> Multipolarity, yes, when there is no alternative. But not when there is. Not when we have the unique imbalance of power that we enjoy today — and that has given the international system a stability and essential tranquillity that it had not known for at least a century. The international environment is far more likely to enjoy peace under a single hegemon. Moreover, we are not just any hegemon. We run a uniquely benign imperium.[3]

Neoconservatism and Christian Zionism

In parallel with the rise of neoconservatism, a particular stream within American evangelical Christian churches has acquired a considerable political significance, especially in relation to the post-9/11 environment. This is Christian Zionism or dispensationalism, a movement that is rigorous in supporting Israel as a Jewish state with Jerusalem as its epicentre. Christian Zionism has only acquired real political significance in the past decade and its current importance stems from three factors. One is the voting power of a significant proportion of evangelical Christians, the second is its intrinsic support for the survival of the State of Israel and the third is the manner in which it links with neoconservatism.

There are some variations within dispensation theology but the essence of it is that God has given a dispensation to the Jews to prepare the way for the Second Coming. There is to be the literal fulfilment of Old Testament promises to biblical Israel in the sense that the 'end of days' will involve a millennium of earthly rule centred on Jerusalem. As such, the State of Israel is a fundamental part of God's plan and it is essential for it to survive and thrive.

Christian Zionism took firm root in US in the interwar years and a particular boost came with the establishment of the State of Israel in 1948, with many dispensationalists seeing this as the beginnings of a fulfilment of biblical prophecies. Yet another boost came when Israel took control of Jerusalem in the Six Day War in 1967, and a third came with the election of Ronald Reagan in 1980, not least because Jimmy Carter, though from an evangelical tradition, had been seen to be too conciliatory towards Palestinian aspirations.

The Clinton years were more difficult for dispensationalists, partly because they came soon after some of the preacher scandals of the late 1980s, but also because Clinton was more at home with the more secular elements of the Israeli political system, not least with the Labour Party. Even so, during his Presidency, the main Israel lobbies in Washington, particularly the American Israel Public Affairs Committee (AIPAC), sought to build close links with the Christian Zionists.[4] In part, organisations such as AIPAC recognised the increasing demographic and political power of the Christian Zionists, but they were doubly important because of the deep divisions among American Jewish communities that resulted in a decrease in support for Israel from a traditional source of influence.

During the first George W. Bush administration there was a remarkable coming together of the movement and of neoconservatism, especially in terms of support for Israel. As the leading evangelical preacher Jerry Falwell put it, 'The Bible Belt is Israel's safety net in the United States.' According to Donald Wagner, a historian of Christian Zionism:

By 2000, a shift had taken place in the Republican Party. It began embracing the doctrines of neoconservative ideologues who advocated US unilateralism and favored military solutions over diplomacy. The more aggressive approach was put into action after Sept. 11, and to no one's surprise, Israel's war against the Palestinians and its other enemies was soon linked to the US 'war on terrorism'.[5]

There are now a number of groups that connect evangelical Christian churches in the United States with support for the State of Israel, with many of them making specific reference to Jerusalem. Stand for Israel, for example, talks of the need 'to mobilise Christians and people of faith to support the State of Israel...' declaring on its home page that

'Anti-Israel = Anti-Zionism = Anti-Semitism'.[6] Christian Zionists may not be particularly significant in the major conservative think tanks in Washington, nor even in the administration itself. Instead, what they do is to provide an electoral pressure that enhances support for a Republican administration with marked neoconservative leanings.

Perhaps what is most interesting is that the growth in Christian Zionism in recent years forms one part of the wider increase in the conservative Evangelism movement, the fastest growing sector within American Christian churches. According to Wagner, estimates of the number of evangelicals range from 100 to 130 million, the latter being close to half the total population of the United States.

By no means all are Christian Zionists, perhaps 20-25 per cent would be described as fundamentalist. Indeed, many evangelical Christians have grave misgivings about aspects of Republican policies. At the same time, larger numbers may be inclined to support Israel because of dispensationalist sympathies, and evangelical Christians seem particularly disposed to vote for, and to be more likely to support the Republican Party. The overall effect of this is that both Israel and US neoconservatives have a particular electoral support from an unexpected and growing source. Moreover, many adherents seriously believe that we may be approaching the end of the world, that salvation can only come through a Christian message linked fundamentally to the success of the State of Israel, and that Islam is necessarily a false faith.

In any other era, Christian Zionism and its links with neoconservative thinking would be interesting but not particularly significant in guiding the policies of the United States. What is relevant here is that there has been a confluence of neoconservatism, the vigorous pursuit of a war on terror that is seen to be primarily against Islamic groups, and the Christian Zionist movement with its electoral strength, support for Israel and anti-Islamic strand. This comes at a time of a particularly hardline government in Israel that looks to neoconservatives and Christian Zionists as the foundation for its support within the United States. All of these have contributed to the policies of the last five years in terms of the war against al-Qaida, the termination of the Saddam Hussein regime in Iraq, and persistent support for the Israeli government. Indeed, in a real sense, Israel and its confrontation with the Palestinians have been widely seen as an integral part of the global war on terror.

Responding to 9/11

The US response to the 9/11 attacks has had three main components, the termination of the Taliban regime in Afghanistan, the pursuit of al-Qaida and the occupation of Iraq. The initial three-month war in Afghanistan, from October to December 2001, appeared to be highly successful from an American perspective. The Taliban regime was terminated, al-Qaida personnel and facilities were dispersed and the United States was able to establish two large military bases at Bagram and Kandahar, in addition to developing military links with a number of Central Asian states. During the course of the war, there were many thousands of people killed, including about 3,000 civilians, a similar number to those killed in the 9/11 attacks. Many more thousands died in refugee camps and as a result of economic and social disruption caused by the conflict.

Within two months of the termination of the Taliban regime, President Bush was able to designate an 'axis of evil' in his January 2002 State of the Union Address — Iraq, Iran and North Korea. His address at West Point three months later elaborated on the new strategy of enhanced pre-emption of presumed threats. Even so, this firm enunciation of policy was already being weakened by persistent problems in Afghanistan and this has resulted in an ongoing low-level insurgency requiring the long-term presence of over ten thousand US combat troops. Moreover, there are severe problems of post-war reconstruction and development in Afghanistan, exacerbated by an opium-fuelled economy and rampant warlordism.[7]

The pursuit of al-Qaida has been worldwide, extending well beyond the immediate region of central Asia. It has involved numerous states that have been in broad alliance with the United States, many of them enacting anti-terrorism legislation that has also served useful purposes against their own political dissidents. In terms of support for al-Qaida, more pertinent has been the use by the United States of imprisonment without trial, the systematic use of torture and the ignoring of the Geneva Conventions.[8] Significantly, these issues have had little political impact within the United States, certainly not enough to affect the outcome of the 2004 Presidential election. They have, though, had a sustained impact on Islamic communities in many parts of the world, an impact heightened by the events in Iraq since March 2003.

Termination of the Saddam Hussein regime was said to be necessary because of the regime's production of weapons of mass destruction and it support of al-Qaida. Neither claim had any substance, but regime termination still went ahead. In the wake of this, the Bush administration expected a rapid and peaceful transition to a secular regime. This client state would be sympathetic to the United States, would embrace free market economics, would welcome US oil interests and would ensure that the US had extended long-term influence in one of the world's most important oil-bearing countries. More generally, it would enhance US power in the region, render Saudi Arabia less significant and, perhaps most important, demonstrate the sheer power of the United States to that other regional member of the 'axis of evil', Iran.

The establishment of the Coalition Provisional Authority (CPA) was expected to preside over a caucus system that would bring the right kind of government to power, and it was certainly expected to take immediate steps to institute a free market low-tax economy likely to prove highly attractive to foreign investors. As far as economic management was concerned, the CPA certainly moved with great speed, but its oversight of the political evolution of Iraq was a very different matter. Within a few months of the end of the old regime, the insurgency was developing with unexpected speed and by the end of 2003 the United States was facing a highly unstable environment, especially in the main Sunni regions of Central Iraq.

In the early months of the insurgency, most of the blame was put on a few 'remnants' of the old regime, groups that were expected to be severely damaged by the deaths of Uday and Qusay Hussein in July 2003 and then by the capture of Saddam Hussein himself at the end of the year. In practice, neither had much impact, and the US authorities put more and more emphasis on two external factors, Islamic paramilitaries linked to al-Qaida and interference from Iran. Neither of these was particularly plausible, even if both may have had a minor impact. Instead, the insurgency gathered pace through 2004, with thousands of Iraqis dying mainly at the hands of coalition forces, not least during periods of intense violence in Fallujah, Najaf, Mosul and elsewhere.

Since the start of the Iraq War, at least 24,000 civilians have been killed and as many as 70,000 have been injured,[9] the insurgency has persisted and the elections of January 2005 have had little impact. At the time of writing, the United States and its partners have deployed over 170,000 troops in Iraq itself, supported by tens of thousands more in neighbouring countries such as Kuwait. The Pentagon is planning to maintain troop numbers at around 130,000 for at least the next two years, and permanent bases continue to be developed. Up to July 2005, the United States had had nearly 1,800 of its troops killed and over 13,000 injured, with at least another 10,000 evacuated because of physical or mental illness.[10]

While US military planners may wish to limit their presence, and certainly want to avoid a substantial presence in urban areas, it is proving excessively difficult to train Iraqi security forces to replace them. Indeed, the training programme is something akin to a disaster, so much so that the Pentagon is no longer giving figures for the numbers of indigenous combat-ready troops available. *The Economist*, which has a track record of caution tempered with realism on this issue, was scathing in its assessment:

The Iraqi forces are utterly feeble. At present only 5,000 of them are a match for the insurgents; perhaps as many as 12,000 are fairly self-sufficient. Most of the rest are unmotivated, unreliable, ill-trained, ill-equipped, prone to desertion, even ready to switch sides. If the Americans left today, they would be thrashed. Indeed, as things now stand, politically and militarily, the war is unwinnable.[11]

Meanwhile, the US predicament in Iraq has been a welcome development for the al-Qaida network, not least in its impact on anti-American sentiments among Islamic communities across the world. The attack on Fallujah, the 'city of mosques', in November 2004 was particularly significant. The use of massive firepower and overwhelming military forces caused city-wide destruction, many hundreds of casualties and over 200,000 refugees, and has given the attack an iconic status across the Arab world not dissimilar to the impact of the 9/11 attacks in the United States.

The Status of al-Qaida

It is in this context that it is appropriate to analyse the current status of the al-Qaida network, and to do so in terms of its origins and early development. Although al-Qaida became significant in the 1990s it was rooted in experiences in Afghanistan in the previous decade and owed much to the influence of radical Islamists, not least Sayyed Qutb in Egypt. Much of the early activity was concentrated in western Gulf States, notably Saudi Arabia, and included attacks on US facilities such as the Khobar Towers bomb in 1996 at the Dhahran Air Base that killed 19 and injured 500. Later attacks included the US embassies in Nairobi and Dar es Salaam, and there may also have been some links with the first attempt to destroy the World Trade Center in New York back in 1993.

Al-Qaida has been variously described as an idea, a consortium, a network of like-minded groups, a loose affiliation or a structured hierarchical organisation. While some controversy persists, the weight of analysis points markedly away from early post-9/11 insistence on a clearly structured hierarchical group, and there is also an acceptance that al-Qaida is an evolving and adaptive entity. Although there have been repeated claims, principally from the Bush administration, that al-Qaida has been thoroughly disrupted and dispersed, substantial evidence suggests otherwise, with clear indications that radical Islamic movements are substantially stronger than prior to 9/11.

Since September 2001 al-Qaida-linked actions have included major attacks on western or Israeli targets in Spain, the United Kingdom, Turkey, Morocco, Saudi Arabia, Egypt, Kenya, Pakistan, Indonesia and Uzbekistan. Independent and reputable military analysts report that al-Qaida and its associates are gaining in support in many parts of the world. Moreover, this is coming at a time of increasing anti-Americanism, as demonstrated by the Pew Center's international opinion surveys,[12] especially but not only in states with a substantial Islamic population, and also in Islamic communities in other states including those in Western Europe.

According to a November 2004 assessment from the International Institute of Strategic Studies (IISS), the invasion of Iraq has seriously weakened the US capacity to engage in other possible confrontations.[13] While up to 1,000 foreign paramilitaries may have infiltrated into Iraq, this is a small fraction of the potential 18,000 paramilitaries available to al-Qaida. According to the IISS analysis '...the substantially exposed US military deployment in Iraq represents al-Qaida with perhaps its most 'iconic' target outside US territory'; 'Galvanised by Iraq, if compromised by Afghanistan, al-Qaida remains a viable and effective 'network of networks'.' Although the termination of the Taliban destroyed its command base and training facilities, it has dispersed effectively, with some activities such as bomb-making still more decentralised and therefore 'potentially more efficient and sophisticated'. Overall, al-Qaida is a dynamic and evolving phenomenon that is maintaining a high level of activity across many countries. Two regime terminations have failed to curtail its development and one of these, in Iraq, is providing a new focus for the organisation and like-minded groups.

Even so, there is little indication that Washington has an appreciation of the aims and intentions of al-Qaida and its associates. Although some individual analysts in the United States and elsewhere have some understanding of the political aims of al-Qaida, this does not appear to figure in US policy formulation. Instead, al-Qaida is simply seen as a radical Islamist terrorist entity that is close to being nihilist in its outlook, does not have a political agenda and can only be countered by force. There is no possibility of engagement with any substantive aspect of the organisation and its affiliates. This fails to recognise that al-Qaida has both short-term and long-term aims and that these are relatively easy to identify, both from the writings and speeches of leading figures and, more importantly, from their strategies and tactics.

There are five main short-term aims, although not all involve all the affiliates in the network. The most immediate is the removal of foreign, especially US, forces from the Islamic world, with Saudi Arabia being the priority. This is followed by the termination of the House of Saud as the unacceptably corrupt and illegitimate Keeper of the Two Holy Places. The third aim follows on from this and involves the downfall of other elite state structures across the Islamic world but primarily in the Middle East, and their replacement by what will be considered to be 'genuine' Islamist regimes.

An underlying theme of statements, web-links and videos coming from al-Qaida sources is this concern with ruling elites. It is at least as significant as the commitment to expel foreign forces from the Islamic world. Moreover, existing rulers are, to an extent, seen as worse than Western occupiers in that they have acquiesced in a process of control that actually blocks the development of true Islamic governance.

A fourth requirement is the establishment of an independent Palestine centred on Jerusalem, and a fifth requirement is the liberation of Islamic societies where they are controlled by secular or other non-Islamist forms of governance. This last requirement includes support for separatist movements in Thailand and the Philippines, Chechen rebels in Russia and radical Islamist groups in countries such as Uzbekistan.

The establishment of a Palestinian state has not been a central aim of the al-Qaida group until recently. There are two reasons for this. One is that the educated Palestinian Diaspora in western Gulf States has been singularly successful in areas such as education and public administration, to the extent that indigenous populations, from where al-Qaida might draw support, have not been sympathetic to the Palestinians and their cause. Against this, with the advent of particularly hard-line policies by the Israeli government of Ariel Sharon, particularly the destruction in the West Bank in early 2002, the coverage of these activities across the region has made it possible for al-Qaida to embrace this cause, whatever the wishes of the Palestinians themselves.

Beyond these short-term aims lies the longer-term intention to establish some kind of pan-Islamic Caliphate, involving ideas dating back to a mythical golden age at the time of the Abbasid Caliphate, centred on Baghdad in the early years of Islam. Such a governance might be seen as a prelude to wider processes of proselytisation and conversion beyond the Middle East, but it is also probable that these are distant aims to be measured in many decades rather than years.

Given that al-Qaida is best described as a loose affiliation of groups, a network of networks, it is unwise to see a firm sense of central direction in all of the many activities of the past four years. At the same time, the major emphasis has been on attacking US interests and those of its close allies, as well as Israel and regional ruling elites, especially in Saudi Arabia. The original 9/11 attacks may well have been aimed at a crude and devastating demonstration of capabilities against the centre of US business and the military, but may also have been intended to bring large US troop concentrations into Afghanistan, where a Taliban/al-Qaida combination could have engaged them in guerrilla warfare.

In the event, the US used a combination of air power, special forces and the rearming of the Northern Alliance — taking sides in the ongoing civil war and thereby ensuring the termination of the Taliban regime. A result of this was the dispersal of al-Qaida and its metamorphosis into a more dispersed system of affiliated groups, benefiting from years of training given to young paramilitaries and from the huge boost to recruitment given by US actions such as the Guantanamo detentions and the heavy use of force in Iraq.

Iraq, indeed, has been of exceptional value to al-Qaida in three quite different ways. One is that it has opened up an entirely new front in the confrontation with the United States, bringing in tens of thousands of paramilitaries who are participating in an insurgency directed against US occupation. Secondly, while most of these insurgents are indigenous to Iraq, a small but significant proportion of them are paramilitaries from neighbouring countries, so that Iraq is providing combat experience in much the same way as the Afghan civil war did previously.

Finally, the persistent use of high levels of military force, as in the attack on Fallujah, has been widely publicised across the region and beyond, especially by the new generation of Arab satellite TV news channels. This has resulted in a widespread increase in anti-Americanism, in turn adding to support for al-Qaida and its associates.

The US predicament in Iraq will not be readily ended, given the importance of Iraqi oil reserves. The Gulf states as a whole have over 65 per cent of world oil reserves, with Iraq alone having 11 per cent, about four times as much as the United States itself. Much of the recent history of US involvement in the Gulf, including the establishment of the Rapid Deployment Force at the end of the 1970s and its later development into Central Command, is connected with the strategic importance of Gulf oil reserves.[14] With the United States intending to maintain a military presence in Iraq and the wider region for many years, al-Qaida and other oppositional forces are in the position of having a long-term focus for their activities in a way that far exceeds any guerrilla war in Afghanistan.

Moreover, Iraq is not just any 'Arab state'; it will be seen by supporters of al-Qaida as the successor to the most integrated and successful of the Islamic caliphates. From their perspective, they are now witnessing the extraordinary circumstance of the occupation of the former capital of the Abbasid Caliphate, Baghdad, by neo-Christian forces, a 'gift' to Islamist paramilitaries that is frankly difficult to exaggerate.

Iran and Syria

Since the November 2004 US presidential election, there has been a hope in some political circles in Europe that the second Bush administration would adopt more moderate policies on issues such as detention of suspects and the extensive use of force in Iraq, and would also be genuinely supportive of a viable two-state solution in Israel/Palestine. At the same time, there has been recognition that other areas of US security policy might conflict directly with European opinion. One concerns the increasing rhetoric in Washington over the status of Syria, with some neoconservative elements demanding regime change, but the more significant area of difference is over Iran.

Part of the opposition to the current regime in Damascus is the belief that much support for the insurgency in Iraq is coming from elements in Syria, with regular movements of insurgents across the border. There is also opposition to Syrian support for Hezbollah in Southern Lebanon. Some neoconservative commentators are calling for US military engagement across the Iraq border into Syria involving air raids on presumed centres of insurgency support.[15]

In the case of Iran, at root is the fundamental American opposition to Iran developing even the theoretical capability to produce nuclear weapons. There is a recognition in Berlin, Paris, London and Washington that Iran has a civil nuclear power programme, and some dispute over whether the International Atomic Energy Agency can continue to verify that it is only a civil programme.

The European view is that diplomacy is the best option, the aim being to allow Iran to develop a relatively small nuclear power programme but without an indigenous capacity for uranium enrichment, given that this can, under certain circumstances, form the basis for enriching uranium to weapons grade. In response to Iran agreeing to this, there would be progressive improvements in trade and other forms of interstate relations.

Even this policy is deeply unpopular within a wide range of political and religious circles in Iran. From an Iranian perspective, the country has been labelled part of an 'axis of evil' by the world's sole superpower that has adopted a clear strategy of pre-empting perceived threats. Furthermore, the United States has already terminated regimes on either side of Iran — the Taliban in Afghanistan and the Saddam Hussein regime in Iraq. The US may be facing formidable problems in Iraq, but does have 150,000 troops there and is still building permanent bases. Moreover, it sanctions an Israeli military presence in the Kurdish region of Iraq close to Iran's western border, and is about to construct a large new military base near Herat in western Afghanistan, close to Iran's eastern border. Finally, the US Navy has almost total control of the Persian Gulf and the Arabian Sea.

The Iranian perspective goes further than this perception of vulnerability in that there is a failure to accept that countries such as Britain and France can modernise their own nuclear forces and turn a blind eye to Israel's formidable nuclear forces, while failing to see Iranian arguments for developing their own deterrent. Such thinking cuts no ice in the United States or Israel, where Iran is regarded as a far more significant threat than Saddam Hussein's Iraq ever was, and where there are deep suspicions of an oil-rich country even wanting to consider a civil nuclear power programme. The problem is that the Washington outlook goes further and is in fundamental disagreement with the Europeans. What is opposed is any Iranian involvement in a substantive nuclear power programme on the grounds that it provides Iran with technical competences that could be applied to the development of nuclear weapons. Elements of the neoconservative agenda extend to the desire for regime change in Tehran, but the minimum requirement is for Iran to give up its nuclear power programme in an irreversible and fully verifiable manner.

Whether or not Iran has any nuclear weapons ambitions, it is highly unlikely that the Tehran government will halt its civil nuclear power programme, although it may well be prepared for closer IAEA inspection than is required by current agreements or, indeed, is required of any other state. It follows that there is real scope for a confrontation, even allowing for the problems currently faced by the United States in Iraq.

Impact on the Conduct of War

Many issues arise for the future conduct of warfare in the light of the first four years of the global war on terror, not least in approaching the question of whether the conduct of the war has increased a tendency towards the barbarisation of war. These issues should be considered on the basis that there is unlikely to be any major change in the conduct of that particular war, at least until there is a change of administration in Washington, and they may have wider implications, not just for the conduct of war by the United States.

For the specific war on terror, it is wise to assume a long-term conflict. Since Iraq and the other oil-rich Gulf states are of great security concern to the United States, there should be expected to be a long-term presence of US forces in the region, with a consequent violent reaction from those opposed to such a presence. Given the extent of the region's oil reserves, it is appropriate to think in terms of a 30-year period of potential instability and conflict, although always on the assumption of no major changes in US security policy.

In terms of the conduct of war, the 9/11 attacks and their aftermath have resulted in a marked increase in US defence budgets, and they are now approaching the peak levels of the Cold War era in the mid-1980s. There has also been the embracing of a much more overt policy of pre-emption of possible threats to US interests, including the termination of two regimes within two years. Accompanying these military developments have been vigorous processes of detention of those thought to be in any way involved in terrorism, including detention without trial. As of early 2006, at least 10,000 and possibly as many as 20,000 people are so detained. The numbers brought to trial in open court, either by the United States or by its coalition partners, are very small. In undertaking such detentions, the United States military has embraced interrogation techniques that involve high levels of harassment and some instances of torture.

In the context of a difficult and persistent insurgency, mostly conducted in crowded urban environments in Iraq, the US military have frequently fallen back on the use of their overwhelming superiority in conventional firepower, with this resulting in numerous civilian casualties, often described as collateral damage. There have also been numerous counter-insurgency innovations, many of them involving practices and equipment borrowed from the Israeli experience in the occupied territories. Even so, the practices of the insurgents have frequently evolved even faster than those of the coalition forces, and asymmetric warfare techniques have included very low-cost actions by insurgents matched against high-cost actions by the coalition. For example, one development has been the use by the US Air Force of the JSTARS surveillance aircraft in the role of attempting to identify vehicle bombs. It has not been entirely successful in this role but costs over $180 million per plane against the current cost of a car bomb in Iraq of around $2,000.

More generally, Donald Rumsfeld has sought, over the past five years, to instigate a major draw-down of numbers of US military personnel, especially in the US Army, and move the armed forces towards much more of a stand-off high-tech role with a minimum number of troops on the ground in any zone of conflict. The experience in both Iraq and Afghanistan indicates that the global war on terror negates this trend. Indeed, the Fiscal Year 2006 Defence Budget involves withdrawal of funds from a number of advanced projects in favour of improved conditions of service and equipment for the US Army. In terms of the wider pursuit of the global war on terror, three issues are prominent in relation to the changing conduct of war and the risk of increasing barbarisation — trends in asymmetric warfare, the intensity of responses from advanced military powers, and the changing impact of the media.

With regard to asymmetric warfare, the 9/11 attacks were seen as being as significant as Pearl Harbour, not least in terms of their human and political effects, yet they actually represented part of an existing trend towards high profile mass casualty attacks. These included major city-centre bombings in Sri Lanka in the mid-1990s in the context of the LTTE insurgency, one such incident being the bombing of the Central Bank in Colombo, on 31 January 1996, which killed nearly 100 people and injured 1,400. Another example of the trend was the attempt of a group of Algerian radicals to crash an A300 Airbus on the centre of Paris, a year earlier, an attempt averted by French special forces.

In between these two attacks, the Aum Shinrikyo sect in Japan attempted to kill hundreds of people with a Sarin nerve gas attack on the Tokyo underground railway on 12 March 1995. Twelve people died and several thousand were made ill, but the attack failed in its main objective. Perhaps the most significant attack was the attempt to collapse the north and south towers of the New York World Trade Center on 26 February 1993. If this had succeeded, the loss of life would have been ten times as high as in the 9/11 attacks.

The point about these incidents is that they demonstrate the capacity of paramilitary groups to identify vulnerable locations in urban-industrial societies and to cause casualties and damage that may be massively greater than the costs of the attacks. It is an aspect of the evolution of conflict that was also demonstrated by the economic targeting campaign of the Provisional IRA in London and Manchester and against transport targets in Britain between 1992 and 1997. While they were not intended to cause mass casualties, the economic impact was considerable, and did much to push the Northern Ireland conflict up the political agenda in Britain at that time.

The second issue concerns the conduct of the Iraq War by the US military. The 9/11 attacks had a profound impact in the United States, not least because the neoconservative agenda of a move towards a New American Century appeared to suffer a major reversal. In terminating the regimes in Afghanistan and Iraq, the Bush administration believed that major progress was being made in their 'war on terror' and that this was likely to ensure that their longer-term security agenda could be maintained.

In practice this has proved extremely difficult, especially in Iraq. One of the key features of the Iraq War is that the US forces are finding it almost impossible to control the insurgency. Their young men and women may have very advanced levels of protection, abundant firepower and superior observation and reconnaissance technologies, yet they are continually threatened by sniper fire, improvised explosive devices and rocket-propelled grenades that are employed by people able to operate in their communities with near impunity. The US military on the ground are therefore experiencing yet another form of asymmetric warfare for which most of them have little training or experience and which leads to high levels of stress.

A significant consequence of this is that there is little ordinary engagement with Iraqis and there is, instead, a persistent propensity to respond with substantial force against suspected insurgents. This was clearly in evidence in the assault on Fallujah in November 2004, yet neither the large-scale destruction in that city, nor the heavy forms of control maintained since have been sufficient to prevent it being a focus of continuing insurgent activity.

The final development adds to the impact of such 'collateral damage' and this is the effect of independent satellite TV news channels such as al-Jazeera and al-Arabiya and their associated web sites. These channels have persistently provided copious amounts on information of the developing insurgencies in Iraq and Afghanistan. The sheer destructiveness of US firepower in Iraq, especially in Fallujah, has had a cumulative effect on audiences, especially young Muslims, in many parts of the non-Western world and in diaspora communities in the West.

Given the continuing viability of the al-Qaida network and the effect such TV images have on a pervasive anti-Americanism, it is possible that the broadcast media may be every bit as significant in the
evolution of the global war on terror as domestic TV coverage of the
Vietnam War was in the United States was in the late 1960s. In the
light of the probable involvement of suicide bombers in the London
attacks of July 2005, the possibility of a greater occurrence of such
attacks in Western countries should not be discounted.

In overall terms, the US military posture in 2001, prior to the
9/11 attacks, was one of developing a range of advanced forces that
could protect US interests wherever they were considered to be at
risk, but to do so with a minimum commitment of US service personnel in the field. This appeared to be vindicated after 9/11 by the rapid
termination of the Taliban regime in Afghanistan, using air power,
special forces and the re-arming of the Northern Alliance rather than
large scale commitments of ground forces.

What has become apparent since, though, is that an ongoing insurgency in Afghanistan is requiring a long-term commitment of up
to 20,000 ground troops. Similarly in Iraq, the three-week-long termination of the Saddam Hussein regime resulted in an early belief
in 'mission accomplished' that was to prove utterly false. Instead, a
deep-rooted and persistent insurgency has resulted that seems likely
to be maintained for as long as coalition troops are present in the
country.

More generally, the Iraq occupation has been of great value to the
al-Qaida movement, enhancing its recruitment base and helping it to
maintain an effective presence in many countries with substantially
more attacks in the past four years than in a similar period prior to
9/11. In relation to the situation in Afghanistan and Iraq, and the
wider 'global war on terror', it is by no means certain that the United
States and its closest allies are succeeding in maintaining control of
a potentially fractured global security environment.[16] Moreover, the
United States, in particular, is persistently reduced to using concentrated military firepower in circumstances that do little to defeat its
opponents and instead result in greater antagonism, not least because
of the high levels of civilian casualties that often result.

Barbarisation Enhanced?

In four different senses it could be argued that the experience of the war on terror in its first four years has enhanced barbarisation. Firstly, the 9/11 attacks and other instances such as the Bali, Madrid and London bombings all show a determination by radical paramilitaries to conduct extreme asymmetric warfare involving mass civilian casualties. While there have been other instances of mass casualty attacks in recent decades, not least the 1993 World Trade Center bombing, 9/11 and the other incidents that have followed have been at a substantially higher level of effect.

Secondly, there is the forceful manner of the US response, especially the use of large-scale firepower in urban environments, to an extent in Afghanistan but on a much more substantial scale in Iraq. Thirdly, the failure of coalition occupying forces in Iraq to establish post-occupation public order has resulted in exceptional levels of criminality leading to many thousands of murders and kidnappings, adding to the more direct impact of the use of firepower on Iraqi civilians.

Finally, there is the use of mass detentions without trial, with those detained not having the full status of prisoner of war, yet not being subject to conventional judicial processes either. These activities are not being undertaken by an autocratic regime in a 'rogue state', but by an advanced industrial power claiming to be acting under international law. At the very least this may have established a significant precedent for other states.

At the same time, these trends do not represent a transformation in the barbarisation of war when compared with many other modern conflicts, whether in Vietnam, Afghanistan, the Horn of Africa, Israel/Palestine or elsewhere since 1945. There have been all too many instances of mass civilian casualties inflicted by states and by paramilitaries, and the use of massive firepower was a frequent feature of US operations in Vietnam and Soviet operations in Afghanistan.

Furthermore, the globalisation of the mass media and of the newer forms of communication such as the internet, DVDs and e-mail has meant that coverage of the war on terror has been even more intense than, for example, that of the Vietnam War. Much of this coverage has been in the non-Western media, especially by the new Middle East sat-

ellite TV news channels such as al-Jazeera. Although these have little
impact on Western populations, they are acting in a sustained manner
to illuminate the effects of the coalition occupation of Iraq, inevitably
resulting in strong reactions, especially within Islamic communities.

Moreover, the powerful images of prisoner abuse from Abu Ghraib
came to public attention via the internet. While this might also have
happened if it had taken place in the pre-internet age it would have
been slower and far less widespread in its immediate impact. In other
words, it is possible that these particular aspects of globalisation may
tend to have a limiting effect on the barbarisation of warfare.

Perhaps the most significant development in the war on terror comes
not so much from the actual conduct of war as from the markedly increased tendency of the United States, in the post-9/11 environment,
to take pre-emptive action against potential threats to its security, most
notably in the termination of the Saddam Hussein regime. While this
cannot be claimed to have set a precedent, it has certainly taken the
concept of pre-emption to a new level, involving an immensely powerful state acting with apparent impunity in a manner that has caused
evident concern among some of its otherwise close allies.

The issue of pre-emption on this scale is therefore the most significant aspect of the changed post-9/11 environment and is one that
may well make it easier for other states to do likewise, also on a larger
scale than has previously been common. Against this, the substantial
problems that the United States is experiencing in Iraq may have the
effect of questioning this development. Given, though, that the United
States is engaged in a conflict in Iraq that may last for some years, it is
too early to be sure that a precedent will indeed be set. That will depend
to an extent on the US domestic political environment and whether the
manifest problems being faced are sufficient to cause a substantive re-as-
sessment of the conduct of the war on terror.

THE TEXTS OF TORTURE

David Simpson

Much of the popular awareness of the torture carried out by the coalition forces in Iraq has been anchored in visual images. The oddly amateur, home-movie quality of the Abu Ghraib photographs proved mesmerising as they were circulated worldwide in April 2004, and they were followed some months later by the lookalike images from Camp Breadbasket in the British sector around Basra. Both events had the quality of happenstance. Private Joseph Darby just happened to feel radically uncomfortable with the culture at Abu Ghraib, and brought the photos to the attention of a supervisor who acted promptly: the events they depicted had been known to the military for at least four months before they went global. A British soldier on leave in his home town just happened to leave off his film for developing at a photo shop in his local high street, at which point they were turned over to the police. Despite the familiarity of these images, especially those from Abu Ghraib, and the now instant worldwide recognition of the hooded man standing on the box, it is not hard to imagine that they might never have seen the light of day in the public sphere. Indeed nearly two hundred more photos from Abu Ghraib have not been released, despite their having been seen by the US Congress and pronounced unspeakably horrible: they show rape and sodomy with chemical lights, among other things.

Visual images claiming documentary status have been commonly subject to critique and disbelief for a long time. Matthew Brady's famous photos of the American Civil War dead are known to have been staged (though the bodies were real); numerous investigations of Holocaust photos have shown that what is being claimed is not what is being shown (though there were millions of deaths); and very recently it has come to light that the famous photo of the helicopter evacuating people from the roof of the American embassy in Saigon in 1975 was actually a shot of the roof of a nearby apartment building occupied by the CIA (though it was an evacuation).[1] In each case the photographs tell a kind of truth, but not a straightforward one. Some photos are outright fakes. But with the Abu Ghraib pictures no one raised the question of authenticity. They were believable from the start and have remained so, because they revealed what everyone felt to be true.

The instability and time-specific nature of photographs invite a certain kind of interpretation; they are preserved through time but they repre-sent only an instant in time, and can seem spontaneous and anomalous, since no instant is quite like any other. Certainly there has been concern that the Abu Ghraib pictures may do as much to inhibit as to encourage the kind of sustained analysis that many feel is called for. They may prove all too easily available to those who would propose the exceptionality of these instances, and who are trying to pin the blame on a few bad apples. We have not had similar photos from Bagram or Guantanamo or from any of the various prisons across the world to which persons detained by the US forces have been 'rendered'. It seems especially important, for these reasons, that we pay close attention to the printed record that has been made available, and to that by no means superseded techno-logical miracle, the book. The book, with its aura of slow time, perpetual records, and careful scrutiny, is far more convenient for certain kinds of scholarly and critical attention than the Web, which is replacing it in so many ways and which has indeed been an important medium for the dissemination of all sorts of vital information and evidence, including the Abu Ghraib images themselves. But the printed record can assemble in one portable and ready to hand object, the book, an important archive for the understanding of events as implicated in long-durational timescales and historical traditions; and in coming to us in the form of language it reminds us that words as well as images matter to a full comprehension of the instances shown in photographs, and may even contribute to making them happen in the ways that they did. Beyond this function of exhaustive and complex record keeping, books are or can be reflexive – they are in language and about language. In contextualising the events at Abu Ghraib and others like them, they reveal that in these cases the violence that is deployed against human beings is embedded in a violent appropriation of the language of protocol and procedure that makes it relatively easy to avoid facing up to the brute facts of what happens between guards and their prisoners. Acronyms, euphemisms and purposely vague attributions of cause and effect play an important part in the maintenance of a culture of torture where, for the body of the victim as for the language of description, nothing is what it is supposed to be.

Reading and Responding

The published record of the political deliberations preceding Abu Ghraib and the military and other inquiries that came after it — the proverbial small print that we should all read— is now available in several forms, the two most useful being Mark Danner's *Torture and Truth* and Karen Greenberg and Joshua Dratel's *The Torture Papers*.[2]

The first is a substantial volume, the second a massive one. Here are the records of the formative exchanges in 2001-2 between lawyers in the White House, the US Department of Defence and the State Department discussing the Geneva protocols, interrogation techniques and POW treatment; the official reports on Abu Ghraib generated by the army (Taguba), military intelligence (Fay-Jones) and the Department of Defence (Schlesinger); the prisoner testimonies and the Red Cross reports; and (in Greenberg and Dratel) a host of Bush administration memoranda along with reports from the New York Bar Association and the American Bar Association, and the 300-page report of Army Inspector General Mikolashek on detainee operations. Since these books were published the executive summary of the report of the Navy's Inspector General Albert T. Church III has also been published on the Web, and there is more to come.

Mark Danner's opening thesis is that the wide circulation of the Abu Ghraib photographs, startling as they were when first released, has increasingly worked to 'block a full public understanding of how the scandal arose and how what Americans did at Abu Ghraib was, ultimately, tied to what they had been doing in Afghanistan, Guantanamo, and elsewhere' in the so-called war on terror (p. xiii). It has been widely claimed, as it is by Danner himself, that the establishment of separate inquiries reporting on bits and pieces of the Abu Ghraib affair as they involved the army, military intelligence, the Department of Defence and so on has had the intended effect of diminishing the awareness of the connectedness and deliberate coherence of the torture-abuse pattern, and particularly its relation to policies originating at the top of the chain of command. The value of these published records is that a careful reading of them produces much that should impede any such displacement. The soldiers on trial for their part in the Abu Ghraib atrocities were not unique, but were following routines established (and continued) in Afghanistan, at Guantanamo, and at other sites in occupied Iraq. They are not so different from the routines familiar to British troops (the MoD has admitted that there have been seven deaths of Iraqis in British custody) and to torturers the world over. One memo (October 2002) actually discusses the legal implications of the aggressive interrogation techniques of the British in Northern Ireland: hooding, loud noise, prolonged standing, deprivation of food, water and sleep.

This is presented as good news since the European Court did not find these acts equivalent to torture but only to 'cruel, inhumane and degrading treatment'.[3] The rhetorical emphasis shared by all the reports on the 'few bad apples' argument, where the events at Abu Ghraib are variously framed as 'wanton acts of select soldiers' (D p. 324; G&D p. 443), as 'aberrant behaviour' carried out by 'a small group of morally corrupt soldiers and civilians' (D pp. 336, 405; G&D pp. 914, 989), is constantly undercut by the honest evidence of the writers of the reports themselves, who argue for 'institutional and personal responsibility at higher levels' (D p. 331; G&D p. 909), discover clear or ambiguous permission for stronger than normal interrogation techniques in a number of memos and findings, and point to intense pressure for results from frustrated military officers. In the light of these accounts, Abu Ghraib does seem to have been exceptional in its vulnerability to mortar attack, its radically overcrowded conditions, its low morale and obscure command structure, its lack of coherent record keeping and prisoner identification, and for the sense among those running it that it was a 'forgotten outpost receiving little support from the army' (D p. 481; D&G p. 1049). There is agreement that upwards of 80-90 per cent of those rounded up were innocents with no information of any use to the coalition. But the goings on there were not categorically different from procedures at other internment camps and prisons. They just happened to generate some unforgettable photographs that found their way into the public domain and generated an intense pressure for explanations.

The earliest records show the various lobbies at the highest levels of the US administration each jostling to impose its own understanding of the relevance or irrelevance of the Geneva Conventions to the 'war on terror'. (Alberto Gonzales, who would become Attorney General in the Bush administration, called the Geneva protocols 'quaint' in the light of what he perceived to be the radically new conditions prevailing after 9/11.) Over the objections of Colin Powell's State Department, President George W. Bush decided in February 2002 that captured al-Qaida and Taliban 'detainees' were not entitled to protection under the terms of the Geneva Prisoner of War provision, but he affirmed that humane policies would govern US practice anyway, and that persons would be treated 'in a manner consistent with the principles of Geneva', though only 'to the extent appropriate and consistent with military necessity' (D p.106; G&D p. 134-5). This circumlocution may have been crucial both in its claim that the US does not need Geneva because it is committed to humane behaviour as a matter of course, and in its introduction of the weasel-clause about military necessity. It also set the terms of a policy that was not revised or revisited when the 'enemy' ceased to be al-Qaida or the Taliban and became Iraq, whose citizens, as Fay-Jones admits, do obviously qualify for the protections of Geneva. These are some of the legal and political obfuscations that followed from the ruthless and reckless running together of the war in Afghanistan and the invasion of Iraq, as if one were the natural continuation of the other.

Managing Pain

The disturbing record of the effort to rationalise and legitimate various degrees of pain and suffering as essential to a military need or as not quite in breach of humane behaviour is written into the three major official reports, which were in progress even before Abu Ghraib became public knowledge. Acronyms constantly distract the reader's mind from any actualised agents or victims under discussion: thus the global war on terror becomes simply GWOT, and the location, history and nature of Guantanamo are erased by its renomination as GTMO. Iraq, with all its political and human complexities, becomes simply the site of the Iraqi

Theater of Operations, thence abbreviated as ITO. EPW is Enemy Prisoner of War, even though they all had names and hardly any of them had done anything deserving of being called enemies or justifying detention or interrogation — which might or might not proceed according to the IROE (Interrogation Rules of Engagement — note the transposing of combat terminology to the scene of investigation). Detainees are numbered rather than named. The monotonous reiteration of one acronym after another characterises almost all of these reports and gives them an aura of robotic routine. Laborious disambiguation operates to assure us, for example, that 'adjusting the sleeping times of the detainee . . . is NOT sleep deprivation' (D p. 202, G&D p. 362); 'segregation' should not be confused with 'isolation', notwithstanding the tendency to identify them in practice (D p. 463 only). Euphemisms abound. We are told that relations between interrogators and detainees are 'frequently adversarial' (D p. 363, G&D p. 938), but that (as if one were applying for a bank loan) 'detainee interrogation involves developing a plan tailored to an individual and approved by senior interrogators' (D p. 203, G&D p. 364): elsewhere this turns out to include 'use of detainees' individual phobias (such as fear of dogs) to induce stress', and something called 'forced grooming' (D pp. 458, 463 only). Detainee-28, who died in custody, received his fatal injury from being 'butt-stroked', a weirdly punning and oxymoronic coinage that (one infers) indicates being hit in the head with a rifle butt to 'suppress the threat he posed' (D p. 489, G&D p. 1056). Dogs are kept around to 'help provide a controlled atmosphere . . . that helps reduce risk of detainee demonstrations or acts of violence' (D 494, G&D p. 1061). The New York Bar Association tends to be explicit in using the word 'torture' for these acts, whereas the more decorous Red Cross report, whose explicit strategy is persuasion, favours such locutions as 'ill-treatment'.

This same rhetoric of decorous and delicate specification, friendly and confiding, as if all measures taken are for the detainees' own good, informs the discussions of what is and is not torture. Assistant Attorney General Jay Bybee (since appointed by Bush to the federal bench) opens his August 2002 memo with the assurance that 'certain acts may be cruel, inhuman or degrading, but still not produce pain and suffering of the requisite intensity to fall within Section 2340A's prescription against torture.' To qualify as torture, the pain must be 'equivalent in intensity to the

pain accompanying serious physical injury, such as organ failure, impair-
ment of bodily function, even death' (D p. 115, G&D p. 172). Imagine
an interrogator getting his or her hands on this and trying to decide at
precisely what point the inhuman and degrading turns into torture! Are
we there yet? Reading on, we find that Section 2340A might need to be
violated anyway in conditions of 'necessity or self-defense': all of this to
argue against the possibility of criminal liability on the part of US interrogators (D p. 116, G&D p. 173). A request for clarification of Guantanamo
protocols begins its listing with polite questioning– 'the detainee should
be provided a chair and the environment should be generally comfortable'– moves up through four-hour stress positions and 30-day isolation,
and ends in Category III where the notorious water treatment, described
as 'use of a wet towel and dripping water to induce the misperception
of suffocation', sits alongside the bland and mildly incommodious 'use
of mild, non-injurious physical contact such as grabbing, poking in the
chest with the finger, and light pushing' (D p. 167-8, G&D p. 227-8).
How could anyone imagine that a light push incurs a comparable response
to being almost suffocated in a wet towel? 20-hour interrogations are
permissible as long as they 'are not done for the purpose of causing harm
or . . . prolonged mental suffering'. The water treatment can similarly be
approved if there is a 'compelling government interest' and provided that
it is not carried out 'with the specific intent to cause prolonged mental
harm' (D p.176, G&D p. 234). Similar evasions, sometimes artful and
sometimes so bizarre as to appear invented, govern much of the language
of these documents, which seem designed to make almost anything permissible under the right conditions, or to justify anything that happened
on the assumption that the right conditions might have been deemed by
somebody to have accrued. We are in the world of *1984*. Before and after
humans are tortured (or is it just inhumane abuse?) the language itself is
dismembered and disjoined. The lawyers do the work.

Understanding euphemism is not just a matter of acknowledging the
traditional American proclivity for suppressing 'cock' in favour of 'roost-
er'; it contributes to a rhetoric that is both grandiose and dishonest in its
avoidance of direct definition and in its translations of human agency into
the passive voice. Things happen with mechanical facility rather than in
the disruptive rhythms of human bodily experience. In the lingo of the
IROE, it is either nobody's fault or the other person's when things get

messy. The Church Report contains an extraordinary instance of this as it describes the unusually harsh, customised methods employed on two Guantanamo prisoners suspected of possessing critical intelligence: 'both [plans] successfully neutralised the two detainees' resistance training and yielded valuable intelligence.'[4] In other words the task of the interrogators was to unsettle prisoners whose training in torture resistance made it incumbent upon them to use methods not normally employed: the fault is the prisoner's for being so well-prepared. Torture is not torture but the undoing of training in resistance to torture.

One of the most chilling items in this long record of graduated cruelty and implausibly rationalised measurement of pain is the transcription of a hand written note commenting on the four-hour standing technique in the approved section of the interrogator's manual: '*However, I stand for 8-10 hours a day. Why is standing limited to 4 hours? D.R.*' (D p. 182, G&D p. 237). D.R. is apparently Donald Rumsfeld, Secretary of Defence, who signed this memo — the same Rumsfeld who was revealed, as US military deaths in Iraq were pushing 1,300, to have signed all the letters of condolence with a machine signature, and who chastised an impertinent combat soldier asking for more body armour with a reminder that he served in the army he had and not the one he wanted. According to his employer, President George Bush, this man's gruff exterior hides a heart of gold. It does not apparently hide an imagination minimal enough to even begin to feel what the body of the other might be experiencing, standing stock still in threatening conditions under interrogation (with or without clothes, the womens' underpants, the hood or the electrodes). Why only four hours? Why not ten or twelve, so that the detainees suffer at least as much as the poor public servant working at his lectern and shuttled between one big decision and the next, chaperoned by bodyguards and ministered unto by faithful employees? It is easy to be sarcastic, harder to know how else to respond. What goes on in the mind and heart of a man who could write that note? What does it bode for the fate of nations that he occupies one of the most powerful positions in the world? It was Rumsfeld who approved more forceful interrogation techniques at Guantanamo in December 2002, only to rescind the approval under pressure from Navy lawyers six weeks later. Various modifications and limited permissions for such obscure tactics as 'pride and ego down' and 'environmental manipulation' continued to be devised and approved, and various items from the menu were taken up by interrogators in Iraq after the invasion of March 2003.

Conjuring with Terror

Much evident in these records is the beguiling 'ticking bomb' scenario beloved of classroom theorists and house intellectuals. This is the question of whether and how much to torture a prisoner in possession of vital information that would save lives but only if revealed promptly. The special conditions deemed by many to obtain after 9/11 have made this syndrome very popular. Thus Alberto Gonzales, now Bush's Attorney General, found the original post-9/11 debate about the Geneva provisions and legal protocol 'quaint' in the light of the need to 'quickly obtain information . . . to avoid further atrocities' (D p. 84, G&D p. 119). A DoD working group reported in April 2003 that the possibility of 'catastrophic harm' might justify the use of 'exceptional' techniques of interrogation (D p. 193, G&D p. 344). And Bush's memo of February 2002, we recall, left open a window for more extreme actions in conditions of 'military necessity'. The Schlesinger Report indeed tells of a case where unauthorised violence against a detainee is said to have succeeded in saving American lives, and mentions two cases at Guantanamo where 'additional techniques' gained 'important and time-urgent information' (D p. 333, G&D p. 911): these are the same cases mentioned in the Church Report, already discussed. Schelsinger finds these situations to involve a 'perplexing moral problem' and resolves it by opining that violating the norms may be 'understandable but not necessarily correct' (D p. 401, G&D p. 974). In other words, it will happen but we don't permit it. At the same time, the Bush specification of 'military necessity' appears to leave all options open to those who decide where that necessity applies, and the White House lawyers from the very start were anxious that nothing must interfere with the President's ability to do whatever he deemed necessary for the security of the country.

The ticking bomb scenario is by all accounts extremely rare: Alan Dershowitz, who has written a widely circulating essay about it, mentions only one case in the official history of Israeli intelligence.[5] The claims made for the successfully timely torture of Abdul Hakim Murad in the Philippines in 1995 as responsible for preventing the destruction of eleven

US airliners have been disputed by journalists who found that the critical information was circumstantially discovered on a computer, though the torture did indeed take place.[6] What must be very common, however, is the situation in which the interrogator does not know whether the detainee has such information or not, and is thus unsure how to proceed. By its vary nature 'time-urgent information' cannot wait for complex official approval. How would one expect an interrogator who is not sure what he has or what he is looking for to respond to the ticking-bomb example? How can the constant production of this largely hypothetical case fail to create an atmosphere which pressures interrogators into thinking that they *might* have such a case on their hands, and had better act as if they do? Here is an instance of the language of the interrogation manuals presupposing a situation which it cannot be sure exists, while planting the idea of its likelihood in the minds of anxious interrogators. Reinforcing this is the fact that the state of exception or emergency presumed by the ticking-bomb scenario is the normative state of a nation at war, and the US is now indefinitely at war. Giorgio Agamben's theories tell us that the power of the modern state is always premised on the state of exception and on its ability to dispose of bare life as it sees fit and with impunity. The Jay Bybee memo provides empirical evidence of just this, as it argues away any limits on the president's 'constitutional power to conduct a military campaign'. Indeed it finds that any efforts to impose limits must themselves be 'unconstitutional': even Congress is deemed to have no say in how troops are deployed or how prisoners are interrogated (D p. 116, G&D p. 173).

There is no single cause to which the Abu Ghraib events and others like them can be attributed. The one major foray into academic evidence found in the Schlesinger Report refers to the findings of a 1973 Stanford University experiment simulating prison conditions wherein the participants rapidly began to exhibit 'pathological reactions': 'We witnessed a sample of normal, healthy American college students fractionate into a group of prison guards who seemed to derive pleasure from insulting, threatening, humiliating and dehumanising their peers' (D p. 394-5; G&D p. 970). The worse it got the worse it got; each level of cruel behaviour encouraged a yet higher level of cruelty. As more and more evidence comes out of similar events in Afghanistan, Guantanamo, Mosul, Basra, and so on, it does begin to be clear that abusive behaviour, even torture, is not the exception and not to be accounted for simply by the 'few bad apples' argument. Records released in December 2004 under the terms of the US Freedom of Information Act — some 10,000 pages with more to come — make clear that abuse / torture has been generic rather than exceptional in all branches of the military. This is by no means an exclusively American problem: stories from Deepcut barracks in England suggest that if no foreign enemy is at hand then plenty of proxies can be created.

The confidential Red Cross Report on Guantanamo, details of which became public at the end of November, made the accusation that the treatment of prisoners there 'amounted to torture' — this finding was the result of a visit in June 2004, *after* the worldwide circulation of the Abu Ghraib photos. But a similar Red Cross report concerning British treatment of Iraqis delivered to the British government in February 2004 was kept confidential (by the standard agreement), despite requests for a public accounting. Blair's government, responding to accusations by Amnesty International and others of stalling or inaction on complaints about the deaths and abuse of civilians, has also defended itself preemptively by claiming that the European Convention on Human Rights does not apply in Iraq. In Britain too wordsmithing has played its part in the effort to dress up torture as something less than it is. Former Archbishop of Canterbury Lord Carey was quoted in the press in May 2004 as distinguishing between the 'barbaric' televised executions of Westerners and the merely 'shameful' abuses of Iraqis by Westerners. This effort to tabulate degrees of cruelty (in our favour) is not comfortably distinct from the verbal ingenuities of the lawyers. Those lawyers turned gratefully to decisions of the European Court of Human Rights that certain Abu Ghraib-like procedures employed by the British in Northern Ireland were not extreme enough to be called torture; the Israeli Supreme Court was similarly complacent about deciding that behaviour could be 'cruel and inhuman' without amounting to torture. Meanwhile, a self-exonerating essay by a former Israeli interrogator claiming the use of only 'very low levels' of physical coercion was answered by the executive director of Amnesty International in the letters column of the *New York Times* (27 December 2004) with evidence that during the period in question (1987-93) torture was routine in Israel.

Rumsfeld is reported to have faced down the increasing evidence of widespread torture by responding that nothing that the coalition has done is as bad as 'chopping someone's head off on television': shameful, perhaps, rather than barbaric. Efforts to fine tune the language in the face of complex experience might normally be welcomed as the sign of an active and critical intelligence at work. When it comes to deciding whether near-suffocation with a wet towel is torture or just cruel and inhuman behaviour, critical taxonomy itself has been suborned in the service of power. The damage being done works upon the perpetrators as well as the victims. It is also replicated in the language of their legitimators, like house intellectual Michael Ignatieff (a vocal supporter of the war) who found in the videotaped beheadings comforting evidence that the 'Muslims' can only be described as 'evil', a term which 'holds the line' between them and us.[7] At Abu Ghraib the Schlesinger Report speculates that the employment of euphemistic language could have led to 'moral disengagement' (D p. 397; G&D p. 972): the language of evasion increases the likelihood of cruel behaviour, so that I am more likely to feel justified in beating someone to a pulp if I know I am arguably within the law or sheltered by a benign definition of what I am doing. This is radical damage to the other but also significant damage to the self. It is not just the detainees who suffer, though they suffer most. Many ordinary soldiers pressed or tempted into dehumanising others, even in critical life and death situations, come to feel very bad about what they have done: many such persons have already returned from Iraq and spoken their stories. A yet more serious self-loathing is likely to be attached to gratuitous brutality directed at internees of whom up to 90 per cent are innocent. The cost of victory is partly (though never equally) paid by the victors. We do not suffer as much as those we make suffer, but neither do we escape without damage. Part of that damage is to the language whose distortions and diminishments are themselves also agents in the legitimation and dissemination of torture.

The lesson to be drawn from the Abu Ghraib syndrome and these investigations of it is then indeed one about the widespread culpability of US and other nations' military personnel; but it is also, more chillingly and with fewer extenuating arguments, about the lawyers and politicians who give them their orders and of the intellectuals who justify them. By offering themselves for slow reading and rereading, the printed records

open up for discussion some of the deeper issues governing how we perpetrate and respond to behaviour that many of us deem inhuman and
appalling. Among these issues are the consequences of the language we
use, consequences not just for others but for ourselves. The tendency of
all such violence to corrupt those who imagine and deploy it is one of
the most important lessons of Abu Ghraib, and it cannot be answered by
handing out long prison sentences to a few bad apples. It goes to the heart
of the imperial imagination, as revealed in the Rumsfeld annotation and in
the hair-splittings according to which legal lackeys attempt to draw a line
between abusive behaviour and torture, evil and mere brutality. There is
nothing in the record that convinces us that with the best will in the world
on the part of officers in the field any and all future acts of torture could
be completely prevented. But it is equally clear that in a climate where
official opportunism, devious euphemism and cynical ambiguity seem to
allow for and even encourage extreme brutality, such acts are much more
likely than not. The amazing Victor Klemperer, who kept scholarly and
critical diaries throughout the Second World War under the most har-
rowing conditions, noted that even the victims of the Third Reich began
to speak its language: 'there were no great differences to be registered
. . . it reigned supreme, as omnipotent as it was wretched, omnipotent
indeed in its very poverty'.[8] Given the state of our own language, we are
nowhere near having created a climate in which there might be *only* a few
bad apples.

THE LAWS OF WAR IN THE AGE OF ASYMMETRIC CONFLICT

Anthony Dworkin

Since 11 September 2001, the United States has been engaged in a proclaimed 'war on terror' that has challenged many of the existing ways of thinking about armed conflict. The Bush administration framed its anti-terrorist campaign to put it outside the bulk of the laws that have historically set standards for humane conduct in war, in particular the Geneva Conventions of 1949. Against the resulting background of legal uncertainty, the United States has pursued policies that are widely seen as a regression from previously accepted rules: the indefinite captivity of people who deny that they were involved in any conflict, coercive or humiliating interrogation, the holding of 'ghost detainees', extra-legal renditions to countries that are known to practice torture. Beyond these officially acknowledged practices, reports of the mistreatment of prisoners held by the United States have surfaced with such regularity that they appear to indicate a systematic pattern of brutality that was either explicitly condoned or at least allowed to develop by military and political authorities.

Remarkably, all these actions were taken by a country that nevertheless continues to insist that it leads the world in its commitment to the laws of war (or international humanitarian law, as it is sometimes known). This fact raises urgently the question of whether the laws of war in their current form have lost their effectiveness as a way of promoting humane standards in armed conflict. The world seems threatened by a degradation of conflict, as the rising capacity for massive violence of terrorist groups is met with highly troubling responses from states that claim legal as well as moral justification for their actions. Many people have reacted by suggesting that the answer lies in a revision of the law; that the Geneva Conventions should be updated to provide a better balance between the legitimate demands of counter-terrorism and the protection of humanitarian standards. Even groups that do not support revising the laws of war recognise that the challenge they face is intense. The International Committee of the Red Cross, institutional guardian of the Geneva Conventions, acknowledged the uncertainty surrounding the regulation of warfare by launching a 'project on the reaffirmation and development of international humanitarian law'.[1]

How should we understand this debate? Does the failure of international law to control American actions indicate a gap in the law, so that the remedy (for those concerned by US policies) should take the form of additional legislation? Or does the problem lie not with the law itself but simply with the failure of the United States to observe it — so that the standards of international law remain adequate, but the global power of the United States allows it to get away with violating them (while cynically claiming to respect them according to its own interpretation)? These questions are central to any debate about the apparent barbarisation of contemporary armed conflict, because they go to the heart of the ability of international society to define rules of humane warfare and work collectively toward their implementation.

I believe that in order to account for what is distinctive — and, from a humanitarian standpoint, particularly dangerous — about the present situation, we need to reject both the simple responses outlined above. The inability of international law to control American actions in the 'war on terror' cannot simply be ascribed either to a gap in the law or to an explicit decision by the United States to act outside the law. Although both these factors may have contributed, the principal cause is to be found in conflicting views about the meaning of the law, and in the failure of the law to constrain soldiers' behaviour at the points where it departs most significantly from traditional military codes of honour. In both these ways, the crisis facing the law of armed conflict must be understood at least partly as a normative crisis; it is rooted in a debate about the law's scope and purpose that is not merely technical but relates to its underlying principles. American policies are based on a vision of international law that has a certain intuitive appeal, but that is ill-suited to protect humanitarian standards in the conditions of modern conflict. In order to reassert international law as an effective guarantor of these standards, it is necessary to promote an alternative interpretation of the law that is more in keeping with contemporary values, but that has not always been identified as clearly as is necessary.

In responding to a new kind of challenge to its national security, the United States has appealed to a vision of the laws of war that sees the protection of the law as an incentive and reward for legitimate fighters. Critics of the United States look to a picture of international law based on fundamental rights that apply to all human beings across the spectrum of peace and war. Since the Second World War, international law has moved substantially towards the second vision — but the extent of the shift remains disputed, and public understanding of the interplay between the relevant branches of the law remains confused. The evolution of transnational terrorism has exposed the gulf between these two conflicting visions at precisely their widest point. However, the questions raised by the war on terror should be seen as only a particularly acute instance of a wider dilemma relevant to many of the wars that Western countries are likely to fight in the future. This is the problem of promoting respect for the law in asymmetric conflicts — the problem of persuading soldiers to recognise legal and moral obligations to fighters who do not themselves observe the law. The difficulty lies in a misalignment between the values that the laws of war have traditionally appealed to and the principles that would be most likely to ensure respect for law in military operations today.

Reciprocity and Legitimacy in the Laws of War

The distinction between conventional and asymmetric conflict is essentially marked out by the limits of two related concepts that have been central to the laws of war since their origins in the chivalric codes of the Middle Ages: reciprocity and entitlement to fight. The international law of armed conflict (or *jus in bello*) began and remained for most of its history as a set of rules that applied only in contests between two groups of authorised combatants whose rights and responsibilities were equal. In medieval law this was *bellum hostile*: 'the open, public war fought between two Christian sovereigns.'[2] This was the only form of conflict to which the term 'war' properly applied, and the only one in which 'adversaries were considered enemies'.[3] By the early modern period, the sovereign authority to engage in war had come to attach exclusively to states, and the laws of war were only applicable in inter-state conflict. Moreover, the only groups authorised under the law to take part in combat were national armed forces or groups attached to them — only they were entitled to the 'combatant's privilege' which meant that they could not be held criminally responsible for any lawful acts of war, and must be treated as prisoners of war if captured. Implicit in this scheme was the assumption that a hierarchy of responsible command would ensure that soldiers generally fought in line with accepted lawful methods.

In effect, the law reflected the extent to which forces that were adversaries nevertheless shared a set of common interests and values — not least the aim of limiting who was entitled to fight. By the modern period the laws of war had evolved as a mutual contract to avoid actions that were both militarily inessential and inhumane, and they appealed to a mutual commitment to keeping war within limits so that a stable peace was more likely to succeed it.[4] The reciprocal nature of the law was reflected in the doctrine of reprisals. If your enemy violated the law, for instance by deliberately targeting civilians, you were entitled to breach the law in reprisal as a way of making them stop.

Outside these specific circumstances, before 1949, the international laws of war did not apply. From the medieval notion of *bellum Romanum*, war against pagans who could not be expected to abide by the law and were not entitled to its protection, to the colonial and civil conflicts of the early modern era, the prevailing idea was that restraint was a matter of policy or conscience rather than legal obligation.[5] In wars of rebellion, especially, the lack of legal protection for rebels was linked explicitly to the fact that they were not legitimate combatants since they had no right to take up arms. The sixteenth century Spanish scholar Balthasar Ayala expressed a representative view when he argued that rebels 'ought not to be classed as enemies, the two being quite distinct, and so it is more correct to term the armed contention with rebel subjects execution of legal process, or prosecution, not war.' For this reason, Ayala maintained, the laws of war 'which apply to enemies, do not apply to rebels.'[6] Police actions were not regarded as an appropriate subject for the law of nations. This came into force only where neither party to a conflict had to acknowledge a legally superior body.

The place of reciprocity and legitimacy in the laws of war was re-affirmed in the modern codification of the law that began in the mid-nineteenth century and culminated in the Geneva Conventions of 1949. Viewed from one perspective, the Geneva Conventions of 1949 illustrate all the trends discussed above. They are applicable only in a conflict between two or more High Contracting Parties — which can only be states — and only binding in relation to non-signatory powers if these accept and apply the Conventions' provisions (although in fact all militarily significant countries have signed the Geneva Conventions). The Conventions set strict criteria for lawful combat and the associated status of prisoners of war — it is essentially limited to members of regular armed forces and groups attached to them who are organised in such a way as to ensure that they comply with the law themselves. The Conventions also implicitly allow acts of reprisal against civilians in enemy territory, by forbidding reprisals only against specific groups defined as 'protected persons' — the wounded, prisoners of war, and enemy civilians in detention or occupied territory.

Human Rights: a New Set of Values

In all these ways the Geneva Conventions marked the ultimate development of a picture of the laws of war as a contract between sovereign military powers. Yet at the same time as they seemed to affirm a traditional vision of the law, the 1949 Conventions also opened a decisive breach in it by importing a set of provisions derived from a historically quite distinct stream of thought. This stream was founded on the notion of individual human dignity, and it was finding new expression following the atrocities of the Second World War in the nascent human rights movement. The human rights movement based its claims not only on natural right but (like *jus in bello*) on its essential contribution to a stable international order. The 1948 Universal Declaration of Human Rights said that 'recognition of the inherent dignity and of the equal and inalienable rights of all members of the human family' was the foundation of 'freedom, justice and peace' in the world.

One area where old and new concerns merged was in the treatment of irregular fighters — guerrillas, partisan fighters, or others who joined in hostilities without being entitled to combatant status under the law. Traditionally, not being legitimate combatants, these irregular fighters had stood outside the protection of the laws of war. If captured, they were entirely at the mercy of the enemy.[7] However, some thinkers had always held that the inhabitants of countries that had been invaded and occupied had a moral right to resist the occupying power; the notion of legitimacy under these specific circumstances was historically disputed.[8] Against this background, the suffering of the inhabitants of occupied countries during the Second World War gave the impetus for an enormous advance in protection for such fighters in the fourth Geneva Convention of 1949 (often known as the Civilians' Convention). According to the Convention, inhabitants of occupied territories who were suspected of being saboteurs or engaging in 'activity hostile to the security of the Occupying Power' without being lawful combatants remained as 'protected persons'. They could be tried for criminal acts, as long as they were given the benefit of due process, or detained — but if detained they had the right of appeal and regular review, and were entitled to the same regime of protection as other civilian internees.

The protection of irregular fighters in occupied territory reflected the confluence of several streams of thought. At one level — as noted above — it looked back to a long-standing feeling that inhabitants of occupied territories had some kind of moral right to resist, even if they fell short of the status of lawful combatants. At another level, it was simply part of a broader concern with the fate of the civilian population of occupied territories as a whole: measures that might be seen as offering due process rights to irregular fighters could more properly be seen as protecting the safety of innocent civilians, in circumstances where distinguishing between the two might be difficult (as is true with the debate over 'unlawful combatants' today)[9]. Finally, these provisions of the fourth Geneva Convention were indicative of a new feeling that all citizens of a state caught up in war were entitled to a minimum standard of humane treatment, even where this involved some sacrifice of military effectiveness.[10]

The fourth Geneva Convention marked a shift in the orientation of the laws of war in a more humanitarian direction, but the extent of the change was limited. For a start, while the law now clearly protected irregular fighters in occupied territories, there remained some question about whether it also protected irregular fighters during ongoing hostilities in the period before one army had established decisive control. In his influential 1951 article on 'unprivileged belligerency', Richard Baxter claimed the fourth Geneva Convention did not protect unlawful belligerents 'where fighting is in progress outside occupied territory'.[11] Persuasive arguments have also been made on the other side.[12] Beyond this, the law did not cover irregular fighters from countries that were members of a military coalition with the detaining power. These seemingly arcane points have come to acquire a new significance in the context of US military action in Afghanistan and Iraq against al-Qaida, and have recently generated an enormous literature. For the purposes of this essay, the most important point to recognise is that the Civilians' Convention incorporated two different streams of thought about the laws of war — one based on the idea of a contract between legitimate combatants and one based on emergent ideas of human rights — and that contemporary disagreements about how to interpret the Convention are often rooted in divergent views about how much weight to attach to the principles embodied in these different visions.

The Civilians' Convention addressed one form of asymmetric combat — the participation by irregular fighters in a conventional inter-state war. But the Geneva Conventions also contained a more radical innovation: for the first time they extended the scope of international law to cover conflicts that were *wholly* asymmetric, in that one or more of the parties was not a sovereign state. Common Article 3 of the Conventions laid down a set of fundamental rights that were applicable in the case of 'armed conflict not of an international character occurring in the territory of one of the High Contracting Parties'. Wars of rebellion were henceforth to be seen not simply as a domestic matter, but as a legitimate international concern. At a stroke, Common Article 3 severed the link between the international laws of armed conflict and the concepts of reciprocity and legitimacy. The obligation of states to respect the provisions of the Article was not made dependent on any undertaking by rebels to obey them, and the text of the article explicitly rejected any idea that its application might give insurgents the right to take up arms.[13] The protections offered by Common Article 3 were much more limited than those granted to 'protected persons' in conventional inter-state war; effectively they represented a direct transfer of fundamental human rights into the framework of the laws of war, at least in the context of conflicts that remained within one country's sovereign territory.

Development and Disagreement

Since 1949 international law has continued to develop in ways that have extended the reach of humanitarian values and further challenged the reciprocity/legitimacy paradigm.[14] The first Additional Protocol to the Geneva Conventions of 1977, applicable in international conflicts, included a list of 'fundamental guarantees' that protected anyone in captivity, no matter what his status. It therefore filled the gaps in protection for irregular fighters that remained from the fourth Geneva Convention, offering them guarantees against murder, torture, and humiliating or degrading treatment, and requiring that any charges against them be tried according to generally recognised principles of due process. Additional Protocol I also overturned the traditional argument that violations of the law by one side might legitimise limited violations by the other, stating bluntly that 'attacks against the civilian population or civilians by way of reprisals are prohibited.'

Another important development has been the progressive recognition and elaboration of customary law, which is held to be binding on everyone involved in conflict irrespective of any treaty. Customary law has been particularly significant in the case of non-international conflict, where the reach of treaty law remains more limited; it has been recognised and applied by the war crimes tribunals for the former Yugoslavia and Rwanda, and is incorporated into the statute of the International Criminal Court. In non-international conflicts, customary law has substantially fleshed out the basic principles of Common Article 3 of the Geneva Conventions and established beyond challenge the idea that humane standards apply even in counter-insurgency campaigns where the enemy is both deceitful and illegitimate. At the same time, since 1945 more general human rights laws and principles have been recognised as having force during both peace and war. Prohibitions against torture, arbitrary deprivation of life, and prolonged arbitrary detention would now be seen as limiting the actions of states against anyone in their power as a matter of fundamental human rights.[15]

A traditional vision of the laws of war based on reciprocity and legitimacy has thus been modified but not superseded by an ideal of the inalienable dignity of all individuals involved in armed conflict. However the balance to be struck between these two principles remains disputed. The United States, Britain, and some of their regular allies have all to varying degrees tried to resist what they see as an excessively humanitarian drift in the way international law is formulated and interpreted. The United States refused to sign the first Additional Protocol (primarily on the grounds that it made too many concessions to guerrilla warfare), while Britain entered a reservation saying that it continued to regard reprisals as legitimate in some circumstances. In the United States, particularly, a moral vision of the laws of war based around a clear distinction between legitimate and illegitimate methods of warfare retains a strong appeal for a number of military law professionals and scholars.[16] One manifestation of this has been a tendency among some commentators to interpret the law so as to assign to guerrilla fighters the primary responsibility for civilians endangered by their methods of urban warfare, and to promote a comparatively permissive attitude to the targeting decisions of lawful combatants.[17]

Terrorism and the Laws of War

Against this background of overlapping legal regimes and value systems, we can begin to understand the subtext to debates about the war on terror. The intuition that terrorists do not meet the requirements of reciprocity and legitimacy, and are therefore not entitled to receive the benefit of the laws of war, lies behind the Bush administration's various legal arguments. The attacks of September 11 revealed that al-Qaida was able to pose a threat to American security on a par with an attack by another state, and President Bush responded by declaring that the United States was at war with those responsible. The US armed forces were thus given the implicit prerogatives of war — to target enemy fighters or detain them until the end of hostilities — but at the same time the White House announced that the protection of the Geneva Conventions did not apply in the war on terror because al-Qaida 'is not a state party to the Geneva Convention; it is a foreign terrorist group.' Members of the Taliban captured during the fighting in Afghanistan were theoretically covered by the

Geneva Conventions, but were not entitled, the administration said, to be treated either as prisoners of war or civilian 'protected persons'.[18]

In the past, countries facing terrorist campaigns have generally sought to deny being involved in a war, out of concern that such an admission might lend legitimacy to the terrorists' cause.[19] The uniqueness of the US response to September 11 lay in gesturing towards the concept of war to legitimise American actions while simultaneously denying the protection of the laws of war to the enemy. The legal framework associated with the laws of armed conflict was invoked and repudiated at the same time. According to the key White House directive on the subject, the terrorist threat to the United States departed from a traditional model based on 'the existence of 'regular' armed forces fighting on behalf of states' and ushered in a 'new paradigm...in which groups with broad international reach commit horrific acts against innocent civilians'; this required 'new thinking in the law of war'.[20] The legal scholar John Yoo, who worked in the Justice Department during this period and was influential in shaping the administration's policies, later defended them with reference to the fact that 'historically, there were people so bad that they were not given protection of the laws...If you were an illegal combatant, you didn't deserve the protection of the laws of war.'[21]

As we have seen, the law of armed conflict taken in its entirety, as it stood on 10 September 2001, recognised forms of conflict that extended well beyond the clash of 'regular' armed forces fighting on behalf of states'. However the essence of the White House argument is that the laws of war specifically did not envisage a conflict between a country and a non-state group based outside its borders (and therefore outside its notional territorial control); that they do not control a form of warfare that is wholly asymmetrical and yet not internal. The war on terror, in the White House's paradoxical formulation, should be understood as a form of armed conflict that is in legal terms neither 'international' (in the technical sense of inter-state) nor 'non-international'. Because the enemy is not a state, the Geneva Conventions are inapplicable. Yet because the threat comes from abroad, the restraints associated with internal rebellion (principally Common Article 3) are inappropriate also. Although the administration has not always spoken consistently on this point, its official position appears to be that even customary international law does not constrain US actions, since (according to a line of argument favoured by conservative American legal thinkers) it cannot legally be enforced by US courts against the president.[22]

A striking feature of the conceptual framework of the 'war on terror' is that the asymmetric conflict against al-Qaida was made to absorb and at least partly subsume a conventional war against Afghanistan. This latter war, in which the United States invaded Afghanistan, engaged with the forces of the Taliban regime, and installed a new president, would seem to fit within a traditional picture of inter-state conflict. The Bush administration appeared to acknowledge this fact by determining that the Geneva Conventions applied to Taliban detainees.[23] Yet the United States denied the status of prisoner of war to Taliban fighters, classifying them along with suspected terrorists as 'unlawful combatants' on the grounds that they did not observe the laws of war or distinguish themselves from civilians.[24] Instead of framing the war in Afghanistan as a conflict in which all participants were protected by the law in some form, the United States hived off suspected terrorists into a notionally separate conflict that escaped legal regulation, and used the Taliban's association with terrorism as a public justification for depriving them of the legal entitlement to use force.[25] Armed resistance by Afghanistan's *de facto* ruling regime against an invasion aimed at toppling it was characterised as illegitimate and rendered anyone who engaged in it potentially liable to trial by military commission at Guantanamo Bay for the crime of 'murder by an unprivileged belligerent'.[26] The US government has regularly elided the distinction between Taliban and al-Qaida detainees by claiming the right to hold all detainees until al-Qaida no longer presents a threat to the United States.[27]

As a matter of law, some of the Bush administration's arguments appear extremely unconvincing. It would be more in keeping with the evolution of international law to say that the law of armed conflict now applies as a matter of principle to all forms of armed conflict, and extends some protection to all participants in it. Under this view, the war in Afghanistan would be regarded as an international armed conflict in which all fighters (even irregular ones) were protected either as prisoners of war or civilians under the Geneva Conventions, or by fundamental guarantees incorporated in customary international law. An orthodox interpretation of the law would suggest that Taliban fighters were presumptively entitled to prisoner of war status, unless a tribunal ruling in each individual case determined otherwise.

Outside Afghanistan, if one accepts the unconventional idea that there could be an armed conflict between a state and a foreign terrorist group — a formula that would require regular and intense hostilities between two organised parties — it might best be regarded as a novel form of 'non-international armed conflict' by analogy with domestic insurgency, and thus regulated by Common Article 3 of the Geneva Conventions.[28] In any case, fundamental human rights including prohibitions against arbitrary deprivation of life, prolonged arbitrary detention and torture would apply to the actions of US forces, whether or not they were said to be taking part in such an armed conflict. Indeed, the global campaign against al-Qaida — like any anti-terrorist campaign — is precisely the kind of military operation in which human rights principles have most significance. In a fight against a loose-knit group that operates covertly, does not aim to control territory or operate across a front line of military engagement, and may never be decisively defeated, the question of whether any given individual is actually involved in hostile activity can be extraordinarily difficult to resolve; the indefinite nature of the contest makes the consequences of wrongful captivity much more severe. Detention and targeting policies that may be appropriate in a conventional war between armed forces (where attempting to kill enemy combatants or holding them until the end of hostilities presents no problems of due process) become much more problematic in an asymmetrical anti-terrorist or anti-insurgent campaign. For instance, the right not to be held in prolonged arbitrary detention appears to demand that all detained terrorist suspects be given a chance to appeal against their detention before a neutral tribunal, as well as regular review of the continued need for holding them.

Human Rights and the Military Ethic

Human rights principles based on a notion of individual dignity provide the most appropriate normative framework for regulating asymmetric forms of conflict like those associated with the US military campaign against al-Qaida. The notion of 'war' seems particularly misplaced in this context, since strictly speaking it has always referred to a limited category of armed conflicts fought between authorised groups of combatants operating on the basis of formal equality. In this sense, the Bush administration's 'war on terror' appears to have things precisely the wrong way round: the White House framed the struggle as a war to which the laws of war are not applicable, but it would seem more accurate to describe it as an armed campaign that (outside the limited 'real' wars in Afghanistan and Iraq) does not meet the criteria for war, but which is nevertheless governed by international law. The problem is that by tradition and culture, armed forces are habituated to operate according to normative principles associated with war, and the way the Bush administration framed and pursued its anti-terrorist campaign reinforced this tendency.

Rules of military conduct are by their nature directed at situations of extreme danger and disorder, and it is widely acknowledged that their effectiveness depends on factors beyond the law itself. To be capable of constraining the behaviour of soldiers in battle, military codes must be 'in accord with the prevailing cultural climate, clear to all, and capable of being enforced'.[29] Above all, the law may require support from the innate professional values of military forces; according to John Keegan, '[t]here is no substitute for honour as a medium of enforcing decency on the battlefield, never has been and never will be.'[30] The place of honour and custom is likely to be particularly important at times when the nature of conflict is changing — as with the rise of transnational terrorism — and written law may not apply in a clear way or may seem outdated in its assumptions.[31]

The distinction between legitimate and illegitimate opponents — between symmetric and asymmetric fighters — has traditionally been at the centre of the military understanding of war. By contrast, the notion that even 'unlawful' fighters are entitled to respect on the basis of their dignity as individuals is not well grounded in military values and culture. Since 1945, violations of humane standards by professional military forces have taken place most often in situations where members of enemy were not regarded as legitimate combatants and fought using unlawful methods themselves — as with the French in Algeria, the British in Kenya, or the Russians in Chechnya. In the present context of the armed campaign against al-Qaida there is neither a theoretical nor a practical incentive for reciprocity, since soldiers cannot expect that humane actions on their part will influence the behaviour of their opponents.[32]

Instead of reinforcing protections for terrorist suspects based on fundamental rights, US leaders and military officers emphasised detainees' unlawful status and created an atmosphere of legal uncertainty that appears to have contributed directly to the widespread torture and abuse that took place. In his presidential directive of 7 February 2002, President Bush wrote that American values 'call for us to treat detainees humanely, including those who are not legally entitled to such treatment.' In addition, he said, US armed forces should treat detainees 'to the extent appropriate and consistent with military necessity, in a manner consistent with the principles of Geneva.'[33] The message given to American forces was that formal restraints were unclear or non-existent. One army reservist told military investigators looking into the killing of two Afghan detainees at the Bagram collection point in December 2002 that soldiers felt they could 'deviate slightly from the rules' normally applied to the interrogation of prisoners because authorities had determined that they were not covered by the laws relating to prisoners of war. 'There was the Geneva Conventions for enemy prisoners of war, but nothing for terrorists,' the soldier is quoted as saying.[34] Other testimony relating to the killings at Bagram reveals that the officer in charge of interrogations there asked repeatedly for clear legal guidelines from her superiors about the methods she could use, but was never given a response.[35]

It was not only in Afghanistan that the uncertain parameters of the war on terror undermined the enforcement of humane standards in armed conflict. In March 2003, US forces attacked Iraq and quickly occupied the country. The US war against Iraq was indisputably an international armed conflict (in the technical sense of a war between states); both it and the subsequent occupation of the country were — as US authorities acknowledged — without doubt governed by the Geneva Conventions. This meant that both Iraqi soldiers and irregular fighters detained by occupying US troops were 'protected persons' under the law. However, the war on Iraq was presented by the White House as another front in the war on terror.[36] Some US soldiers went into battle with 9/11-inspired phrases like 'Let's Roll' stencilled on their vehicles.[37] Following their occupation of the country, US forces found themselves faced with an insurgency conducted jointly by Iraqis and foreign fighters and employing terrorist tactics like suicide bombs to often devastating effect.

Interrogation in Asymmetric Conflict

The results have been well documented: not only the lurid photographs from Abu Ghraib but a systematic pattern of humiliation and coercive interrogation applied to both civilian and military detainees. As the war in Iraq metamorphosed into an asymmetrical counter-insurgency campaign, the constraining effect of the rules of war was progressively weakened. Above all, it was evidently seen as legitimate to apply pressure to force prisoners to talk, despite the fact that the Geneva Conventions forbid any use of coercion to obtain information from prisoners of war or civilian detainees. The official investigations into Abu Ghraib and the related detention scandals reveal that repeated demands were made of field interrogators to produce 'actionable' intelligence.[38] An email message from US Army headquarters in Baghdad to field interrogators sent in August 2003 said that 'the gloves are coming off' because of the need to obtain better intelligence to combat the growing insurgency.[39]

Although those directly responsible for the torture or killing of detainees in Iraq are being prosecuted, there seems to be no recognition by US authorities that the urgent demand to obtain intelligence from prisoners was always likely to encourage violations of the Geneva Conventions. The fact that such manifestly unlawful actions were carried out so widely by forces supposedly committed to the laws of war is difficult to account for unless we understand these acts (in terms of the culture from which they emerged) as *excesses:* as an extreme case of methods that would have been seen as justifiable if they had not been carried so far. The independent Schlesinger Report into US detention operations — commissioned to assess the problems that had led to the abuse of detainees — itself endorsed the idea that 'the need for human intelligence has dramatically increased in the new threat environment of asymmetric warfare.'[40]

The report stressed that 'certain insurgent and terrorist organisations represent a higher level of threat [than traditional terrorism], characterised by an ability and willingness to violate the political sovereignty and territorial integrity of sovereign nations' and that in order to defeat them it was essential to obtain intelligence that could be used to 'locate cells, kill or detain key leaders, and interdict operational and financial networks.'[41] Compare this notion to the familiar doctrine that prisoners of war should not be pressured to reveal more than their name, rank and serial number. The intuition that aggressive questioning of detainees that would be inappropriate in conventional warfare may be acceptable — even necessary — in asymmetric conflict is widely shared, even where it is not recognised by the law. In circumstances where detainees are thought to possess information that may have a direct impact on military security, soldiers may feel that laws protecting the rights of irregular fighters express a perverse set of values. In a parliamentary debate on Iraq, a former British Chief of Defence Staff complained that the current legal code was 'perhaps now weighted as much, if not more, on human rights as on self-defence'.[42]

By appealing to traditional intuitions about the connection between legal protection and legitimate combat, while framing the conflicts so as to magnify the illegitimate nature of the enemy, US authorities laid the ground for a collapse in the standards of behaviour of American forces in both Afghanistan and Iraq. However the contemporary challenge to the laws of war is not limited to the US counter-terrorist campaign. Instead, changes in the nature of armed conflict are likely to put accepted standards of humane war-fighting under continuing strain, by further undermining the idea that the enemies against whom Western nations find themselves fighting are legitimate and worthy opponents.

Reciprocity and Legitimacy: Future Prospects

Looking back at the first US-Iraq war (the so-called 'Gulf War' of 1991), General Anthony Zinni, later to be Commander-in-Chief of US Central Command, commented that 'the only reason Desert Storm worked was because we managed to go up against the only jerk on the planet who actually was stupid enough to confront us symmetrically, with less of everything, including the moral right to do what he did to Kuwait.'[43] Future conflicts in which the United States and its allies are involved appear more likely to resemble the second Iraqi war — a contest in which even the opposing military forces fought out of uniform, side by side with unauthorised fighters, and resorted increasingly to terrorist tactics. The disparity of military power between the United States and any likely opponents will push them to rely on methods of fighting that put them outside the law and deprive them of the moral standing of equal and honourable enemies, while increasing the premium placed on any intelligence that can be extracted from captured fighters.

There is another trend in international affairs that converges with this. The laws of war traditionally presupposed a situation in which no higher body was able to rule on the respective claims of the sovereign bodies who were engaged in armed conflict. But since 1945 — and more plausibly since the end of the Cold War — the United Nations system has asserted the principle that the Security Council can adjudicate on the use of force; only with the imprimatur of the Security Council is an act of war legitimate (apart from self-defence against an immediate threat). This threatens to undermine the idea of the equality of parties to a conflict on which the moral appeal of the laws of war has always relied. Increasingly, when the United States and its allies go to war, they do in the guise of a kind of super-law enforcement operation against a regime that has been condemned as a threat to international peace and security. [44] To return to the categories of Balthasar Ayala, we are moving back to the realm of 'execution of legal process' and away from the traditional moral understanding of war.

If military action has been authorised as an enforcement measure against a regime that is (at least by suggestion) criminal, there is an implication that resistance to the attack is not legitimate. This idea will be even more powerful if the resistance takes the form of terrorism or insurgency, with enemy forces using methods of warfare that are themselves plainly unlawful. In such conflicts, it may be difficult to sustain any support for the laws of war on the basis of the traditional values of reciprocity and equality. Whether or not the Geneva Conventions are formally applicable, governments that want to promote humane standards will have to look to another value system to reinforce them. The further we move away from conventional engagements between military forces towards asymmetric forms of conflict, and the more the boundary between peace and war is eroded, the more important it is to emphasise the values of fundamental human rights and human dignity as the most effective foundation for preserving humane standards in military operations.

If the analysis presented in this essay is correct, the forces behind the degradation of military conduct seen in the 'war on terror' extend far beyond any deficiency in the written law. Some aspects of the law could usefully be revised — for instance, it could be made clear that all irregular fighters in international armed conflict are entitled to the protection accorded to civilian 'protected persons'[45] — but it is doubtful that the United States under its current leadership would accept such a change. In any case, the difficulties of upholding humane standards in asymmetric war are based more on confusion and disagreement about the values and standards that are appropriate than on limitations in the provisions of the law itself. Armed forces that claim to be enforcing a higher law against criminal fighters should be prepared to recognise that they operate under fundamental principles of law themselves, no matter how their enemies behave. Clarification and reinforcement of this principle by governments confronting asymmetric threats may be the most effective way of restoring humane standards in these particularly testing circumstances.

ON BRAINWASHING

Kathleen Taylor

On 7 July 2005 four suicide bombers on London's underground train network killed 52 people and injured more than 700. Mohammad Sidique Khan, Hasib Hussain, Shehzad Tanweer and Jamal Lindsay were British citizens — husbands, fathers, carers, employees. Mohammad Sidique Khan was 'Sid' to former school-friends, who remembered him as a friendly, well-integrated lad who visited the United States and came back enraptured by it. Yet Khan and his colleagues came to see themselves very differently, as his testament made clear. 'We are at war,' he said in the video, 'and I am a soldier'.[1]

War and Terrorism

For suicide bombers (a label the militants do not themselves accept), their actions are the heroic military sacrifices of soldiers fighting in a global war.[2] US President George W. Bush christened this conflict a 'war on terror'. Some of his opponents saw it rather as a war on Islam and its believers waged by immensely powerful Western nations, primarily the United States, whose leaders are not above using terror tactics of their own.[3] In this as in other conflicts, victims on both sides tend to see attacks by their own side in military terms and attacks by the other side as morally unjustifiable, barbaric acts of terrorism. It is as if war is less an interaction between participants than behaviour defined as such by whoever performs it; as if the relevant verb should be conjugated: 'we make war, you attack, they commit terrorist atrocities'. Yet self-sacrifice and killing were intermingled in the attacks of 11 September 2001 as they were in the trenches of the Somme.

One way of rejecting the elision of war and terrorism is to sharpen distinctions between them by laying down codes of conduct for warriors. A fundamental element of these codes in modern warfare is the distinction between military and civilian personnel; enemy combatants are legitimate targets; enemy civilians are not. This categorisation, enshrined in the Hague and Geneva Conventions since the first Hague Convention was signed in 1899, has been repeatedly ignored in practice.[4] As other chapters in this volume demonstrate, barbaric acts are not the sole preserve of terrorists. In the twentieth century, atrocities against civilians committed by military or paramilitary personnel range from individual incidents with death tolls in the tens or hundreds (such as the massacre of up to 500 Vietnamese civilians by US soldiers at My Lai in 1968) to genocidal campaigns in which casualties total hundreds of thousands (e.g. the Rape of Nanking in 1937, Rwanda in 1994), or even millions (e.g. the Holocaust, Khmer Rouge rule in Democratic Kampuchea, Turkish targeting of Armenians during the First World War).[5]

The military atrocities which result from the barbarisation of warfare share certain features in common with terrorist atrocities such as 9/11. Both are especially feared and condemned by civilians because they spread the risk of being a victim from military professionals to the general population. Both are typically perpetrated by small, cohesive groups of men (although women can also be perpetrators: the scandal of prisoner abuse at Abu Ghraib involved female US military personnel and there have been female suicide bombers). In both cases, the perpetrator group is part of a much wider network which draws sustenance and support from a political community and/or government. Group members often share an elite, militaristic ethos and appear to believe that their desired ends justify their murderous means. They ignore the distinction between military and civilian targets, using lethal violence against relatively powerless and often unprepared opponents in operations considered unpleasant but necessary by their instigators. Both military and terrorist perpetrators cite deterrence as a motive, seeing carnage as a useful way of instilling fear; both use revenge and honour narratives to justify their actions, and both behave as if they are unlikely to be punished. This assumption of impunity is obviously justified for suicide bombers. To date it has also proved realistic for perpetrators of war crimes.[6]

Another similarity is that both military and terrorist atrocities are intended at least in part as public events. The message, written in blood, is addressed to the victims, their supporters and their governments. It is not primarily for neutral third parties, and perpetrators can risk widespread condemnation if and when news of their behaviour reaches a wider audience; hence their frequent attempts to conceal or obfuscate their actions. Even in the most serious cases of genocide, however, observer condemnation has rarely translated into effective deterrent action. Terrorists, like soldiers, operate within a strongly cohesive social network. Their controlling organisations emphasise group virtues such as loyalty, obedience and self-sacrifice. Any longstanding terrorist or military campaign additionally relies on the tacit or overt support of the wider community. This support may range from minimal to enthusiastic, from turning a blind eye or refusing to condemn, as some Irish politicians did with the IRA, to large-scale demonstrations of active support as in the Palestinian Intifada. If the societal consensus is against extreme tactics, as it was in Ireland, suicide bombing will not form part of the terrorists' strategy.[7] Similarly, if community support for a military campaign evaporates that campaign becomes unsustainable, as the Americans discovered in Vietnam. Objections from outsiders tend to have much less impact. The US invasion of Iraq in 2003, for instance, was widely condemned internationally, even by traditional US allies. At the time, however, the plan received considerable support from the American population. The invasion went ahead.

To argue that the perpetrators of atrocities in war may be similar, in some respects, to the perpetrators of terrorist attacks is not to make any claims of moral equivalence (or otherwise) between them. What the argument does suggest, however, is that in trying to understand the barbarisation of warfare we may gain useful insights from studying the processes which shape and motivate terrorists. Research has emphasised the social and structural aspects of those processes, yet the ultimate subject of their manipulations remains the individual human being.[8] In this essay, therefore, I will focus on the extreme example of suicide bombing to illustrate the journey from 'normal' to 'killer' taken by previously peaceable individuals like Mohammad Sidique Khan, who end up perpetrating atrocities in what they see as war. Drawing out similarities with the beliefs and motivations of military personnel who use violence to terrorise and slaughter civilians may increase our understanding of why such barbarisation occurs in war.

Popular Reactions to Perpetrators

The modern West owes many of its moral concepts to Christianity. One of that religion's most profound legacies — the concept of evil — is commonly invoked when discussing atrocities. Evil is a problematic concept for believers and sceptics alike because of the tensions it embodies between fatalism and free agency, passivity and moral responsibility.[9] Yet its usefulness as a social judgement has immunised it against philosophical complaints, at least in political and media discourse.

Within the Christian tradition, some strands personified evil as the Devil, blaming a supernatural agent for human barbarity and regarding evildoers as contaminated by contact with this agency, much as we might regard sufferers from some deadly infectious disease. Other strands emphasised the stain of original sin, seeing evil as a character flaw which morally disfigured every human but which could be fought against, imperfectly, by virtue and good works, or entirely erased by the redemptive sacrifice of Jesus Christ. Modern usage has stripped evil of its theological baggage, but the result has been a corresponding simplification of the concept. With no Devil to take responsibility, and the subtleties of 'hate the sin and love the sinner' largely abandoned, we are left with an essentialist view of evil as inherent to, even definitional of, the nature of evildoers.

As long as the evildoers in question are members of an outgroup rather than an ingroup — 'them' rather than 'us', however those categories may come to be defined — thinking of them as essentially evil beings is psychologically comfortable. But when they are not so easily distanced (e.g. the 'home-grown' London bombers) the need to find an alternative target for blame becomes urgent. In earlier times, the standard explanation would have been the theological one of demonic possession. But in the 1950s, as the United States confronted Mao Zedong's China in the Korean War, a new explanation became available. CIA man Edward Hunter coined the term 'brainwashing'.[10]

Subjected to a Chinese 're-education' programme called *szu-hsiang-kai-tsao* ('thought reform'), some Westerners converted to Communism and strongly denounced their governments and their former way of life, a phenomenon as unnerving to Western observers then as suicide bombers' videos are now.[11] In coining the colloquialism 'brainwashing' to name whatever caused this sudden change in ideological enthusiasms, Hunter envisaged a powerful, secret process which could wipe a person clean of old beliefs and then implant new ones. In brainwashing, unlike its predecessor-concept possession, a human mind succumbs to the control of other humans, rather than to a supernatural force.

Brainwashing as Belief Change

Brainwashing threatens cherished notions of free will. It seems to suggest that we may not be safe anywhere, not even inside our own skulls: that we could lose control of our core selves and be held responsible for actions orchestrated by someone else. This taps very deep fears, making brainwashing a potently evocative concept. As such, it has been called upon whenever rational explanations seem inadequate: in 1969 to explain the murders committed by Charles Manson's followers; in November 1978 when followers of the preacher and paranoid socialist Jim Jones willingly drank sugar-flavoured cyanide; and after Waco, 9/11 and other mass killings.[12] The pattern recurred after the London bombings, with Mohammad Khan's family insisting that the kind and loving man they knew must have been brainwashed into perpetrating such an appalling crime.[13]

This view of brainwashing, exemplified by Raymond Shaw in *The Manchurian Candidate*, suggests that people can be reprogrammed to commit atrocities.[14] But human brain cells — neurons — are not microchips; the brain is not a meatier type of personal computer, and ideologies are not transferred like software. Giving a name to the pathway from normal to killer may make us feel better as we look for someone to blame, but simply using the word 'brainwashing' is no more helpful than calling the transformation 'the Devil's work'. Both are concepts of last resort; they are not, by themselves, explanations.

Unlike the appeal to personified forces of evil, however, the notion of brainwashing can be reframed in secular, scientific terms as an extreme example of methods for changing beliefs. People do, in certain circumstances, undergo dramatic changes of belief over startlingly short periods of time. Teenagers join cults and reject their friends and family; church converts disavow their former lifestyles; people adopt new ideologies or abandon old ones. Sometimes the new beliefs are frankly bizarre, as in some cults. Sometimes they are lethal: more than 900 people died in the implosion of Jonestown.[15] But the strangeness or moral repugnance of a belief is no bar to understanding how it can be stamped on a person's mind.

Core Techniques of Brainwashing

Descriptions of brainwashing, whether the context be a prisoner-of-war camp, a cult's headquarters or a terrorist training ground, suggest that the processes involved can be analysed in terms of five core techniques: isolation, control, repetition, uncertainty and emotional manipulation. In combination these can generate radical change, as studies of cults illustrate.[16] If terrorism and the barbarisation of warfare have as much in common as this chapter has suggested then the same five core techniques will also be found in the backgrounds of perpetrators of wartime atrocities.

To illustrate how the core techniques operate, it is useful to combine descriptions of brainwashing, and extract their common features into a standardised 'case study'. For convenience let us take the victim to be a young Western man called Adam; the person attempting to brainwash him will be referred to as Mr X. Mr X is the leader of a small group of ideologues committed to violent struggle against the West. (This is a simplification; groups which use brainwashing techniques often have a single clear leader, but it is not essential that they should.) Mr X's aim is to instil in Adam a set of beliefs which will motivate him to become a suicide bomber. The challenge facing Mr X is that the ideology he wants Adam to accept not only contradicts many beliefs widespread in Western societies — to which Adam may not have given much thought — but also goes against some of Adam's own beliefs. Adam may, for instance, have friends who would be considered immoral by Mr X because of their lifestyles, attitudes or personal characteristics such as ethnicity. Whenever Adam enjoys their company his belief that such friendships are acceptable is reinforced by the pleasure he derives from them. Mr X's claims directly challenge that belief.

Military training evokes a similar conflict. Most human beings find the idea of killing someone strongly aversive. Frightened, dying people — especially children — are potent sources of distress to onlookers; they evoke empathy and the urge to help as well as anxiety and fear. Even a corpse is not just inanimate matter, but the object of awe, disgust, relief and guilt: uncanny, buffered with rituals. Yet if soldiers are to function effectively they must believe that in some circumstances killing is, practically and morally, the appropriate course of action.

Military personnel manage this conflict by compartmentalisation: they divide their beliefs and actions into two distinct domains and keep them separate as far as possible. In the civilian domain killing is morally wrong; in the military domain it is a desired goal. Potential targets, and the actions which can be taken against them, are similarly divided into legitimate and illegitimate. The clearer the differences and the smaller the degree of overlap between the domains, the better the soldier's chance of retaining good psychological health long-term.

Compartmentalisation, however, is not an option open to Mr X, because his ideology is a totalist one. That is, one element of Mr X's ideology is a belief about the ideology: that it constitutes not just a collage of true beliefs but Truth absolute and uncompromising, the whole truth and nothing but the truth. Mr X divides the world into good and evil, saved and damned; its people are either with him or against him. They accept his ideology *in toto* or they reject it utterly.[17] Conflicting beliefs and separate domains of thought and action are intolerable affronts to any believer making a totalist claim about his or her views.

Isolation, Control and Repetition

Human brains depend on their senses to maintain internal models of the way the world is. The information used to build those models is ranked as more or less reliable according to its source.[18] Typically, direct perception trumps indirect inference or reporting; ingroup sources ('us') trump signals from outgroup members ('them'); sources with high social status, such as leaders and experts, trump low-status sources; and something touched feels more real to us than something seen or heard, which in turn trumps something thought about or remembered. Our representations of reality are layered, dynamic composites which draw on all these sources to provide us with useful and up-to-date models of the world around us. Beliefs confirmed by incoming information are reinforced and grow stronger, while beliefs contradicted by it tend to weaken. While this allows brains to adapt to new environments, it leaves them vulnerable to manipulation if those environments are under someone else's control.

Isolation and control work by altering the sensory input, the supply of information brains use to check that their models of the world are still effective. Isolation removes a person's access to previously trusted sources; control supplies him or her with new alternatives. Both squeeze their target's mental horizons, narrowing and coarsening the person's worldview. Removing alternative sources makes the new ideology more prominent (as there is less to contrast it with); while emphasising a single, simplistic vision encourages a superficial analysis which takes little account of the messy complexities inherent in political interactions. It also distracts the target from asking difficult questions about how utopia is actually to be achieved.

Jim Jones achieved isolation by extreme means: physically moving himself and his followers to the Guyanan jungle.[19] More recently, Western recruits to the Islamist cause have been sent to remote training camps in (for them) exotic locations such as Afghanistan. Military training likewise uses isolation to remove personnel from civilian society, and warfare itself compounds isolation by increasing the soldier's immersion in a military environment where most of his or her information about the world comes from other soldiers. The contrary moral voices of the civilian domain become less real in war simply because they are less often heard, especially when the soldier is fighting far from home. The Nazi tactic of exporting the 'Jewish problem' beyond Germany's borders, for example, isolated the Germans involved in the Final Solution from their home communities.[20] Other examples of atrocities committed far from home include My Lai, Abu Ghraib and 9/11.

Isolation and control work by changing the environment, and hence the inputs, on the Marxist premise that environment determines consciousness. Our hypothetical brainwasher Mr X will use isolation to wean his victim, Adam, off the Western media's aspirational fantasies. He will use control to give Adam alternative narratives to ponder: narratives which tie the West's selfish greed to global misery, stories of atrocity and barbarisation which mirror those told by the West about its enemies, but in which Westerners become the hated outgroup. Every time Western moral standards slip, of course, the stories told by Mr X and others like him gain more conviction, and consequently more recruits: surely one of many reasons why the laws of war should not be lightly set aside.

Human brains can be thought of as constant gamblers whose waking hours are spent guessing what the world will do next. They construct hypotheses which predict, moment to moment, what reality will offer, and then test these hypotheses against the inputs they actually receive.[21] Hypotheses which repeatedly pass the tests become stable, accepted beliefs about the way the world is. Every time the news from reality confirms them they become stronger, and hence more likely to be trusted as true. This is why Mr X's third technique, repetition, is an effective way to strengthen the new beliefs in Adam's mind. The more often Adam hears the core message, the more comfortable and familiar it will feel to him and the more likely he is to accept it. Cult leaders use the same principle, as did Chinese thought reform: its academies scheduled hours of lectures, discussions and debates, from early in the morning to late at night, for days, weeks, months or even years on end.[22]

Hypotheses which fail the tests should, one might expect, be discarded at once and the stored knowledge used to construct them altered accordingly. In practice, conflicts between a belief and new information are resolved by a process much more like negotiation, in which the brain's representations of both are adjusted so that they become more similar. Importantly, the degree of adjustment depends on the strength of the representation (in brain terms, how active the relevant neurons are). A clearly-visible, unambiguous video of an Iraqi child being shot, for instance, will generate a strong representation in a viewer's brain, both because of the emotions it arouses (of which more below) and because we tend to trust what our eyes tell us unless the context cues us to do otherwise, as an art gallery does. Watching such images, as Mohammad Khan is said to have done, may thus force the watcher to jettison ideals about the West.[23]

Like incoming information from the senses, beliefs are represented in the brain with varying degrees of strength. Most beliefs are weak enough to make them subservient to reality, in that when they clash with incoming information they undergo considerable change, while the sensory information is adjusted only minimally. Some beliefs, however, can become so strongly-held that, when conflict occurs, they 'win', undergoing relatively little adjustment while new information is massively reinterpreted to fit. (An example is some Western leaders' apparently sincerely-held belief, in the period preceding the 2003 Iraq war, that Saddam Hussein possessed weapons of mass destruction.) In other words, our readiness to abandon or change a particular belief depends on how much we have already invested in its being true; that is, how important it is to us.[24] If we care about it, we may choose, like the Beatles' *Nowhere Man*, to reinterpret what our senses tell us and just see what we want to see.

Mr X knows that Adam's reaction to his claims will be affected by the beliefs he already has, some of which he may cherish as his strongest convictions. If these conflict with Mr X's ideology — for example, if Mr X claims that Western culture is entirely worthless and Adam disagrees because he has a passion for Bach — they will limit his power to change Adam's behaviour. Isolation and control may not be effective in this case, since Adam is likely to respond to such pressures by defending his favourite beliefs. He can do this by using compartmentalisation to move them to a domain out of Mr X's reach, denying the ideologue's claim of totalism by refusing to apply his ideology to classical music. Alternatively, Adam may choose to reinterpret what Mr X tells him so that it is consistent with his beliefs, if this is possible — for instance by redefining Bach as a 'world' composer rather than a Western one. Adam may even fail to register the musical implications of what Mr X is saying unless Mr X explicitly points out that Bach was a Westerner. To alter Adam's convictions directly, therefore, Mr X must turn to the other two techniques in his armoury: uncertainty and emotion.

Uncertainty

One of the techniques which made Communist China's thought reform so feared was a process of 'struggle' carried out in small, supervised groups of students or prisoners. One person was accused of, or confessed to, having 'wrong thoughts' or ideologically suspect beliefs. Other group members then showed their loyalty by competing to challenge and condemn the unfortunate victim and reiterate the Communist message. Struggle sometimes led to physical abuse, but even when it did not it was

often destructively effective, especially when combined with interrogation and sleeplessness. As a doctor who experienced it recalled:

You are annihilated ... exhausted ... you can't control yourself, or remember
what you said two minutes before. You feel that all is lost ... You do whatever
they want. You don't pay any more attention to your life or to your handcuffed
arms. You can't distinguish right from left. You just wonder when you will be shot
— and begin to hope for the end of all this.[25]

Uncertainty is a potent source of stress: ask any relative of a murder
victim whose body cannot be found. Whereas isolation, control and
repetition operate on the information we use to check our beliefs, uncertainty attacks the beliefs themselves. We rely on our beliefs because
they guide our interactions with the world; their accuracy can mean
the difference between success and failure, life and death. We have to
trust them because we do not have time to check each one's continuing validity in a changeable universe. Doubting them leads to alarming
insecurity and the search for some certainty, some mental anchor to
make us feel secure again. If Mr X can make Adam doubt beliefs he used
to take for granted, he will look for alternative certainties to replace
them — at which point the brainwasher stands ready to assist, offering
a simple, coherent belief system. Psychological stress increases reliance
on stereotypes and simplistic thinking.[26] If Adam is stressed, therefore,
he will find a totalist ideology more attractive than if he feels at ease and
in control of his circumstances. Challenging his old beliefs is one method
Mr X can use to make him stressed.

The contrast between the complicated, fragmented muddle of the unbe-
liever's life and the pure simplicity of true belief is inevitably emphasised by
ideologues who understand how uncertainty unnerves people, especially
people who already feel that their lives are out of control. Sayyid Qutb,
whose writings heavily influenced modern radical Islam, used the term
jahiliyyah — literally, ignorance — to describe Western existence, a word
with connotations of darkness, complexity and moral chaos. Qutb's West is
not so much the Great Satan as the Great Void: relativist, postmodern and
meaningless, with no simple truths and no absolute authorities in which to
trust. Mr X, wanting Adam to find certainty with him and his group, will
trade on similar associations to demonise his opponents. By contrast, he
will emphasise how clear and simple his own basic rules are by making his
core message brief, coherent and easy to understand and remember.

The rules and regulations of military conduct can seem to offer a similar escape to certainty. It is noticeable, however, that situations which lead to atrocities often confront the perpetrators with high levels of uncertainty. This may stem from ill-defined orders or a failure to spell out what behaviour is or is not morally acceptable; a recent example is the prevarication of senior US officials over how to define torture before, during and after the 2003 Iraq war. Uncertainty may also surround the likely consequences of challenging an order on moral grounds. Some German soldiers and policemen interviewed after the war, for instance, acknowledged that refusing to shoot defenceless citizens did not, in practice, entail serious adverse consequences; but they claimed that at the time when they were first ordered to kill civilians they were not told what the likely consequences would be, leading to 'not so much an objective necessity to obey orders, more of a subjective one'.[27]

Uncertainty may also relate to the military targets, and specifically to whether they inhabit the civilian or the military domain. Terrorists, paramilitaries, partisans or guerrilla fighters may all be difficult to distinguish from civilians. This similarity makes it easier for the category of 'legitimate target', and its associated well-rehearsed behaviours to spread from military and paramilitary opponents to civilians. In the presence of a socially dominant ideology whose core ideals are consonant with military values, such as Nazi anti-Semitism, Khmer Rouge anti-intellectualism or Hutu extremism, even obviously defenceless civilians can be reinterpreted as a cleverly disguised fifth column. All three belief systems emphasised the treachery and cunning of their enemies and the extent to which those enemies could resemble good citizens.

In short, conditions in which uncertainty is high — whether because of unclear orders, poorly reinforced or actively undermined moral conventions, or difficulty in distinguishing legitimate targets — should increase the likelihood of military atrocities.

Emotion

Isolation, control, repetition and uncertainty help Mr X to weaken Adam's old beliefs and familiarise him with a new way of understanding life. But for the transplant to succeed, Mr X will need the last of the five techniques: emotion. Having absorbed the new beliefs, Adam must be motivated to act accordingly.

Emotions, especially strong negative emotions like anger, fear and disgust, enhance survival by facilitating the learning of efficient and appropriate responses to threats.[28] They are associated with specific facial expressions and patterns of bodily activity as well as with changes in brain function.[29] Disgust, for example, involves nausea; fear increases the heart rate; anger is signalled by a direct and wide-eyed glare; and so on. Time is required — more time than it takes a group of neurons to knit together a thought — for these changes to occur and for the body then to return to its previous state.

In *Homo sapiens'* pre-linguistic past, the slower time-scale over which emotions occurred was not a problem as long as they continued to be triggered by threats from the environment. In fact, the discrepancy between fast thoughts and slower emotions was an advantage. The brain's ability to associate simultaneous perceptions allows any stimulus registered while experiencing a strong emotion to become tinged with it, such that the feeling becomes part of what that stimulus means to the person, an effect especially strong for negative emotions like disgust and fear.[30] Thus individuals who had escaped a predator would in future feel fear not only at the sight, sound or smell of the animal itself, but also in the area where the encounter happened and in similar areas. Consequently they would be warier in places where predators were likely to lurk, thereby increasing their survival chances.

With the development of symbolic thinking, however, the link between immediate threat and emotional response was changed. Symbols, unlike the simpler representations triggered in a brain by sensory information, need have no obvious connection with the object, event, concept or emotion to which they refer.[31] This detachment from sensory perceptions allows them to be manipulated irrespective of what is currently happening, as any daydreamer knows. The links between symbols and their referents are learned from other ingroup members, most dramatically in the childhood acquisition of language. Mr X can thus use symbols, such as descriptions or images of atrocities, to trigger extremely strong negative emotions in Adam, regardless of the fact that Adam is not under any direct threat. By mentioning the West at the same time, Mr X can use association to taint Adam's view of his home society and enhance or even create prejudice against it.[32] The same pattern holds for positive emotions, except that here the association is with Mr X, his group and his ideas. When Mr X speaks of peace and social justice, of caring for the poor and giving the oppressed their freedom, he will emphasise his group's beliefs as well. Such associations sharpen the totalist distinction between ingroup and outgroup, an activation and reinforcement of social boundaries which is crucial if beliefs are to translate into actions. Charles Tilly, for example, notes the 'prominence of 'us-them' categorical distinctions in all varieties of collective violence'.[33]

On the assumption, noted earlier, that the similarities between terrorist and military atrocities reflect similar underlying mechanisms, one would expect wartime barbarisation also to involve emotional manipulation: the arousal of strong negative emotions directed against the victim group coupled with the fostering of positive feelings towards one's colleagues. Considering the wider cultural environment which provides the political justifications for warfare, the language used by ideological leaders to describe their enemies can be extremely emotive. Nazi propaganda is noted for its vivid biomedical metaphors of disease, contamination and corruption, likening Jewishness to an infection or cancer and its 'carriers' to rats, maggots, lice and bacilli; but similar language also permeates perpetrator rhetoric in other atrocities, such as the Rwandan genocide.[34] Military training itself has often involved deliberate attempts at emotion manipulation, although these may be met with scepticism by soldiers with combat experience, 'profoundly aware of the discrepancy between the demonized pictures they were shown of their foe while in training and those they encountered in battle'.[35] However, the emotions aroused, while they need to be extreme in order to produce a suicide bomber, need affect only a subset of soldiers. As Christopher Browning notes, 'A core of eager and committed men, aided by an even larger block of men who complied with the policies of the regime more out of situational and organisational rather than ideological factors, was sufficient to commit genocide' in the Second World War.[36]

When Mr X evokes emotions in Adam, his aim is not to ensure that in future Adam will be overcome by fury or loathing whenever someone mentions the West. That would be counter-productive, as strong emotions could impair his efficiency and perhaps be detectable by his intended targets. The advantages of introducing Adam to Mr X's grievances via provocative videos rather than starting him off with actual combat is that his reactions, while intensely emotional, are unlikely to be extreme enough to induce the kinds of debilitating flashbacks seen in post-traumatic stress disorder. This allows the emotions in question to fulfil their evolutionary function: learning from experience.

Emotions enhance Adam's learning by greatly strengthening whichever beliefs he is thinking about at the time he experiences the emotions. As noted earlier, repetition of a stimulus also strengthens the mental representation of that stimulus; strong emotions enhance this effect considerably. What this means in practice is that Adam becomes more likely to act on the strengthened beliefs. Neurons representing stronger beliefs have stronger interconnections, and this makes it easier for the nerve signals that flow through them to reach areas of Adam's brain responsible for triggering behaviour. However, as the representations become stronger Adam's responses become faster, more efficient and less emotional, a process known as automatisation.[37] The gradual 'numbing' of perpetrators described, for example, in the Holocaust may reflect similar processes.[38]

Brainwashing, Terrorism and the Barbarisation of Warfare

Brainwashing, in the scientific sense described here, is an extreme method of changing beliefs. It combines the use of isolation, control, repetition, uncertainty and emotions to alter a person's perceptions of the world, challenge preconceived ideas, and supply an apparently attractive ideological alternative. These five core techniques can be found in the backgrounds of terrorists, including suicide bombers, and members of destructive cults. They may similarly shape the perpetrators who commit military atrocities. Where soldiers are isolated from their home communities; when their access to information, particularly information about their military opponents, is limited, while ignorance and uncertainty are rife; and when their wider culture and their immediate military environment both repeatedly proclaim the same core messages of us-them hostility — then the stresses and emotions of war can and will combine with these other factors to increase the likelihood of barbarisation occurring.

Human beings exhibit three unfortunate tendencies in stressful, emotive situations such as warfare. They fall back on simplistic thinking and stereotypes; they trust messages from their own leaders more than usual while distrusting information from the enemy more; and they forget to take into account the fact that their own realities are partial and fallible. In short, they cling to known and trusted beliefs and are less inclined to seek out new information. This behaviour, which is protective when the threat is immediate and direct, can be dangerously counter-productive when threats are symbolic, as they often are in situations which lead to atrocities. As long as the human response to symbolic threats is to retreat into totalism the barbarisation of warfare will continue.

EPILOGUE

REFLECTIONS ON WAR AND BARBARISM

Jay Winter

The conduct of war has undeniably changed since 1914. The exponential increase in the lethality and range of weapons has meant that war-related deaths number in the millions, and that over time, the majority have been civilians. Given levels of male mobilisation in wartime, the extension of the killing fields to cities and towns both democratised suffering and brought about a rough gender balance in terms of loss of life in wartime. No one knows whether more men than women died during the Second World War. Part of the point is that the question no longer mattered. War was capable of killing everybody, as both the Holocaust and the nuclear attacks on Hiroshima and Nagasaki proved.

What made war change was not so much a difference in degree of ferocity but in kind. Genocide has precedents before 1914, but the twentieth century was the age of war-related genocide. Here we come to a central element in the story, one worth emphasising in an epilogue to this volume. What has made war more destructive than before is the intersection of two separate vectors: one arising out of international conflict and another arising out of civil war. Each vector became increasingly lethal over the century; and their conflation has been multiplicative in terms of destructive power. International war among industrialised countries precipitating or precipitated by a civil war has brought about a new form of conflict, which over the century we have termed 'total war.' It is warfare with barbarism at its core.

254

The term 'total war' is more about a process than a product. No war is ever fully 'total', but the mix of civil war and international conflict lets loose forces which make each more lethal and more savage, and which undermine the chances of terminating either one. The totalising effects of twentieth century warfare, which certainly are with us still, are asymptotic; they approach, in the manner of Xeno's paradox, but never reach totality. Near enough is bad enough.

Two additional ideological elements helped ensure that warfare and civil war in the twentieth century turned more toxic and more barbaric than ever before. The first was the widespread circulation of ideas about the survival of the fittest and the struggle for domination, forms of vulgar and debased Darwinism. As Richard Overy shows above, this strain of belief was central to much of Hitler's thinking. If the German people were 'weak' enough to lose the war, he opined, they did not deserve to survive. Biologism clearly underlay anti-Semitism and anti-Slavic beliefs on the Eastern front in the Second World War. Racism did the same in the Pacific theatre. This was not only true of Japanese attitudes towards the Chinese, but also of American attitudes towards the Japanese.

The second pollutant of both war and civil war was the language of class conflict. In the Soviet case, as Amir Wiener has noted, this pillar of Soviet terror stood as a bulwark of the war against the German invasion. And in varying forms, the language of class hatred and class struggle informed virtually every partisan or resistance movement in Western Europe too, not to mention the long and vicious triangulation of conflict between the Communist party, the Kuomintang, and the Japanese in China.

War Cultures

In this context it may be useful to introduce some elements of French historiography to the debate. In the literature of the 1914-18 war, Stéphane Audoin-Rouzeau and Annette Becker have developed the term 'war culture'. They take the term to mean 'a collection of representations of the conflict that crystallised into a system of thought which gave the war its deep significance'. Intrinsic to 'war culture' was the notion that the fight was between the civilised world and the barbarians, hatred for whom grew from the very first months of the conflict. 'Deep down,' they write, 'the 1914-1918 "war culture" harboured a true drive to "exterminate" the enemy'.[1] In effect, the emergence and efflorescence of 'war culture' account for the consent of populations to carry on wars of unprecedented murderousness as well as for their demonisation and dehumanisation of the enemy. From this perspective, the Second World War deepened and amplified what was already there.

The thesis advanced by Audoin-Rouzeau and Becker about 'war culture' carries only part of the truth. The first reason for hesitancy about this interpretation is that it is too singular. There were multiple 'war cultures', inflected by class, region, religion, geographical proximity to the fighting, memories of earlier conflicts, and so on. Secondly, it exaggerates the extent to which soldiers and civilians shared the same assumptions about what they were enduring. Soldiers insisted on their own 'war cultures', and made a great deal of fuss about being different from those who had no idea what trench warfare was like. And among those who fought, there was a vast range of views about the enemy. Only a minority of those who served actually killed someone; the weight of artillery ensured that killing was more anonymous than ever before. Only a minority of those who killed enjoyed it, or relished the chance to exterminate the enemy. Such people were there, but to generalise their attitudes to those of armies as a whole, let alone populations as a whole, is to fall into what I would term the Goldhagen trap, the treatment of cultural history as a dense fog covering the ground of historical reality so fully that no real human beings can be seen. Thirdly, soldiers served and put up with the unpleasantness of war for myriad reasons; some did so out of belief; others, out of inertia; others still out of fear of the military police just behind the lines. Getting out of the mess was no easy matter. Better in most cases to justify what they were going through, out of loyalty to the men on their right and left or loyalty to their families rather than commitment to any sense of fighting for civilisation against the barbarians, however this view was configured.

What remains valuable about the thesis of 'war cultures', though, is that it enables us to understand better the linkage between international war and civil war in the twentieth century. That linkage, I argue, is the source of the increasingly barbarous character of armed conflict.

International War, Civil War and Genocide

Let us consider two of the most heavily documented instances of these linkages. First there is the case of the Armenian genocide in Turkey beginning in 1915. The reverses in the early months of the war suffered by the Turkish army on the Russian front helped precipitate a plan carried out by military and paramilitary agents of the regime to deport and exterminate the Armenian population of eastern Turkey. Their aim was to wipe out this 'fifth column' and to thereby stabilise a regime which feared dismemberment of Turkey itself. Thus the two vectors of international war and civil war combined. International conflict of a long-standing kind about the territorial integrity of Turkey transformed into genocide domestic conflict of a long-standing kind about the place of ethnic minorities within the new Turkish state.

To use the term 'civil war' is to describe the collision between Turkish national aspirations and Armenian survival in a way which Turkish politicians time and again have deployed to deny the genocide. That is the opposite of my view. There is a clear parallel here, not in terms of Hitler's famous adage 'who remembers the Armenians?', but in terms of the way the Holocaust emerged out of the concatenation of international war and civil war, made more toxic by the language of biologism central to Nazi ideology.[2]

I want to consider in more detail a second instance where the notion of barbarism is best understood through an appreciation of the intersection of war and civil war. Consider this interpretation, controversial to be sure, about the unfolding of Hitler's decision to kill the Jews.[3] On 15 August 1941, Hitler held a series of meetings with the high command — Himmler, Goebbels, Heydrich — in Berlin, and then issued a series of decisive orders. The first was to reverse the strategic objectives of the military campaign against Russia. It was just two months after the 22 June invasion of the Soviet Union, and in that brief period, a very large portion of European Russia and the fruits of Stalin's five-year plans of industrialisation had been swept up and placed under Nazi control. The German army's northern command was poised to launch an assault on Moscow. Then on 15 August, the order came through to pull back from Moscow, and to turn south. The Army High Command was stupefied. They begged Hitler to reverse his order. Moscow, they said, was within their reach. The Red Army could not hold out against the weight of German artillery and mobile infantry power. Once taken, Moscow would be the place where Hitler would dictate terms to Stalin, and then, as in the First World War, when Lenin had capitulated to the Kaiser's army, the German war machine could turn west. It would soon be Britain's turn. Standing alone, Britain would make peace, removing the last remaining obstacle to total victory in the war.

On 15 August 1941, Hitler refused to listen to these arguments. He had made up his mind. He had set a new course. Northern command stood down its units poised to initiate the thrust towards Moscow. The weight of German armour shifted south and east, towards the oil-rich regions of the Caucasus. The march to Stalingrad had begun.

It was not only military strategy that Hitler reconfigured on 15 August 1941. It was also the moment when crucial elements of the 'Final Solution of the Jewish problem' were set in motion. In secret meetings with Himmler and Heydrich, Hitler ordered that Jews wear the yellow star, that efforts to concentrate them in Eastern Europe be intensified, and that the killing of Jews — until then conducted by rear group units of the German army, the notorious *Einsatzgruppen* — be turned into a systematic, comprehensive, industrial operation.

What is the connection between these two decisions of 15 August 1941? The crucial and decisive link between military operations in the east and the extermination of the Jews was the publication in Washington on 14 August of what we now term the Atlantic Charter, a statement of common aims signed by Winston Churchill and Franklin Delano Roosevelt. Here is its sixth and critical point in the Charter; the two heads of government affirmed that:

after the final destruction of the Nazi tyranny, they hope to see established a peace which will afford to all nations the means of dwelling in safety within their own boundaries, and which will afford assurance that all the men in all lands may live out their lives in freedom from fear and want;...(my italics)

We now know for certain that Hitler received, read and annotated a transcript of this document in the early morning of 15 August 1941. He was furious. Reports from his doctor and his closest aides indicate that he went through one of his periodic rages, marked by a mixture of seclusion and introspection on one hand and violent, apocalyptic outbursts on the other hand. It was at this precise moment that he decided to turn the

German army around, and it is at this precise moment, according to this interpretation, that he set in motion the extermination of all the Jews of Europe trapped behind the front lines from the Pyrenees to the Caucasus.

Let me qualify this argument. There is no document in Hitler's hand dated 15 August 1941, saying to Himmler, now we will kill all the Jews. This new interpretation is circumstantial and contextual; it is located in the geometry of power rather than in a single piece of evidence. But I believe that it makes sense, and does so in a way illustrating the braiding together of international conflict and civil war, in this case the war against the Jews.

What Hitler saw in the Atlantic Charter was that whatever happened in the Soviet Union, whether or not Moscow was taken, whether or not Stalin sued for peace, the Second World War would go on and on, just as the First World War had done. The Atlantic Charter stated that Britain and the United States would carry on the fight until Nazi tyranny had been defeated and until a new order in Europe had established. This was four months *before* Pearl Harbor, well before American entry into the war was certain. And this seems to be what made Hitler furious, because even a victory over the Soviet Union would not present him with a decisive advantage over Britain, which now — as Churchill and Roosevelt stated unequivocally — had American power to back it up.

We might speculate that in 1941 Hitler returned to the First World War, and realised that a nightmare was returning. Just as in 1917, when the United States entered the war and bolstered the shaky and stretched Allied war effort in significant ways, so in 1941, Roosevelt and Churchill promised that the Second World War would be just that — a world war, with the might of America arrayed against the Germans. It would be a war that would go on and on whatever happened in Russia.

And for this transformation of a euphoric moment — the period of gigantic victories in European Russia from June to August 1941 — into a vista of unending war, Hitler blamed the Jews. In 1939, he had made a promise and a prophesy. If, he told German army officers, the Jews succeed in provoking a second world war, then whatever its outcome, they would pay the price. That price was extermination. Now, on 15 August 1941, and in the subsequent three and a half years, Hitler decided to fulfil that prophecy.

One of the attractive features of this new interpretation of the onset of the Holocaust is that it bypasses the question as to whether Hitler's plan to kill the Jews of Europe was built into his programme from its earliest days or whether it was a product of the conquest of Poland and European Russia, and with it, of the heartland of Eastern European Jewry. This debate has gone round and round without any resolution. Now we have an alternative. Hitler spent much time thinking about how to rid Europe of its Jewish 'cancer', and flirted over years with ideas of deportation to extra-European destinations. There is little doubt that his long-term and deep-seated objective was to remove Jews from Europe. When the Second World War broke out, these notions of solving the Jewish problem were not at the top of his agenda. Mass emigration was no longer a realistic option, since it required at least the tacit cooperation of countries with which Germany was now at war.

The invasion of Russia in June 1941 opened new possibilities and posed new problems. Now, with millions more Jews in his hands, Hitler could act against them with impunity. Jews and communists were shot by the thousands from the earliest days of Operation Barbarossa. But it seems clear that his approach to the Jewish problem was that he would 'solve' it — whatever that meant — *after* the war.

Here is the critical meaning of the Atlantic Charter. It convinced Hitler that there would be no 'after the war' for years and years. Just as the entry of America into the First World War in 1917 had created a vision of unending conflict for the German army, so Hitler saw the Second World War going on and on into a grey and bloody future. It was this transformation of the war that made him see that it no longer mattered whether or not he forced a Soviet capitulation, as Hindenberg and Ludendorff had done to the Bolsheviks at Brest-Litovsk in March 1918. The war would go on anyway. And that is why his approach to the Jewish problem changed. It would be 'solved' now not after the war, but during it. Intention turned into operational thinking. Thus what Hitler did with his armies was to draw an iron line around his European conquests, from Norway to the Caucasus, and then turn that whole area into a killing field for the European Jews.

Consider the following small, but significant, steps taken in the wake of this momentous decision. There are many minor indications that a new phase of the war had begun. On 15 August 1941 a meeting was held at the

Ministry of Propaganda in Berlin. The minister's director, Leopold Gut-
terer, was in the chair. He stated that the Jewish problem had to be solved
then and there because soldiers on leave were furious to see Jews still
strolling around the capital. Getting rid of them would help alleviate the
housing shortage too. An estimated 70,000 Jews were still left in Berlin.
Of these about 20,000 were working. 'All the rest should be checked out
to find which of them are capable of working, and the others should be
cast out [*abkarren*] into Russia'. Further restrictions on Jewish rations and
on Jewish travel — only in special trolley cars — were mooted. Then,
as the minutes show, these officials were prepared to go one giant step
further. Goebbels' deputy noted in bold type: 'the best thing would be
to kill them altogether'. It was time, they decided, to designate a special
sign, to facilitate the separation of the Jews from the rest. That was the
Yellow Badge or Star. Within two weeks, a regulation stipulated that all
Jews in the Reich had to wear the Star.

Even more ominously, Goebbels met with Hitler and received word
that there was a new order of priorities in the war effort. On 15 August,
the Führer told Goebbels and Heydrich that he would now approve the
release of rolling stock and train consignments to help deport Jews to the
east, 'where', in Hitler's words, 'they would be dealt with in a harsher
climate'. This surprised both men, who had understood that Hitler's intention was to deal with the Jews after the war. Now the organisation
of human shipments to the east was to be started during the war, and
right away. The next week, on 23 August 1941, Heinrich Himmler issued an order that 'the emigration of Jews to be stopped immediately'.
There would be no escape abroad. The next day Alfred Rosenberg sent
his deputy Otto Bräutigam to obtain Hitler's approval for the deportation
of Jews from the Reich as a retaliation for the Soviet deportation of Volga
Germans to the Urals. Hitler approved the idea, subject to discussions
with the Foreign Office, which took place the following day. Foreign Office records provide the same story; surprise at the Führer's reversal of
his earlier line. Clearly everyone knew that there was a new agenda in
the east.

This interpretation puts the Wannsee meeting of 20 January 1942 in an
entirely different light. There, in the suburbs of Berlin, Adolf Eichmann
and other second-order bureaucrats began to work out the modalities of
murder. These men were simply registering and working out a decision

that had been taken six months before by Hitler and Hitler alone, furious at how the war was unfolding, furious at history, furious at the Jews, whom he blamed for this turn of affairs. Only by locating this chain of events in the intersection of international and civil war, braiding together his hatred of the Jews with his thinking about military planning in the east and geopolitics in the west, can we understand fully the critical turning point leading to the extermination of the Jews of Europe. In the wake of the Atlantic Charter, Hitler turned the Second World War into the war against the Jews.

It is tempting to offer a psychological interpretation of this turn in Hitler's strategy and outlook. His experiences of the First World War were certainly traumatic. He was a brave and decorated soldier, operating as a runner on the Western Front. It was one of the most dangerous positions that any soldier could occupy. He was gassed near the end of the war, and, temporarily blinded, he received the news of Germany's defeat in hospital. He cried, he said, only twice in his life: when his mother died and when he learned of Germany's defeat. If, he fumed, only some 20,000 Jews had been gassed during the war, the defeat, all the sufferings of the German army, and the deaths of two million men, could have been avoided.

In 1941, he returned to that moment. And this time, he was the one who would inflict the suffering. He was the one who would make the Jews know what it was like to be gassed. He was the one who would blind his victims and make them choke on bitter tears. To be sure, there is an element of conjecture in this interpretation. I prefer to view the evidence in another context. Hitler's thinking and his entire outlook make no sense outside the context of the totalising effects of industrial war in the twentieth century. What Hitler was doing, as he said time and again, was to wage total war, a kind of war which completely obliterated the distinction between civilian and military targets or any legal limits whatsoever. That barrier had been broken long before the outbreak of the Second World War. As noted above, the Turks had demolished it in their genocide of the Armenian population. The U-boat commanders had broken it, when they attacked civilian shipping in the First World War. And the Allies had broken it, when they continued their blockade of Germany after the Armistice of 11 November 1918, and thereby made war on civilians, while the new regime tried to come to terms with the disaster bequeathed to it by the Kaiser and the German military clique that had brought Germany to disaster.

What Hitler did was to take a new form of barbarism — the barbarism imbedded in total war — and turn it into an instrument to carry out a unique crime. That intrinsic otherness, strangeness, ineffable quality of the Holocaust precludes its firm location within any comparative framework. What is relevant here is the way the unfolding of the war against the Jews disclosed the complex process of barbarisation, bringing together different levels of armed conflict — those against nations, those against the internal enemies of warring powers, and those against Resistance fighters acting to overthrow the occupier.

What happened in the unfolding of the Holocaust is but an extreme instance of what happened in every occupied country of Europe. In each one, a vertical conflict between occupied and occupier was framed by a horizontal conflict between nation states. The longer the horizontal, international conflict went on, the worse the vertical, domestic conflict became. Partisans and Resistance fighters carried out two wars at once: one against the occupier, and another against those parts of their own population who were implicated in the workings of the occupation or who used the occupation to gain power, settle scores and ruthlessly eliminate their old and new domestic enemies. The history of Vichy France provides abundant evidence about these two vectors of conflict; so does the history of every other occupied country in the Second World War.

Warfare is a State of Being

What are the implications of this argument for the history of twentieth century warfare? Does this set of evidence support the notion of the 'barbarisation' of warfare in the era of total war? I believe the answer is 'yes. Let us consider for heuristic purposes a rough typology of barbarism in warfare since 1914. I take barbarisation to mean changes along three lines:

1. The expansion of the space for unnecessary, gratuitous, and irrational violence against both enemy combatants and non-combatants. The notion of gratuitous conduct is based on the view that the achievement of military goals in and of themselves requires a degree of violence, which

when exceeded renders the acts barbarous and the men and women who perform them barbaric.

2. The intensification of the ferocity of combat to the point that no one can escape from the field of battle or of aerial bombardment, even by surrendering. Thus without any possibility of surrender, the ferocity of war continues unnecessarily, at times until one side slaughters the other. Battles end, as Ferguson argues, later than they need to. To limit unnecessary killing, soldiers must believe that surrender is not suicide.

3. The transformation of the norms whereby war is fought as an extension of politics into norms through which war is fought as an extension of ideologies of extermination. Thus the end of 'barbarised' war is not primarily the achievement of political goals, as Clausewitz posited, but the achievement of the annihilation of the enemy not only on the field of battle but behind the lines, in their homes, their factories, their villages.

My argument is that these three deleterious changes in the history of warfare arose out of the braiding together of international conflict and civil war. Nothing in the history of warfare after 1945 persuades me that this story is over. Let us pause for a moment to consider contemporary affairs, reference to which a number of contributors have made.

The intervention of the United States and other Western states in the civil war within Islam fits the model of the barbarism inherent in total war. In this case, though, we have clear echoes of the West's colonial and imperial past. The language of civilisation and barbarism is with us again. Anyone who glances at Conrad's *Lord Jim* or his *Heart of Darkness*, both published at the turn of the twentieth century, will encounter a discursive field vividly present a century later.

To be sure, the context is different now. The emergence of fundamentalist Islam as a force trying to save the Islamic faith from disaster antedated American military intervention in the Middle East by decades. To radicals who believed that the clock was set at one minute to midnight, that Islam — what they took to be 'true' Islam — was dying, their only hope was to overthrow those corrupt Muslim regimes — Saudi Arabia, Egypt, Algeria — being propped up by Western interests and Western power. Barbaric methods were and are used by both sides in this Islamic civil war. When al-Qaida moved to cut off the American hand propping up these regimes through attacking the United States in the World Trade Center, its operatives were fully engaged in the barbarism of total war.

The only difference is that this war is asymmetric, in that one side is an industrial power, and the other is a loosely-organised trans-national movement. In effect, the United States agreed to the terms of the conflict, accepting, indeed relishing, the chance to fight barbarism with barbarism. Civilian casualties, devastation, daily cruelties, the loss of civil liberties both in the United States and elsewhere, were a trivial cost in this war; torture was inevitable, and so was the dissemination of the notion of war without end.

What links the two world wars with the current history of conflict in the 'war against terror' is the notion that warfare is a state of being, not a state of conflict; shades of vulgar Darwinism indeed. Now is a time when complacency is suicidal. You may not be interested in war, so Trotsky is supposed to have remarked, but it is very interested in you. For many reasons, therefore, it is essential that we continue the thinking presented in this volume, and develop a fuller understanding of the barbarism of total war, because this phenomenon is not only our past, but our future as well.

NOTES

1. THE BARBARISATION OF WARFARE: A USER'S MANUAL

[1] ICTY press release, CC/PIO/026-E, The Hague, 16 November 1995; see also Jan Willem Honig and Norbert Both, *Srebrenica: a Record of a War Crime* (London, 1996)

[2] See Iris Chang's important book, *The Rape of Nanking: the Forgotten Holocaust of World War II* (New York, 1997). Chang, whose own grandparents were survivors recounts the massacre with understandable outrage. So sickening was the spectacle, she writes in the book's introduction, that even Nazis in the city were horrified by what took place.

[3] See Philip Gourevitch, *We Wish to Inform you that Tomorrow We will be Killed with our Families* (London, 1999); Jean Hatzfeld, *Machete Season: the Killers in Rwanda Speak* (London, 2005).

[4] Omer Bartov, *The Eastern Front, 1941-45, German Troops and the Barbarisation of Warfare* (Basingstoke, 1985); see also Catherine Merridale, *Ivan's War: the Red Army 1939-45* (London, 2005); Anonymous, 'A Woman in Berlin: Eight Weeks in the Conquered City' (New York, 2005).

[5] See Antony Beevor's magisterial *Stalingrad and Berlin: the Downfall, 1945* (London, 1998 and 2002).

[6] See David Anderson, *Histories of the Hanged: Britain's Dirty War in Kenya and the End of Empire* (London, 2005); Caroline Elkins, *Britain's Gulag: the Brutal End of Empire in Kenya* (London, 2005), and a review of both books entitled 'English Atrocities' by John Newsinger, *New Left Review* (March-April 2005).

[7] See James Tatum, *The Mourner's Song: War and Remembrance from the Iliad to Vietnam* (Chicago, 2004).

[8] See Michael Ignatieff, 'The Gods of War', *New York Review of Books* (9 October 1997); see also Vannevar Bush, 'Can Men Live Without War?', *Atlantic Monthly* (vol.197, no. 2 February 1956).

[9] Barbara Ehrenreich, *Blood Rites: Origins and the History of the Passions of War* (New York, 1997); Joanna Bourke, *An Intimate History of Killing: Face-to-Face Killing in Twentieth Century Warfare* (London, 1999); Philippe Delmas, *The Rosy*

Future of War (New York, 1997).

10 See Chris Hedges, *War is a Force that Gives us Meaning* (New York, 2002), p.14.

11 William Broyles, 'Why Men Love War' in *Esquire* magazine (1984) and in Walter Capps (ed.), *The Vietnam Reader* (New York, 1991).

12 See, for instance, the last piece *Wall Street Journal* journalist Matt Pottinger wrote before he left the newspaper in 2005 to join the US Marines. 'Friends ask me,' writes Pottinger in a piece entitled 'Mightier than the pen', 'if I worry about going from a life of independent thought and action to a life of hierarchy and teamwork. At the moment, I find that appealing because it means being part of something bigger than I am. As for how different it's going to be, that too has its appeal because it's the opposite of what I've been doing up to now.' *Wall Street Journal Europe*, 15 December 2005.

13 *The Iliad*, trans. Robert Fagles (New York, 1990), Book 19, line 179.

14 See Eric Hobsbawm, 'Barbarism: a User's Guide', *Interesting Times: a Twentieth-Century Life* (New York, 2003).

15 Jonathan Glover, *Humanity: a Moral History of the Twentieth Century* (London, 1999), p.6.

16 Michael Ignatieff, *The Warrior's Honor: Ethnic War and the Modern Conscience* (London, 1998), p.18. See also Eric Hobsbawm, 'War and Peace in the 20th Century', *London Review of Books*, 21 February 2002.

17 See Geoffrey Best's classic *Humanity in Warfare: the Modern History of the International Law of Armed Conflicts* (London, 1980); for a more contemporary take on the subject see Rupert Smith's *The Utility of Force: the Art of War in the Modern World* (London, 2005), pp.377-83. However, the best available treatment of the history of laws of war is a collection edited by Michael Howard, George Andreopoulos and Mark R. Shulman, *The Laws of War: Constraints on Warfare in the Western World* (London, 1997).

18 John Keegan, *A History of Warfare* (London, 2004); see also Keegan's magisterial *The Face of Battle: a Study of Agincourt, Waterloo and the Somme* (London, 2004).

19 See Caroline Moorehead's essay, 'The Warrior Children' in the *New York Review of Books* (vol.52, no. 19, 1 December 2005).

20 P.W. Singer, *Children at War* (New York, 2005).

21 See Alephonsion Deng, Benson Deng and Benjamin Ajak, *They Poured Fire on Us from the Sky: the True Story of Three Lost Boys from Sudan* (New York, 2005); Richard Maclure and Myriam Denov, ' "I Didn't Want to Die So I Joined Them": Structuration and the Process of Becoming Boy Soldiers in Sierra Leone', *Terrorism and Political Violence* (vol.18, no. 1, 2006) pp.119-36.

22 See *The Scars of Death: Children Abducted by the Lord's Resistance Army in Uganda*, a report by Human Rights Watch, September 1997.

23 Cited in Michael Ignatieff, *The Warrior's Honor*, p.162.

24 Slavenka Drakulić, *They Would Never Hurt a Fly: War Criminals on Trial in The*

Hague (London, 2004), p.165.

25   ibid, p.166.

26   ibid, p.168.

27   See Christopher Browning, *Ordinary Men: Reserve Battalion 101 and the Final Solution in Poland* (New York, 1992).

28   This paragraph draws heavily on Jason Epstein's essay, 'Always Time to Kill', *New York Review of Books*, 4 November 2004.

29   Ervin Staub, *The Roots of Evil: the Origins of Genocide and Other Group Violence* (Cambridge, 1989), p.26. Staub argues rather emphatically that 'ordinary psychological processes and normal, common human motivations and certain basic but not inevitable tendencies in human thought and feeling' are the 'primary sources' of the human capacity for mass destruction of human life. p.126.

30   *Humanity*, Glover, p.131; see also Joanna Bourke, *Fear: a Cultural History* (London, 2005).

31   Sebastian Faulks, 'The Creation of Hell', *Sunday Telegraph Magazine*, 25 August 2005; on what drove men to atrocities in the First World War see John Keegan's classic *The First World War* (London, 2001) and Chapter 12 in Niall Ferguson's 'The Death Instinct: Why Men Fought' in his *The Pity of War* (London, 1998), pp.339-66.

32   Glover, *A Moral History*, p.50.

33   On psychological distancing and dehumanisation see John W. Dower's *War Without Mercy: Race and Power in the Pacific War* (London, 1986), pp.3-15.

34   Michael Bilton and Kevin Sim, *Four Hours in My Lai* (London, 1993), p.7.

35   Cited in a *Financial Times Magazine* review essay on Jean Hatzfeld's book on Rwanda, *Machete Season: the Killers in Rwanda Speak*, 16 July 2005.

36   Lebanon was locked in a civil war from 1975 to 1990 between dozens of rival militias that were backed in shifting alliances with foreign governments. The Palestinian Liberation Organisation (PLO), which was by then based in the refuge camps of Beirut and southern Lebanon, soon became involved in the long-running tensions between the Lebanese Muslims and the Maronite community. The rival groups fought against each other and then among themselves, and when the war ended, 15 years later, at least 100,000 were dead and another 100,000 seriously injured.

37   See Anatol Lieven's study, *Chechnya: Tombstone of Russian Power*, (London, 1998); Anna Politkovskaya, *A Dirty War: a Russian Reporter in Chechnya* (London, 2001) and Anne Nivat, *Chienne de Guerre: a Woman Reporter Behind the Lines of the War in Chechnya* (New York, 2001).

38   Mark Bowden, 'Lessons of Abu Ghraib' in *Atlantic Monthly* (July/August 2004).

39   Susan Sontag, 'What have we done?', *The Guardian*, 24 May 2005.

40   On the new face of American war see Evan Wright, *Generation Kill: the Story*

Bravo Company in Iraq- Marines Who Deal in Bullets, Bombs and Ultraviolence (London, 2004); see also Anthony Swofford, *Jarhead: a Soldier's Story of Modern War* (London, 2003).

41   Bowden, 'Lessons of Abu Ghraib'.

42   On the-end-justifies-the-means approach of the Bush administration in conducting its 'war on terror' strategy see Mark Danner, *Torture and Truth: America, Abu Ghraib and the War on Terror* (London, 2005); Karen J. Greenberg and Joshua L. Dragel (eds), *The Torture Papers: the Road to Abu Ghraib* (Cambridge, 2005); John Yoo, *The Powers of War and Peace: the Constitution and Foreign Affairs after 9/11* (Chicago, 2005).

43   Ian Buruma, 'Just Following Orders', *Financial Times Magazine*, 3 July 2004; See also Joanna Bourke, 'Torture as pornography', *The Guardian*, 7 May 2004 and Katherine Viner, 'The Sexual Sadism of Our Culture, in Peace and in War', *The Guardian*, 22 May 2004.

44   On America's flagrant violation of the established international codes of behaviour concerning prisoners of war see Philippe Sands' critique *Lawless World: America and the Making and Breaking of Global Rules* (London, 2005); Michael Byers, 'A New Type of War: Blair and Bush's attempt to change international law', *London Review of Books* (6 May 2004); and David Scheffer, 'Terror suspects are entitled to legal protection', *Financial Times*, 5 December 2005.

45   Graydon Carter, *What We've Lost: How the Bush Administration Has Curtailed Freedoms, Ravaged the Environment and Damaged America and the World* (London, 2004).

46   Francis Fukuyama, 'The Bush Doctrine, Before and After', *Financial Times,* 10 October 2005.

47   See Anatol Lieven, 'A Second Chance to Learn the Lesson of Vietnam', *Financial Times*, 8 June 2004.

48   See David Rose's *Guantanamo: America's War on Human Rights* (London, 2004), chapter 4 in particular; see also Jan Banning's 'Traces of War: Dutch and Indonesian Survivors', www.openDemocracy.net, 19 August 2005. The photojournalist Jan Banning listens and portrays Dutch and Indonesian prisoners-of-war under forced labour who were denied even minimal rights by their Japanese captors during the Pacific war of 1941-5.

49   See Human Rights Watch report on torture in Iraq entitled 'Leadership Failure: Firsthand Accounts of Torture of Iraqi Detainees by US Army's 82nd Airborne Division', 25 September 2005. Available at hrw.org/reports/2005/us0905

50   'Orders to Torture', *The Nation*, 7 June 2004. On America's Iraqi adventure see George Parker, *The Assassin's Gate: America in Iraq* (New York, 2005) and Andrew J. Bacevich, *The New American Militarism: How Americans Are Seduced by War* (New York, 2005); see also Tony Judt's polemical essay 'The New World

Order', *New York Review of Books*, 14 July 2005.

51   For a polemical take on the Iraq war see John Gray's essay 'Power and Vainglory: Iraq Isn't Another Vietnam – It's Much Worse' in *The Independent*, 19 May 2004; see also David Runciman, *The Politics of Good Intentions: History, Fear and Hypocrisy in the New World Order* (Oxford, 2006).

52   Sheik Mohammed Bashir, Friday prayers, Um al-Oura, Baghdad, 11 June 2004. Cited in Edward Coy's *Washington Post* article 'Iraqis Put Contempt for Troops on Display', 12 June 2004.

53   See Moazzam Begg, *Enemy Combatant: a British Muslim's Journey to Guantanamo and Back* (London, 2006). Moazzam Begg, a former Wolverhampton University law student, was arrested in 2002 in Pakistan, where he was helping set up education programmes for children, in the panic-stricken months after the 9/11 attacks. He was then sent to Guantanamo where he spent three years in prison, much of it in solitary confinement, and was subjected to over 300 interrogations, death threats and torture, witnessing the killings of two detainees. He was released early in 2005 without explanation or apology. See also Joseph Lelyveld's essay, 'Interrogating Ourselves', *New York Times*, 12 June 2005.

54   See Anthony Lewis, 'Making Torture Legal' in *New York Review of Books*, 15 July 2004. See also Stanley Cohen, 'Post Moral Torture: from Guantanamo to Abu Ghraib', *Index on Censorship*, special issue on torture (vol.34, no.1, 2005), pp.24-30; James Clasper, 'The Rotten Tree of Torture', *The Liberal* (February-March 2005).

55   See David Rose, 'Using Terror to fight Terror', *The Observer*, 26 February 2006.

56   Alistair Horne, *A Savage War of Peace* (New York, reissued, 2006); see also Adam Shatz's essay 'Torture of Algiers', *New York Review of Books*, 21 November 2002.

57   See Raphaelle Branche, *La Torture et l'armée pendant la guerre d'Algérie* (Paris, 2002); Sylvie Thénault, *Une drôle de justice. Les magistrats dans la guerre d'Algérie* (Paris, 2002); and Irwin M. Wall, *France, the United States and the Algerian War* (Berkeley, 2002).

2. BARBARISATION VS CIVILISATION IN TIME OF WAR

1   Primo Levi, *If This is a Man and the Truce* (London, 1987), p.108.

2   'A Truthseeker', *Thoughts on Barbarism and Civilisation or Bloodhounds* (Dublin, 1869), p.6.

3   Interview with General Bernard Trainor, for 'Frontline', http://www.pbs.org/wgbh/pages/frontline/gulf/weapons/tomahawk.html.

4   Philip C. Winslow, *Sowing the Dragon's Teeth: Land Mines and the Global Legacy of*

War (Boston, 1997), p.2.

5 Human Rights Watch and Vietnam Veterans of America Foundation, *In Its Own Words: the US Army and Antipersonnel Mines in the Korean and Vietnam Wars* (Washington, DC, 1997), p.2.

6 Edward C. McDonald, 'Social Adjustment to Militarism', *Sociology and Social Research*, 29, July–August 1945, pp.445-50.

7 Robert Jay Lifton, *Home from the War. Vietnam Veterans: Neither Victims Nor Executioners* (London, 1974), p.347.

8 James W. Garner, 'Proposed Rules for the Regulation of Aerial Warfare', *American Journal of International Law*, 18, January 1924, p.66.

9 Ronald Schaffer, 'American Military Ethics in World War Two: The Bombing of German Civilians', *The Journal of American History*, 67, September 1980, p.322.

10 United States Strategic Bombing Survey, *Overall Report (European War)*, (Washington, DC, 1945), p.71.

11 Both statistics are from Hans Rumpf, *The Bombing of Germany*, translated by Edward Fitzgerald, (London, 1963), pp.160-61.

12 Fred Branfman, 'The Era of the Blue Machine: Laos', *Washington Monthly*, July 1971, cited in Robert Jay Lifton, *Home from the War. Vietnam Veterans: Neither Victims Nor Executioners*, (New York, 1974), p.349.

13 J. Glenn Gray, *The Warriors: Reflections on Men in Battle*, New York, 1959, p.173. Also see the similar comments by Therese Benedek, *Insight and Personality Adjustment: A Study of the Psychological Effects of War* (New York, 1946), pp.54-5; Irvin L. Child, 'Morale: A Bibliographical Review', *Psychological Bulletin*, 38, 1941, p.411; Robert L. Garrard, 'Combat Guilt Reactions', *North Carolina Medical Journal*, 10, September 1949, p.489.

14 Ted Van Kirk in *Newsweek*, July 1985, p.44, quoted by Bernard J. Kerkamp, *The Moral Treatment of Returning Warriors in Early Medieval and Modern Times* (Scranton, 1993), p.151.

15 Jimmy Roberson of Washington DC, aged 19 when enlisted, interviewed by Mark Lane, *Conversations with Americans* (New York, 1970), p.59.

16 William L. Calley, *Body Count* (London, 1971), p.8.

17 Michal R. Belknap, *The Vietnam War on Trial* (Lawrence, 2002), p.191.

18 Wayne Greenhaw, *The Making of a Hero: the Story of Lieut. William Calley, Jr.* (Louisville, KY, 1971), p.191.

19 'Judgement at Fort Benning', *Newsweek*, 12 April 1971, p.28.

20 Wayne Greenhaw, *The Making of a Hero: the Story of Lieut. William Calley, Jr.* (Louisville, KY, 1971).

21 Leon Mann, 'Attitudes Towards My Lai and Obedience to Orders: An Australian Survey', *Australian Journal of Psychology*, 25, 1973, pp.11, 20.

22 Herbert C. Kelman and Lee H. Lawrence, 'Assignment of Responsibility in the Case of Lt. Calley: Preliminary Report on a National Survey', *Journal of*

Social Issues, 28, 1972, p.196.

23 Stanley Milgram, *Obedience to Authority*, NewYork, 1974. Also see Herbert C. Kelman and V. Lee Hamilton, *Crimes of Obedience: Toward a Social Psychology of Authority and Responsibility* (New Haven, 1989); Ervin Staub, *The Roots of Evil*, (NewYork, 1989).

24 Desmond Fennell, *Uncertain Dawn: Hiroshima and the Beginning of Post-Western Civilisation* (Dublin, 1996), p.2.

25 Lawrence Freedman, 'Nuclear Weapons Today', in The Royal United Services Institute for Defence Studies (ed.), *Nuclear Attack: Civil Defence. Aspects of Civil Defence in the Nuclear Age. A Symposium*, (Oxford, 1982), p.42.

26 Michel Foucault, *The History of Sexuality. Volume I: An Introduction*, (London, 1978), p.143.

27 Hannah Arendt, 'Europe and the Atom Bomb', in her *Essays in Understanding, 1930-1954*, edited by Jerome Kohn (NewYork, 1994), pp.421-2.

28 For all this, I am indebted to Eric Prokosch, *The Technology of Killing. A Military and Political History of Antipersonnel Weapons* (London, 1995), pp.20-1.

29 Cited in ibid, p.53.

30 ibid, p.194.

31 Max Horkheimer and Theodor W. Adorno, *Dialectic of Enlightenment: Philosophical Fragments*, ed. Gunzelin Schmid Noerr and trans. Edmund Jephcott (Stanford, 2002), 1st published 1944, xvii-xviii. Also see Zygmunt Bauman, *Modernity and the Holocaust* (Cambridge, 1989).

32 Jan Gross, *Revolution from Abroad: the Soviet Conquest of Poland's West Ukraine and Western Belorussia* (Princeton, NJ, 1988).

33 Mehmed Reşid, cited in Vahakn N. Dadrian, *The Role of Turkish Physicians in the World War I Genocide of Ottoman Armenians* (Oxford, 1986), p.175.

34 Florence Mazian, *Why Genocide? The Armenian and Jewish Experiences in Perspective* (Ames, IA, 1990), p.78

35 David Andrew Schmidt, *Ianfu: The Comfort Women of the Japanese Imperial Army of the Pacific War: Broken Silence* (Lewiston, 2000), p.87.

36 Eugene B. ('Sledgehammer') Sledge, interviewed in Studs Terkel, *'The Good War': an Oral History of World War Two* (London, 1985), p.62.

37 Sergeant Scott Camil, in 'Vietnam Veterans Against the War', *The Winter Soldier Investigation: An Inquiry into American War Crimes* (Boston, 1972), p.14.

38 John W. Dower, *War Without Mercy: Race and Power in the Pacific War*, (New York, 1986) p.147. Also see Seymour Leventman and Paul Comacho, 'The 'Gook' Syndrome: the Vietnam War as a Racial Encounter', in Charles R. Figley and Seymour Leventman (eds), *Strangers at Home: Vietnam Veterans Since the War* (New York, 1990), pp.55-70 and James J. Weingartner, 'Trophies of War: US Troops and the Mutilation of Japanese War Dead, 1941-1945', *Pacific Historical Review*, lxi, February 1992, pp.53-67.

39 Gérard Prunier, *The Rwanda Crisis: History of a Genocide* (London 1998),

p.247.
40 Gavin Hart, 'Sexual Behavior in a War Environment', *The Journal of Sex Research*, 11, August 1975, p.223.
41 Alan M. Dershowitz, *Why Terrorism Works. Understanding the Threat, Responding to the Challenge* (New Haven, 2002), pp.135, 144, 182.
42 Leonard Wantchekon and Andrew Healy, 'The 'Game' of Torture', *The Journal of Conflict Resolution*, 43, October 1999, pp.596-609. The three techniques of dealing with torture were initially proposed by Victor Serge, *Ce que tout révolutionnaire doit savoir sur la répression* (Paris, 1970), pp.69-70.
43 Simone de Beauvoir, *La force des choses* 2 (Paris, 1963), pp.125-265.
44 Eric Hobsbawm, 'Barbarism: a User's Guide', *New Left Review*, 206, July/August 1994, p.44.
45 Omar Rivabella, *Requiem for a Woman's Soul* (New York, 1986), p.86. Also see Adolfo Pérez Esquivel, *Christ in a Poncho* (New York, 1984), p.13.
46 Rita Maran, *Torture: the Role of Ideology in the French-Algerian War* (New York, 1989), p.188.
47 Stephen Harper, *Miracle of Deliverance: the Case for the Bombing of Hiroshima and Nagasaki*, (London, 1985), p.200.
48 Human Rights Watch, *Needless Deaths in the Gulf War: Civilian Casualties During the Air Campaign and Violations of the Laws of War*, (New York, 1991), p.15.
49 'Nobody is Talking', *The Guardian*, 18 February 2005.
50 For a detailed examination, see Human Rights Watch, *Still at Risk: Diplomatic Assurances No Safeguard Against Torture*, col. 17, no. 3(D), 2005, in http://hrw.org/reports/2005/eca0405/.
51 R.G. Collingwood, *The New Leviathan. Or Man, Society, Civilisation and Barbarism*, revised edition, edited and introduced by David Boucher, first published in 1942 (Oxford, 1992), p.342.
52 Daniel A. Bell, 'Why Rights are Universal?', *Political Theory*, 27, December 1999, p.851.
53 George Steiner, *Language and Silence. Essays 1958-1966* (Harmondsworth, 1979), pp.119-20.
54 'A Truthseeker', *Thoughts on Barbarism and Civilisation or Bloodhounds* (Dublin, 1869), p.7.

3. THE SECOND WORLD WAR: A BARBAROUS CONFLICT?

1   Cited in M. Straight, *Make This the Last War: the Future of the United Nations* (New York, 1943), p.xi.
2   See R.J. Overy, *Interrogations: the Nazi Elite in Allied Hands* (London, 2001), pp.46-53.
3   Statistics on war casualties are notoriously unreliable, but the different

pattern is nevertheless clear. In the First World War an estimated 10.5 million
military casualties, an estimated 100,000 civilian casualties from military
action; in addition an estimated 4.6 million died in Europe from hunger or
disease attributed to the effects of war. In the Second World War there were
an estimated 21 million military dead in all theatres, but civilian deaths as a
direct result of the war in excess of 34 million.

4   O. Bartov, *The Eastern Front 1941-1945: German Troops and the Barbarisation
     of Warfare* (New York, 1985). On the subsequent debate see particularly
     R-D. Müller and H-E. Volkmann (eds), *Die Wehrmacht: Mythos und Realität*
     (Munich, 1999); K. H. Pohl (ed.), *Wehrmacht und Vernichtungspolitik: Militär
     im nationalsozialistischen System* (Göttingen, 1999); H. Heer and K. Naumann
     (eds), *Vernichtungskrieg: Verbrechen der Wehrmacht, 1941-1944* (Hamburg,
     1995); C. Hartmann, J. Hürter, U. Jureit (eds), *Verbrechen der Wehrmacht:
     Bilanz einer Debatte* (Munich, 2005).

5   C. Streit, *Keine Kamaraden:die Wehrmacht und die sowjetischen Kriegsgefangen,
     1941-1945* (Stuttgart, 1978); C. Gerlach *Kalkulierte Morde: Die deutsche
     Wirtschafts-und Vernichtungspolitik in Weissrussland 1941-1944* (Hamburg,
     1999).

6   J.P.Reemtsma, 'On War Crimes' in O. Bartov, A. Grossmann and M. Nolan
     (eds), *Crimes of War: Guilt and Denial in the Twentieth Century* (New York, 2002),
     pp.13-16; O. Bartov, 'The Wehrmacht Exhibition Controversy: the Politics
     of Evidence' in ibid, pp.41-60.

7   See J. Förster, 'Operation Barbarossa as a War of Conquest and Annihilation'
     in H. Boog *et al Germany and the Second World War: Vol IV* (Oxford, 1998),
     pp.485-510 for details of these orders.

8   *Russkii Arkhiv 13: Nemetskii Voennoplennye v SSSR* (Moscow, 1999), p.17:
     document 1, Molotov to International Red Cross, 27 June 1941.

9   See for example T. Schulte, *The German Army and Nazi Policies in Occupied Russia*
     (Oxford, 1989), pp. 317-20 for German views of the Soviet soldier. For life
     on the front see J. Lucas, *War on the Eastern Front: the German Soldier in Russia
     1941-1945* (London, 1991); E. Hesse, *Der sowjetische Partisanenkrieg 1941-
     1944 im Spiegel deutscher Kampfanweisungen und Befehle* (Göttingen, 1993).

10   Schulte, *German Army*, for a general discussion of the impact of environment.
     See too B. Shepherd, 'The Continuum of Brutality: *Wehrmacht* Security
     Divisions in Central Russia 1942', *German History*, 21 (2003), pp.49-81.

11   See for example G. Chianese, 'I massacri nazisti nel Mezzogiorno d'Italia',
     Italia Contemporanea, 209/10 (Dec. 1997-Mar. 1998), pp.143-54.

12   National Archives II, College Park, MD, RG107 McCloy Papers, Box 1,
     United Nations War Crimes Commission memorandum, 6 Oct. 1944,
     Annex A.

13   Archivio centrale dello Stato, Rome, Ministero dell'Aeronautica Gabinetto,
     1940, letter from Commissar for War Production to Minister of War, 24

June 1940.

[14] Archivio centrale dello Stato, Ministero dell'Interno, A5G, Busta 21, Genova carabinieri to ministry, 16 Nov. 1942, enclosing leaflet 'Perché vi bombardiamo'.

[15] J. Horne, 'Les civils et la violence de guerre' in S. Audoin-Rouzeau, A. Becker, C. Ingrao, H. Rousso (eds), *La violence de guerre, 1914-1945* (Paris, 2002), pp.135-50.

[16] Z. Bauman, *Modernity and the Holocaust* (New York, 1992); O. Bartov, *Mirrors of Destruction:War, Genocide , and Modern Identity* (New York, 2000).

[17] See for example R.Weikart, *From Darwin to Hitler: Evolutionary Ethics, Eugenics and Racism in Germany* (London, 2004); P.Weindling, *Health, Race and German Politics between National Unification and Nazism, 1870-1945* (Cambridge, 1989); M. Hawkins, *Social Darwinism in European and American Thought* (Cambridge, 1997); D. Gasman, *The Scientific Origins of National Socialism: Social Darwinism in Ernst Haeckel and the German Monist League* (London, 1971).

[18] Weikart, *From Darwin to Hitler*, p.210.

[19] G.L. Weinberg (ed.), *Hitlers Zweites Buch: ein Dokument aus dem Jahr 1928* (Stuttgart, 1961); on Mussolini see particularly R. Ben-Ghiat, *Fascist Modernities: Italy, 1922-1945* (Berkeley, 2001), chs. 5-6 on war and culture.

[20] D. Fensch and O. Groehler 'Imperialistische Ökonomie und militärische Strategie: eine Denkschrift Wilhelm Groeners', *Zeitschrift für Geschichtswissenschaft*, 19 (1971), pp.1167-77.

[21] Cited in B.A. Carroll, *Design for Total War: Arms and Economics in the Third Reich* (The Hague, 1968), p.40.

[22] S. Freud, 'Thoughts for the Times on War and Death' in S. Freud, *Collected Papers:Volume IV* (London, 1956), p.299; P.E. Stepansky, *A History of Aggression in Freud* (New York, 1977), p.159.

[23] 'Warum Krieg' in S. Freud *Collected Papers:Volume V* (London, 1956), p.204, letter from Freud to Albert Einstein, Sept. 1932.

[24] ibid, pp.209, 213. For a general discussion of the psychoanalytic discourses see D. Pick, *War Machine: the Rationalisation of Slaughter in the Modern Age* (New Haven, 1993), pp.211-57.

[25] H. G.Wells, *The Salvaging of Civilisation* (London, 1921), p.1.

[26] ibid, p.5.

[27] R. J. Lifton and E. Markusen, *The Genocidal Mentality: Nazi Holocaust and Nuclear Threat* (New York, 1990). See also M. J. Sherry, *The Rise of American Air Power: the Creation of Armageddon* (New York, 1987); E. Markusen, D. Kopf (eds) *The Holocaust and Strategic Bombing: Genocide and Total War in the Twentieth Century* (Boulder, 1995).

[28] 'Warum Krieg' in S. Freud, *Collected Papers:V*, p.199, letter from Einstein to Freud, 30 July 1932.

[29] Wells, *Salvaging of Civilisation*, p.197.

30   H. Schnädelbach, *Philosophy in Germany 1831-1933* (Cambridge, 1984), esp. pp.151-7 for the impact of Spengler's work. There are numerous titles about the post-war 'catastrophe'. See an account that directly challenged Spengler in R. T. Flewelling, *The Survival of Western Culture: an Inquiry into the Problem of Decline and Resurgence* (New York, 1943).

31   A. Toynbee, *Civilisation on Trial* (New York, 1948), p.25.

32   'How Can Civilisation be Saved?' in E. Jones, *Essays in Applied Psycho-Analysis: Volume I, Miscellaneous Essays* (London, 1951), pp.250-4.

33   W. Treue, 'Hitlers Denkschrift zum Vierjahresplan 1936', *Vierteljahreshefte für Zeitgeschichte*, 3 (1955), p.205.

34   See for example G. Eghigian, 'Injury, Fate, Resentment and Sacrifice in German Political Culture, 1914-1939' in G. Eghigian (ed.), *Sacrifice and National Belonging in Twentieth-Century Germany* (College Station, TX, 2002), pp.90-110; K.-U. Merz, *Das Schreckbild: Deutschland und der Bolschewismus 1917 bis 1921*(Frankfurt/Main, 1995).

35   M. Rader, *No Compromise: The Conflict between Two Worlds* (London, 1939), pp.viii-ix.

36   PRO, PREM 3/88 (3), Churchill to Gen. Ismay, 26 Dec. 1940; Portal (CAS) to Churchill, 13 Feb. 1940.

37   See R. J. Overy, 'Strategic Bombardment before 1939: Doctrine, Planning and Operations' in R. Cargill Hall (ed.), *Case Studies in Strategic Bombardment* (Washington, DC, 1998), pp.11-90; and for a general account of the genesis of modern air strategy J. Buckley, *Air Power in the Age of Total War* (London, 1999).

38   For example U. Bialer, *The Shadow of the Bomber: the Fear of Air Attack and British Bombing 1932-1939* (London, 1980); P. Fritzsche, *A Nation of Fliers: German Aviation and the Popular Imagination* (Cambridge, MA, 1992).

39   PRO, AIR 9/8 Chiefs-of-Staff, note by the First Sea Lord, 21 May 1928, p.2.

40   USAF Academy, Colorado Springs, Macdonald papers, Ser. V, Box 8, Folder 8, 'Development of the US Air Forces' Philosophy of Air Warfare prior to our entry into World War II', pp.15-16.

41   PRO, AIR 9/8, War Office staff exercise, address by the Chief of Air Staff, 17 May 1923.

42   PRO, AIR 9/8, Chiefs-of-Staff paper, 'The War Object of an Air Force', 22 May 1928, p.2.

43   PRO, AIR 9/39, lecture by Air Vice-Marshal Barrett, 'Air Policy and Strategy', 23 Mar 1936, pp.5-6.

44   Archivio centrale dello Stato, Rome, Ministero dell'Aeronautica Gabinetto, 1940, letter from Italian Air Force Staff to Air Minister, 18 April 1939.

45   USAFA, Macdonald Papers, Ser V, Box 8, Folder 8, p.25.

46   RAF Museum, Hendon, London, Harris Papers H47, Harris to Air Ministry,

7 Mar. 1944.

[47] J.S. Underwood, *The Winds of Democracy: The Influence of Airpower upon the Roosevelt Administration, 1933-1941* (College Station, TX, 1991), p.170.

[48] Letter, Churchill to Beaverbrook, 8 July 1940 in W. S. Churchill, *The Second WorldWar* (6 vols, London, 1948-54), pp.ii, 567.

[49] D.A. Rosenberg, 'American Atomic Strategy and the Hydrogen Bomb Decision', *Journal of American History*, 66/1 (1979), p.68.

[50] See B. Davis, 'Experience, Identity, and Memory: the Legacy of World War I', *The Journal of Modern History*, 75 (2003), pp.111-31 for a discussion of the centrality of the deforming experiences of the Great War.

4. TIME, SPACE AND BARBARISATION

[1] See Brian W. Blouet, *Halford Mackinder: a Biography* (College Station, TX, 1987); W.H. Parkes, *Mackinder: Geography as an Aid to Statecraft* (Oxford, 1982).

[2] H.J. Mackinder, 'The Geographical Pivot of History', *The Geographical Journal*, 23, 1904, p.422.

[3] ibid, p.423.

[4] ibid, p.434.

[5] quoted by Blouet, *Mackinder*, p.168.

[6] Current military history and much military theory tend to ignore geography despite its self-evidently decisive effect: Henri Coutau Bégarie, *Traité de stratégie* (Paris, 1999), is the deeply impressive exception that proves the rule. In English, see also Patrick O'Sullivan and Jesse W. Miller, *The Geography of Warfare* (Beckenham, 1983). Geographical studies of the First World War focus on the Western Front: see Robert Villate, *Les conditions géographiques de la guerre: étude de géographie militaire sur le front français de 1914 à 1918* (Paris, 1925), and Douglas W. Johnson, *Battlefields of the World War: Western and Southern Fronts: a Study in Military Geography* (2 vols, New York, 1921). Johnson's wartime book did embrace the Eastern Front: see Douglas W. Johnson, *Topography and Strategy in the War* (London, 1918). Vejas Gabriel Liulevicius, *War Land on the Eastern Front: Culture, National Identity and German Occupation inWorldWar I* (Cambridge, 2000) is concerned with the geography of the Eastern Front but not for its operational consequences. For the Second World War, and particularly Germany, see Rainer Mennel, *Die Schlussphase des ZweitenWeltkrieges im Westen (1944/45). Eine Studie zur politischen Geographie* (Osnabrück, 1981), esp. pp.3-7.

[7] Montgomery's commentary on Cyril Falls, 'Geography and War Strategy', *Geographical Journal*, 112, July-Sept. 1948, p.16. See also Rupert Smith, *The Utility of Force* (London, 2005), pp.153-5.

8 Mackinder, *Democratic Ideals and Reality: a Study in the Politics of Reconstruction* (London, 1919), p.26, quoted by G. Nicolas-O. and C. Guanzini, *Halford John Mackinder: géographie et politique* (Lausanne, 1988), pp.49-58.

9 Holger Afflerbach, *Falkenhayn. Politisches Denken und Handeln im Kaiserreich* (Munich, 1994), pp.11, 294-5, 303-5.

10 Keith Neilson,'Russia', in KeithWilson (ed.), *Decisions forWar, 1914* (London, 1995), p.98; Dietrich Geyer, *Russian Imperialism: the Interaction of Domestic and Foreign Policy 1860-1914* (Leamington Spa, 1987), p.265; Peter Gatrell, *Government, Industry and Rearmament in Russia, 1900-1914: the Last Argument of Tsarism* (Cambridge, 1994), pp.139, 176-8.

11 Norman Stone, *The Eastern Front 1914-1917* (London, 1975), pp.35-6.

12 Gerhard Ritter, *The Sword and the Sceptre: the Problem of Militarism in Germany* (4 vols, London, 1970-73), vol.I, pp.228-9; see also Moltke's letter of 28 August 1856, in Max Horst (ed.), *Moltke. Leben und Werk in Selbstzeugnissen* (Bremen, n.d.), pp.229-36.

13 Eberhard Kessel (ed.), *Generalfeldmarschall Graf Alfred von Schlieffen. Briefe* (Göttingen,Vandenhoeck und Ruprecht, 1958), p.296

14 John Röhl, 'An der Schwelle zum Weltkrieg. Eine Dokumentation über den 'Kriegsrat' vom 8. Dezember 1912', *Militärgeschichtliche Mitteilungen*, 21, 1977, pp.77-134.

15 Scott Lackey, *The Birth of the Habsburg Army: Friedrich Beck and the Rise of the General Staff* (Westport, CT, 1995), pp.114-17, 161-2; GraydonTunstall, Jr, *Planning forWar against Russia and Serbia: Austro-Hungarian and German Military Strategies, 1897-1914* (Boulder, 1993), pp.16-48; Günther Kronenbitter, *"Krieg im Frieden". Die Führung der k.u.k Armee und Grossmachtpolitik Österreichs-Ungarns 1906-1914* (Munich, 2003), pp.293-6.

16 Jehuda Wallach, *Das Dogma der Vernichtungsschlacht. Die Lehren von Clausewitz und Schlieffen und ihreWirkung in zweiWeltkriegen* (first published 1967; Munich, 1970), p.139, fn. 27.

17 'General Staff Ride (East), 1894, quoted by Robert Foley (ed.), *Alfred von Schlieffen's Military Writings* (London, 2003), p.14.

18 Alfred C. Macdonnell, *The Outlines of Military Geography* (London, 1911), pp.76-7. For Mackinder's own reflections on this front, see Halford Mackinder, *TheWorldWar and After: a Concise Narrative and Some Tentative Ideas* (London, 1924), pp.36-9.

19 Mackinder,'Geographical Pivot', p.434. As early as 1899,T. Miller Maguire, *Outlines of Military Geography* (Cambridge, 1899), pp.151-2, made the same point.

20 Arden Bucholz, *Moltke, Schlieffen and PrussianWar Planning* (NewYork, 1991), pp.184-5.

21 Friedrich Ratzel, *Politische Geographie* (Munich and Leipzig, 1897), p.193

22 ibid, p.322.

23 ibid (1903 edn), p.374.

24 ibid (1903 edn), p.471.

25 Carl von Clausewitz, *On War*, edited and translated by Michael Howard and Peter Paret (Princeton, NJ, 1976), p.480. See also Carl von Clausewitz, *Strategie aus dem Jahr 1804 mit Zusätzen von 1808 and 1809*, edited by Eberhard Kessel (Hamburg, 1937), pp.40-2; Carl von Clausewitz, *The Campaign of 1812 in Russia* (first published in English 1843; reprint, Cambridge, MA, 1995).

26 Ratzel, *Politische Geographie* (1903 edn), p.375.

27 Terence Zuber, *Inventing the Schlieffen Plan: German War Planning 1871-1914* (Oxford, 2002), is the most recent and most revisionist discussion of these issues; see especially pp.63, 102, 181. On the origins of the Tannenberg manoeuvre, see Dennis Showalter, *Tannenberg: Clash of Empires* (Hamden, CT, 1991).

28 Sigismund von Schlichting, *Taktische und strategische Grundsätze der Gegenwart* (3 vols, Berlin, 1897-9), vol.II, p.26.

29 ibid, vol.II, pp.30-3, 47.

30 Grossen Generalstabe Kriegsgeschichtliche Abteilung I, *Heerespflegung* (Berlin, 1913), p.50.

31 ibid, p.290.

32 It is not one given much weight by John Horne and Alan Kramer, *German Atrocities 1914: a History of Denial* (New Haven, 2001), but the part played by requisitioning and plundering in promoting clashes between indigenous populations and armies is even more evident on more mobile fronts.

33 Hew Strachan, *The First World War*, vol.1, *To arms* (Oxford, 2001), pp.1005-14; Stig Förster, 'Der deutsche Generalstab und die Illusion des kurzen Krieges, 1871-1914. Metakritik eines Mythos', *Militärgeschichtliche Mitteilungen*, 54, 1995, pp.61-95.

34 Hans Delbrück, *Krieg und Politik 1914-1916* (Berlin, 1918), p.114.

35 ibid, p.128.

36 Alfred Franke, 'Wehrgeographisches zum Russlandfeldzug Napoleons', *Zeitschrift für Geopolitik*, 12, 1934, p.459.

37 quoted by Holger Herwig, *The First World War: Germany and Austria-Hungary 1914-1918* (London, 1997), p.392.

38 The argument followed here is that of Karl-Heinz Frieser, *Blitzkrieg-Legende. Der Westfeldzug 1940* (2nd edn, Munich, 1996). The planning documents are to be found in Hans-Adolf Jacobsen, *Fall Gelb. Der Kampf um den deutschen Operationsplan zur Westoffensive 1940* (Wiesbaden, 1957). For a recent English-language account, see Ernest May, *Strange Victory: Hitler's Conquest of France* (New York, 2000).

39 Hans-Adolf Jacobsen, *Karl Haushofer. Leben und Werk* (2 vols, Boppard am Rhein, 1979), vol.1, p.633.

40 The details of Niedermayer's life are drawn from Hans-Ulrich Seidt, *Berlin Kabul Moskau. Oskar Ritter von Niedermayer und Deutschlands Geopolitik* (Munich, 2002).

41 Oskar von Niedermayer, 'Wehrgeographische Betrachtungen über die Sowjet-Union', *Sonderabdruck aus der Zeitschrift für Geopolitik*, 1933, pp.1-11.

42 Oskar von Niedermayer, 'Wehrgeographie am Beispiel Sowjetrusslands', *Zeitschrift der Gesellschaft für Erdkunde zu Berlin*, Heft 1:2, March 1940, pp.1-28

43 Franke, 'Wehrgeographisches zum Russlandfeldzug Napoleons', *Zeitschrift für Geopolitik*, 11, 1934, pp.449-61.

44 Ulrich Marwedel, *Carl von Clausewitz. Persönlichkeit und Wirkungsgeschichte seines Werkes bis 1918* (Boppard am Rhein, 1978), pp.196, 216-20.

45 Karl von Clausewitz, *Vom Kriege*, abridged edition edited by Friedrich Cochenhausen (Leipzig, 1937), pp.24-5.

46 Jacobsen, *Haushofer*, vol.1, p.627.

47 Bruce Condell and David T. Zabecki (eds), *On the German Art of War: Truppenführung* (Boulder, 2001), p.148.

48 Franz Halder, *The Halder Diaries, 1939-1942* (Boulder, 1975), trans. and ed. Trevor Dupuy, p.314. See also Militärgeschichtliches Forschungsamt, *Germany and the Second World War, vol.4, The Attack on the Soviet Union* (first published in German, 1996; English edn, Oxford, 1998), pp.21-2, 243-4, 252.

49 Andreas Hillgruber, 'Das Russland-Bild der führenden Deutschen Militärs vor Beginn des Angriffs auf die Sowjetunion', in *Russland-Deutschland-Amerika. Russia-Germany-America. Festschrift für Fritz T. Epstein zum 80. Geburtstag* (Wiesbaden, Frankfurter historische Abhandlungen 17, 1978), p.297.

50 Bundesarchiv-Militärarchiv Freiburg, RH 20-8/45, and outlined in Militärgeschichtliches Forschungsamt, *Germany and the Second World War*, vol.4, pp.257-70.

51 Seidt, *Berlin Kabul Moskau*, pp.321-3; for the later stages of Niedermayer's career, see also Christoph Jahr, 'Generalmajor Oskar Ritter von Niedermayer', in Gerd R. Ueberschär (ed.), *Hitlers militärische Elite* (Darmstadt, 1998), vol.1, pp.178-84 .

52 Hillgruber, 'Das Russland-Bild', p.306.

53 Militärgeschichtliches Forschungsamt, *Germany and the Second World War*, vol.4, p.294.

54 ibid, p.482.

55 Halder, *The Halder Diaries, 1939-1942*, p.833.

5. THE MODERN AND THE PRIMITIVE

1 Stephen G. Fritz, *Frontsoldaten: the German Soldier in World War II* (Lexington, 1995), pp.53-54; Omer Bartov, *The Eastern Front, 1941-45, German Troops and*

the *Barbarisation of Warfare* (Hampshire, 2001); Omer Bartov, *Hitler's Army: Soldiers, Nazis, and War in the Third Reich* (New York, 1991).

2 The common phrase in Nazi as well as German soldiers' writings was 'Sein oder Nichtsein,' literally existence or nonexistence. See e.g. 'Befehl Keitels über die Anwendung beliebiger Mittel im Kampf gegen Partisanen und Einwohner, die ihnen Unterstützung erweisen,' Führerhauptquartier, 16 December 1942, TsGAOR, f. 7445, op.2, d. 96, ll. pp.86-7, reprinted in *Wehrmachtsverbrechen. Dokumente aus sowjetischen Archiven* (Cologne, 1997), 116.

3 Michael Burleigh, *The Racial State: Germany, 1933-1945* (Cambridge, 1991).

4 For the development of the laws of war in Europe and the United States up to World War II see Jörg Friedrich, *Das Gesetz des Krieges. Das Deutsche Heer in Rußland 1941 bis 1945. Der Prozeß gegen das Oberkommando der Wehrmacht* (Munich, 1993), pp.15-122.

5 For a good discussion of the legal implications of the 'special circumstances' in Barbarossa, see Alfred Streim, 'International Law and Soviet Prisoners of War,' in Bernd Wegner (ed.), *From Peace to War: Germany, Soviet Russia and the World, 1939-1941* (Providence, 1997), p.293.

6 See the deriding of the Geneva Convention in particular in Document NOKW-2961, 'Keitel Order Concerning Anti-Band Warfare, 16 December 1942; Letter of Transmittal and Distribution List, 29 December 1942,' *Trials of War Criminals Before the Nuernburg Military Tribunals, Vol. X* (Washington, DC, 1951), [hereafter *TWC, Vol. X*], 1168.

7 Document NOKW-2672, 'Extracts from Activity Report No. 2 of Panzer Group 3, January-July 1941, Concerning Treatment of Commissars, Partisans, etc,' *TWC, Vol. X*, p.1133.

8 Document EC-338, 'Comments by Canaris (Chief of Intelligence, OKW), 15 September 1941, Concerning OKW Directive, 8 September 1941, On the Treatment of Soviet Russian PW's,' *Trials of War Criminals before the Nuernburg Military Tribunals, Vol. XI* (Washington, 1950), (hereafter *TWC, Vol. XI*), p.3.

9 Föster shows well how Hitler used this particular decree to get the Wehrmacht to participate in his war of annihilation in Jürgen Förster, 'Das Unternehmen 'Barbarossa' als Eroberungs- und Vernichtungskrieg,' in Horst Boog, Jürgen Förster *et al*, (eds), *Das Deutsch Reich und der zweite Weltkrieg, Band 4: Der Angriff auf die Sowjetunion* (Stuttgart, 1983), pp.426-35.

10 Document C-50, 'Decree Concerning the Exercise of Military Jurisdiction in the 'Barbarossa' Area and Special Measures To Be Taken by the Troops,' 13 May 1941, in *TWC, Vol. X*, 1116; Document 877-PS, 'Army High Command Draft of Barbarossa Order, May 1941, Addressed to Army and Army Group Commanders,' in *TWC, Vol. X*, pp.1124-1125.

11 22 August 1939: 'Means to this end [annihilating Poland]: It does not matter

what they are. The victor is never called upon to vindicate his actions. The question is not one of the justice of our cause, but exclusively of achieving victory.' Charles Burdick and Hans-Adolf Jacobsen, *The Halder War Diary, 1939-1942* (Novato, CA, 1988), p.31.

12 Document C-50, 'Decree Concerning the Exercise of Military Jursidiction in the 'Barbarossa' Area and Special Measures To Be Taken by the Troops,' 13 May 1941, in *TWC,Vol.X*, p.1117.

13 Document NOKW-2672, 'Extracts from Activity Report No. 2 of Panzer Group 3, January-July 1941, Concerning Treatment of Commissars, Partisans, etc,' in ibid, p.1133.

14 'Bestimmungen über das Kriegsgefangenenwesen im Fall Barbarossa,' 16 June 1941, reprinted in Gerd R. Ueberschär and Wolfram Wette (eds), *'Unternehmen Barbarossa' Der deutsche Überfall auf die sowjetunion 1941* (Paderborn, 1984), p.315.

15 Document NO-3417: 'Letter of 26 September 1941, from Heydrich's Office, Enclosing Letter of Transmittal, Signed by defendant Reinecke, and Directives for the Treatment of Soviet Prisoners of War, 8 September 1941,' *TWC, Vol.XI*, pp.11-13.

16 Bartov, *The Eastern Front*, p.107.

17 Burdick and Jacobsen, *The Halder War Diary, 1939-1942*, p.339.

18 ibid, p.346.

19 Document 1471-PS, 'Draft of Commissar Order, undated, prepared according to directives of 31 March 1941, and comment by defendant Lehmann, 8 May 1941,' *TWC,Vol.X*, p.1061.

20 Document NOKW-1076, 'The Commissar Order with distribution list, and covering letter by General von Brauchitsch, Commander in Chief of the Army, 8 June 1941, containing supplements to the order,' ibid, p.1057.

21 ibid, p.1058.

22 'Befehl des Befehlshabers der Panzergruppe 4, Generaloberst Hoepner, zur bevorstehenden Kampfführung im Osten, 2 May 1941,' BA-MA, LVI. AK., 17956/7a, reprinted in Ueberschär and Wette, *'Unternehmen Barbarossa'*, p.305.

23 Jürgen Förster, 'Hitler's Entscheidung für den Krieg gegen die Sowjetunion,' in Horst Boog, Jürgen Förster *et al*, (eds), *Das Deutsch Reich und der zweite Weltkrieg, Band 4: Der Angriff auf die Sowjetunion* (Stuttgart, 1983), p.19.

24 See e.g. Aktenvermerk des Oberstleutnants von Lahousen über die Besprechung im Führerzug am 12. 9. 1939 in Ilnau. Wien, 14 September 1939. BA-MA, N 104/3, reprinted in Helmuth Groscurth, *Tagebücher eines Abwehroffiziers 1938-1940* (Stuttgart, 1970), p.358; Burdick and Jacobsen, *The Halder War Diary, 1939-1942*, p.57.

25 Groscurth, *Tagebücher eines Abwehroffiziers 1938-1940*, p.201.

26 Document NOKW-3485, 'Special Instructions for Case Barbarossa, Issued

by OKW ON, 19 May 1941, with enclosed, 'Directive for the Conduct of the Troops in Russia',' *TWC,Vol.X*, p.994.

[27] Peter Neumann, *The Black March: the Personal Story of an SS Man* (New York, 1959), 131.

[28] For a good overall discussion of the Wehrmacht's participation in the Holocaust, see Hannes Heer, 'Killing Fields. Die Wehrmacht und der Holocaust,' in Hannes Heer and Klaus Naumann (eds), *Vernichtungskrieg. Verbrechen der Wehrmacht, 1941-1944* (Frankfurt, 1999), pp.57-77.

[29] 'Aktenvermerk, Reichsleiter M. Bormann, 16 July 1941,' reprinted in Ueberschär and Wette, *'Unternehmen Barbarossa'*, p.330.

[30] Document C-50, 'The Barbarossa Jurisdiction Order, 13 May 1941, with Transmittal Letters from the High Command of the Armed Forces, 14 May 1941, and from the Naval War Staff, 17 June 1941,' *TWC,Vol.X*, 1116.

[31] Document 877-PS, 'Army High Command Draft of Barbarossa Order, May 1941, Addressed to Army and Army Group Commanders,' *TWC,Vol.X*, p.1125.

[32] 'Befehl Keitels über die schonungslose Unterdrückung der Befreiungsbewegung in den besetzten Ländern und Geiselerschießung,' 16 September 1941, TsGAOR, f. 7445, op.2, d. 140, ll. 502-504, reprinted in *Wehrmachtsverbrechen. Dokumente aus sowjetischen Archiven* (Cologne, 1997), p.82.

[33] 'Befehl Keitels über die Anwendung beliebiger Mittel im Kampf gegen Partisanen und Einwohner, die ihnen Unterstützung erweisen,' Führerhauptquartier, 16 December 1942, TsGAOR, f. 7445, op.2, d. 96, ll. 86-7, reprinted in *Wehrmachtsverbrechen*, p.116.

[34] Hannes Heer, 'Der Logik des Vernichtungskrieges: Wehrmacht und Partisanenkampf,' in Hannes Heer and Klaus Naumann (eds), *Vernichtungskrieg. Verbrechen der Wehrmacht, 1941-1944* (Frankfurt, 1999), p.115ff.

[35] The following discussion is taken from 'Aus dem Befehl des Oberbefehlshabers der 6. Armee, Generalfeldmarschall von Reichenau, über das Verhalten der Truppe im Ostraum,' 10 October 1941, TsGAOR, f. 7021, op.148, d. 454, l. 25 reprinted in *Wehrmachtsverbrechen*, pp.65-69 and NOKW-3411, ' 'Reichenau Order', of 10 October 1941, Distributed by XXVII Army Corps of the 18th Army, Commanded by Defendant von Küchler,' *TWC,Vol. X*, pp.1212-14.

[36] Quoted in Hannes Heer, 'Der Logik des Vernichtungskrieges: Wehrmacht und Partisanenkampf,' in Heer and Naumann (eds), *Vernichtungskrieg*, p.116.

[37] 'Besondere Anordnungen Nr. 1 zur Weisung Nr 21 (Fall 'Barbarossa') 19 May 1941 with Anlage I: Gliederung und Aufgaben der im Raum 'Barbarossa' einzusetzenden Wirtschaftsorganisation, and Anlage 3: Richtlinien für das Verhalten der Truppe in Rußland,' BA-MA, RW4/v.524, reprinted in Ueberschär und Wette (eds), *'Unternehmen Barbarossa'*, pp.308-312; 'Aus den

Richtlinien Görings für die wirtschaftliche Ausplünderung der zu besetzenden Gebiete der UdSSR,' ~16 June 1941, TsGAOR, f. 7021, op.148, d. 14, ll. pp.3-11, reprinted in *Wehrmachtsverbrechen*, pp.39-40; 'Befehl des Chefs des Oberkommandos der Wehrmacht zur Inkraftsetzung der richlinine 'Grüne Mappe'' 16 June 1941, TsGAOR, f. 7021, op.148, d. 14, l. 1, ibid, pp.42-3.

[38] Rolf-Dieter Müller, 'Menschenjagd: Die Rekrutierung von Zwangsarbeitern in der besetzten Sowjetunion,' in Heer and Naumann (eds), *Vernichtungskrieg*, pp.92-103.

[39] Document NOKW-2341: 'Report from Commander Army Rear Area 590, Group VII, (Military Administration), to 3d Panzer Army, 29 November 1942, Concerning Recruitment and Use of Civilians for Labour,' *TWC,Vol. XI*, pp.261-3.

[40] Document NOKW-2340: 'Order from 3d Panzer Army to Subordinate Units, 19 July 1943, Concerning Drafting of Eastern Workers for Labour in the Reich and Labor Draft Proclamation,' *TWC, Vol.XI*, 267; Document NOKW-3475: 'Order from High Command of the Army, 12 September 1943,' *TWC,Vol.XI*, p.272.

[41] Document NOKW-2351: 'Administrative Orders from 263d Infantry Division to Ortskommandanturen, 30 March 1943, Concerning Use of Civilians for Building Fortifications,' *TWC,Vol.XI*, p.264.

[42] Document NOKW-2100: 'Order from XLII Army Corps Headquarters to Subordinate Units, 2 June 1943, Concerning Drafting of Able-Bodied Population for Labor,' *TWC,Vol.XI*, pp.264-5.

[43] Entry for 8 July 1941 in Burdick and Jacobsen, *The Halder War Diary, 1939-1942*, p.458.

[44] 'Vertragsnotiz Leningrad,' 21 September 1941, BA-MA, RW 4/v. 578, in Ueberschär and Wette (eds), *'Unternehmen Barbarossa'*, pp.333-4.

[45] NOKW-3411, 'Letter of Transmittal and, 'Reichenau Order', of 10 October 1941, Distributed by XXVII Army Corps of the 18th Army, Commanded by defendant von Küchler,' *TWC,Vol.X*, pp.1212-14.

[46] See e.g. Letter 137: Wachtmeister A.R., 4.Kp./Korps-Nacht.Abt. 427, 23 October 1941, Ortwin Buchbender and Reinhold Sterz, (eds), *Das andere Gesicht des Krieges. Deutsche Feldpostbriefe, 1939-1945* (Munich, 1982), p.85.

[47] Letter from Sold. E. L., Geb. Div., [Russia], 17 August 1941, in Walter Manoschek (ed.), *'Es gibt nur eines für das Judentum:Vernichtung,' Das Judenbild in deutschen Soldatenbriefen 1939-1944* (Hamburg, 1995), p.41.

[48] Letter 108: From Soldat R.L., 4.Kp/Ln.Rgt. 12, 1 August 1941, Buchbender and Sterz (eds), *Das andere Gesicht des Krieges*, p.76.

[49] Siegfried Knappe and Ted Brusaw, *Soldat: Reflections of a German Soldier, 1936-1949* (NewYork, 1992), p.190.

[50] Hans von Luck, *Panzer Commander:The Memoirs of Colonel Hans von Luck* (New

York, 1989), p.60.

[51] Christoph Faulhaber, *Der Krieg, wie ich ihn erlebte. Aus dem Kriegstagebuch eines Landsers* (Frankfurt, 1986), p.26.

[52] Eberhard Rupp, November 1942, quoted in Klaus Latzel, *Deutsche Soldaten— nationalsozialistischer Krieg? Kriegserlebnis-Kriegserfahrung 1939-1945* (Paderborn, 1998), p.301; Letter from Soldier E. L., Geb. Div., [Russia], 17 August 1941, in Walter Manoschek (ed.), *'Es gibt nur eines für das Judentum: Vernichtung,' Das Judenbild in deutschen Soldatenbriefen 1939-1944* (Hamburg, 1995), p.41.

[53] Letter from O'Gefr.A. G., Kurierstaffel des Führers, Roslawl, 1 March 1942, Manoschek (ed.), *'Es gibt nur eines für das Judentum:Vernichtung'*, 52; Letter 128: Unteroffizier H.G., 7.Kp/Inf.Rgr. 208, 79. Inf.Div., 24 September 1941, Buchbender and Sterz (eds), *Das andere Gesicht des Krieges*, p.82.

[54] José María Sánchez Diana, *Cabeza de puente. Diario de un soldado de Hitler* (Alicante, 1990), pp.27, 73.

[55] 'Tagebuch, beiTschernigow, 13 September 1941,' Johannes Hürter, (ed.), *Ein deutscher General an der Ostfront. Die Briefe und Tagebücher des Gotthard Heinrici, 1941/42* (Erfurt, 2001), p.82; 'Kreigsbericht an seine Familie, Grjasnowo, 19 November 1941,' in ibid, p.112; Groscurth, *Tagebücher eines Abwehroffiziers 1938-1940*, p.526.

[56] Horst Lange, *Tagebücher aus dem zweitenWeltkrieg* (Mainz, 1979), p.73.

[57] Albert Pretzel, January 1944, quoted in Latzel, *Deutsche Soldaten*, p.290.

[58] Letter 139: Unteroffizier L.K., 10.Kp./Inf.Rgt. 351, 183. Inf.Div., 29 October 1941, Buchbender and Sterz (eds), *Das andere Gesicht des Krieges*, p.85; Letter 104: From Unteroffizier (without any other address), 10 July 1941, ibid, p.74.

[59] Neumann, *The Black March*, p.203.

[60] Alexander Stahlberg, *Bound Duty: the Memoirs of a German Officer, 1932-45* (London, 1990), p.159.

[61] Letter 105: From Soldier H., Stab II/Ln. Rgt. 38, 16 July 1941, in Buchbender and Sterz (eds), *Das andere Gesicht des Krieges*, p.74; Siegfried Knappe andTed Brusaw, *Soldat: Reflections of a German Soldier, 1936-1949* (New York, 1992), p.175.

[62] Neumann, *The Black March*, 110; Stahlberg, *Bound Duty*, p.159.

[63] Letter 351: San.-Unteroffizier K.G., Stab/Lw.Bau-Btl. 6/VII, 18 July 1942, Buchbender and Sterz (eds), *Das andere Gesicht des Krieges*, p.171.

[64] Helmut Kober, *Jugend im Dritten Reich. Erinnerung an Rußland, 1942/43* (Cologne, 1993), pp.20-1, 54-5; Bericht Groscurths vom 21. 8. 1941 für den Chef des Generalstabes der Heeresgruppe Süd, General von Sodenstern, über dieVorgänge in Bjelaja Zerkow am 20. 8. 1941 reprinted in Groscurth, *Tagebücher eines Abwehroffiziers 1938-1940*, pp.534-9.

[65] Neumann, *The Black March*, p.131.

66 Letter from Franzl to his parents, Tarnopol, 6 July 1941, Manoschek, (ed.), *'Es gibt nur eines für das Judentum: Vernichtung'*, p.33. The discovery of thousands of mutilated bodies at Lwów (Lemberg) in particular seems to have radicalised a large number of German soldiers. See Letter from Gefr. F. B., Inf. Div., [on the march to Russia], 3 July 1941, ibid, p.31; Letter from Lt. K., Korps-Nachr.Abt., [Russia], 13 February 1942, ibid, 51; Burdick and Jacobsen, *The Halder War Diary, 1939-1942*, p.439; Neumann, *The Black March*, pp.127-8.

67 Letter 349: Gefreiter H.W., Stab/Inf.Div.Nachr.Abt. 387, 387.Inf.Div., 12 April 1942, Buchbender and Sterz, (eds), *Das andere Gesicht des Krieges*, p.171.

68 Letter from Fw. E. E., Marsch-Batallion, [Russia], 18 December 1942, Manoschek, (ed.), *'Es gibt nur eines für das Judentum: Vernichtung'*, 65. See also Letter from E., Inf. Div., [Poland], 17 November 1940, ibid, 18; Letter from Gefr. W. H., Stab/Bau-Btl, [Poland], 28 May 1941, ibid, 25; Letter from Sold. X. M., Inf.Div., [Russia], 2 November 1941, ibid, p.49.

69 Hannes Heer, 'Der Logik des Vernichtungskrieges: Wehrmacht und Partisanenkampf,' in Heer and Naumann (eds), *Vernichtungskrieg*, p.105.

70 Document NOKW-2181, 'Extracts from War Diary of Commander of Army Rear Area 580, September 1942, Concerning Antipartisan Warfare,' *TWC, Vol.X*, p.1161.

71 'Befehl des Kommandanten an die Dnepropetrowsker Stadtverwaltung über die Verhaftung und Erschießung von Geiseln wegen Unterstützung der Roten Armee,' 22 September 1941, TsGAOR, Sammlung von Flugblättern und Briefen, Mappe 1, reprinted in *Wehrmachtsverbrechen*, p.83.

72 Document NOKW-2538, 'Orders to Subordinate Units, 21 and 26 November 1941, signed by defendant von Salmut Concerning Antipartisan Warfare; and Implementation Instructions Thereto Distributed by Subordinate 72d Infantry Division, 28 November 1941,' *TWC, Vol.XI*, p.64.

73 'Bekanntmachung des Stadtkommandanten von Kiew, Generalmajor Eberhard, über Erschießung von Kiewer Einwohnern,' 2 November 1941, TsGAOR, f. 7021, op.148, d. 60, l. 2, reprinted in *Wehrmachtsverbrechen*, 86-87; 'Bekanntmachung des Stadtkommandanten von Charkow über die Erschießung von Einwohnern der Stadt,' 14 November 1941, Gosudarstvennyi Arkhiv Kharkovsoi Oblasti, f. R-3086, op.1, d. 2, l. 23, reprinted in ibid, pp.87-8.

74 'Bekanntmachung des Stadtkommandanten von Kiew, Generalmajor Eberhard, über die Erschießung von Kiewer Einwohnern,' 29 November 1941, TsGAOR, f. 7021, op.148, d. 60, l, reprinted in ibid, p.89.

75 'Anordnung des Generalkommissars von Shitomir, Klemm, an die Gebiets- und Stadtkommissare über Geiselverhaftungen und erschießungen,' 18 December 1941, Gosudarstvennyi Arkhiv Zhitomirskoi Oblasti, f. 1151,

[76] op.1, d. 4, l. 1, reprinted in *Wehrmachtsverbrechen*, p.93.

[76] 'Bekanntmachung des Divisionskommandeurs über die Verbrennung von Dörfern und die Erschießung von Einwohnern wegen Unterstützung der Partisanen,' 28 November 1941, Gosudarstvennyi Arkhiv Poltovskoi Oblasti, f. 2368, op.1, d. 4, l. 2, reprinted in ibid, pp.88-89.

[77] Document NOKW-2599, 'Extract from Evening Reports of Subordinate Units of 4th Panzer Army, 2 August 1942, Regarding Shooting of Male Civilians over 15 Years of Age,' *TWC, Vol. X*, p.1160.

[78] Helmut Pabst, *The Outermost Frontier: a German Soldier in the Russian Campaign* (London, 1986), p.22.

[79] Neumann, *The Black March*, p.151.

[80] 'Letter from Hermann to Lieber Kamerad, 16 November 1942,' Anatoly Golovchansky, Valentin Osipov, *et al*, (eds), *'Ich will raus aus diesem Wahnsinn.' Deutsche Brief von der Ostfront 1941-1945. Aus sowjestischen Archiven* (Wuppertal, 1991), p.109.

[81] Letter from K.V.-Insp.H. K., H.K.P., Baranowice, 18 April 1942, in Manoschek (ed.), *'Es gibt nur eines für das Judentum: Vernichtung'*, 54; Letter from Gefr. L. B., Inf. Div., [Russia], 28 September 1941, ibid, p.45.

[82] Letter 346: Reichsbahn-Inspektor K.S., Haupteisenbahn-Direktion Minsk, 8 October 1941, Buchbender and Sterz (eds), *Das andere Gesicht des Krieges*, 170; Neumann, *The Black March*, pp.161-4.

[83] Letter 308: Gefreiter H.M., 4. Kp./Korps-Nachr.Abt. 452, 17 November 1943, Buchbender and Sterz (eds), *Das andere Gesicht des Krieges*, p.152; Lange, *Tagebücher*, p.87; 'Tagebuch, Grjasnowo, 7 November 1941,' in Hürter (ed.), *Ein deutscher General an der Ostfront*, p.112; Neumann, *The Black March*, pp.168-72, 219.

[84] Benno Zieser, *The Road to Stalingrad* (New York, 1956), pp.13-14.

[85] ibid, pp.32-3.

[86] Neumann, *The Black March*, pp.114-15, 182. This transformation of sensibilities toward atrocities is quite similar to that which occurred during the Holocaust, as pointed out by Browning in Christopher R. Browning, *Ordinary Men: Reserve Police Battalion 101 and the Final Solution in Poland* (New York, 1998).

[87] Brief an seine Frau, Kozow, 6 July 1941, in Hürter (ed.), *Ein deutscher General an der Ostfront*, p.65; Diana, *Cabeza de puente*, pp.118, 146; Knappe and Brusaw, *Soldat*, pp.193-4.

[88] Letter 116: Soldat M.M., 2.Kp./Lw.bau-Btl 6/XIII, 20 August 1941, Buchbender and Sterz, (eds), *Das andere Gesicht des Krieges*, p.78.

[89] Letter 302: Leutnant A.B., Eisb.Bau-Kp.115, 19 October 1942, ibid, pp.150-1.

[90] Claus Hansmann, *Vorüber—nicht vorbei. Russische Impressionen 1941-1943* (Frankfurt, 1989), p.21.

[91]   Bernd Boll and Hans Safrian, 'Auf dem Weg nach Stalingrad. Die 6. Armee
        1941/42,' in Heer and Naumann, (eds), *Vernichtungskrieg*, 283.

[92]   Brief an seine Familie, Tomaszow, 9 May 1941, Hürter, (ed.), *Ein deutscher
        General an der Ostfront*, 58; Brief an seine Familie, Siedlce, 17 May 1941, ibid,
        p.60.

[93]   This was such a normal activity that almost every account of the war
        contains descriptions of foraging. See e.g. Zieser *The Road to Stalingrad*, p.17;
        Kreigsbericht an seine Familie, östlich des Bug, 24 June 1941, in Hürter
        (ed.), *Ein deutscher General an der Ostfront*, p.63; Neumann, *The Black March*,
        pp.119-121; Knappe and Brusaw, *Soldat*, p.184; Pabst, *The Outermost Frontier*,
        p.34.

[94]   Otto Auer, *Als Kriegsteilnehmer an der russischen Front, 1941-1945* (Munich,
        1995), pp.123-4.

[95]   Neumann, *The Black March*, p.156.

[96]   'Aus einem Schreiben des Bürgermeisters von Kiew an Stadtkommissar
        Oberst Muss über Hunger unter der Bevölkerung infolge knapper
        Lebensmittelrationen,' December 1941, TsGAOR, Sammlung von
        Flugblättern und Briefen, Mappe 1, reprinted in *Wehrmachtsverbrechen*, p.94.

[97]   Bernd Boll and Hans Safrian, 'Auf dem Weg nach Stalingrad. Die 6. Armee
        1941/42,' in Heer and Naumann (eds), *Vernichtungskrieg*, p.286.

[98]   Richard Zimmermann, *Überlebt—Erlebt. Ein ehemaliger SS-Rottenführer
        berichtet* (Berlin, 1995), p.72.

[99]   'So im Graben...denkt man unwillkürlich an ganz bestimmte
        Ungezogenheiten,' in Ingrid Hammer and Susanne zur Nieden (eds), *Sehr
        selten habe ich geweint. Briefe und Tagebücher aus dem Zweiten Weltkrieg von
        Menschen aus Berlin* (Zürich, 1992), p.127; Gottlob Herbert Bidermann, *In
        Deadly Combat: a German Soldier's Memoir of the Eastern Front* (Lawrence, KS,
        2000), p.16; Wilhelm Eichner, *Zurück in die grosse Freiheit. Tagebuch aus dem
        Rußlandfeldzug 1942-1944.Vom Kaukasus bis Rumänien* (Leoni am Starnberger
        See, 1991). Earlier, the German army had also been involved in plundering
        the Jews of Poland as well. See e.g. Letter from K.V.-Insp.H. K., H.K.P.,
        Brest/Bug, 14 May 1942, in Manoschek (ed.), *'Es gibt nur eines für das
        Judentum:Vernichtung'*, p.57.

[100] John Stieber, *Against the Odds. Survival on the Russian Front, 1944-1945* (Dublin,
        1995), p.97.

[101] For a detailed discussion of both the troops pillaging and larger-scale
        plundering, see Rolf-Dieter Müller, 'Das 'Unternehmen Barabarossa' als
        wirtschaftlicher Raubkrieg,' in Ueberschär and Wette, (eds) *'Unternehmen
        Barbarossa'*, pp.173-96.

[102] 'Aus dem Erfahrungsbericht über den Verlauf der Aktion zur Vernichtung
        von Ortschaften laut Auftrag des Bataillons vom 22. September 1942,' 30
        September 1942,TsGAOR, f. 7021, op.148, d. 2, ll. pp.342-3, reprinted in

Wehrmachtsverbrechen, p.110; 'Tagesmeldungen der Einsatzgruppen über die Ergebnisse von Strafaktionen zur Vernichtung von Dörfern und friedlichen Einwohnern in Belorußland,' 26 February-4 March 1943, Gosudarstennyi Tsentralnyi Arkhiv Lettiskogo SSR, f. 256, op.1, d. 10, l. pp.18-19 and d. 9, l. 147, reprinted in ibid, pp.122-6.

[103] 'Aus dem Tätigkeits- und Lagebericht des Chefs der Einsatzgruppe B der Sicherheitspolizei und des SD für die Zeit vom 15. November bis 15. Dezember 1942,' 29 December 1942, TsGAOR Belorusskogo SSSR, f. 655, op.1, d. 3, ll. 203, reprinted in ibid, pp.117-19.

[104] 'Telegramm des Hauptstrumfahrers SS Wilke an den Chef der Sicherheitspolizei und des SD in Minsk über die Ergebnisse des Unternehmens 'Fritz' zur Plünderung der Bevölkerung des Kreises Wilejka, Gebiet Molodetschno, in der Zeit vom 24. September bis 10. Oktober 1943 und Bericht über die Besprechung der Ergebnisse des Unternehmens,' 13 October-3 November 1943, TsGAOR Belorusskogo SSR, f. 370, op.6, d. 138, l. 1, reprinted in ibid, pp.272-3.

[105] 'Brief an seine Frau, Siedlce, 25 April 1941,' in Hürter (ed.), *Ein deutscher General an der Ostfront*, p.56.

[106] Rolf-Dieter Müller, 'Menschenjagd: Die Rekrutierung von Zwangsarbeitern in der besetzten Sowjetunion,' in Heer and Naumann (eds), *Vernichtungskrieg*, pp.92-103.

6. SOMETHING TO DIE FOR, A LOT TO KILL FOR

[1]   Laurence Rees, *War of the Century:When Hitler Fought Stalin* (New York, 1999), p.167.

[2]   Alexander Werth, *Russia at War* (New York, 1964), p.763.

[3]   John Armstrong, *The Soviet Partisans in World War II* (Madison, 1964), pp. 751-2.

[4]   For the role of the forthcoming war in the terror of the late 1930s, see Hiroaki Kuromiya, 'Accounting for the Great Terror,' *Jahrbücher für Geschichte Osteuropas* 53 (2005), pp.86-101; Oleg Khlevniuk, 'The Objectives of the Great Terror, 1937-1938' in R.W. Davies *et al* (eds), *Soviet History, 1917-53* (London, 1995), pp.158-76.

[5]   I.V. Stalin, *Sochineniia* 3 (16): 2.

[6]   Mark von Hagen, 'Soviet Soldiers and Officers on the Eve of the German Invasion:Towards a Description of Social Psychology and Political Attitudes,' *Soviet Union/Union Soviétique* 18: 1-3 (1991), pp.79-101. See also the indispensable collection of correspondence between Red Army soldiers and their families, gathered by Vladimir Zenzinov from the bodies of fallen soldiers and POWs in Finland and published as *Vstrecha s Rossiei: Kak i chem*

zhivut v Sovetskom Soiuze. Pis'ma v Krasnuiu Armiiu, 1939-1940 (New York, 1944), esp. pp.133-78.

7   Peter Gornev, 'The Life of a Soviet Soldier,' in Louis Fischer (ed.), *Thirteen Who Fled* (New York, 1949), p.37.

8   Pavel Negretov, *Vse dorogi vedut na Vorkutu* (Vermont, 1985), pp.24-5.

9   Lazar Lazarev, *Konstantin Simonov: Ocherki zhizni i tvorchestva* (Moscow, 1985), p.57.

10   Vladimir Nevezhin, *Sindrom nastupatel'noi voiny: Sovetskaia propaganda v preddverii 'sviashchennykh boev,' 1939-1941 gg.* (Moscow, 1997), pp.95-112; M. N. Mel'tiukhov, 'Narashchivanie sovetskogo voennogo prisutsviia v pribaltike v 1939-1941 godakh,' *Otechestvennaia istoriia* 4 (1999), pp.46-70; Rossiiskii gosudarstvennyi voennyi arkhiv (Hereafter RGVA), fond 9, opis 36, delo 3574, l.72 (hereafter fond/opis/delo/list); 9/36/3773/204.

11   Leo Heiman, pp.17-18.

12   RGVA: 9/31/292; 9/39/70; Ann Lehtmets, *Sentence: Siberia—A Story of Survival* (Kent Town, Australia, 1994), pp.6-11.

13   Geoffrey Hosking, 'The Second World War and Russian National Consciousness,' *Past & Present* 175:1 (2002), p.167; Elena Seniavskaia, p.263.

14   Derzhavnyi arkhiv Vinnyts'koi oblasti f.136, op.3, d.392, l.144; G.A. Stefanovskii *et al* (eds), *Poslednie pis'ma s fronta* (Moscow, 1991), 2:341-44.

15   Gosudarstvennyi arkhiv Rossiiskoi Federatsii (GARF) 9478/1/643/109.

16   Rossiiskii gosudarstvennyi arkhiv sotsial'no-politicheskoi istorii (RGASPI) 17/125/46/7.

17   Werth, p.617.

18   Antony Beevor, *Stalingrad* (New York, 1998), pp.166-86; Catherine Merridale, *Night of Stone: Death and Memory in Twentieth-Century Russia* (New York, 2001), p.217; Richard Overy, *Russia's War* (London, 1997), pp.158-61. In a recent interview, Alexander Iakovlev claimed that 954,000 soldiers (*sic!*) were executed for cowardice and other offenses during the war. http://www.newsru.com/russia/5 May 2005.

19   Gornev, pp.33-4; Norman Naimark, *The Russians in Germany* (New York, 1995), p.112.

20   See the astute observations by Overy, pp.212-17.

21   Elena Seniavskaia, *1941-1945, Frontovoe pokolenie: Istoriko-psikhologicheskoe issledovanie* (Moscow, 1995), p.133, citing Viacheslav Kondrat'ev 'Ne tol'ko o svoem pokolenii: zametki pistalia,' *Kommunist*, no. 7 (1990), p.113. Belash's poem 'Chto vesego strashnee na voine' is cited in Kondrat'ev, 'Paradoksy frontovoi nostal'gii,' *Literaturnaia gazeta*, 9 May 1990, p.9.

22   Hosking, 'The Second World War,' p.174; Merridale, pp.217-18.

23   Gabriel Temkin, *My Just War: the Memoir of a Jewish Red Army Soldier in World War II* (Novato, 1998).

[24] GARF 9479/1/140/12; 9414/1/330/61.

[25] GARF 9414/4/145/11-12b.

[26] Rees, pp.137-8

[27] GARF 9414/1/325/65.

[28] Amir Weiner, *Making Sense of War* (Princeton, 2001), pp.69-70.

[29] Temkin, pp.67-8, 71, 81-2; Weiner, pp.298-331.

[30] Anatol Goldberg, *Ilya Ehrenburg: Revolutionary, Novelist, Poet, War Correspondent, Propagandist* (London, 1984), p.197; Werth, p.965.

[31] Stalin, *Sochineniia* 15:24, pp.43-44 (23 February 1942).

[32] See Niall Ferguson's piece in this volume; For a comprehensive treatment of German POWs in the Soviet Union, see Andreas Hilger, *Deutsche Kriegsgefangene in der Sowjetunion, 1941-1956: Kriegsgefangenenpolitik, Lageralltag und Erinnerung* (Essen, 2000).

[33] Milovan Djilas, *Conversations with Stalin* (New York, 1962), p.76.

[34] Weiner, pp.222-3.

[35] Leonid Rabichev, 'Voina vse spishet,' *Znamia* 2 (February 2005), p.163.

[36] For a comprehensive treatment of the mass rapes in Germany, see Naimark, *The Russians in Germany*, pp.69-140.

[37] Werth, p.986.

[38] See the warning issued in *Pravda* in September 1944 in Werth, pp.947-8.

[39] Werth, p.983.

[40] Weiner, p.155.

[41] Grigorii Linkov, *Voina v tylu vraga* (Moscow, 1951), p.92.

[42] Rees, p.115.

[43] Iurii Shapoval, 'The Ukrainian Years, 1894-1949,' in William Taubman *et al.* (eds), *Nikita Khrushchev* (New Haven, 2000), pp.37-8.

[44] Tsentral'nyi derzhavnyi arkhiv hromads'kykh ob'iednan Ukrainy (TsDAHOU) 28/1/1/41-42, p.128.

[45] Weiner, p.174.

[46] Leo Heiman, *I Was a Soviet Guerrilla* (London, 1959), pp.37, 49, 53, 59-60, pp.125-7. SS-Policemen who did not conceal their own atrocities or excuse them claimed to be especially motivated by the view of mutilated corpses of their comrades whose 'ears had been cut off, eyes had been gauged out and their genitals had been cut off.' Rees, p.118; Ben Shepherd, *War in the Wild East: the German Army and Soviet Partisans* (Cambridge, MA, 2004), p.72.

[47] William Taubman, *Khrushchev: the Man and his Era* (New York, 2003), pp.195-6.

[48] Rees, pp.112-13.

[49] Heiman, p.155.

[50] Martin C. Dean, *Collaboration in the Holocaust: Crimes of the Local Police in Belorussia and Ukraine, 1941-1944* (New York, 1999); Dieter Pohl,

Natsionalsozialistische Judenverfolgung in Ostgalizien, 1941-1944: Organisation und Durchführung eines staatlichen Masseverbrechens (Munich, 1996); Heiman, p.77.

51	On mass violence in the non-Russian Soviet territories, see Karel Berkhoff, *Harvest of Despair: Life and Death in Ukraine under Nazi Rule* (Cambridge, MA, 2004); Bernhard Chiari, *Alltag hinter der Front: Besatzung, Kollaboration und Widerstand in Weissrussland 1941-1944* (Düsseldorf, 1998); Timothy Snyder, 'To Resolve the Ukrainian Problem once and for All': the Ethnic Cleansing of Ukrainians in Poland, 1943-1947,' *Journal of Cold War Studies*, 1:2 (Spring 1999), pp.86-120 and 'The Causes of the Ukrainian-Polish Ethnic Cleansing 1943,' *Past & Present* 179 (May 2003), pp.197-234; Weiner, pp.239-97.

52	Waldemar Lotnik with Julian Preece, *Nine Lives: Ethnic Conflict in the Polish-Ukrainian Borderlands* (London, 1999), esp.pp.54-79.

53	Heiman, pp.17, 19.

54	Weiner, p.152; Arch Getty *et al.*, 'Victims of the Soviet Penal System in the Pre-War Years: a First Approach on the Basis of Archival Evidence,' *American Historical Review* 98 (October 1993), pp.1039-41.

55	Rees, pp.195, 197.

56	Norman Naimark, *Fires of Hatred: Ethnic Cleansing in Twentieth-Century Europe* (Cambridge, MA, 2001), p.97.

57	Tatyana Senkevich, 'A Soviet Girl's Diary,' in Fischer *op.cit*, pp.114, 117, 123-4.

58	Rees, p.168.

59	Vasilii Grossman, *Life and Fate*, trans. Robert Chandler (London, 1995), p.141 as cited in Merridale, p.223.

60	Milovan Djilas, 'Christ and the Commissar,' in George Urban (ed.), *Stalinism: its Impact on Russia and the World* (Wildwood, 1982), p.207.

61	*Literaturnaia gazeta*, 23 September 1987, cited in Chris Ward, *Stalin's Russia* (London, 1993), pp.184-5.

7. PRISONER TAKING AND PRISONER KILLING

1	Gottlob Herbert Bidermann, *In Deadly Combat: a German Soldier's Memoir of the Eastern Front* (Lawrence, KS, 2000), p.291.

2	Niall Ferguson, *The Pity of War* (London, 1998), ch. 13.

3	For a stimulating if somewhat undifferentiated discussion, see Joanna Bourke, *An Intimate History of Killing: Face-to-face Killing in Twentieth-Century Warfare* (London, 1999).

4	Quoted in Christopher Coker, *War and the 20th Century: The Impact of War on Modern Consciousness* (London/Washington, 1994), p.93.

5	Carl von Clausewitz, *On War*, ed., Anatol Rappaport (London, 1982 [1832]),

p.309.
6   Op.cit.
7   Op.cit., pp.311ff.
8   Peter G. Tsouras, *The Greenhill Dictionary of Military Quotations* (London, 2000), p.379.
9   John Hussey, 'Kiggell and the Prisoners: Was He Guilty of a War Crime?' in *British Army Review* (1993), p.48. These were explicitly incorporated in the British *Manual of Military Law*. See also Hisakazu Fujita, 'POWs and Internatonal Law', in Philip Towle, Margaret Kosuge and Yoichi Kibata (eds), *Japanese Prisoners of War* (London/New York, 2000), pp.87-94.
10 William L. Hauser, 'The Will to Fight', in Sam C. Sarkesian, *Combat Effectiveness: Cohesion, Stress, and the Volunteer Military* (Beverly Hills/London, 1980), pp.186-211.
11 See e.g. M. Brewster Smith, 'Combat Motivations among Ground Troops', in S. A. Stouffer *et al.* (eds), *The American Soldier: Combat and its Aftermath* (New York, 1965 [1949]), pp.108ff., 136ff., and the brilliant case study by M. Janowitz and E. A. Shils, 'Cohesion and Disintegration in the Wehrmacht in World War II', in Janowitz (ed.), *Military Conflict: Essays in the Institutional Analysis of War and Peace* (Beverly Hills/London, 1975), pp.177-220.
12 Stephen D. Wesbrook, 'The Potential for Military Disintegration', in Sarkesian (ed.), *Combat Effectiveness*, esp.pp.256ff. See also the discussion in Stasiu Labuc, 'Cultural and Societal Factors in Military Organisations', in Reuven Gal and A. David Mangelsdorff (eds), *Handbook of Military Psychology* (Chichester, 1991), pp.471-90, and Shabtai Noy, 'Combat Stress Reactions', in Gal and Mangelsdorff (eds), *Handbook of Military Psychology*, pp.507-530. The paramount importance of 'political awareness' to morale was of course a Soviet axiom: V.V. Shelyag, A.D. Glotochkin and K.K. Platonov, *Military Psychology: a Soviet View* [*Soviet Military Thought*, No. 8] (Moscow, 1972), pp.392ff.
13 On the importance of reciprocity rather than international law in Churchill's repeated interventions to ensure good treatment of German POWs, see Bob Moore, 'Unruly Allies: British Problems with the French Treatment of Axis Prisoners of War, 1943-1945', *War in History*, 7, 2 (2000), pp.183, 190. Churchill worried that the killing of Italian and German prisoners by the Free French might lead to retaliatory massacres of British POWs in Axis hands.
14 Hussey, 'Kiggell and the Prisoners', p.47. Cf. Gary Sheffield, *The Redcaps: a History of the Royal Military Police and its Antecedents from the Middle Ages to the Gulf War* (London/New York, 1994), p.56.
15 Frederic Manning, *The Middle Parts of Fortune* (London, 2000 [1929]), pp.216f.
16 Tsouras, *Dictionary*, p.380.

17   Loc. cit.
18   On Caporetto, see Ronald Seth, *Caporetto: the Scapegoat Battle* (London, 1965), esp.pp.80-3, 156-9; Cyril Falls, *Caporetto 1917* (London, 1965), pp.64-9.
19   Richard Garrett, *P.O.W.* (Newton Abbot/London, 1981), pp.100f.
20   See Ferguson, *Pity of War*, p.368 and plates 25 to 28.
21   Herbert C. Fooks, *Prisoners of War* (Federalsburg, Maryland, 1924), pp.97f.
22   Stories about such incidents abounded on both sides and can be found not only in post-war memoirs but also in contemporary letters and dairies. The examples given here are all additional to those cited in Ferguson, *Pity of War*, ch. 13.
23   Bourke, *Intimate History*, p.183.
24   Richard Holmes, *The Western Front* (London, 1999), p.179.
25   Yale University, Beinecke Rare Book and Manuscript Library, Henri Gaudier-Brzeska to Ezra Pound, 22 May 1915.
26   Hussey, 'Kiggell and the Prisoners', p.47.
27   Malcolm Brown, in association with the Imperial War Museum, *Tommy Goes to War* (London, 1999), p.116.
28   Paddy Griffith, *Battle Tactics of the Western Front: the British Army's Art of Attack, 1916-18* (New Haven/London, 1994), p.72.
29   Loc. cit.
30   Brown, *Tommy*, p.28.
31   Bourke, *Intimate History*, p.182.
32   Op.cit. Bourke cites three other Irish examples on p.439n.
33   Bourke, *Intimate History*, p.189.
34   Brown, *Tommy*, p.73.
35   Brown, *Tommy*, pp.117, 183.
36   Imperial War Museum, *Kriegsflugblätter*, 29 January 1915.
37   Keegan, *The Face of Battle*, p.50.
38   Ferguson, *Pity of War*, ch. 10.
39   Deist, 'Military Collapse'. See also George. G. Bruntz, *Allied Propaganda and the Collapse of the German Empire in 1918* [Hoover War Library Publications, no.13] (Stanford, 1938), pp.207-21.
40   Bob Moore and Kent Fedorowich, 'Prisoners of War in the Second World War: An Overview', in Moore and Fedorowich (eds), *Prisoners of War and their Captors in World War II* (Oxford/Washington, DC, 1996), p.1.
41   Eugen Weber, *The Hollow Years: France in the 1930s* (London, 1995), p.275n.
42   Alistair Horne, *To Lose a Battle: France 1940* (London, 1990), pp.150-5, 361. Cf. William L. Shirer, *The Collapse of the Third Republic: An Inquiry into the Fall of France in 1940* (London, 1972), pp.739-55; George Forty and John Duncan, *The Fall of France: Disaster in the West, 1939-1940* (London, 1990).
43   Horne, *To Lose a Battle*, pp.411, 479.

[44]   Weber, *Hollow Years*, p.282.

[45]   Horne, *To Lose a Battle*, p.416.

[46]   Robert Gayler, *Private Prisoner: An Astonishing Story of Survival under the Nazis* (Wellingborough, 1984), p.23; David Rolf, *Prisoners of the Reich: Germany's Captives, 1939-1945* (Dunton Green, 1989), p.30. For a good example of the mood of the ordinary French soldier, see Gustave Folcher, *Marching to Captivity: the War Diaries of a French Peasant, 1939-45* (London/Washington, 1996), pp.122-31 ('My bed at home, how much I thought of it at that time!').

[47]   See in general Yves Durand, *Des prisonniers de guerre dans les Stalags, les Oflags et les Kommandos, 1939-1945* (Paris, 1987).

[48]   Op.cit., p.23.

[49]   Myron Echenberg, *Colonial Conscripts: the Tirailleurs Sénégalese in French West Africa, 1857-1960* (London, 1991), pp.92-6.

[50]   Marc Bloch, *Etrange défaite: Témoignage écrit en 1940* (Paris, 1946).

[51]   Ernest May, *Strange Victory: Hitler's Conquest of France* (New York, 2000).

[52]   R.G. Waldeck, *Athene Palace, Bucharest: Hitler's 'New Order' Comes to Rumania* (London, 1943), pp.196ff.

[53]   Weber, *Hollow Years*, p.19.

[54]   John Erickson, *The Road to Stalingrad: Stalin's War with Germany*, vol.I (London, 1975), p.159.

[55]   Gabriel Gorodetsky, *Grand Delusion: Stalin and the German Invasion of Russia* (New Haven, 1999).

[56]   But also partly because they fought overseas and therefore had more discretion about when they engaged the enemy. The British were also lucky in 1940. Had Hitler pressed home the German advantage before the Dunkirk evacuation could be completed, many more prisoners would have been taken.

[57]   See e.g. James Stedman, *Life of a British POW in Poland, 31 May 1940 to 30 April 1945* (Braunton, Devon, 1992), p.8; Sam Kydd, *For YOU the War is Over* (London, 1973), pp.50ff; Philip Kindersley, *For You the War is Over* (Tunbridge Wells, 1983), p.11; Ernest Walker, *The Price of Surrender. 1941: The War in Crete* (London, 1992), pp.31-5; Harry Spiller (ed.), *Prisoners of Nazis: Accounts by American POWs in World War II* (Jefferson, NC/London, 1998), p.36; John Baxter, *Not Much of a Picnic: Memoirs of a Conscript and Japanese Prisoner of War, 1941-1945* (Trowbridge, 1995) p.37.

[58]   C.P. Stacey, *The Canadian Army 1939-1945: An Official Historical Summary* (Ottawa, 1948), pp.80, 179.

[59]   Donald T. Giles Jr. (ed.), *Captive of the Rising Sun: The POW Memoirs of Rear Admiral Donald T. Giles, Jr.* (Annapolis, MD, 1994), pp.44-7. Cf. Bernard T. FitzPatrick and John. A. Sweetser III (eds), *The Hike into the Sun: Memoir of an American Soldier Captured on Bataan in 1942 and Imprisoned by the Japanese*

until 1945 (Jefferson, NC/London, 1993), pp.54ff.; Dick Bilyeu, *Lost in Action: A World War II Soldier's Account of Capture on Bataan and Imprisonment by the Japanese* (Jefferson, NC, 1991), pp.64ff., 73ff.

60   Chester M. Biggs Junior, *Behind the Barbed Wire: Memoir of a World War II U.S. Marine Captured in North China in 1941 and Imprisoned by the Japanese Until 1945* (Jefferson, NC/London, 1995), p.10.

61   See e.g. Fooks, *Prisoners of War*, pp.127ff.; Carter, *POW*, p.71; Buckledee, *For You the War is Over*, pp.2ff.; Begg and Liddle (eds), *For Five Shillings a Day*, p.199.

62   No matter how solid the primary group loyalties and patriotism of a unit, few soldiers could endure more than two hundred combat days without cracking in some way: Wendy Holden, *Shell Shock* (London/Basingstoke, 1998), pp.101-3.

63   Gilbert Broadbent, *Behind Enemy Lines* (Bognor Regis, 1985), p.6.

64   See e.g. Rolf, *Prisoners of the Reich*, p.22; Donald Edgar, *The Stalag Men: the Story of one of the 110,000 Other Ranks who were P.O.W.s of the Germans in the 1939-45 War* (London, 1982), pp.1-13; Garrett, *P.O.W.*, pp.10-15; Spiller (ed.), *Prisoners of Nazis*, p.154. Cf. Hunter, 'Prisoners', pp.743ff; Samuel Hynes, *The Soldier's Tale: Bearing Witness to Modern War* (New York, 1997), pp.232ff., 245; Frank. J. Grady and Rebecca Dickson, *Surviving the Day: An American POW in Japan* (Shrewsbury, 1997), p.43.

65   Andrew D. Carson, *My Time in Hell: Memoir of an American Soldier Imprisoned by the Japanese in World War II* (Jefferson, NC/London, 1997), pp.8-15.

66   Gayler, *Private Prisoner*, p.13.

67   Donald Watt, *Stoker: The Story of an Australian who Survived Auschwitz-Birkenau* (East Roseville, 1995), pp.11ff. For examples of very reluctant Antipodean surrender in the Pacific theatre see James Bertram, *The Shadow of a War: a New Zealander in the Far East 1939–1946* (London, 1947), p.135; Kenneth Harrison, *The Brave Japanese* (Adelaide, 1967), p.90; Baxter, *Not Much of Picnic*, p.37.

68   Overmans, 'German Historiography', p.153.

69   Zabecki, *World War II*, p.1249.

70   Maschke *et al.*, *Deutsche Kriegsgefangenen*, pp.194f, 200f. (Tables 2, 5).

71   Overmans, 'German Historiography', p.141.

72   *Op.cit.*, p.269.

73   Clifford Kinvig, 'Allied POWs and the Burma-Thailand Railway', in Philip Towle, Margaret Kosuge and Yoichi Kibata (eds), *Japanese Prisoners of War* (London/New York, 2000), p.48.

74   Allison B. Gilmore, *You Can't Fight Tanks with Bayonets: Psychological Warfare against the Japanese Army in the Southwest Pacific* (Lincoln/London, 1998), pp.77ff.

75   Louis Allen and David Steeds, 'Burma: the Longest War, 1941-45' in Saki

Dockrill (ed.), *From Pearl Harbour to Hiroshima: the Second World War in Asia and the Pacific, 1941–45* (Basingstoke, 1994), pp.116f.

[76]   Op.cit, p.271.

[77]   Hiroo Onoda, *No Surrender: My Thirty Year War* (London, 1975).

[78]   Anthony Babington, *For The Sake of Example: Capital Courts-Martial, 1914-1920* (London, rev. edn 1993), p.189. Cf. Christoph Jahr, *Gewöhnliche Soldaten: Desertion und Deserteure im deutschen und britischen Heer 1914-1918* (Göttingen, 1998). These are figures for executions for desertion. For total death sentences, the figures were Germany 150, France 2,000 and Britain 3,080; for sentences carried out, Germany 48, France 700 and Britain 346. Official figures do not include deserters who were summarily shot by their officers or comrades for trying to desert.

[79]   Bruntz, *Allied Propaganda*, p.206. See also p.210.

[80]   Leonard Sellers, *For God's Sake Shoot Straight! The Story of the Court Martial and Execution of Temporary Sub-Lieutenant Edwin Leopold Arthur Dyett Nelson Battalion 63rd (RN) Division during the First World War* (London, 1995), p.125.

[81]   Apart from his famous 'never surrender' speech of 4 June 1940, Churchill also exhorted the Singapore garrison to fight to the death.

[82]   Jean Paul Pallud, 'Crime in WWII. The Execution of Eddie Slovik', *After the Battle*, 32 (1981), pp.28-42.

[83]   Dmitri Volkogonov, *Trotsky: The Eternal Revolutionary* (London, 1996), pp.178ff.

[84]   Anthony Beevor, *Stalingrad* (London, 1998), p.169.

[85]   Laurence Rees, *War of the Century: When Hitler Fought Stalin* (London, 1999), p.223.

[86]   Bidermann, *In Deadly Combat*, p.9. See also Omer Bartov, *Hitler's Army: Soldiers, Nazis, and War in the Third Reich* (New York/Oxford, 1992), pp.71ff.; Stephen G. Fritz, *Frontsoldaten: The German Soldier in World War II* (Lexington, 1995), p.90.

[87]   See for details Omer Bartov, *The Eastern Front, 1941-45, German Troops and the Barbarisation of Warfare* (Basingstoke, 1985), pp.29-36; Bartov, *Hitler's Army*, pp.98-101. Cf. Burleigh, *Third Reich*, pp.524ff.

[88]   Fritz, *Frontsoldaten*, p.95.

[89]   Bartov, *Hitler's Army*, p.99.

[90]   One reason for the discrepancy is the very high desertion rate in the first year of the First World War, when there had been no selection of volunteers beyond a basic physical check, allowing many psychologically unsuitable recruits to join the army.

[91]   The phrase 'shame culture' was coined by the anthropologist Ruth Benedict during the war: Ikuhiko Hata, 'From Consideration to Contempt: the Changing Nature of Japanese Military and Popular Perceptions of Prisoners of War Through the Ages', in Moore and Fedorowich (eds), *Prisoners of War*,

p.269. Cf. Gilmore, *You Can't Fight Tanks with Bayonets*, p.97.

92 Hata, 'Consideration to Contempt', pp.260ff.

93 Mackenzie, 'The Treatment of Prisoners of War', pp.513-7. Cf. Teruhiko Asada, *The Night of a Thousand Suicides: the Japanese Outbreak at Cowra* (London, 1970), pp.2, 7.

94 Op.cit., pp.139ff.

95 Hata, 'Consideration to Contempt', p.263. Cf. Aida, *Prisoner*, p.6: 'If there was a surrender all on fronts, we too would surrender ... without bearing the stigma of being called "prisoner".' See also op.cit., p.50, for the distinction between 'prisoners of war' and 'disarmed military personnel'.

96 Adolf Hitler, *Mein Kampf*, transl. Ralph Manheim (London, 1992), p.183. See also pp.172f.

97 Ian Kershaw, *Hitler, 1936-45: Nemesis* (London, 2000), p.117.

98 Op.cit., p.217.

99 Hans Mommsen, 'The Dissolution of the Third Reich: Crisis Management and Collapse, 1943-1945', *German Historical Institute Bulletin*, 27 (2000), pp.9-24, p.17.

100 Saul K. Padover, *Psychologist in Germany: The Story of an American Intelligence Officer* (London, 1946), p.169.

101 Op.cit, p.166.

102 Günter K. Koschorrek, *Blood Red Snow: The Memoirs of a German Soldier on the Eastern Front*, transl. Olav R. Crone-Aamot (London, 2002), p.309.

103 Martin Pöppel, *Heaven and Hell: The War Diary of a German Paratrooper*, transl. Dr Louise Willmot (Staplehurst, 2000 [1988]), p.237.

104 Stephen E. Ambrose, 'The Last Barrier', in Robert Cowley (ed.), *No End Save Victory: New Second World War Writing* (London, 2002), p.548.

105 Volkogonov, *Trotsky*, p.185. On the other hand, the new regime never expressly acknowledged the 1895/1907 Hague Laws of Land Warfare; nor did it adhere to the Geneva Convention of 1929. Only in July 1941 did Stalin propose a reciprocal adherence to the Hague Convention, but the German government pointedly ignored the suggestion: Burleigh, *Third Reich*, pp.512ff.

106 Jürgen Forster, 'The German Army and the Ideological War against the Soviet Union', in Gerhard Hirschfeld (ed.), *The Policies of Genocide: Jews and Soviet Prisoners of War in Nazi Germany* (London, 1986), p.20.

107 Kershaw, *Nemesis*, p.358.

108 Forster, 'German Army', p.20.

109 Op.cit, p.21.

110 Bartov, *Hitler's Army*, p.84.

111 Op.cit, p.83.

112 Op.cit, p.84.

113 Omer Bartov, 'Savage War', in Michael Burleigh (ed.), *Confronting the Nazi*

Past: New Debates on Modern German History (London, 1996), p.131. Cf. idem, *Mirrors of Destruction: War, Genocide and Modern Identity* (Oxford/New York, 2000), pp.25-30.

[114] Fritz, *Frontsoldaten*, pp.53f.

[115] Beevor, *Stalingrad*, p.60.

[116] Rees, *War of the Century*, p.67.

[117] Forster, 'German Army', p.21.

[118] Bartov, *Hitler's Army*, p.87.

[119] Op.cit, p.88.

[120] Op.cit, pp.85f.

[121] Fritz, *Frontsoldaten*, p.55.

[122] Beevor, *Stalingrad*, p.59.

[123] Hans Dibold, *Doctor at Stalingrad: the Passion of a Captivity* (London, 1958), pp.24, 31.

[124] Bob Carruthers and Simon Trew (eds), *Servants of Evil: New First-hand Accounts of the Second World War from Survivors of Hitler's Armed Forces* (London, 2001), pp.231f.

[125] Op.cit, p.235.

[126] Bidermann, *In Deadly Combat*, pp.282-93.

[127] Bartov, *Eastern Front*, p.38.

[128] Quoted in Bartov, *Mirrors of Destruction*, p.236n.

[129] Rees, *War of the Century*, p.167.

[130] *Op.cit*, p.369.

[131] Beevor, *Stalingrad*, p.182.

[132] Carruthers and Trew (eds), *Servants of Evil*, p.232.

[133] Mackenzie, 'Treatment of Prisoners of War', p.488.

[134] John W. Dower, *War Without Mercy: Race and Power in the Pacific War* (London/Boston, 1986), pp.63ff.

[135] Op.cit, p.68.

[136] Op.cit, p.70.

[137] Bourke, *Intimate History*, p.184.

[138] Op.cit, pp.185f.

[139] Gerhard L. Weinberg, *A World at Arms: a Global History of World War II* (New York, 1994), p.695.

[140] Bruce I. Gudmundsson, 'Okinawa', in Robert Cowley (ed.), *No End Save Victory: New Second World War Writing* (London, 2002), pp.637ff.

[141] Andrew D. Carson, *My Time in Hell: Memoir of an American Soldier Imprisoned by the Japanese in World War II* (Jefferson, NC/London, 1997), p.231.

[142] Dower, *War Without Mercy*, p.64.

[143] Bourke, *Intimate History*, pp.255.

[144] Op.cit, p.293.

[145] Dower, *War Without Mercy*, pp.63, 70.

146 Op.cit, p.68.
147 Bourke, *Intimate History*, p.184.
148 Op.cit, p.71.
149 *Life*, 22 May 1944.
150 Dower, *War Without Mercy*, pp.64f. Ears, bones and teeth were also collected. In April 1943 the *Baltimore Sun* ran a story about a mother who petitioned the authorities to let her son post her a Japanese ear so that she could nail it to her front door.
151 S. Hart, R. Hart and M. Hughes, *The German Soldier in World War II* (Staplehurst, 2000), p.186.
152 Spiller (ed.), *Prisoners of Nazis*, pp.87, 149; Rolf, *Prisoners of the Reich*, p.21. For incidents of massacres of British and American troops by SS units see Garrett, *P.O.W.*, p.142.
153 Bourke, *Intimate History*, p.183.
154 Spiller (ed.), *Prisoners of Nazis*, p.11.
155 Moore, 'Unruly Allies', p.190.
156 Stephen E. Ambrose, *Band of Brothers: E Company, 506th Regiment, 101st Airborne from Normandy to Hitler's Eagle's Nest* (London, 2001 [1992]), pp.150, 206, 277. It is nevertheless worth noting that Ambrose could only obtain second-hand accounts of the most flagrant story he heard about prisoner killing, when Lieutenant Ronald C. Spiers allegedly gunned down ten German POWs who were at work digging a ditch. No one actually saw it happen.
157 Moore, 'Unruly Allies', p.191.
158 Bourke, *Intimate History*, p.183.
159 Op.cit, p.184.
160 Padover, *Psychologist in Germany*, p.166.
161 Eric Bull, *Go Right, Young Man* (Hornby, 1997), p.19; Jeffrey E. Geiger, *German Prisoners of War at Camp Cooke, California: Personal Accounts of 14 Soldiers, 1944–1946* (Jefferson, NC/London, 1996), pp.13, 18ff.
162 Op.cit, p.174.
163 Begg and Liddle (eds), *For Five Shillings a Day*, p.327.
164 John Verney, *Going to the Wars* (London, 1955).
165 Ambrose, 'Last Barrier', p.547.
166 Michael Burleigh, 'Political Religion and Social Evil' in *Totalitarian Movements and Political Religions*, 3, 2 (2002), pp.1-60.
167 Richard Garrett, *P.O.W.* (London, 1981), pp.182ff.; Martin Gilbert, *Second World War* (London, 1989), p.745.
168 Begg and Liddle (eds), *For Five Shillings a Day*, pp.404ff.
169 Philip Towle, 'Introduction', in idem, Margaret Kosuge and Yoichi Kibata (eds), *Japanese Prisoners of War* (London/New York, 2000), p.xv; Clifford Kinvig, 'Allied POWs and the Burma-Thailand Railway', in op.cit, pp.17-57.

170 Hynes, *Soldier's Tale*, p.246.

171 For mortality rates of prisoners in Japanese hands, see Kinvig, 'Allied POWs', p.47n.

172 Yoichi Kibata, 'Japanese Treatment of British Prisoners: The Historical Context', in Philip Towle, Margaret Kosuge and Yoichi Kibata (eds), *Japanese Prisoners of War* (London/New York, 2000), p.143.

173 Philip Towle, 'The Japanese Army and Prisoners of War', in Towle, Kosuge and Kibata (eds), *Japanese Prisoners of War*, pp.1-16.

174 Beevor, *Stalingrad*, p.199. One might of course ask how Russian wives knew that German prison camps were 'worse than death', given the much more limited news available to them? The answer is, of course, that their government told them so.

175 Koschorrek, *Blood Red Snow*, pp.309ff.

176 Daniel Lerner, *Psychological Warfare against Nazi Germany: The Sykewar Campaign, D-Day to VE-Day* (Cambridge, MA, 1971 [1949]), pp.23, 43, 101, 133, 136, 184, 208, 216.

177 Op.cit, pp.174, 279, 358. As one 'Sykewar' veteran commented, 'Much casuistical effort was expended to make surrender compatible with soldierly honour'. Note the case of Generalmajor Elster, who was reluctant to surrender to the American 39th Infantry without a token exchange of fire. Notions of military honour were remarkably persistent even in the face of inevitable defeat: Ramsey, 'Germany Surrenders', p.4. See also Jordan (ed.), *Conditions of Surrender*, p.130.

178 Lerner, *Psychological Warfare*, p.216.

179 Op.cit, p.311. On the questionnaires' results, see op.cit, chart V.

180 M. Janowitz and E. A. Shils, 'Cohesion and Disintegration in the Wehrmacht in World War II', in Janowitz (ed.), *Military Conflict: Essays in the Institutional Analysis of War and Peace* (Beverly Hills/London, 1975), esp.pp.202, 211ff.

181 Koshorrek, *Blood Red* Snow, pp.309ff. Cf. e.g. Geiger (ed.), *German Prisoners of War*, pp.20-3; Murdoch, *The Other Side*, pp.138ff.

182 Contrary to the terms of the Geneva Convention of 1929, a substantial number of German prisoners were transferred to other powers by those they surrendered to. The Americans handed over 765,000 to France, 76,000 to the Benelux countries and 200,000 to Russia. They also refused to accept the surrender of German troops in Saxony and Bohemia, who were handed over to the Russians: Heinz Nawratil, *Die deutschen Nachkriegsverluste unter Vertriebenen, Gefangenen und Verschleppten. Mit einer Übersicht über die europäischen Nachkriegsverluste* (Munich/Berlin, 1988), pp.36ff.

183 Gilmore, *You Can't Fight Tanks with Bayonets*, p.60.

184 Op.cit, p.61.

185 Op.cit, p.66.

8. SURROGATES OF THE STATE

1   The best textbook account is Wunyabari Maloba, *Mau Mau and Kenya: an Analysis of a Peasant Revolt* (Bloomington, 1993), but the first full history by Carl G. Rosberg and John Nottingham, *The Myth of Mau Mau: Nationalism in Kenya* (Stanford, 1966), remains indispensable. For revisionism, see E.S. Atieno Odhiambo and John Lonsdale (eds), *Mau Mau and Nationhood: Arms, Authority and Narration* (Oxford, 2003).

2   The evidence for combat deaths is set out in David Anderson, *Histories of the Hanged: Britain's Dirty War in Kenya and the End of Empire* (London and New York, 2005). Caroline Elkins, *Britain's Gulag: the Brutal End of Empire in Kenya* (London, 2005), p.xvi, suggests the numbers detained and the numbers killed could have been significantly higher, though the evidence offered for this claim is not explicit.

3   Joanna Lewis, 'Daddy Wouldn't Buy Me a Mau Mau: British Popular Press and the Demoralisation of Empire', in Odhiambo and Lonsdale (eds), *Mau Mau and Nationhood*, pp.227-50; and for the influence of the Kenya government's Office of Information, Susan Carruthers, *Winning Hearts and Minds: the British Government, the Media and Colonial Counter-Insurgency 1944-1960* (London, 1995).

4   For a sophisticated analysis of the historiography, see John Lonsdale, 'Mau Maus of the Mind: Making Mau Mau and Remaking Kenya', *Journal of African History*, 31, 1990, pp.393-421.

5   On mechanical violence and face-to-face killing, see Joanna Bourke, *An Intimate History of Killing: Face-to-Face Killing in Twentieth-Century Warfare* (London, 1999), pp.5-8. On intimate violence and the hunting of the quarry, Jean Hatzfeld, *A Time for Machetes: the Rwanda Genocide – The Killers Speak* (London, 2005) provides a chilling example.

6   A summary of the official figures is to be found in J.D. Corfield, *The Origins and Growth of Mau Mau (Corfield Report)* (London, HMSO Cmd.1030, 1960), appendix.

7   For a succinct refutation of this idea, see Bourke, *Intimate History*, pp.171-214.

8   Christopher Hibbert, *Redcoats and Rebels: a British View of the American War of Independence* (New York, 1990). For Ireland, Charles Townshend, *Britain's Civil Wars: Counter-insurgency in the Twentieth Century* (London, 1986).

9   The politics that opened the way to this are explained in Anderson, *Histories of the Hanged*, pp.240-1.

10   Anderson, *Histories of the Hanged*, citing figures from the Kenya National Archive [KNA], file MAA/7/761.

11   M.P.K. Sorrenson, *Land Reform in Kikuyu Country* (London, 1967), p.109.

12   Daniel Branch, 'Loyalists in Kenya's Mau Mau War, 1952-1963' (DPhil thesis,

Oxford University, 2005), and Daniel Branch, 'The Enemy Within: Loyalists and the War Against Mau Mau in Kenya', *Journal of African History*, forthcoming.

13   For an insightful model that holds for the Kenya case and has influenced my thinking, see Anthony Oberschall and Michael Seidman, 'Food Coercion in Revolutions and Civil Wars: Who Wins and How They Do It', *Comparative Studies in Society & History*, 47 (2), (2005), pp.372-402.

14   For Lari and its aftermath, including details of the newspaper reports of subsequent Home Guard atrocities, see Anderson, *Histories of the Hanged*, pp.129-34, 177-8, 256-7. See also Greet Kershaw, *Mau Mau From Below* (Oxford, 1997), pp.251-7, and E.N. Wanyoike, *An African Pastor* (Nairobi, 1974), pp.198-202.

15   Photographs of the body appear in John Pinney, *A History of the Kikuyu Guard 1953-1955 (Fort Hall)* (Privately published, David Lovatt-Smith, 2002), p.20.

16   Sidney Fazan, *History of the Loyalists* (Nairobi, 1958); Anthony Lavers, *The Kikuyu Who Fought Mau Mau* (Nairobi, 1955), pp.24-6; Pinney, *History*, pp.19-21.

17   Elkins, *Britain's Gulag*, pp.78-9. Elkins cites no sources on the massacre other than oral testimony.

18   The following account is drawn from Virginia Blakeslee, *Beyond the Kikuyu Curtain* (Chicago, 1956), pp.254-8.

19   Blakeslee, *Beyond*, pp.254-5. The claim that Thigiru was decapitated is often repeated in oral accounts of this tale, but it appears to be untrue. The head is to be seen in photographs of his body, taken at the scene of the murder: Pinney, *History*, p.20.

20   Leonard J. Gill, *Military Musings* (Victoria BC, 2003), p.91

21   Gill, *Military Musings*, p.91.

22   ibid, p.90.

23   ibid, pp.89-90.

24   For accounts of Kago's activities, see Pinney, *History*, pp.26-35, Frank Kitson, *Gangs and Counter-gangs* (London, 1960), and Anderson, *Histories of the Hanged*, pp.250, 265-7.

25   Oberschall and Seidman, 'Food Coercion', 377-9, explains the comparative model for this statement.

26   For a parallel, see the description of the Bosnian War of 1992-95, another 'war fought more against civilians than between soldiers', in Oberschall and Seidman, 'Food Coercion', pp.381-2.

27   Anthony Clayton, *Counter-insurgency in Kenya* (Nairobi, 1976).

28   For a sample of the evidence, see the following material held in the Rhodes House Library [RHL], Oxford: Whyatt (Attorney General) to Governor Baring, 10 June 1954 and 21 August 1954, G. Hill to District Commissioner, Nyeri, 4 December 1954, K.P.Hadingham to C.M. Johnston, 14 December 1954, and D. MacPherson to Young, 23 December 1954, all in RHL Mss Afr s 1694; O. Hughes to C.M. Johnston, 11 September 1954, C.M. Johnston to

C.I.D. Nyeri, 16 September 1954, C.M. Johnston to Asst Commissioner of Police, 16 October 1954, K.P.Hadingham to Young, 22 November 1954, and 'Record of Interview between C.M. Johnston and H.R. Walker (CID)', 27 November 1954, all in RHL Mss Brit Emp s 486, Box 5, File 5.

29   The following is taken from the full transcript of the trial papers: Criminal Case 240/1954 'Muriu Wamai & 5 others', KNA MLA 1/1179.

30   A detailed precise of the relevant documents appears in PRO CO 822/1293. There are further materials in Young's own papers, at Rhodes House, Oxford.

31   For an informed discussion, see Randall Heather, 'Intelligence and counter-insurgency in Kenya, 1952-56' (PhD thesis, University of Cambridge, 1993), pp.227-8.

32   Baring to Lennox-Boyd, 9 January 1955, PRO CO 822/775; 'Text of Governor's Speech at Nyeri, 18 January 1955', KNA (TA) Nbi/PC/Arch/Adm/15/1.

33   These have been most rigorously documented by Daniel Branch, 'Loyalists and Mau Mau', ch. 3.

34   Barbara Castle, 'What Price Justice in the Land of Fear?', *Daily Mirror*, 7 December 1955, p.3; 'Why Was This Report Kept Dark?', *Daily Mirror*, 10 December 1955, p.3; 'Justice in Kenya', *New Statesman and Nation*, 17 December 1955, pp.821-2;

35   'Statement by David Martin', 17 May 1953, RHL Mss Perham 467, File 1.

36   E. Carey Francis, 'Kenya's Problems as seen by a Schoolmaster in Kikuyu Country', *African Affairs*, 54 (1955), p.193.

9 . THE AMERICAN EMPIRE AT WAR

1   Joe Haldeman, *The Forever War* (New York, reissue, 1996). Haldeman, himself a Vietnam veteran, published this story of an intergalactic war that had been going on for 1,200 years in 1972.

2   George H.W. Bush, Address Before a Joint Session of Congress on the End of the Gulf War, March 6, 1991. On line at www.millercenter.virginia.edu. Although Bush quoted Winston Churchill in this speech, some listeners were chilled by the phrase, which owed more to the Axis than the Allies.

3   See for example, Anthony Swofford's *Jarhead*. In the conclusion of his bitter memoir, Swofford observes: 'The men who go to war and live are spared for the single purpose of spreading bad news when they return, the bad news about the way war is fought and why, and by whom for whom, and the more men who survive the war, the higher the number of men who might speak. Unfortunately, many of the men who live through the war don't understand why they were spared. They think they are still alive in order to return home and make money and fuck their wives and get drunk and wave the flag.

These men spread what they call good news, the good news about war and warriors. Some of the men who spread good news have never fought — so what could they have to say about the purity of war and warriors? These men are liars and cheats and they gamble with your freedom and your life and the lives of your sons and daughters and the reputation of your country.'

4   It is important to remember that during the entire build-up to war, poll data indicated substantial popular opposition to war despite the media barrage orchestrated by the administration. See Scott McConnell, 'Gulf War One – Reconsidered,' 22 Jaunary 2004, www.antiwar.com: 'In the weeks prior to the beginning of the bombardment, the don't-go-to-war-party was gradually winning the day. Polls showed public opinion almost evenly divided on whether to "give sanctions a chance" or to attack Iraq. The leaders of the main Christian churches urged a negotiated solution to the crisis. While there were few anti-war demonstrations, there was serious argument among opinion leaders at nearly all levels.' Once the bombing started, poll data shifted dramatically, as they always do in the immediate aftermath of a US military demarche. Had the war lasted longer than a month it is likely public opinion would have shifted again.

5   Erik Dean, *Shook Over Hell: Post-traumatic Stress Disorder, Vietnam and the Civil War* (Cambridge, MA, 1997), pp.183,194.

6   As quoted in Jeet Heer and Dave Wagner, 'Man of the World: Michael Ledeen's Adventures in History,' www.bostonreviewonline.com, 10 October 2004, [accessed Oct. 14, 2005]; Michael Ledeen, 'Machiavelli on War,' www. nationalreviewonline.com, [accessed 14 Oct. 2005].

7   President Richard Milhaus Nixon, Cambodian Invasion, May, 1970, http://www.presidentialrhetoric/historicspeeches/nixon/cambodianinvasion. html [accessed 14 Sept. 2005].

8   Madeline Albright interview with Phil Ponce, www.onlinedailynewshour. com, April 4, 1999; [accessed 14 Sept. 2004]; praise for Clinton quoted in Andrew J. Bacevich, *American Empire: the Realities and Consequences of U.S. Diplomacy* (Cambridge, MA, 2002), p.272, fn. 22.

9   Thomas Friedman, 'One War, Two Fronts,' *New York Times*, 11 January 2001. Friedman used the slogan on several TV interview programmes as well.

10   Thomas Friedman, 'Osama and Katrina,' *New York Times*, 9 September 2005.

11   Norman Podhoretz, 'How to Win World War IV,' *Commentary*, Feb 2002, vol.113, no. 2, pp.19-29.

12   Stephen Peter Rosen, 'The Future of War and the American Military,' *Harvard Magazine*, May-June 2002, available on line at www.harvardmagazine.com/ on-line, [accessed 14 Sept. 2005]; 14 October 2005.

13   See The National Security Strategy of the United States of America, Sept. 17, 2002, p.1, 20, 3. (on line at www.whitehouse.gov/nsc). See David Armstrong, 'Dick Cheney's song of America,' *Harper's,* October 2002 for an

interesting account of the document in comparison to earlier versions under discussion since 1992.

[14] Interview with Margaret Warner on Jim Lehrer News Hour, 25 Sept. 2002, www.pbs.org [accessed 27 Sept. 2002].

[15] Greg Palast BBC interview with Garner, www.gregpalast.com

[16] On February 26, 2004, the PBS documentary series 'Frontline' posted transcripts of its account of the 'Invasion of Iraq' including an analysis of why the general was forced into retirement by the journalist James Fallon. See 'The Invasion of Iraq,' www.pbs.org/wgbh/frontline/shows/invasion.

[17] Ullman was everywhere in the weeks before the war. These quotes are drawn from his interview on the CBS Evening News, 24 January 2003. See also January 2003 News Log on Alternet. Ullman and a colleague, James P. Wade, had published a book on the subject in 1996: *Shock and Awe: Achieving Rapid Dominance*, National Defense University Press, 1996). This was their shining hour.

[18] Wolfgang Schivelbusch, 'The Loneliest Victors,' *New York Times*, 22 April 2003.

[19] Angst as to the capacity of Americans to exercise the necessary will power to deal with the situation was most impressively voiced by David Brooks, a regular TV commentator and *New York Times* columnist. Brooks worried about the impact inevitable atrocities committed by US troops would have on the public's stamina. He lamented the tendency of Americans, faced with an insurgency led by the 'scum of the earth', reluctant to stare into the 'face of evil,' wanted nothing more than to withdraw from a 'tangled morass we don't understand.' Brooks was sympathetic. It wasn't that Americans could not 'accept casualties. ... the real doubts come when we see ourselves inflicting them.' Inevitably there would be atrocities that would try the soul of the country. 'The president,' Brooks urged, 'will have to remind us that we live in a fallen world, that we have to take morally hazardous action if we are to defeat the killers who confront us.'

[20] The revelations of torture in US detention camps in Guantanamo, Iraq and Afghanistan demonstrated the capacity of Americans troops to follow orders and resist what Brooks had called the 'paradise of our own innocence'.

[21] Quoted in Chris Hedges, 'On War,' *New York Review of Books*, 16 December 2004, vol.51,

[22] Edward Wong, 'Marines Face New Kind of War in Iraq,' *New York Times*, 24 October 2004,

[23] Jospeph Galloway, 'Army lowers standards and increases bonuses, but still may fall short of recruiting goal,' posted 13 June 2005, KnightRidder Washington Bureau, accessed 14 June 2005; Jamie Wilson, 'US army lowers standards in recruitment crisis,' 4 June 2005, *The Guardian* www.guardian. co.uk, [accessed 14 June 2005]. Recruiting for the National Guard and

the Army Reserve (which comprise 40 per cent of the troops in Iraq) has suffered even more.

[24] See poll date on CNN.com for 10 September 2005 [accessed 13 September 2005].

[25] See PollingReport.com for September 8-11, 2005 [accessed 13 September 2005].

[26] Dana Milbank and Claudia Deane, 'Poll Finds Dimmer View of Iraq War,' *Washington Post*, June 8, 2005, www.washingtonpost.com, [accessed 14 June 2005].

[27] Tom Lasseter, 'Military action won't end insurgency, growing number of US officers believe,' posted 12 June 2005, Knight Ridder Washington Bureau, on line, [accessed 14 June 2005.]

[28] Susan Milligan, 'More in Congress Want Iraq Exit Strategy,' *Boston Globe*, June 11, 2005, [accessed via commondreams.com, 14 June 2005].

[29] See for one of hundreds of examples, 'Casey's Peace Page,' at www.angelfire. com/sk3/spkhntrca/Casey.html [accessed 16 Sept. 2005]. In Vermont as of the spring of 2005, 48 Vermont towns had voted against the war. See democracynow.com, March 2, 2005 [accessed 16 Sept. 2005] Sheehan's son Casey died in Iraq on 4 April 2004. Deeply unhappy with what she considered to be the President's lame response to the grieving families with whom he met in June 2004, she carried her protest to the President's vacation home in Crawford, Texas in June 2005 where she set up 'Camp Casey,' as a magnet for anti-war protests seeking to confront Bush during his long summer vacation — a vacation interrupted only by the disastrous impact of Hurricane Katrina on New Orleans — and his administration.

[30] J.M. Coetzee, *Waiting for the Barbarians* (New York, 1980), p.133.

[31] Niall Ferguson, 'The Empire Slinks Back: Why Americans Don't Really Have What It Takes to Rule the World,' *New York Times Magazine*, 27 April 2003.

10. THE GLOBAL WAR ON TERROR AND ITS IMPACT ON THE CONDUCT OF WAR

[1] Details available at www.newamericancentury.org/

[2] See an earlier briefing in this series for a more detailed discussion of the neoconservative orientation: Paul Rogers and Scilla Elworthy, 'The United States, Europe and the Majority World after 11 September', Oxford Research Group Briefing Paper, October 2001, available at: www.oxfordresearchgroup. org.uk/publications/briefings/spet11.htm

[3] See Charles Krauthammer, 'The Bush Doctrine: ABM, Kyoto and the New American Unilateralism', *The Weekly Standard*, 4 June 2001.

[4] Details available at www.aiopac.org/

[5] Donald Wagner, 'A Heavenly Match: Bush and the Christian Zionists' www.

informationclearinghouse.info/article4960.htm This is the last of five articles about the development of Christian Zionism and provides links to the other four in the series.

6   See www.standforisrael.org/

7   Details of current opium production in Afghanistan are available in: World Drugs Report 2004, UN Office on Drugs and Crime, Vienna, 2004.

8   The most comprehensive account is in Mark Danner, *Torture and Truth: America, Abu Ghraib and the War on Terror* (London, 2005).

9   Civilian casualties estimates are from www.iraqbodycount.net, and use a careful and conservative methodology based on press reports and therefore involving direct counts. Other studies, using sampling methods, give much higher figures. The figures for those injured are based on an estimated ratio or three people injured for every person killed.

10   Information on coalition casualties is available at: www.icasualties.org/oif/.

11   *The Economist*, 29 January 2005.

12   See, in particular, the Pew Center's Global Attitudes Project, details available at: www.people-press.org/pgap/

13   *The Military Balance, 2004-2005*, The International Institute for Strategic Studies, (London, 2004).

14   A detailed discussion of oil and US security is Michael Clare, *Blood and Oil*, (London, 2004).

15   William Kristol, 'Getting Serious About Syria', *The Weekly Standard*, 20 December 2004.

16   Paul Rogers, *Losing Control: Global Security in the 21st Century*, (London, 2002).

11. THE TEXTS OF TORTURE

1   Hubert Van Es, 'Thirty Years at 300 Millimeters', *The New York Times*, 29 April 2005, p.A27. For a summary of the Holocaust photographic record see Barbie Zelizer, *Remembering to Forget: Holocaust Memory Through the Camera's Eye*, (Chicago, 1998).

2   Mark Danner, *Torture and Truth: America, Abu Ghraib and the War on Terror* (New York, 2004); Karen J. Greenberg and Joshua L. Dratel, *The Torture Papers: the Road to Abu Ghraib* (Cambridge, 2005). I will refer to these texts as D and G&D in giving page references.

3   D p.172; G&D p.230-1. Further details of that treatment can be found in James Meek, 'How torture became acceptable', *The Guardian* 18 Feb. 2005.

4   Unclassified Executive Summary of Naval Inspector General Vice Admiral Albert T. Church's Report, available at http://www.defenselink.mil/news/Mar2005/d20050310exe.pdf, p.10.

5   'Should the Ticking Bomb Terrorist be Tortured?', in Alan M. Dershowitz
    Why Terrorism Works: Understanding the Threat, Responding to the Challenge (New
    Haven/London, 2002), pp.131-63.
6   See Meek, 'How torture became acceptable'.
7   Michael Ignatieff, 'The Terrorist as Auteur', *The New York Times Magazine*, 14
    Nov. 2004, p.8.
8   Victor Klemperer, *The Language of the Third Reich: LTI-Lingua Tertii Imperii: a
    Philologist's Notebook,* trans. Martin Brady (London/New York, 2002), pp.12,
    20.

12. THE LAWS OF WAR IN THE AGE OF ASYMMETRIC CONFLICT

1   International Committee of the Red Cross, 'Project on the Reaffirmation and
    Development of International Humanitarian Law', 1 Sept. 2003, available
    online at http://www.icrc.org/Web/Eng/siteeng0.nsf/iwpList575/
    795CACB6D4D247C9C1256DDE00568298 [accessed 8 Sept. 2005].
2   Robert C. Stacey, 'The Age of Chivalry', in M. Howard, G. Andreopoulos
    and M. Shulman, (eds), *The Laws of War* (London, 1994), p.34.
3   M.H. Keen, *The Laws of War in the Late Middle Ages* (London, 1965), pp.70,
    81.
4   Michael Howard, *The Invention of Peace* (London, 2001), p.25.
5   Leslie C. Green, *The Contemporary Law of Armed Conflict* (Manchester, 2nd
    edn., 2000), pp.54-5.
6   Quoted in Geoffrey Parker, 'Early Modern Europe' in Howard, Andreopoulos
    and Shulman (note 2); p.44.
7   Richard R. Baxter, 'So-Called 'Unprivileged Belligerency': Spies, Guerrillas
    and Saboteurs', reprinted in *Military Law Review*, Bicentennial Edition
    (September 1975), pp.490-1.
8   Geoffrey Best, *Humanity in Warfare* (New York, 1980), pp.112-21, 179-90.
9   See the discussion of Article 5 in International Committee of the Red Cross,
    *Commentary: Convention (IV) Relative to the Protection of Civilian Persons in Time of
    War, Geneva, Aug. 1949* (Geneva, 1958), p.52.
10 Geoffrey Best, *War and Law Since 1945* (Oxford, 1994), pp.118-19; see also
    Kenneth Watkin, 'Warriors Without Rights? Combatants, Unprivileged
    Belligerents and the Struggle over Legitimacy', *Program on Humanitarian
    Policy and Conflict Research, Harvard University, Occasional Paper Series*, 2 (2005),
    pp.53-4.
11 Baxter, (note 7), pp.492-3.
12 Watkin, (note 10), pp.55-6.
13 The head of the British delegation to the Diplomatic Conference at which the
    Conventions were drafted, Sir Robert Craigie, questioned whether rebels

could be bound by a treaty to which they were not a party, but concluded that 'any civilized government should feel bound to apply the principles of the Convention even if the insurgents failed to apply them.' See Best, (note 10), p.178. The final provision of Common Article 3 states that 'the application of the preceding provisions shall not affect the legal status of the Parties to the conflict.'

14 See, generally on this subject, Theodor Meron, 'The Humanization of Humanitarian Law', *American Journal of International Law,* 94 (2000) 2, pp.239-78.

15 This has been formally acknowledged by the US government. See US Department of Defense, *Operational Law Handbook (2005)*, p.45.

16 See, for instance, LTC Michael Newton, 'Unlawful Belligerency After September 11', in D. Wippman and M. Evangelista (eds), *New Wars, New Laws?*, (Ardsley, NY, 2005), pp.76-9.

17 Kenneth Anderson, 'Who Owns the Rules of War?', *The New York Times Magazine*, 13 April 2003. See also Eyal Benvenisti , 'Excessive Force and Human Dignity during Military Conflict', *Tel Aviv University Legal Working Paper Series*, 11 Jan. 2005.

18 White House, Office of the Press Secretary, 'Fact Sheet: Status of Detainees at Guantanamo', 7 Feb. 2002.

19 Michael Howard, 'What's in a Name: How to Fight Terrorism', *Foreign Affairs*, 81 (1), Jan./Feb. 2002.

20 The White House, 'Memorandum: Humane Treatment of al Qaeda and Taliban Detainees', 7 Feb. 2002, available at http://www.humanrightsfirst. org/us_law/etn/gonzales/memos_dir/dir_20020207_Bush_Det.pdf [accessed 1 Sept. 2005].

21 Quoted in Jane Mayer, 'Outsourcing Torture', *The New Yorker*, 14 Feb. 2005.

22 See the discussion of a January 2002 memo written by John Yoo and Robert Delahunty of the US Department of Justice in Michael Isikoff, 'Double Standards', *Newsweek* web exclusive, 25 May 2004, available at http://www. msnbc.msn.com/id/5032094/site/newsweek [accessed 9 Sept. 2005]. It is notable that, in line with the arguments made by Yoo and Delahunty, prosecutors at the military commissions in Guantanamo Bay did not claim to be enforcing customary international law, but 'commission law'. See Amnesty International Public Statement, 'Guantanamo: Military Commissions -- Amnesty International Observer's Notes from Proceedings', 3 Nov. 2004. For a contrary view, see the statement of Charles Allen, Deputy General Counsel at the Department of Defense, that 'the regime of law that applies [to the war on terror] is the customary law of armed conflict,' in Anthony Dworkin, 'Law and the Campaign Against Terrorism: The View from the Pentagon', *Crimes of War Project*, 16 Dec. 2002, available at http://www. crimesofwar.org/onnews/news-pentagon.html [accessed 9 Sept. 2005].

23 Fact Sheet (note 18).

24 The arguments that apparently prevailed with the White House were
    set out in Jay Bybee, Office of Legal Counsel, 'Memorandum for Alberto
    R. Gonzales, Counsel to the President and William J. Haynes II, General
    Counsel of the Department of Defense, Re: *Application of Treaties and Laws
    to al Qaeda and Taliban Detainees*', 22 January, 2002 available at http://
    www.washingtonpost.com/wp-srv/nation/documents/012202bybee.pdf
    [accessed 9 Sept. 2005].

25 See for instance the statement by Vice President Dick Cheney regarding
    the detainees being held at Guantanamo Bay, including both Taliban and al-
    Qaida suspects: 'They are not lawful combatants. These are the worst of a
    very bad lot...They are devoted to killing millions of Americans, innocent
    Americans, if they can, and they are perfectly prepared to die in the effort.'
    Dick Cheney, appearing on 'Fox News Sunday', Fox News, 27 Jan. 2002,
    transcript available at http://www.whitehouse.gov/vicepresident/news-
    speeches/speeches/vp20020127-1.html [accessed 10 Sept. 2005].

26 Department of Defense, 'Military Commission Instruction No.2: Crimes
    and Elements for Trials by Military Commissions', 30 Apr. 2003, pp.13-14.

27 William Taft, 'Guantanamo Detention is Legal and Essential', *Financial Times*,
    12 Jan. 2004, p.19.

28 For a fuller exposition of the arguments in this paragraph, see Anthony
    Dworkin, 'Military Necessity and Due Process: the Place of Human Rights
    in the War on Terror', in Wippman and Evangelista, (note 16), pp.53-75.

29 Martin van Creveld, *The Transformation of War*, (New York, 1991), p.89.

30 John Keegan, 'If You Won't, We Won't: Honour and the Decencies of Battle',
    Times Literary Supplement, 24 Nov. 1995, p.11.

31 For a discussion of this point with reference to the Second World War, see
    Adam Roberts, 'Land Warfare: From The Hague to Nuremberg', in Howard,
    Andreopoulos and Shulman, (note 2), p.137.

32 For a discussion of this point, and a wider analysis of reciprocity and the war
    on terror, see Noah Feldman, 'Ugly Americans', *The New Republic*, 30 May
    2005, pp.23-9.

33 The White House, 'Memorandum: Humane Treatment of al Qaida and
    Taliban Detainees', 7 Feb. 2002, available at http://www.humanrightsfirst.
    org/us_law/etn/gonzales/memos_dir/dir_20020207_Bush_Det.pdf
    [accessed 1 Sept. 2005].

34 Tim Golden, 'In US Report, Brutal Details of Two Afghan Inmates' Deaths',
    The New York Times, 20 May 2005.

35 Tim Golden, 'Abuse Cases Open Command Issues at Army Prison', *The New
    York Times*, 8 Aug. 2005.

36 See for instance the statement of President Bush announcing the end of
    major combat operations, in which he said, 'The battle of Iraq is one victory

in a war on terror that began on September the 11, 2001 — and still goes on.' White House, Office of the Press Secretary, 'President Bush Announces Major Combat Operations in Iraq Have Ended', 1 May 2003.

[37] Evan Wright, *Generation Kill* (New York, 2004), p.77.

[38] See for instance 'Final Report of the Independent Panel to Review DoD Detention Operations', August 2004 [the 'Schlesinger Report'] p.65.

[39] Josh White, 'Soldiers' 'Wish Lists' of Detainee Tactics Cited', *The Washington Post*, 19 April 2005.

[40] Final Report, (note 22), p.64.

[41] ibid, p.31.

[42] Lord Bramall, *Lords Hansard*, vol.673 (33), 14 July 2005, Col. 1226.

[43] Dana Priest, *The Mission* (New York, 2004), p.69.

[44] See the comment by Michael Walzer that 'without the equal right to kill, war as a rule-governed activity would disappear and be replaced by crime and punishment, by evil conspiracies and military law enforcement.' Walzer, *Just and Unjust Wars* (New York, 2nd edn, 1992), p.41.

[45] This recommendation is made in Watkin, (note 10), pp.74-5.

13. ON BRAINWASHING

[1] Nasreen Suleaman, 'Biography of a suicide bomber', in the series *Koran and Country*, BBC Radio Four, 17 November 2005. Available online at http://www.bbc.co.uk/koranandcountry/pip/q8q01 [accessed 30 November 2005].

[2] Diego Gambetta (ed.), *Making Sense of Suicide Missions* (New York, 2005).

[3] Malise Ruthven, *Fundamentalism: the Search for Meaning* (Oxford, 2004); William Blum, *Rogue State: a Guide to the World's Only Superpower* (London, 2nd edn, 2003); Noam Chomsky, *Hegemony or Survival: America's Quest for Global Dominance* (London, 2004).

[4] The texts of the Hague Conventions 1899-1954 are available online from Brigham Young University, http://www.lib.byu.edu/~rdh/wwi/hague.html [accessed 30 November 2005].

[5] Eric D. Weitz, *A Century of Genocide: Utopias of Race and Nation* (Princeton, NJ, 2003); Samantha Power, *'A Problem from Hell': America and the Age of Genocide* (London, 2003); Jonathan Glover, *Humanity: a Moral History of the Twentieth Century* (London, 2001); Donald G. Dutton, Ehor O. Boyanowsky, Michael Harris Bond, 'Extreme Mass Homicide: From Military Massacre to Genocide', *Aggression and Violent Behavior*, 10, 2005, pp.437-73.

[6] Samantha Power, *'A Problem from Hell'*.

[7] Diego Gambetta (ed.), *Making Sense of Suicide Missions*.

[8] Charles Tilly, *The Politics of Collective Violence* (New York, 2003); Christopher

Browning, *Ordinary Men* (New York, 1991).

9   Mary Midgley, *Wickedness* (London, 2001).

10   Edward Hunter, *Brainwashing in Red China: the Calculated Destruction of Men's Minds* (New York, 1951).

11   Robert Jay Lifton, *Thought Reform and the Psychology of Totalism: a Study of 'Brainwashing' in China* (London, 1961).

12   Kathleen Taylor, *Brainwashing: the Science of Thought Control* (Oxford, 2004).

13   Nasreen Suleaman, 'Biography of a Suicide Bomber'.

14   The film of Robert Condon's 1959 novel *The Manchurian Candidate* (Harmondsworth, 1973) was directed by John Frankenheimer (United Artists, 1962).

15   Shiva Naipaul, *Black and White* (London, 1981).

16   Kathleen Taylor, *Brainwashing*; Kathleen Taylor, 'Thought Crime', *The Guardian*, 8 October 2005; Marc Galanter, *Cults: Faith, Healing, and Coercion*, (New York, 2nd edn, 1999); Robert Jay Lifton, *Thought Reform and the Psychology of Totalism*.

17   Core beliefs are often codified in written form as a 'sacred' (religious or nonreligious) text, which may be taken at face value, or read as an allegorical or historical document, or some combination thereof. The defining characteristic of religious (and secular) fundamentalists may, it has been argued, be less an insistence on returning to first principles ('fundamentals') than a tendency to treat sacred texts as literally true in their entirety; that is, to adopt a totalist approach towards them. See Ralph W. Hood and Peter C. Hill, W. Paul Williamson, *The Psychology of Religious Fundamentalism* (New York, 2005).

18   Robert B. Cialdini, *Influence: Science and Practice* (Needham Heights, MA, 4th edn, 2002).

19   Shiva Naipaul, *Black and White*.

20   Christopher Browning, *Ordinary Men*.

21   Ulrich Hillenbrand and J. Leo van Hemmen, 'Adaptation in the Corticothalamic Loop: Computational Prospects of Tuning the Senses', *Philosophical Transactions of the Royal Society: Biological Sciences*, 357, 2002, pp.1859-67.

22   Robert Jay Lifton, *Thought Reform and the Psychology of Totalism*.

23   Nasreen Suleaman, 'Biography of a Suicide Bomber'.

24   Jody L. Davis and Caryl E. Rusbult, 'Attitude Alignment in Close Relationships', *Journal of Personality and Social Psychology*, 81, 2001, pp.65-84.

25   Robert Jay Lifton, *Thought Reform and the Psychology of Totalism*, p.23.

26   Nehemia Friedland, Giora Keinan and Talia Tytiun, 'The Effect of Psychological Stress and Tolerance of Ambiguity on Stereotypic

Attributions', *Anxiety, Stress and Coping*, 12, 1999, pp.397-410.

27 Ernst Klee, Willi Dressen Volker Riess (eds), *'The Good Old Days': the Holocaust as seen by its Perpetrators and Bystanders* (NewYork, 1991), p.85. In *Ordinary Men*, his study of policemen who became mass killers under the Nazi regime, Christopher Browning describes an occasion when explicit reassurance about consequences was given prior to an operation, but this may not have been standard practice.

28 Catherine A. Cottrell and Stephen L. Neuberg, 'Different Emotional Reactions to Different Groups: a Sociofunctional Threat-based Approach to 'Prejudice', *Journal of Personality and Social Psychology*, 88, 2005, pp.770-89.

29 Jennifer S. Lerner, Roxana M. Gonzalez, Ronald E. Dahl, Ahmad R. Hariri and Shelley E. Taylor, 'Facial Expressions of Emotion Reveal Neuroendocrine and Cardiovascular Stress Responses', *Biological Psychiatry*, 58, 2005, pp.743-50.

30 Midori Inaba, Michio Nomura and Hideki Ohira, 'Neural Evidence of Effects of Emotional Valence on Word Recognition', *International Journal of Psychophysiology*, 57, 2005, pp.165-73.

31 Terrence W. Deacon, *The Symbolic Species: the Co-evolution of Language and the Human Brain* (London, 1997).

32 David DeSteno, Nilanjana Dasgupta, Monica Y. Bartlett and Aida Cajdric, 'Prejudice from Thin Air', *Psychological Science*, 15, 2004, pp.319-24.

33 Charles Tilly, *The Politics of Collective Violence*, p.11.

34 Robert Jay Lifton, *The Nazi Doctors: Medical Killing and the Psychology of Genocide* (New York, 2000); Vahakn N. Dadrian, 'Patterns of Twentieth Century Genocides: the Armenian, Jewish and Rwandan Cases', *Journal of Genocide Research*, 6, 2004, pp.487-522; Christopher C. Taylor, 'The Cultural Face of Terror in the Rwandan Genocide of 1994' in A.L. Hinton (ed.), *Annihilating Difference: the Anthropology of Genocide* (Berkeley, 2002), pp.137-78.

35 Joanna Bourke, *An Intimate History of Killing: Face-to-face Killing in Twentieth-century Warfare* (London, 2000), pp.139-70; quotation from p.165.

36 Christopher Browning, 'Holocaust Perpetrators: Ideologues, Managers, Ordinary Men', United States Holocaust Memorial Museum: Committee on Conscience, 6 March 2002, p.16. Available online at http://www.ushmm.org/conscience/analysis/details/2002-03-06/browning.pdf [accessed 3 December 2005].

37 Robert S. Wyer (ed.), *The Automaticity of Everyday Life. Advances in Social Cognition. Volume X* (Mahwah, NJ, 1997); Kathleen Taylor, 'Applying Continuous Modelling to Consciousness', *Journal of Consciousness Studies*, 8, 2001, pp.45-60.

38 Christopher Browning, *Ordinary Men*; Ernst Klee, Willi Dressen, Volker

Riess (eds), *'The Good Old Days'*.

14. EPILOGUE: REFLECTIONS ON WAR AND BARBARISM

1   Stéphane Audoin-Rouzeau and Annette Becker, *Understanding the Great War* (New York, 2000), pp.102-3.

2   Jay Winter, introduction to J. Winter (ed.), *America and the Armenian Genocide* (Cambridge, 2000).

3   The evidence and citations underlying this interpretation may be found in the work of Tobias Jersak. See his Cambridge PhD dissertation 'Hitler and the Interaction of War and Holocaust' (2000), and his article, Tobias Jersak, 'Die Interaktion von Krieg und Judenvernichtung. Ein Blick aufs Hitlers Strategie im Spätsommer 1941', *Historisches Zeitschrift*, 268 (1999), pp.313-74.

INDEX